Contents

Abbreviations

9 Discriminatory redundancy

Abbreviations

Courts

ECJ	European Court of Justice
ECHR	European Court of Human Rights
PC	Privy Council
SC	Supreme Court
HL	House of Lords
CA	Court of Appeal
Ct Sess	Court of Session
NICA	Northern Ireland Court of Appeal
QBD	Queen's Bench Division
Div Ct	(Queen's Bench) Divisional Court
KBD	King's Bench Division
ChD	Chancery Division
NIRC	National Industrial Relations Court
EAT	Employment Appeal Tribunal
ET	Employment Tribunal

Case references

AC	Law Reports, Appeal Cases
All ER	All England Law Reports
Ch	Law Reports, Chancery Division
CMLR	Common Market Law Reports
COET	Employment Tribunal folio number
EAT	Employment Appeal Tribunal unreported case number
ECR	European Case Reports
ET	Employment Tribunal unreported case number
EWCA	Court of Appeal unreported case number
ICR	Industrial Cases Reports
IRLR	Industrial Relations Law Reports
ITR	Industrial Tribunal Reports
KB	Law Reports, King's Bench Division
QB	Law Reports, Queen's Bench Division
SCOET	Scottish Employment Tribunal folio number
SLT	Scots Law Times
TLR	Times Law Reports
UKSC	Supreme Court unreported case number
WLR	Weekly Law Reports

Legislation

DDA	Disability Discrimination Act 1995
EA	Employment Act 2002
EqA	Equality Act 2010
EqPA	Equal Pay Act 1970
ERA	Employment Rights Act 1996
ETA	Employment Tribunals Act 1996
RRA	Race Relations Act 1976
SDA	Sex Discrimination Act 1975
TULR(C)A	Trade Union and Labour Relations (Consolidation) Act 1992

Statutory references, unless otherwise stated, are to the ERA, except in Chapter 12 where references are to the TULR(C)A.

Some of the cases mentioned in this Handbook were decided under legislation that preceded the ERA. Reference is made throughout to the corresponding provisions in the later statute and not to their antecedents in repealed legislation.

Introduction

This Handbook is primarily concerned with the law relating to statutory redundancy payments, which was first introduced in the Redundancy Payments Act 1965 but is now largely contained in Part XI of the Employment Rights Act 1996 (ERA). It does not deal with contractual or ex gratia schemes in any detail (unless these have legal consequences for the statutory scheme), except in Chapter 6, where the payment of enhanced redundancy pay is considered.

In addition to explaining the law as it pertains to individual employees' statutory redundancy pay entitlement, this Handbook also deals with the rules governing unfair and discriminatory redundancy dismissals and, in the final chapter, focuses on the somewhat different regime relating to collective redundancies. It is important to note in this regard that the definition of redundancy for collective consultation purposes, which is contained in the Trade Union and Labour Relations (Consolidation) Act 1992 (TULR(C)A), differs significantly from the ERA definition for the purposes of individual claims for redundancy payments or unfair dismissal. This difference has important implications as there will be circumstances in which the ERA definition of redundancy will not be engaged, and so no liability to make statutory redundancy payments will arise, but the wider definition in the TULR(C)A will apply, thereby triggering the statutory consultation procedure.

This Handbook updates and replaces IDS Employment Law Handbook, 'Redundancy', which was published in 2008, and takes into account the changes in both statute and case law that have taken place since then. Economic instability in the years since the last edition was published has once again made redundancy a familiar feature of working life, and this Handbook draws many of its factual examples from real-life first instance employment tribunal decisions. However, the substantial law at the core of this area has not changed significantly over the past few years. The test of what amounts to a redundancy situation – first developed by Judge Peter Clark in Safeway Stores plc v Burrell 1997 ICR 523, EAT, and later approved by the House of Lords in Murray v Foyle Meats Ltd 1999 ICR 827 – has stood the test of time. The most significant developments since the last edition of this Handbook, so far as the fairness of individual redundancy dismissals are concerned, include the repeal of the statutory dismissal procedures in 2009 and the growth in the number of grounds on which selection for redundancy will be automatically unfair. In the context of collective redundancies, there have been some significant higher court decisions – such as the Court of Appeal's reference to the European Court of Justice in United States of America v Nolan 2011 IRLR 40, CA, for clarification as to when an employer must start collective consultation. Unfair redundancies are dealt with in Chapter 8, and collective redundancy consultation in Chapter 12.

i

Scheme of the Handbook

The scheme of this Handbook is as follows:

- Chapters 1 and 2 describe the fundamental concepts of 'dismissal' and 'redundancy'

- Chapter 3 explains how an employer's liability to make a redundancy payment can be avoided if the employer makes an offer of suitable alternative employment which the employee unreasonably refuses

- Chapter 4 deals with the complex statutory scheme for claiming a redundancy payment when an employee is laid off or kept on short-time

- Chapter 5 examines who is and who is not entitled to claim statutory redundancy pay – i.e. the various classes of excluded employee and the various kinds of personal disqualification that can disentitle an employee to a redundancy payment

- Chapter 6 is concerned with the calculation of redundancy pay and considers the position of enhanced redundancy pay schemes

- Chapter 7 describes the circumstances in which an employee may apply to the Secretary of State for payment of redundancy pay where the employer either refuses to make a payment or has become insolvent

- Chapter 8 explains the law governing unfair redundancies and describes the circumstances in which an employee unfairly selected for redundancy can bring an unfair dismissal claim

- Chapter 9 considers the circumstances in which discrimination may occur in the context of redundancy. It also looks at the special provisions prohibiting less favourable treatment on the grounds of part-time or fixed-term status

- Chapter 10 deals with the procedural requirements with which an individual must comply in order to be able to bring a claim under the redundancy legislation

- Chapter 11 sets out the statutory right of an employee under notice for redundancy to take time off to look for work or make arrangements for training

- Chapter 12 is concerned with the legal obligations on employers to consult 'appropriate representatives' and to notify the Secretary of State where collective redundancies are proposed.

It should be noted that where decisions cited in this Handbook are decisions of employment tribunals, these are intended to be illustrative only and are not binding on other tribunals, even if the facts and circumstances of the two cases appear to be identical.

The law is stated as at 1 November 2011. This Handbook completely replaces the IDS Employment Law Handbook, 'Redundancy' (2008), which should now be discarded.

> **This publication aims to provide accurate, authoritative information and comment on the subjects it covers. It is offered to subscribers on the understanding that the publisher is not in business as a lawyer or consultant.**

1 Dismissal

Definition of 'dismissal'

Burden of proof

Dismissal by employer

Expiry of limited-term contract

Constructive dismissal

Dismissal by operation of law

Special dismissals by statute

Transfer of Undertakings Regulations

Non-dismissals and problem areas

To be entitled to a redundancy payment an employee will normally first have to **1.1** show that he or she has been dismissed. The exceptions to this rule are where the employee has been laid off or kept on short-time. These special situations are discussed in Chapter 4. In this chapter we examine the various situations that might amount to a 'dismissal' for the purposes of the redundancy legislation. Then, in Chapter 2, we go on to explain when such a dismissal will be categorised as being by reason of redundancy: that is, where it arises because the business at which the employee is employed closes, or closes in the place where he or she works; or where the requirements of that business for employees to carry out work of a particular kind, or work of a particular kind in a particular place, have ceased or diminished – S.139(1) Employment Rights Act 1996 (ERA).

Definition of 'dismissal'   1.2

The basic definition of dismissal for the purposes of the statutory redundancy scheme is found in S.136(1) ERA. (A similar, though not identical, definition of dismissal for unfair dismissal purposes is found in S.95(1).) S.136(1) states that an employee will be treated as dismissed if:

- his or her contract of employment is terminated by the employer, either with or without notice – S.136(1)(a), or

- he or she is employed under a limited-term contract and the contract expires by virtue of the limiting event without being renewed under the same terms – S.136(1)(b), or

- he or she has been constructively dismissed – S.136(1)(c). A constructive dismissal occurs when an employee resigns, with or without notice, because of a repudiatory breach of contract by the employer. However, this subsection does not apply where the employee terminates the contract without notice in circumstances in which he or she is entitled to do so by reason of a lock-out by the employer – S.136(2).

1.3 To these basic definitions are added two further circumstances which also amount to dismissal for the purposes of the statutory redundancy scheme. These are:

- the resignation of an employee under notice of dismissal – S.136(3) (this also applies to unfair dismissal), and

- the termination of a contract by operation of law – S.136(5).

The wording of S.136(1) indicates that this is an exhaustive list of the circumstances in which an employee may be dismissed by his or her employer for the purposes of the statutory redundancy scheme. However, as discussed under 'Special dismissals by statute' below, dismissal may also be deemed in certain situations involving the termination of membership of specified bodies, even where the individuals concerned are not employees but statutory office holders – S.172 ERA.

1.4 Burden of proof

In a claim for a statutory redundancy payment, it is the employee who has to prove, on the balance of probabilities, that there has been a dismissal. Although there is a statutory presumption that a dismissed employee claiming a redundancy payment has been dismissed *by reason of redundancy* (see Chapter 2 under 'Presumption of redundancy'), there is no presumption that an employee has been dismissed in the first place. Thus, if an employee fails to prove that he or she has been dismissed, any claim for a redundancy payment (or for unfair dismissal) will fail.

In Morris v London Iron and Steel Co Ltd 1987 ICR 855, CA (an unfair dismissal case), M claimed that he had been unfairly dismissed while the employer claimed that he had resigned. The tribunal was unable to decide whose evidence was more likely to be true and so it dismissed M's claim. The Court of Appeal upheld this decision saying that, in such exceptional circumstances, the tribunal would have to fall back on where the onus of proof lay. As the employee had failed to prove that he had been dismissed, the tribunal had been entitled to dismiss his claim.

Dismissal by employer 1.5

Under S.136(1)(a) ERA termination of an employment contract by the employer, either with or without notice, constitutes a dismissal for redundancy purposes. If the employer says that the employee's job has come to an immediate end, that is a summary dismissal. If, on the other hand, the employer says that the contract will come to an end on a future date, that is a dismissal with notice (even if the employee is not required to work out that notice).

Notice period 1.6

The amount of notice an employee is entitled to receive will depend on either the terms of the employment contract or S.86 ERA. S.86 lays down minimum periods of notice. Although the contract of employment may specify the period of notice which must be given, if it specifies a shorter notice period than is required by S.86 then it is the statutory minimum notice which applies. (Note, however, that it is open to an employee to waive his or her right to notice or to accept a payment in lieu of notice – S.86(3).)

The statutory notice period depends on the length of the employee's continuous employment. An employer is not statutorily bound to give any notice to an employee who has not been continuously employed for at least one month. To an employee who has been continuously employed for more than one month but less than two years, however, the employer must give at least one week's notice and to an employee who has been continuously employed for more than two years the employer must give at least one week's notice for each year of continuous employment subject to a statutory maximum of 12 weeks' notice.

Limited-term contracts. The contract of employment of an employee who is 1.7 on a limited-term contract terminates on expiry of his or her contract, without the need for notice, subject to S.86(4). This provides that an employee on a fixed-term contract of one month or less who has been continuously employed for three months or more should be treated as though he or she has a contract for an indefinite period.

Remedy. If an employer fails to give adequate notice then, unless it has made a 1.8 payment in lieu of notice, the employee will be entitled to claim damages for breach of contract, either in an employment tribunal (for claims up to £25,000) or in the civil courts. Any such claim will not affect the employee's right to claim a redundancy payment in a tribunal, although, in practice, both claims will be heard together if the employee pursues the breach of contract claim in a tribunal.

For more information on contractual and statutory notice, see IDS Employment Law Supplement, 'Notice Rights' (2006).

1.9 **Withdrawal of notice**

Redundancy decisions are often made as a response to volatile economic conditions. The fluidity of the situation can sometimes lead the employer to rethink the decision to make redundancies already announced. However, an employer cannot unilaterally withdraw notice of dismissal once it has been given – Harris and Russell Ltd v Slingsby 1973 ICR 454, NIRC. Notice may only be rescinded if both parties agree, as the following cases demonstrate:

- **Arthurs v Fairfield Control Systems Ltd** ET Case No.2601627/08: A was employed by FCS Ltd, but from 2000 onwards was contracted out to work at another company, R. During 2007 R advised FCS Ltd that it would terminate their contract at the end of the year. FCS Ltd wrote to A on 5 November giving him 'notice of the potential termination of your employment' and saying that as he was entitled to nine weeks' notice, this would end on 5 January 2008, but that it could 'withdraw this notice at any time'. On 5 December R offered to employ A directly to do the same work after his employment with FCS Ltd was terminated. A did not inform FCS Ltd of this. On 10 December FCS Ltd won a large new contract and wrote to A saying that it was withdrawing his redundancy notice. It offered him a new position, which A did not accept. A tribunal upheld A's claim for a redundancy payment. The letter of 5 November amounted to notice to terminate the contract and FCS Ltd had no right to withdraw that notice unilaterally. Furthermore, A did not act unreasonably in refusing the offer of suitable alternative employment

- **Hedley v J and J Nichol** ET Case No.2505828/09: H was given notice of dismissal for redundancy. The next day his employer heard from a contractor that a project it had tendered for had been successful and it decided that redundancies were no longer required. At a meeting with H later the same day the employer purported to rescind the notice of dismissal, but H refused to accept this. An employment tribunal held that the notice of dismissal for redundancy stood, since it could only be withdrawn by mutual agreement. However, by failing to accept reinstatement, H had failed to mitigate his loss and this had a significant impact on the level of his award for unfair dismissal.

1.10 The fact that notice of dismissal cannot be withdrawn unilaterally can cause problems for employers where they have agreed enhanced contractual redundancy terms. In British Polythene Ltd t/a BPI Stretchfilms v Bishop EAT 1048/02 difficulties occurred within a business that led to a call for volunteers for redundancy and B put himself forward. An agreement for B to be made redundant was reached but before it could be implemented the employer's needs changed and BP Ltd sought to revoke the agreement. B maintained that the agreement was binding. He resigned and claimed that BP Ltd was in breach of contract. A tribunal upheld his claim and awarded a sum representing the

4

promised contractual redundancy pay under the agreement. On appeal, BP Ltd contended that the tribunal had failed to recognise that the agreement was subject to a condition precedent that the voluntary redundancy would only take effect if there was a genuine need for it prior to the date assigned for termination of B's employment. In rejecting this, the EAT held that there was nothing in the agreement to indicate any conditionality. It provided for dismissal on the ground of redundancy, and B was entitled to rely on it. In the absence of any conditionality, the agreement could only be changed by the consent of both sides.

Date of dismissal   1.11

A dismissal with notice generally takes effect on the date on which the notice expires and this remains so even if the employer does not actually require the employee to work out the notice – S.145(2)(a). Where, however, the employer dismisses summarily, i.e. without notice, the dismissal normally takes immediate effect – S.145(2)(b). This is the case even if a payment is made in lieu of notice – Dedman v British Building and Engineering Appliances Ltd 1974 ICR 53, CA.

In certain circumstances, though, where the employer has given no notice or inadequate notice, the date of termination of the contract may be postponed, for certain purposes, to the date when the proper statutory notice under S.86 would have expired. S.145(5)–(6) provides that notice is postponed in this way for the following purposes in connection with the statutory redundancy scheme:

- calculating the two-year qualifying period under S.155 (see Chapter 5 under 'Qualifying service')

- computing the employee's total length of service in order to calculate his or her redundancy pay entitlement – S.162(1) (see Chapter 6 under 'Statutory redundancy pay scheme – relevant date and calculation date').

So, for example, an employee with ten years, ten months of continuous service 1.12
who is summarily dismissed because of redundancy will have a notional ten weeks of statutory notice added on to his or her length of service. This means that he or she will be treated as having completed 11 years' service and being entitled to a redundancy payment on that basis. Note that it is only statutory notice under S.86 that can be added on in this way: more generous contractual notice terms are disregarded.

It used to be the case that the termination date was also postponed for the purpose of assessing the maximum allowed for a 'week's pay' in circumstances where, between an employee's actual dismissal date and the date upon which dismissal would have taken effect had the correct statutory notice been given, the Secretary of State raised the level of the maximum week's pay under S.227(3). However, S.227(3) was repealed by the Employment Relations Act 1999 and replaced by S.34 of that Act, which is not referred to in S.145(5)

5

ERA. This seems to suggest that the postponement of the relevant date for the purposes of calculating a week's pay no longer applies (although the reference to S.227(3) in S.145(5) ERA still remains). In the many years since S.227(3) was repealed, we have not seen a case addressing this point.

1.13 **Cutting short the notice period.** Where an employer gives notice but attempts to curtail the notice period by giving a payment in lieu of notice and asking the employee to leave early then, unless there is very clear evidence that both parties agreed to early termination, the courts will tend to hold that the original date for the expiry of the notice period has been preserved. In HW Smith (Cabinets) Ltd v Brindle 1973 ICR 12, CA, B was given a month's notice but after three days was told not to come to work any more. This was obviously not a consensual termination and B's date of termination was the date that her notice expired. An employment tribunal followed Brindle in the following decision:

- **Page v Telecom Protection Technologies Ltd** ET Case No.1701930/09: P was given notice of redundancy on 13 January 2009. On 29 January he was handed a letter which stated that he was entitled to receive 12 weeks' notice, that he was not required to work out his notice, that his employer would pay him a 'compensatory payment which is your net notice payment in lieu of working your notice', and that his last day of employment would be 30 January. P believed his dismissal was unfair and lodged a tribunal claim on 10 August. The tribunal found that his claim was made within the three-month time limit from his effective date of termination, which was the date on which the 12 weeks' notice expired.

(Note that different rules apply where it is the employee who wishes to leave before the notice period has expired – see 'Leaving before notice expires' below.)

1.14 **Limited-term contracts.** As indicated above under 'Notice period – limited-term contracts', where an employee is employed under a limited-term contract which is not renewed before its expiry, the date of dismissal will be the date the limited-term contract expires – S.145(2)(c).

1.15 **Death of employee.** If the employee dies during the notice period, the contract is treated as having expired by notice terminating on the date of the employee's death – S.176(1). If the employee dies after the contract has been terminated, but S.145(5) applies to postpone the date of termination to the end of the statutory notice period and this later date has not yet been reached, then the contract is also treated as having been ended by notice expiring on the date of the employee's death – S.176(2).

1.16 **Warning of future redundancies**
A warning of future redundancies is not a dismissal with notice (or at all) under S.136(1)(a). If an employee leaves following such a warning, he or she will be treated as having resigned and will not be entitled to a redundancy payment. A

true notice of dismissal will not only inform the employee that his or her employment will end but will also inform him or her either directly or indirectly of the date upon which the employment will end. The leading case is:

- **Morton Sundour Fabrics Ltd v Shaw** 1967 ITR 84, Div Ct: S was warned by his employer that the department in which he worked would have to be closed down. S found another job, gave 28 days' notice and left. A tribunal awarded him a redundancy payment, but the Divisional Court overturned this. As Mr Justice Widgery put it: 'As a matter of law an employer cannot dismiss his employee by saying "I intend to dispense with your services at some time in the coming months". In order to terminate the contract of employment the notice must either specify the date or contain material from which that date is positively ascertainable.' This had not happened, and the event that actually terminated the contract was the notice given by S and not any action taken by the employer. It followed that S had not been dismissed and had no claim to a redundancy payment.

Similarly, in Kinmond v Rushton Connections Ltd EAT 799/97 the EAT found **1.17** that a letter informing employees that, from a provisional date, the employer would be closing down its premises and relocating did not amount to a notice of dismissal. However, a later memo giving the actual date of the move did constitute such a notice.

A warning which states that employment will end *on or after* a certain date is not a notice of dismissal:

- **Pritchard-Rhodes Ltd v Boon and anor** 1979 IRLR 19, EAT: the employees were sent a letter explaining that the company was in a perilous situation, but continuing: 'After careful consideration it is felt that the job which you are currently undertaking will last for at least seven months from 1.3.77.' The EAT held that all the employer was doing was giving a warning that the employment might well terminate at the end of the seven months' period but that it was not certain to do so. There was not enough certainty about the date when the employment would end for this to be a notice of dismissal.

Similarly, there is no notice of dismissal where the warning states that **1.18** employment will end *on or before* a certain date. Two examples:

- **Burton Group Ltd v Smith** 1977 IRLR 351, EAT: S was told that he would be dismissed between 31 October and 26 December, the actual date to be confirmed later. On 24 October the unions and the employer agreed that the redundancies would take effect on 26 December, but S died on 26 October without hearing of this. The EAT held that no formal notice of dismissal had been given to S, since all he knew was that the date of termination would be 26 December or such earlier date as the employer might select. There was

7

an arrangement that S would be dismissed for redundancy, but no notice of dismissal

● **International Computers Ltd v Kennedy** 1981 IRLR 28, EAT: in October 1979 an employer told 900 employees that the factory where they worked would close by the end of September 1980 and that they would receive statutory redundancy payments and other severance payments. K found another job and left shortly afterwards. The EAT held that the employer's announcement was not a dismissal. The date of closure of the factory might have been stated clearly, but it was quite unknown when K's individual employment would come to an end.

1.19 Even where it appears that the dismissal date is clear there may be no notice of dismissal. Two examples:

● **Doble v Firestone Tyre and Rubber Co Ltd** 1981 IRLR 300, EAT: F Ltd proposed to close its factory on 15 February 1980 and issued a written statement informing the workforce of its intention. The statement went on to say that separate notices of dismissal would be issued to each employee at the appropriate time, and that although the employer intended to continue production until 15 February it would keep the matter under constant review. The EAT held that there was no firm date on which the employees' contracts were due to come to an end since those matters were to be kept under review. In any case, the proposal could not itself be a notice of dismissal because it had stated that notices of dismissal would follow at the appropriate time

● **Carder v Kvaerner Services Ltd** ET Case No.35933/95: C, a contracts manager involved in the supervision of building works contracts, received a letter from his employer on 23 February saying that it was obliged to consider him for an alternative position, and that if it were not successful in finding him alternative employment by 31 March 'then there will be no alternative but to terminate your employment by reason of redundancy'. An employment tribunal found that this letter did not amount to a dismissal. In reaching this conclusion, it took into account the fact that the employer wrote to C on 9 March stating that he, C, had not been notified of redundancy, which would only arise if the company failed to find him a suitable alternative appointment.

1.20 A valid notice of dismissal, if it does not specify the actual date of termination, must contain material from which that date is positively ascertainable. It is a question of fact for the tribunal whether a specific date was ascertainable. An illustration:

● **Wadham Kenning Motor Group t/a Wadham Stringer v Avery and ors** EAT 405/91: on 4 January 1991 K, a director, told the workforce that W's garage was to be closed down. Later that day, A, F and J were offered alternative employment at another garage. A and F resigned and J resigned after trying out the new job. Thinking that their garage was to close, all three claimed redundancy payments. The tribunal found that either K had informed the staff on 4 January that the garage was to close on 28 February or it was common knowledge among the workforce that this was to happen. Letters to the garage's customers, for example, gave 28 February as the day of closure. The tribunal thought that a reasonable employee would have understood from all the events of 4 January that his or her employment was to terminate on 28 February. It found that A, F and J had been given valid notice of termination on 4 January. The EAT refused to interfere with that decision as there was some evidence to support the tribunal's finding.

1.21 Tribunals will take account of all the surrounding circumstances when ascertaining whether a valid notice of dismissal was given and, if so, when it was given. In Pole v NIACE ET Case No.22836/95, for example, the employer, embarking on a reorganisation, wrote to P on 12 December 1994 saying, in part, that it had decided 'to issue initial and precautionary notices of redundancy... This letter is formal notice that these decisions are to be implemented, and constitutes therefore a formal precautionary notice of redundancy, since your current post will be deleted from 1 April 1995.' P was later interviewed for one of the new posts that were available but was unsuccessful. The employer wrote to her again on 28 February saying that 'your present post has been declared redundant... therefore, I am writing to confirm formally the termination of your employment at NIACE on 31 March 1995'. P, who was entitled to 12 weeks' notice, claimed that the February letter was the notice of dismissal, while the employer argued that the December letter had been the notice of dismissal – meaning that P had been given more than adequate notice. A tribunal held that the December letter was ambiguous but, noting the use of the words 'initial' and 'cautionary', found that it was simply a warning of impending redundancies to take effect on 31 March. It found that the actual letter of termination was the February letter. It was influenced by its belief that the employer's intention had been to use the notice period to carry out interviews, thereby avoiding having to give notice once the interviewing process had been completed and risking having to make payments in lieu of notice.

There is no reason why an employee should not be given a very long period of notice. In Hicks v Humphrey 1967 ITR 214, ET, for example, a tenant employer told his employee in February 1966 that he had given notice to terminate the tenancy of the farm to take effect on 11 October of that year. The employee left before that date and claimed a redundancy payment. The tribunal held that the notice was a notice of dismissal, albeit a very long one.

1.22 Note that the rule in Morton Sundour Fabrics Ltd v Shaw (see above), applies to notice given by an employee as well as to notice given by an employer. In

Mabert v Ellerman Lines plc ET Case No.07680/83 M and her husband were accepted as prospective adopters and she wrote to her employer to say that she intended to leave at short notice as soon as a child became available for adoption. A redundancy situation arose and M was made redundant. The employer claimed that she was not entitled to a redundancy payment because she had announced her resignation. But a tribunal pointed out that all M had done was state her intention to resign in the future: this was not a valid resignation because no firm date had been set, so that what terminated M's employment was the employer's dismissal. M was therefore entitled to a redundancy payment.

1.23 **Warning of redundancy and constructive dismissal.** It has been argued that a warning of redundancy amounts to a fundamental breach of contract that can give rise to a constructive dismissal (for the definition of which see 'Definition of "dismissal"' above). However, this argument was rejected by the EAT in Secretary of State for Employment v Greenfield EAT 147/89. In that case a tribunal found that there had been a constructive dismissal when an employer told all its employees, including the claimants, that they would be made redundant at some unknown time in the future. On appeal, the EAT overturned the tribunal's decision, saying that it was clear from the authorities that an indication of impending redundancy does not constitute a repudiation of contract or dismissal, actual or constructive.

However, in Greenaway Harrison Ltd v Wiles 1994 IRLR 380, EAT, the Appeal Tribunal appeared to suggest that a threat to dismiss with notice could be a fundamental anticipatory breach of contract, where the threat was made in the context of a unilateral variation of contract by the employer. In that case W was given notice that her hours of work were to be changed and that if she did not accept those hours she would be given notice of dismissal. W's manager informed her that she could speak to the managing director about the issue, but that there was little possibility of him changing his mind. W decided that it would be pointless to do so and resigned. The EAT held that although the contract of employment had not actually been breached, the employer was in anticipatory breach of contract and that breach – the threat to terminate the employee's contract by giving notice of termination in accordance with the contract – was a fundamental breach of contract for the purpose of claiming constructive dismissal.

1.24 It is difficult to reconcile the Greenaway Harrison case with the Greenfield case. The upshot of the two cases appears to be that where an employer informs employees that if they do not accept certain variations to their contracts of employment they may face redundancy, the employer may well be acting in fundamental anticipatory breach of the contract of employment, allowing the employees to resign and claim constructive dismissal. However, if the employer merely informs the employees that they may face redundancy, but makes no suggestion of varying the employees' contracts, then that will not amount to a fundamental anticipatory breach of contract. Obviously, such an inconsistency in the law is highly undesirable and it is somewhat surprising that a definitive answer has yet to be provided by either the EAT or the Court of Appeal. In Kerry Foods Ltd v Lynch 2005 IRLR 680, EAT, the EAT considered Greenaway Harrison and expressed some concern at the decision – but pointedly refused to reach a conclusion about whether it had been wrongly decided. In our view, Greenaway Harrison should be treated with some caution, not least because it appears to suggest that a threat to terminate a contract with notice in accordance with the terms of the contract can amount to an anticipatory breach of contract, while it is established case law that an actual termination in these circumstances can never amount to such a breach (see Haseltine Lake and Co v Dowler 1981 ICR 222, EAT).

Of course, if an employer clearly intends to commit a breach of contract, there will be scope for a constructive dismissal. For example, a warning that an employer would require an employee to move premises where it had no contractual right to do so would amount to a fundamental breach – see Maher v Fram Gerrard Ltd and anor 1974 ICR 31, NIRC.

In certain circumstances it may be possible to argue that a warning of future **1.25** redundancies amounts to a breach of the implied duty of mutual trust and confidence inherent in an employment relationship. It is unlikely that a normal warning, such as in the above cases, would constitute such a breach. However, if the warning is couched in such a way that the employee is faced with a situation in which there is no prospect of his or her remaining in employment, it might lead to a finding of constructive dismissal. An example:

- **Valor Heating Ltd v Nelder** EAT 292/92: N, a regional service engineer, was selected for redundancy after 26 years' service. He was told that he had been selected because he had failed a Gas Regulation course. At a later meeting, he was offered the choice of taking over another region or accepting redundancy. N chose the latter because he did not want to move and he did not expect to remain in employment for very long after failing the Gas Regulation course. N brought tribunal proceedings, claiming that he had no choice but to accept redundancy. The employer gave a different version of events and said that N had been given the choice of accepting redundancy or remaining in the same job. The tribunal decided that N had been constructively dismissed. A situation was allowed to develop in N's mind in which he believed that, whatever happened, he would lose his job. Even if his belief was not in fact 'an accurate assessment of the situation', the employer had breached the implied term of mutual trust and confidence. The EAT, however, allowed the employer's appeal on the ground that the tribunal had failed to establish exactly what had been said to N at his meetings with management and whether he had, in fact, been faced with an intolerable choice. It remitted the case for the tribunal to make such a finding and then to determine whether there had been a breach of contract. In doing so, however, the EAT seemed to accept that it is possible for there to be a constructive dismissal in these circumstances.

1.26 Leaving before notice expires

An employee under notice of dismissal may wish to leave work before the notice expires, perhaps to go to another job. An important question, if the employee does leave early, is whether he or she is still entitled to a redundancy payment.

An employee can leave early and claim a redundancy payment only if he or she either:

- agrees with the employer to vary the notice period, or

- complies with the statutory provisions relating to counter-notice.

1.27 **Agreement with employer.** If the employer agrees that the employee can leave before the expiry of the notice period, there is still a dismissal by the employer. All that has happened is that the employer has agreed to substitute an earlier termination date – McAlwane v Boughton Estates Ltd 1973 ICR 470, NIRC. It is important, however, that there is actual agreement between the parties. An employee's unilateral decision to leave early will amount to a resignation and, unless the employee has followed the counter-notice provisions (see below), he or she will have no right to a redundancy payment.

1.28 **Statutory counter-notice.** The basic requirements, which must be followed precisely, are:

- the employer must have given notice to the employee to terminate the contract – S.136(3)(a). A mere warning of a pending redundancy is not enough

- the employee must give counter-notice in writing within the 'obligatory period' of the employer's notice, to terminate on a date earlier than the expiry of the employer's notice – S.136(3)(b). (A failure to provide the notice in writing will defeat a redundancy pay claim. Note, however, that for the purpose of an unfair dismissal claim similar provisions under S.95(2) do not require the counter-notice to be in writing.)

1.29 *Obligatory period.* The 'obligatory period' is defined in S.136(4). It is the period, ending on the date of expiry of the employer's notice, which is equal in length to the statutory notice period under S.86 ERA or to the employee's contractual notice entitlement, whichever is the longer. If, for example, an employee has three years' service, he or she will be entitled to a minimum of three weeks' statutory notice under S.86. If the employer gives three weeks' notice, then the obligatory period and the notice period are one and the same.

12

If the employer gives six weeks' notice of redundancy then – if the employee has no separate contractual entitlement to notice – the last three weeks of the employer's six weeks' notice will be the obligatory period. If, however, the same employee is entitled to four weeks' notice under the contract, then the last four weeks of the employer's notice will be the obligatory period. If the employer gives less than lawful notice, the obligatory period will still be the minimum notice period required (statutory or contractual) ending with the date of expiry of the employer's notice.

There is a trap for employees where the employer gives longer notice than required. If an employee gives counter-notice during the notice period but before the obligatory period starts and then leaves his or her employment, he or she will be treated as having resigned and not as having been dismissed and will lose entitlement to redundancy pay. In Nicholas v George Payne and Co Ltd ET Case No.25139/95 N was entitled to three weeks' notice. He was in fact given ten weeks' notice and told that he would get more than double his statutory entitlement to redundancy pay. N found a new job and his new employer wanted him to start seven weeks before the end of his notice period. N served his counter-notice. An employment tribunal found that he was not entitled to redundancy pay because he had failed to give his counter-notice during the obligatory period, which was three weeks prior to the end of his notice period.

Length of counter-notice. How much counter-notice should be given is **1.30** uncertain. The length of the employee's counter-notice is not specified in the ERA, which only requires that notice must be given. However, it could be argued that the employee should be required to give the amount of notice which he or she is bound to give lawfully to terminate the contract of employment. That would be either the statutory minimum of one week (S.86(2)) or a longer period of contractual notice, if any. This proposition, however, was rejected in Ready Case Ltd v Jackson 1981 IRLR 312, EAT, where the Appeal Tribunal held that the word 'notice' in S.95(2) (the equivalent unfair dismissal provision) was to be construed not as 'valid notice' (i.e. not as the amount of notice the employee is obliged to give) but as notice of any period. In that case the employee had given five days' notice.

In Millington v Roberts and Hewett Agriculture Ltd ET Case No.00977/84 a tribunal held that it followed from Ready Case that a notice to leave immediately was a valid counter-notice. The tribunal, however, doubted whether Ready Case was correct and said that had it not been for that case it would have said that a counter-notice was only valid if it was the notice which the employee was either contractually or statutorily bound to give to terminate the contract. Unfortunately, as far as we know, there is no other authority on the point. The only advice which can safely be given to employees is that, to be on the safe

13

side, they should give the notice which they are lawfully required to give to terminate their contracts of employment.

1.31 What is clear is that an employee must give *some* notice. In Walker v Cotswold Chine Home School 1977 ITR 342, EAT, a school cook was told that her job would end at the end of term, which was about seven weeks away. She simply left at the end of the afternoon, never returned to work, and did not answer letters from the school. The EAT said there was no evidence of anything she said or did which could sensibly be construed as amounting to notice.

An employee who has served a valid counter-notice is still deemed to have been dismissed by the employer, but on the date of the expiry of the counter-notice and not of the original notice of the employer. However, if the employer wishes to stick with the original dismissal date, it may serve a further notice under the Act, requiring the employee to work out the original notice period.

1.32 **Employer's further notice.** Serving a valid counter-notice does not always ensure the employee's entitlement to a redundancy payment since the employer can serve a further notice calling on the employee to work out the full term of notice – S.142(1). This further notice must:

- be in writing and be given to the employee before the employee's counter-notice expires

- tell the employee that the employer requires him or her to withdraw the counter-notice and continue to work until the employer's original notice expires, and

- state that unless the employee complies the employer will contest any liability to pay a redundancy payment – S.142(1)–(2).

If the employee complies with the employer's further notice and withdraws his or her counter-notice, the employer's original notice of dismissal will remain in effect.

1.33 An employee who does not comply with the employer's further notice is deemed to have been dismissed by the employer on the date specified in the employee's counter-notice. The employee is not, however, entitled *as of right* to a redundancy payment by reason of that dismissal. He or she must apply to a tribunal, which, having considered the reasons the employee had for leaving early and the reasons the employer had for wishing to retain the employee for the full notice period, must decide whether it is just and equitable for the employee to receive a payment. The tribunal may award the whole, part or none of the payment to which the employee would have been entitled but for the employer's further notice – S.142(3)–(4).

Cases in this area are infrequent, but if an employee wants to leave early because he or she has found another job a tribunal will often decide in his or her favour and award a full redundancy payment. In Simon v HA Stradling and Sons Ltd ET Case No.3926/85, for example, S, a construction site agent, was given three months' notice of redundancy. He rapidly found two other jobs, but in both cases the employer wanted him to start promptly, while his current employer needed him up to the end of the contract on which he was working. S gave counter-notice, refused to comply with the employer's further notice, and applied to a tribunal for a redundancy payment. Weighing up the facts, the tribunal said that it was essential for S to safeguard his future given the difficult climate for the construction industry; while the employer would be inconvenienced by the loss of a site agent, it could, at a pinch, hire a temporary replacement at no extra cost. In the circumstances it was fair for S to receive the whole of his redundancy payment.

It all depends on the facts, however. In Harrison v Walsh t/a LLG Wheelchairs **1.34** ET Case No.2401814/98 H was under notice of redundancy, to expire on 31 March. On 17 March he gave notice to his employer that he was leaving on 25 March as he had new employment commencing on 26 March. The employer served a further notice requiring H to work until 31 March and stating that he would lose his entitlement to redundancy pay unless he did so. H left on 25 March. The tribunal ordered the employer to pay just 25 per cent of the redundancy pay. It found that the employer had compelling business and financial reasons for wanting H to remain until 31 March, and that H did not believe he would lose his new job if he delayed his start date – he simply believed that it would not be a good start to the employment relationship.

Death of employee following counter-notice. Note that if an employee dies **1.35** after having served a counter-notice, then the employer is deemed to have served a further notice under S.142(1), whether it has done so or not, and the employee is deemed not to have complied with it – S.176(5). The result is that a tribunal will have to exercise its discretion, under S.142(3), whether to award a redundancy payment (to the employee's estate).

Working on after notice expires   1.36

We have seen that the parties to an employment contract can agree to bring forward the employee's leaving date without the employee losing the right to a redundancy payment. It follows from this that the parties should also be able to set a new leaving date *later* than the original date without affecting that right. The ERA makes no provision for such an eventuality but the EAT seems to have accepted in principle that the leaving date can be postponed by agreement:

- **Mowlem Northern Ltd v Watson** 1990 ICR 751, EAT: MN Ltd had a contract to carry out work at a particular power station where it employed W as a foreman. In January 1988 the contract was coming to an end and the company gave W notice of redundancy to expire on 11 March 1988. A few weeks before the expiry of that notice the employer asked W to transfer temporarily to another site, and to stay there beyond 11 March, in the hope that it would get a new construction contract at the original site to which W would then return. If the new contract failed to materialise, it would be up to W to decide what to do. W was told that, in the meantime, the redundancy notice would 'lie on the table'. In the event, the company failed to secure the new contract and W left in June 1989. MN Ltd refused to give him a redundancy payment, saying that the reason for the termination of employment was W's resignation and not redundancy. The EAT held that the employer's notice of dismissal stood but it had been suspended by mutual agreement. It became reactivated when it became clear that W would not be able to return to the original site.

1.37 Unfortunately, the reasoning behind this decision is not entirely clear. Presumably, the EAT was not saying that the parties varied the date of dismissal, since no new leaving date was fixed – and Morton Sundour Fabrics Ltd v Shaw 1967 ITR 84, Div Ct (see 'Dismissal by employer – warning of future redundancies' above), makes it clear that there is no notice of dismissal where the exact date of leaving is not ascertainable. Rather, it seems that it was saying that the parties agreed to suspend the operation of the notice. The EAT went on to hold that in these circumstances there was nothing to prevent W claiming a statutory redundancy payment. It would appear that the EAT, in reaching this decision, did not consider S.138(1) ERA, which provides that where an employee's contract of employment is renewed, or he or she is re-engaged under a new contract of employment in pursuance of an offer (in certain circumstances which applied in this case), the employee will not be regarded as dismissed by reason of the ending of his or her employment under the previous contract. Although it is possible that W might have been able to argue that he never really accepted the offer because acceptance was dependent on a condition – that he would be able to return to the original site – which was not met, the EAT did not mention the section at all and therefore some doubt must be cast on the decision.

The decision in the Mowlem case was relied upon by the employer in S Jones Industrial Holdings v (1) Jarvis (2) Webb EAT 641/93. There, J and W were employed as lorry drivers in the contracts division of a road haulage firm. They were given notice that they would be made redundant on 24 July. The employer did not want to lose them, however, and found them different driving duties after that date. J and W were then given a revised date of termination of 4 September, but both left shortly before then. A tribunal found that the employees' original contracts had terminated on 24 July and that they were entitled to a redundancy payment. The employer challenged that decision on the basis of the Mowlem case and argued that the original notice of redundancy had been varied by mutual consent to take effect on 4 September. Therefore, as both employees had resigned before 4 September, they had not been dismissed and were not entitled to a redundancy payment. In contrast to the Mowlem case, there had been no agreement with the employees that the redundancy would 'lie on the table'.

The EAT held that the case was governed by ordinary contractual principles **1.38** and found no agreement on the employees' part to accept a deferred redundancy date, even though they had been retained in a different capacity after 24 July. The EAT pointed out that an employee who continues to work after the date specified in the original redundancy notice and who has agreed to the continuation of his or her existing contract may, subject to the issue of suitable alternative employment, lose the right to a redundancy payment. Employers who wish to extend the contract beyond the expiry date should therefore make their proposals clear and obtain the employee's consent to them. In the instant case the employer had not made it plain what it was seeking to do. It was not clear that the contracts were being extended and, consequently, the employees remained entitled to their redundancy payments.

Unlike the Mowlem case, the question of suitable alternative employment does seem to have been raised before the tribunal in the above case. However, it is unclear from the EAT's decision how this issue was dealt with and since it does not appear to have been raised on appeal it is impossible to comment on whether S.138(1) might have applied in the circumstances. Note that S.138 is discussed in Chapter 3, 'Alternative job offers'.

Family leave-related dismissals   1.39

Prior to the changes introduced by the Employment Relations Act 1999, special provisions existed allowing women on maternity leave, whose contracts of employment did not subsist during that leave, to claim a deemed dismissal in the event of their employer refusing to allow them to return to work on the ground of redundancy. These provisions, contained in S.137 ERA, were repealed by the 1999 Act, and the Maternity and Parental Leave etc Regulations 1999 SI 1999/3312 make it clear that the contract of employment of a woman on maternity leave subsists throughout her leave. If the employee is dismissed during that leave, or is not allowed to return at the end of her leave, this will be an ordinary dismissal by the employer and the employee will not have to rely on a 'deemed' dismissal to enforce her rights. Redundancy during maternity leave is discussed in IDS Employment Law Handbook, 'Maternity and Parental Rights' (2009), Chapters 3 and 4.

Similarly, the employment contract of an employee on paternity, adoption or parental leave subsists during the leave period and any redundancy during that period or refusal to allow the employee to return at the end of the leave will amount to a dismissal in the normal way.

1.40 Expiry of limited-term contract

The Fixed-term Employees (Prevention of Less Favourable Treatment) Regulations 2002 SI 2002/2034 made a number of changes to redundancy law, giving fixed-term and limited-term employees greater protection than they previously enjoyed.

Prior to the Regulations' coming into force, S.136(1)(b) ERA provided that where a fixed-term contract – which was defined as a contract with both a defined date of commencement and a defined date of expiry – expired and was not renewed on the same terms, then a dismissal had taken place. This definition did not cover a contract for a particular purpose designed to expire whenever the task in question was completed (hereafter referred to as a 'task contract'). As a result, such contracts – examples of which could include a sailor who is employed for a voyage of uncertain duration or a person who is engaged to fell an area of trees and whose employment will end when all the trees have been felled – came to an end by performance and there was no dismissal for ERA purposes.

1.41 However, task contracts are now included in the definition of 'fixed-term contract' found in Reg 1(2) of the Fixed-term Regulations. In addition, S.136(1)(b) ERA was amended from 1 October 2002 to provide that an employee is dismissed if he or she is 'employed under a limited term contract and that contract terminates by virtue of the limiting event without being renewed under the same contract'. S.235(2A) ERA states that a contract of employment is a limited-term contract if:

- the employment under the contract is not intended to be permanent, and

- provision is accordingly made in the contract for it to terminate by virtue of a limiting event.

Subsection (2B) goes on to define a 'limiting event' as:

- in the case of a contract for a fixed term, the expiry of the term

- in the case of a contract made in contemplation of the performance of a specific task, the performance of that task, and

- in the case of a contract which provides for its termination on the occurrence of an event (or the failure of an event to occur), the occurrence of the event (or the failure of the event to occur).

1.42 Among other things, the changes brought about by the Regulations put to bed a body of case law examining the often narrow distinction between contracts of a fixed term and task contracts. Another change introduced by the Regulations means that it is no longer possible for parties to exclude the right to claim a redundancy payment on expiry of a fixed-term contract when the contract is

18

for a term of two years or more – this was previously permitted by S.197 ERA, which the Regulations repealed.

Where an employee works under a succession of limited-term contracts he or she may be dismissed for redundancy on the expiration of each contract, and will be entitled to a redundancy payment provided he or she has been employed for at least two years. In Pfaffinger v City of Liverpool Community College 1997 ICR 142, EAT, P had been a part-time lecturer under a series of fixed-term contracts, each for a single academic term, for 13 years. The last relevant contract was issued on 23 April 1993 and ran until 25 June, when term ended and the summer vacation began. Over the summer, P's employer introduced a new system of payment which had the effect of substantially reducing P's hourly rate. P did not return to work and claimed, among other things, a redundancy payment. Her employer argued that she had not been dismissed but that her employment had terminated by reason of the expiry of her contract on 25 June, and denied that she had the requisite continuity of employment. The EAT found that when P's contract expired at the end of each term she was dismissed for redundancy, since during a vacation the need for teachers ceases or diminishes. It said that, in situations like P's, a redundancy payment entitlement is not lost when the employee returns to work under a new contract the following term unless, in accordance with S.138, an offer of re-engagement was made before the previous contract had ended. The fact that P's fixed-term contracts gave her continuity of employment for the purposes of making certain claims in respect of her dismissal did not prevent the expiry of her fixed-term contract from being a dismissal or that dismissal being for redundancy. P was therefore entitled to a redundancy payment.

1.43 Note that a contract is still a fixed-term contract even if it can be brought to an end by notice within the term – Dixon and anor v BBC 1979 ICR 281, CA. Thus, a provision in a three-year fixed-term contract that it can be terminated by three months' notice on either side does not change its character.

Constructive dismissal **1.44**

By virtue of S.136(1)(c) ERA there is a dismissal when 'the employee terminates the contract… (with or without notice) in circumstances in which he is entitled to terminate it without notice by reason of the employer's conduct'. This section refers to those cases where the employer has committed, or is threatening to commit, a repudiatory breach of contract, thereby entitling the employee under the law of contract to leave without notice. If the employee in fact leaves, with or without notice, there is a constructive dismissal: see IDS Employment Law Handbook, 'Unfair Dismissal' (2010), Chapter 1.

The employer's reason for dismissal in a case of constructive dismissal is the reason for the employer's breach of contract that caused the employee to resign

– Berriman v Delabole Slate Ltd 1985 ICR 546, CA. If the reason for the breach of contract fits the statutory definition of redundancy (see Chapter 2), then the employee will be redundant. (As to whether such a redundancy dismissal is fair or unfair for the purposes of the unfair dismissal legislation, see Chapter 8 under 'Unreasonable redundancy'.)

1.45 Common breaches of contract that could lead to a constructive dismissal on the ground of redundancy include the following:

- *laying off employees* when there is no contractual right to do so. For example, in Wootton v Quinney's Auto Services Ltd ET Case No.2465/96 W's employer, acting in breach of the employment contract, laid him off on 11 December but refused to make him redundant, saying that there would be work for him in January. W, however, chose not to return, and a tribunal found that he had been constructively dismissed. (Note that an employee who is laid off where the employer does have a contractual right to do so may be able to claim a redundancy payment under the special statutory scheme set out in Chapter III of Part XI of the ERA, despite the fact that he or she has not been dismissed – see Chapter 4)

- *changing terms of employment* by, for example, switching an employee from one job to another because there is no longer a requirement for the former. For example, in Melia v Green Contract Services Ltd ET Case No.2902217/08 M was a time-served pipe fitter. The contract on which he worked was cancelled at short notice in February 2008 and he was given other work to do, such as gardening, since the employer had no further need for a pipe fitter. However, M was drifting further and further away from his trade so in July he accepted an offer from another company and resigned. An employment tribunal upheld his claim for a redundancy payment on the basis of a constructive dismissal. M had resigned in response to his employer's breach of contract in failing to provide him with the work he was employed to do

- *requiring employees to move to new premises* when there is no contractual right to do so. For example, in David Webster Ltd v Filmer EAT 167/98 the depot at which F worked closed and he was moved, in breach of his contract, to another, more distant, location. F left and the EAT found that he had been constructively dismissed.

1.46 It is important to stress, however, that a constructive dismissal will only amount to a dismissal on the ground of *redundancy* where the underlying reason for the breach of contract satisfies the statutory definition. See Chapter 2 under 'Less work available – same work done under different terms and conditions' for a detailed consideration of when a change in an employee's terms and conditions in breach of contract may or may not amount to redundancy. It should also be borne in mind that a move to new premises or a change of job may rank as an offer of suitable alternative employment, so that the employee may forfeit any right to redundancy pay if he or she unreasonably refuses it – see Chapter 3.

Affirming the contract. An employee may be disqualified from claiming **1.47** constructive dismissal if he or she works on without protest under changed terms and conditions. But it will all depend on the facts. In Melia v Green Contract Services Ltd (above), for example, the tribunal considered that although M had waited for over four months following the loss of his pipe-fitting work, in the circumstances he did not affirm the contract. The new duties he was given changed from week to week, and he continued to hope that he would be put back on pipe-fitting work; he did not accept that he would be doing unskilled work forever.

Anticipatory breach. As noted above, an employee may resign in circumstances **1.48** that amount to a constructive dismissal not only where his or her employer has already committed a fundamental breach of contract, but where the employer has indicated an *intention* to commit such a breach. This is known as an anticipatory breach. Where the employer's intention to breach the contract is clear, the employee does not have wait for the employer to carry out the threat before he or she can resign and claim constructive dismissal – Wellworthy Ltd v Ellis EAT 915/83. However, there is a risk that an employee may act too hastily in resigning before the nature of the threatened breach is clear.

Lock-outs
1.49
The definition of dismissal *for redundancy purposes* is circumscribed by S.136(2) where there has been a 'lock-out' by the employer. 'Lock-out', as defined by S.235(4), means:

- the closing of a place of employment

- the suspension of work, or

- the refusal by an employer to continue to employ any number of persons employed by him in consequence of a dispute,

done with a view to compelling persons employed by the employer, or to aid another employer in compelling persons employed by him, to accept terms or conditions of or affecting employment.

Although a lock-out is a repudiatory breach of contract by the employer, if an **1.50** employee resigns without notice because of that breach, S.136(2) expressly prevents a claim of constructive dismissal with regard to redundancy. This does not prevent an employee claiming constructive dismissal at common law, or indeed pursuing an unfair dismissal claim in respect of a constructive dismissal. However, it means that an employee will not normally be able to claim a redundancy payment in these circumstances.

Note, however, that S.136(2) only applies when the employee resigns *without* notice: if an employee gives notice of resignation, it seems on the literal wording of the statute that a claim for constructive dismissal under S.136(1)(c) can still be made. However, it will still be up to the employee to convince a tribunal that the reason for the employer's lock-out was redundancy, which may not be easy.

1.51 ## Dismissal by operation of law

Section 136(5) ERA provides that certain events which operate to terminate a contract of employment, but which do not normally amount to a 'dismissal', should be treated as a dismissal for the purposes of the statutory redundancy scheme. The subsection applies where a contract is terminated automatically in accordance with an enactment or rule of law by (a) an act on the part of an employer, or (b) an event affecting an employer (including, in the case of an individual, the employer's death).

In such a situation, if the employee's contract is not renewed, and he or she is not re-engaged under a new contract, he or she will be taken to be dismissed by reason of redundancy if the circumstances fall within the definition of redundancy – S.139(4) and (5). Note that it is only the act of the employer or an event affecting the employer that counts under S.136(5). If an employee is disabled from working by an enactment – e.g. for health and safety reasons – or by death or injury, this does not count as a dismissal.

Section 136(5) may be relevant in many situations. For example, in London Borough of Haringey v Reynolds EAT 1070/98 the junior school of which R was head teacher was amalgamated with its sister infant school to create a single 'primary school', pursuant to the requirements of the Education Act 1996. R agreed to accept premature retirement but because her acceptance was based on misrepresentations by her employer, the tribunal found that her agreement had been rescinded. It went on to find that R had been dismissed by virtue of S.136(5). The closure of the junior school in accordance with provisions of the 1996 Act, in conjunction with the employer's erroneous insistence that R had resigned (a rule of law dictates that such insistence amounts to dismissal – see Ely v YKK Fasteners (UK) Ltd 1994 ICR 164, CA), were found to be 'acts or events' for the purposes of that provision. The EAT upheld the tribunal's decision.

1.52 At common law there are several situations where a contract of employment is regarded as having ended automatically as a result of some act or event done or suffered by the employer. These include:

- *death of employer*. At common law, where the contract of employment is with an individual employer, the death of that employer will automatically terminate the contract – Farrow v Wilson 1869 LR 4 CP 744, Court of Common Pleas. An employee who is not re-engaged by the person to whom control of the business passes will be taken to be dismissed for redundancy if failure to renew or re-engage him or her is wholly or mainly attributable to redundancy – S.139(4) and (5)

- *change in employing partnership.* In Brace v Calder and ors 1895 2 QB 253, CA, it was held that a contract of employment with two or more partners is brought to an end by the retirement from the partnership of one or more of the partners, unless the terms of the contract provide otherwise. It may be easy, however, to infer that the party contracting with the partnership is agreeing to work for the partnership as from time to time constituted and that therefore a change in the firm would not of itself automatically terminate the contract – see Briggs v Oates 1990 ICR 473, ChD. However, this may not be true where there is a major change in the partnership such as the splitting of a partnership with both parts remaining in the same business or where one of only two partners retires – see Tunstall and anor v Condon and anor 1980 ICR 786, EAT; Briggs v Oates (above)

- *appointment of receiver by the court.* Receivership by order of the courts automatically terminates the company's contracts of employment – Reid v The Explosives Co Ltd 1887 19 QBD 264, CA

- *appointment of a receiver by debenture holders as agent of the company.* Generally, the appointment of such a receiver does not automatically terminate the employees' contracts of employment – In re Foster Clark Ltd's Indenture Trusts 1966 1 WLR 125, ChD. There are, however, three exceptions to this rule. First, if the receiver sells off the business the contracts of employment are (probably – the position is not entirely clear) automatically terminated at common law. This situation, however, is now altered by the Transfer of Undertakings (Protection of Employment) Regulations 2006 SI 2006/264 (TUPE), as explained below. Secondly, the appointment may terminate the contract of employment of a particular employee if the receiver and that employee enter into a new contract inconsistent with the contract between that employee and the company – In re Mack Trucks (Britain) Ltd 1967 1 All ER 977, ChD. Thirdly, the appointment may terminate the contract of an employee whose continued employment is in conflict with the role and functions of the receiver – In re Mack Trucks. This is most likely to be the case with the directors of the company, whose powers of control and management tend to be suspended during receivership

- *appointment of a receiver by debenture holders as agent of themselves.* This will (probably) terminate the company's contracts of employment – Hopley-Dodd v Highfield Motors (Derby) Ltd 1969 ITR 289, ET; Deaway Trading Ltd v Calverley and ors 1973 ICR 546, NIRC

- *winding-up order.* Where the order is a *compulsory* order the company's contracts of employment are terminated. Any employees kept on are regarded as employed by the liquidator in his or her personal capacity – see, for example, Golding and Howard v Fire Auto and Marine Insurance Co Ltd 1968 ITR 372, ET. A resolution for the *voluntary* winding up of a company, however, does not of itself automatically terminate employment contracts – Fox Brothers (Clothes) Ltd (in liquidation) v Bryant 1979 ICR 64, EAT. Whether or not the contracts are terminated will depend on the facts. Where the business is being discontinued there may well be a termination – Reigate v Union Manufacturing Co (Ramsbottom) Ltd 1918 1 KB 592, CA. Similarly, there may also be a termination of at least some of the employment contracts where the continued employment of the employees is incompatible with any restructuring of the business – Fowler v Commercial Timber Co Ltd 1930 2 KB 1, CA

- *statutory regulations* may have the effect that the employer must terminate contracts of employment and would rank as an event affecting the employer

- *frustration.* A contract of employment may come to an end when an unforeseen event makes performance of the contract impossible or radically different from what the parties originally intended – Davis Contractors Ltd v Fareham UDC 1956 AC 696, HL. The contract is then said to have been 'frustrated'. When a contract is frustrated it ends automatically by operation of law, without a dismissal on the part of the employer or a resignation on the part of the employee, and the parties are discharged from further obligations under it. The employee cannot therefore claim unfair dismissal and is not entitled to any notice or payment in lieu – GF Sharp and Co Ltd v McMillan 1998 IRLR 632, EAT. In relation to redundancy, however, the employee might be able to rely on S.136(5) ERA, which deems a dismissal to be by reason of redundancy where a frustrating event affecting the *employer* operates to terminate the contract. Most cases on frustration in the employment context, however, turn on whether an employee's long-term sickness (or imprisonment) has frustrated the contract (see below under 'Non-dismissals and problem areas – frustration'). These are obviously not events 'affecting an employer' and so S.136(5) will not apply. But what of, for example, the situation where premises have been destroyed by bombing, or burnt down during riots? These situations may well amount to frustrating events automatically terminating the contracts of the employees involved. They are also events 'affecting [the] employer' and as such presumably fall within the scope of S.136(5). It does not matter if the event also affects the employee – British Airports Authority v Fenerty 1976 ICR 361, QBD.

1.53 Intervention of regulatory authorities

In Rose v Dodd 2005 ICR 1776, CA, a legal secretary's contract of employment was not terminated by operation of law when the Law Society intervened in the affairs of the sole practitioner firm for which she worked. Having considered the earlier decision of the EAT in Barnes and ors v Leavesley and ors 2001 ICR

24

38, EAT, the Court confirmed that the effect on contracts of employment caused by the Law Society intervening in the affairs of the employing firm is dependent on the facts of each individual case. Where the intervention leads to a cessation of trading, the contracts of employment are terminated. Where, however, the parties continue to work under the contract after the intervention, and attempts are made to dispose of the firm as a going concern, the contracts of employment continue. If contracts continue, liability for redundancy pay can transfer to a new employer under TUPE (see 'Transfer of Undertakings Regulations' below).

In Merrick (formerly t/a Wm A Merrick and Co Solicitors) v Simpson EAT 0349/10 the EAT confirmed that the principle in Rose v Dodd applies just as much to a situation in which a solicitor is suspended from practice as it does to a situation in which the Law Society is intervening in a solicitor's practice. Neither situation automatically terminates the employment of any of the solicitor's employees.

Note that many of the regulatory responsibilities of the Law Society have now been transferred to the Solicitors Regulations Authority. However, this would not appear to affect the principle established in Rose v Dodd (above).

Transfer of a business   1.54
When a business is transferred from one employer to another, TUPE (see 'Transfer of Undertakings Regulations' below) will usually apply. The main effect of the application of TUPE is that the transfer of the business does not operate to terminate the employees' contracts of employment. Instead, the contracts automatically transfer to the transferee, who then takes responsibility for all the employees' contractual and statutory rights connected with the employment relationship – Reg 4(1)–(2). As a result, there is no dismissal and no redundancy situation.

However, where TUPE does not apply, the contracts of employment are automatically terminated at common law. The employees will then be able to rely on S.136(5) to show a dismissal and may claim redundancy payments if it can be shown that there is a redundancy situation falling within S.139(1). This will not normally be difficult, particularly where the transferor ceases to trade after the transfer has taken place.

Special dismissals by statute   1.55

Under S.172 ERA the Secretary of State may provide by regulations that the termination of certain employments by statute will be deemed to be dismissals by reason of redundancy and that the statutory redundancy scheme will apply to them. Under S.172(2) this may happen even when the individuals concerned are not employees as defined by S.230. S.172 applies when a person is unwilling to be transferred from one statutory body to another. In practice, it has been

25

used in connection with problems that have arisen concerning the amalgamation of police forces and fire brigades – see Chapter 5, 'Employees and excluded employees – office holders'.

1.56 Transfer of Undertakings Regulations

Where the transfer of a business falls within the scope of the Transfer of Undertakings (Protection of Employment) Regulations 2006 SI 2006/246 (TUPE), special rules apply to automatically transfer the contracts of employees employed in the undertaking at the time of the transfer to the new employer (the transferee) – see Reg 4(1) and (2). These rules are discussed briefly below.

1.57 Pre-transfer dismissals

In order for Reg 4(1) and (2) of TUPE to have the effect of automatically transferring an employee's contract to the transferee, the employee must have been employed 'immediately before the transfer' or 'would have been so employed if he had not been dismissed in the circumstances described in Reg 7(1)' – Reg 4(3). The second criterion owes its existence to the House of Lords' decision in Litster and ors v Forth Dry Dock and Engineering Co Ltd (in receivership) and anor 1989 ICR 341, HL – a case that established that a transferee cannot avoid TUPE liability by having the transferor dismiss unwanted transferring employees in advance of, but not 'immediately before', the transfer.

By virtue of Reg 7(1), dismissals for a reason connected with a transfer are automatically unfair unless they fall within the 'economic, technical or organisational' (ETO) reason for dismissal exception set out in Reg 7(2). Put simply, then, where an employer dismisses an employee on the ground of redundancy prior to a transfer to which TUPE applies, liability for unfair dismissal and any redundancy payment will pass to the transferee if the dismissal was for a reason connected with the transfer which was not an ETO reason. If the reason for the dismissal was not connected with the transfer, or if the reason was an ETO reason, then there is no automatically unfair dismissal (although there may be an ordinary unfair dismissal under S.98 ERA). In these circumstances, liability will probably remain with the transferor – see Collins v John Ansell and Partners Ltd EAT 124/99.

1.58 In determining who is liable for a pre-transfer dismissal the key issue, therefore, is whether the employee has been dismissed for a reason connected with the transfer. This is discussed in IDS Employment Law Handbook, 'Transfer of Undertakings' (2011) at Chapter 4. The question of whether the classic redundancy situation involving a diminution in the requirement for employees can constitute an ETO reason is dealt with in Chapter 8 of this Handbook under 'Reason for dismissal – transfer of undertakings'.

Effect of employee objecting to transfer

1.59

The ECJ confirmed in Katsikas v Konstantinidis 1993 IRLR 179, ECJ, that, under the EU Acquired Rights Directive (now No.2001/23), which TUPE implements, an employee is entitled to object to the transfer of his or her employment. This is reflected in Reg 4(7)–(11) of TUPE, which states that the rules in Reg 4(1) and (2) providing for the automatic transfer of employment and of contractual rights and liabilities 'shall not operate to transfer [the employee's] contract of employment and the rights, powers, duties and liabilities under or in connection with it if the employee informs the transferor or the transferee that he objects to becoming employed by the transferee'.

The consequences of expressing such an objection are set out in Reg 4(8), which states that, subject to Reg 4(9) and (11), 'where an employee so objects, the relevant transfer shall operate so as to terminate his contract of employment with the transferor but he shall not be treated, for any purpose, as having been dismissed by the transferor'. The effect of an employee's objection to a transfer, therefore, is to prevent his or her contract of employment from passing to the transferee and to terminate his or her contract with the transferor. However, that termination will not generally – as Reg 4(8) states – amount to a dismissal.

As noted above, the objection provision of Reg 4(8) is subject to Reg 4(9) and **1.60** (11). Reg 4(11) states that Reg 4(1), (2), (8) (and indeed (9)) are 'without prejudice to the right of an employee arising apart from these Regulations to terminate his contract of employment without notice in acceptance of a repudiatory breach of contract by his employer'. This reflects the Court of Appeal's decision in Humphreys v Chancellor, Master and Scholars of the University of Oxford 2000 ICR 405, CA. There, H, who was employed to mark examination papers, left his employer prior to a transfer because the transferee planned to deprive him of the life tenure he had enjoyed under the terms of his employment contract with the transferor. The Court of Appeal found that he had 'objected' to the transfer under what was then Reg 5(4A) of the 1981 Regulations, and that his objection resulted in the termination of his contract of employment, which therefore did not pass to the transferee. Nevertheless, the Court ruled that H's objection did not remove his right to claim constructive dismissal. Furthermore, the Court held that the appropriate respondent for H's constructive dismissal claim was the transferor, since H never had a contractual relationship with the transferee. Thus, in such circumstances, if the transferor's reasons for breaching the employee's contract amount to a redundancy situation, he may be liable to make a redundancy payment.

Regulation 4(9) states that an employee who objects to a transfer on the basis that the 'transfer involves or would involve a substantial change in working conditions to the material detriment of a person whose contract of employment is or would be transferred under paragraph (1), such an employee may treat the

27

contract of employment as having been terminated, and the employee shall be treated for any purpose as having been dismissed by the employer'.

1.61 In many circumstances, Reg 4(9) and Reg 4(11) dismissals will be automatically unfair, as they are carried out for a reason connected with a transfer within the meaning of Reg 7(1). However, if the employer can show an 'economic, technical or organisational' (ETO) reason for the dismissals, they will not be automatically unfair, and might well be carried out by reason of redundancy.

Note that the workings of Reg 4 are exceedingly complex, and it would be impossible for us to provide a thorough examination of them here. For further details, see IDS Employment Law Handbook, 'Transfer of Undertakings' (2011), Chapter 4.

1.62 Non-dismissals and problem areas

As was made clear at the outset of this chapter, dismissal is the gateway through which employees must pass in order to claim a statutory redundancy payment: if there is no dismissal, there is no right to such a payment. Certain specific situations do not count as dismissals and it is important to recognise these.

1.63 Frustration

As discussed in 'Dismissal by operation of law' above, frustration of a contract arises when, through no fault of the parties, an unforeseen event makes performance of the contract impossible or radically different from what was envisaged when the contract was made – Davis Contractors Ltd v Fareham UDC 1956 AC 696, HL. When an employment contract is frustrated there is no dismissal: the contract simply comes to an end and neither party has any further obligations under it.

In the employment context, the situations in which frustration is most likely to occur are where an employee is incapacitated by illness; is prevented from working by a sentence of imprisonment; or is excluded from his or her workplace at the behest of a third party.

Note that certain frustrating events may amount to 'dismissals' for redundancy purposes by virtue of S.136(5) ERA – see 'Dismissal by operation of law' above.

1.64 **An employee's illness.** An employee's prolonged or sudden serious illness or disability is capable of frustrating the employment contract. Whether or not it does so will depend on a number of factors. The EAT in Egg Stores (Stamford Hill) Ltd v Leibovici 1977 ICR 260, EAT, set out the following relevant considerations:

- the length of previous employment
- the expected future duration of employment

- the nature of the job
- the nature, length and effect of the illness or disabling event
- the employer's need for the work to be done and need for a replacement to do it
- the risk to the employer of acquiring employment protection obligations towards a replacement employee
- whether the employee has continued to be paid
- the acts and statements of the employer in relation to the employment, including the dismissal of, or failure to dismiss, the employee
- whether a reasonable employer could be expected to wait any longer for the employee to return.

The judgment in Leibovici was subsequently considered by the EAT in Williams **1.65** v Watsons Luxury Coaches Ltd 1990 ICR 536, EAT. Having reviewed the concept of frustration in the field of employment law, the EAT made it clear that tribunals should guard against too easy an application of the doctrine, especially when redundancy occurs. Moreover, although it is not necessary to determine a specific date upon which frustration occurred, it may be helpful to attempt to do so as it may assist the tribunal in determining whether there is a true frustration situation. The EAT went on to endorse the factors identified in Leibovici, and added two more of its own:

- the contractual terms as to sick pay
- the prospects of recovery.

The EAT also pointed out that as a result of the decision in FC Shepherd and **1.66** Co Ltd v Jerrom 1986 ICR 802, CA, it was clear that a party alleging frustration should not be allowed to rely on the frustrating event if it was caused by the fault of that party. This would appear to prevent an employer treating an employee's contract of employment as frustrated in circumstances where the employee has become unable to work due to injuries sustained as a result of the employer's negligence. In Smith v Wingate Signs Ltd ET Case No.2408674/07, an unfair dismissal case, S was injured in an accident at work and went on sick leave. At the time, his employer had begun to have discussions with him about redundancy and the possibility of alternative work. There was little communication between S and his employer from April 2005, when his right to sick pay expired, until 27 July 2007, when S phoned to say he was fit to return to work. The employer maintained that S had resigned and was no longer an employee. S claimed unfair dismissal and an issue arose as to whether his contract had in fact been frustrated. However, the tribunal held that S had been unfairly dismissed. On the evidence the accident was caused by the employer's breach of duty to provide a safe system of work; that being so, the contract was not frustrated. S was dismissed on 27 July, when he was told that he was no longer an employee.

Two further cases where there was no frustration:

- **Marshall v Harland and Wolff Ltd and anor** 1972 ICR 101, NIRC: M was a shipyard fitter with 23 years' service who had been off work with angina for 18 months. There was no medical evidence of permanent incapacity and M himself expected to recover and return to work after an operation. His employment came to an end when the employer closed his workplace. The NIRC held that the contract had not been frustrated: there was no evidence that future performance would be impossible or radically different from what was originally envisaged

- **Lawton v Bawden International Ltd** EAT 421/90: L was employed by BI Ltd as a crane operator from 1976. He mainly worked offshore where he witnessed several fatal accidents and as a result suffered from depression. In June 1988 some of his friends died in the Piper Alpha disaster. Although L was onshore at the time, he suffered shock-induced depression and was certified as unfit for work until September 1988. On his return to work he suffered a further attack and was eventually certified as unfit for permanent offshore employment. He was told, however, that his job was currently secure. He received disability benefit from the company until 23 May 1989 and statutory sick pay until 11 August 1989. Later BI Ltd claimed that the employment contract had been frustrated. L complained that he had been unfairly dismissed. The tribunal held that the contract had not been frustrated, and no appeal was made against this part of the decision.

1.67 Three cases which went the other way:

- **Notcutt v Universal Equipment Co (London) Ltd** 1986 ICR 414, CA: N suffered a coronary and was off work thereafter. About nine months later the employer asked for a report from N's doctor and this said 'he is unlikely to be able to resume work in the near future. In fact, I doubt whether he will ever be able to work again.' The employer then dismissed N with 12 weeks' notice. N sued for pay during the notice period but a county court judge held that the contract had been frustrated before the employer's purported notice and the Court of Appeal upheld this finding: as soon as it was accepted by the parties that N would not work again, the frustration of the contract was established and the employer's subsequent notice was of no effect

- **Hurst v (1) Bailey Parkinson Tea Ltd (2) Secretary of State for Employment** EAT 842/95: H was off sick from mid-1991 with diabetes. In March 1992 the employer secured a report from H's doctor which said that H's condition was deteriorating and that it was unlikely he would ever work again. The employer took no steps to terminate H's contract. In 1994 the company ceased trading and all the staff were dismissed with redundancy payments. H claimed a redundancy payment. The tribunal decided that H's contract had been frustrated by his illness and that he had no entitlement to redundancy pay

- **Hanif v Secretary of State for Trade and Industry** EAT 1327/97: H was a 'stentor' at a textile firm. He had worked for his employers for nine years when he went off work with knee pain. Five years later the company went into administrative receivership and H had still not returned to work. He had been kept 'on the books' but not paid his salary. He claimed a redundancy payment from the Secretary of State, who refused to pay on the basis that his contract of employment had been frustrated. The EAT upheld this refusal, saying that while long-term sickness is something which every employment contract envisages, five years was so protracted a period that the contract was frustrated.

Once a contract has been frustrated, the parties to it cannot elect to keep it **1.68** alive. In GF Sharp and Co Ltd v McMillan 1998 IRLR 632, EAT, M was working as a joiner for a building company when he suffered a serious injury to his left hand. The injury was sustained in October 1994, and on 4 December 1995 he told his employer that he was rendered permanently incapable of doing joinery work. He was not able to do any other kind of building work. The employer told M that it would 'keep him on the books' and continue to treat him as an employee until March 1996, when he would be 60 and would qualify for higher benefits under a pension scheme. M received no wages but his employer continued to make contributions on his behalf to the pension plan. M then made a redundancy claim in a tribunal but was unsuccessful and his employer wrote to him on 27 August 1996 saying that his contract of employment was terminated. M claimed pay in lieu of notice. The tribunal found that had it not been for the agreement between M and his employer to keep the contract alive, it would have been frustrated in December 1995. However, because of the agreement it was terminated in August 1996 by the employer's letter of dismissal and therefore M was entitled to pay in lieu of notice. The EAT overturned this decision. It found that, once a contract has been declared a nullity in law by operation of the doctrine of frustration, the parties cannot elect to 'keep it alive': any arrangement to keep staff 'on the books' is not an employment contract.

Imprisonment of employee. According to the Court of Appeal in FC Shepherd **1.69** and Co Ltd v Jerrom 1986 ICR 802, CA, a custodial sentence is capable in law of frustrating an employment contract. Whether or not it does so will depend on such factors as the likely length of absence, how necessary it is to replace the employee, and whether it is necessary to find a permanent, rather than a temporary, replacement. In the Jerrom case it was held that a borstal sentence of between six months and two years, which was expected to last nine months, frustrated the four-year contract of a single apprentice in a fairly small company. However, the Court pointed out that such a sentence would not necessarily frustrate the contract of a general labourer in a very large company with a tradition of hiring temporary labour.

In Mecca Ltd v Shepherd EAT 379/78 the EAT held that a short prison sentence of 20 days ('no longer than the period of an annual holiday') was not be enough to frustrate the contract. By contrast, in Johnson v London Borough of Tower Hamlets Council ET Case Nos.3202191/09 and 3202946/09 an employment tribunal found that J's contract was frustrated when he was imprisoned for four months for fraudulently attempting to obtain or renew a driving licence. His imprisonment had made his contractual obligations as a parking enforcement officer incapable of being performed.

1.70 Restrictive bail conditions or a remand in custody may amount to a frustrating event in the same way as a custodial sentence. It will depend on the employee's ability to perform the contract and the surrounding circumstances. In Four Seasons Healthcare Ltd (formerly Cotswold Spa Retirement Hotels Ltd) v Maughan 2005 IRLR 324, EAT, M was employed by FSH Ltd as a nurse at a care home. He was suspended without pay following an allegation that he had abused a patient and was subsequently convicted and sentenced to two years' imprisonment. He brought an unauthorised deduction from wages claim relating to the period of unpaid suspension but FSH Ltd argued that the fact that M's bail conditions prevented his attending work meant that his contract of employment had been frustrated. The EAT rejected this argument. It noted that FSH Ltd had not been able to cite any case in which it was suggested that a period of bail, even if preventing an employee from attending work, might frustrate an employment contract. In any event, the EAT found that FSH Ltd had the power under M's contract to require him to work somewhere other than the care home, but had chosen not to do so. Further, in suspending M rather than dismissing him, FSH Ltd had shown itself willing to continue the contract until the conclusion of the Crown Court proceedings.

1.71 **Exclusion from place of work.** The employee's exclusion from his or her place of work by a third party may also frustrate the employment contract. In Stanley Wattam Ltd v Rippin EAT 355/98 R was employed by SW Ltd as a chicken sexer. From 1993 she had been seconded to work at the employer's most important customer, P. A dispute between R and P arose on a day when P's major supplier was due to make a visit to watch R at work. Fearful of the potential embarrassment that R might cause, P decided to ban her from their premises for good. With no other possibility of seconding R to another site, SW Ltd eventually sent her her P45. In her claim of unfair dismissal, legal argument was based on whether R had been dismissed or her contract frustrated. The tribunal found the former. On appeal, the EAT ruled that the tribunal had erred. Since R had been excluded from her place of work by a third party (P) and P had refused to change its mind, there were no alternative ways of continuing R's contract.

Early retirement
1.72

Enforced early retirement will clearly be a dismissal (and may amount to age discrimination under the Equality Act 2010 – see IDS Employment Law Guide, 'The Equality Act 2010', and IDS Employment Law Supplement, 'Age Discrimination' (2006)).

A request for early retirement can lead to a dismissal if the request is clearly not voluntary. In Vanneck-Murray v Governors of St Mary's College, Twickenham EAT 611/82, for example, it was arranged that V, a teacher, would go on leave until she reached the age of 50 and then receive an accelerated, but reduced, pension. The alternative was disciplinary proceedings likely to result in her dismissal. The EAT upheld a finding that this was a constructive dismissal, not a termination by agreement, although it was justified in view of V's conduct. In Schoon v Unison EAT 850/95, on the other hand, the EAT found that S had agreed to early retirement even though his employer had made it plain that if S did not agree to leave, investigatory procedures, preliminary to a disciplinary hearing, would be reinstated. The EAT said that the tribunal was entitled to find that this did not amount to holding a 'metaphorical pistol' to S's head.

But the distinction between voluntary and enforced early retirement is not 1.73 always an easy one to make. In Birch and anor v University of Liverpool 1985 ICR 470, CA, B and another employee made requests for early retirement under a scheme offered by the university in the context that compulsory redundancies would be needed if not enough volunteers were forthcoming. The requests were granted and the two employees were asked to make formal applications to retire on a stated date, after which the university wrote to them confirming that it was in the 'managerial interest' for them to retire and requesting them to do so on the stated date. The EAT and the Court of Appeal both held that this was not a dismissal but a termination by mutual agreement reached between the employer and the employees.

Where an employee has been issued with a notice of dismissal for redundancy and later takes early retirement instead, the position is not at all clear. In Scott and ors v Coalite Fuels and Chemicals Ltd 1988 ICR 355, EAT, written notices of redundancy were sent to the employees but in the ensuing negotiations they agreed to take early retirement as an alternative to redundancy. A tribunal concluded that the notices had been impliedly withdrawn by the employer and waived by the employees. A majority of the EAT held that there were no dismissals as the notices had been superseded by the subsequent agreement. The notice of dismissal did not prevent the parties agreeing to terminate the contract in some other way. By contrast, in Gateshead Metropolitan Borough

33

Council v Mills EAT 610/92 M was given one year's notice of redundancy. He applied, and was accepted, for early retirement. A tribunal decided that he was also entitled to a redundancy payment on the ground that he had been dismissed and the notice had never been withdrawn. The Council relied on Scott v Coalite (above) and argued that, once the agreement to take early retirement had been reached, it had impliedly withdrawn the notice. The EAT rejected this argument, holding that the notice could not be withdrawn without the consent of the employee. There was no express consent by M and no evidence that he had impliedly consented. The agreement to take early retirement was not inconsistent with a dismissal for redundancy and the tribunal had been correct to find that there had been a dismissal.

Employers would therefore be well advised to seek an employee's written consent to the withdrawal of a notice of redundancy when negotiating early retirement if they want to avoid making a redundancy payment to the employee.

1.74 Termination by mutual consent

Since a dismissal is the unilateral act of the employer, it follows that there is no dismissal where the employer and the employee agree to terminate the employment contract. In Davies v Black and Decker Ltd ET Case No.1601108/97 D, a salesman, became dissatisfied with his job after changes in the way the business was run led to changes in the terms and conditions of his employment. A meeting was convened on 17 January in respect of D's inappropriate behaviour at a recent sales marketing conference. At the meeting the issue of discipline was raised, as was the issue of a 'voluntary severance'. D was not told that his job was gone or going, but he was shown a 'voluntary redundancy package'. He accepted the package on 28 February, when he was told that it was about to be withdrawn. D claimed that he had been unfairly dismissed because he had been coerced into accepting the package. The tribunal found that there had been no dismissal and no coercion, and that D's employment had been consensually terminated.

In theory, the distinction between a dismissal by an employer and a consensual termination seems clear enough but in practice it is not always so easily made. The question of whether the employee was dismissed is a question of fact for the tribunal to decide – Scott and ors v Coalite Fuels and Chemicals Ltd 1988 ICR 355, EAT.

1.75 There is still a dismissal for redundancy if the employee agrees to the employer's proposal of redundancy or if the employee volunteers for redundancy or even if the employee persuades the employer to dismiss him or her. In practice, however, the distinction between a situation where the employee and the employer agree to terminate the contract and the situation where the employee invites the employer to dismiss him or her may be narrow. Some examples:

- **Optare Group Ltd v Transport and General Workers' Union** 2007 IRLR 931, EAT: three employees volunteered to leave their posts at the start of a redundancy exercise. Upholding an employment tribunal's decision, the EAT held that these voluntary redundancies did amount to dismissals, and that it was immaterial that the employees might have accepted a similar package even in the absence of a redundancy situation. However, the EAT noted that the result would have been different had there been evidence that the employees were anxious to leave and had expressed this wish independently of, or prior to, a redundancy situation arising

- **Burton, Allton and Johnson Ltd v Peck** 1975 ICR 193, QBD: P had been off work for several months and on his return it was found that there was no work for him. He claimed a redundancy payment. The employer argued that because P had been 'only too willing to be dismissed for redundancy' there had been a termination by mutual consent. The High Court held that an employee's agreement to redundancy is no ground for holding that a dismissal did not take place

- **Morley and ors v CT Morley Ltd** 1985 ICR 499, EAT: a father and two sons were employees and sole directors of a family business. The business was in financial difficulty and the directors decided that one of them would have to go. The father volunteered to leave and claimed a redundancy payment. Later, the two remaining directors agreed that the company would cease trading. The EAT held that: (i) the father had volunteered for redundancy and had been dismissed; and (ii) although the sons had taken the decision (as directors) to dismiss themselves (as employees), they had still been dismissed by the company

- **Walley v Morgan** 1969 ITR 122, Div Ct: M was employed on W's farm. In 1967 all the livestock was destroyed because of foot-and-mouth disease. M persuaded W to dismiss him and then claimed a redundancy payment. The Court held that the fact that W was persuaded to take the decision to dismiss did not mean that there was no dismissal

- **Kaaba and anor v Hackney Community College and ors** EAT 283/97: K's employer asked for volunteers for its 'voluntary redundancy scheme'. K, a lecturer who felt she had been shabbily treated, volunteered for the scheme and received a substantial payment. She later claimed that she had been unfairly constructively dismissed. The EAT upheld the tribunal's finding that there had been no dismissal. It said that K had not been forced to leave but had carefully considered her situation, including the generous payment on offer, and had freely resigned, although in form it was a dismissal through redundancy.

1.76 Agreement not to renew a fixed-term contract

In Manson and Johnston v (1) University of Strathclyde (2) Automated Microscopy Systems Ltd EAT 356/87 the EAT considered whether an agreement not to renew a fixed-term contract was a dismissal. In that case M and J had been employed on a series of fixed-term contracts by the University of Strathclyde. The latest contract was due to expire on 31 December 1985. In 1984 the university decided to seek outside funding to set up a company for the commercial exploitation of M and J's research. On 1 January 1986 M and J commenced employment with the new company and claimed redundancy payments from the university. In turning down their applications, the EAT found that the university had not told M and J that their fixed-term contracts would not be renewed; that they had agreed to leave the university and go to the company; and that at no time were they put under any pressure to leave. Although non-renewal of a fixed-term contract could be a dismissal (see 'Expiry of limited-term contract' above), in this case there was a termination by mutual consent.

1.77 Alternative employment

It is worth noting here that S.138(1) ERA provides that for the purposes of the statutory redundancy scheme, when an employee accepts a renewal of his or her contract or a re-engagement to take effect within four weeks of the old contract ending, there is no dismissal. The offer may be from the original employer or from an associated employer – S.146. However, S.138(1) applies only for the purposes of the statutory redundancy scheme and does not prevent an employee who has been re-employed from bringing an unfair dismissal claim – Jones v Governing Body of Burdett Coutts School 1997 ICR 390, EAT. Alternative job offers are discussed in Chapter 3.

1.78 Mobility clauses

There will be no dismissal where an employer exercises a contractual mobility clause to move an employee to a different workplace. However, an employer seeking to exercise a mobility clause to avoid a redundancy situation should tread carefully.

First, the employer needs to ensure that the clause in question authorises its actions. In Smith and anor v Westside Day Nursery Ltd ET Case No.1802542/09 WDN Ltd operated four nurseries in Hull, and S and W worked in one of them. Their contracts of employment specified that they 'may be required to work at other locations'. The staff handbook, which neither was ever given, provided that employees might be required to relocate on a permanent basis. In early 2009, WDN Ltd decided to close the nursery where S and W worked and it informed them that they would be relocated to one of the other nurseries. A tribunal upheld their claims for a redundancy payment on the basis that they had not been told where to report for work once the nursery closed, and were thus dismissed. In any event, the tribunal considered that the wording of the mobility clause was ineffective to enable WDN Ltd to transfer employees permanently. The contract described their nursery as their 'usual' place of work. A power to transfer temporarily, however, would have been consistent with the wording of the clause.

Secondly, employers need to take care as to how they exercise the power to **1.79** move the employee. In Curling and ors v Securicor Ltd 1992 IRLR 549, EAT, S Ltd had the benefit of a contractual mobility clause allowing it to relocate staff to Head Office or to one of its branch offices. When the company lost its tender to manage the detention centre where C worked it entered into negotiations over redundancies and alternative employment. At no time during the negotiations did the company seek to invoke the contractual mobility clause. However, when C and a number of his colleagues subsequently brought claims for redundancy payments in the tribunal, S Ltd argued that the existence of the mobility clause meant that there had been no dismissals and that no redundancy situation arose. Overturning the tribunal's finding that none of the employees had been dismissed, the EAT clarified that if an employer seeks to rely on the benefit of a mobility clause when making changes to jobs or the location of work, then it must make its position clear in that respect. It is not open to an employer to 'dodge' between applying redundancy procedures and invoking a mobility clause in the hope of settling on the most advantageous option.

The Curling decision was considered by the Court of Appeal in Home Office v Evans and anor 2008 ICR 302, CA. In that case E and L were employed as immigration officers at Waterloo Station. Their contracts included a clause allowing them to be transferred 'anywhere' in the United Kingdom or abroad. When the Home Office decided that immigration services at Waterloo would be closed down, it considered invoking the redundancy procedures set out in a collective agreement. However, following legal advice, the decision was taken to invoke the mobility clause and affected staff were apprised of this at the time the closure was announced in Spring 2004. When the Home Office informed E and L in August 2004 that they were to be moved to Heathrow, they resigned and claimed constructive dismissal. Both the tribunal and the EAT agreed that the Home Office was not entitled to change its mind on the redundancy/ mobility issue before finally and publicly announcing its position, since this amounted to the kind of dodging identified in the Curling case. Allowing the appeal, the Court of Appeal stated that neither the tribunal nor the EAT had properly understood or applied Curling. In Curling, the employer had shifted from implementing a redundancy procedure to relying upon a mobility clause at a much later stage of the proceedings – in fact, at the tribunal hearing itself. At that point, having already implemented the redundancy procedure, the employer's about-face was too late. By contrast, there was no question in the instant case of the Home Office dodging from one contractual procedure to

37

another; of leaving it too late to invoke the mobility clause; or of waiving its right to invoke that clause. Rather, at all times after its staff announcement, the Home Office clearly and consistently followed the contractual mobility procedure and not the redundancy procedure.

1.80 It follows from these decisions that the announcement to staff that the workplace is to close is likely to be the point of no return. The employer must have made up its mind by that stage whether it intends to invoke a contractual mobility clause or follow a redundancy procedure, which would include consideration of alternative employment.

(Note that mobility clauses may also be relevant when it comes to establishing the place of employment for the purpose of the statutory definition of redundancy. This is discussed in Chapter 2 under 'Closure of workplace – place of employment'.)

2 Redundancy

Presumption of redundancy

Definition of 'redundancy'

Closure of business

Closure of workplace

Diminishing need for employees

Reason for dismissal

A dismissed employee is only entitled to a redundancy payment if he or she has **2.1** been dismissed wholly or mainly *by reason of redundancy*. 'Redundancy' is exhaustively defined in S.139(1) of the Employment Rights Act 1996 (ERA) and covers three broad scenarios: the closure of the business, the closure of the workplace, and where there is a diminishing need for employees to do the available work. In this chapter we examine the meaning of redundancy and consider when a dismissal will be 'by reason of' redundancy. The concept of 'dismissal' is discussed in Chapter 1.

Presumption of redundancy   2.2

There is a presumption that an employee who has been dismissed has been dismissed for redundancy unless the contrary is proved – S.163(2) ERA. In practice, therefore, if an employer wants to resist making a redundancy payment it must prove, on the balance of probabilities, that the dismissal was *not* for redundancy.

An example of the application of the presumption is given by Willcox and anor v Hastings and anor 1987 IRLR 298, CA. In that case the two claimants were employed by H. One of their posts became redundant and H wished to give the other to his son. Both claimants were dismissed and claimed redundancy payments. The tribunal was unable to decide which claimant had been dismissed for which reason and therefore dismissed the claims. The Court of Appeal held that the tribunal had failed to have regard to the statutory presumption. If the presumption had been taken into account, the tribunal would have concluded that the employer had failed to rebut it in respect of both claims and that both claimants were entitled to a redundancy payment.

The presumption of redundancy only applies in claims for a redundancy **2.3** payment and not in unfair dismissal cases. This can cause curious results where the employee brings a claim for both redundancy and unfair dismissal. In

39

Midland Foot Comfort Centre v Moppett and anor 1973 ICR 219, NIRC, for example, M brought claims for a redundancy payment and unfair dismissal. The tribunal was unable to determine from the employer's vague evidence what the real reason for the dismissal was so it held that the presumption of redundancy had not been rebutted and allowed M's redundancy pay claim to succeed. It went on to find that the employer had failed to show a reason for the dismissal (although redundancy would have been an 'acceptable' reason) and allowed M's unfair dismissal claim to succeed as well. The decision was upheld by the NIRC on appeal.

2.4 Definition of 'redundancy'

Redundancy is defined in S.139(1) ERA and the definition applies both to claims for redundancy payments (see Chapter 6) and to unfair dismissal claims (see Chapter 8). The statutory words are:

'For the purposes of this Act an employee who is dismissed shall be taken to be dismissed by reason of redundancy if the dismissal is wholly or mainly attributable to –

  (a) the fact that his employer has ceased or intends to cease –

   (i) to carry on the business for the purposes of which the employee was employed by him, or

   (ii) to carry on that business in the place where the employee was so employed, or

  (b) the fact that the requirements of that business –

   (i) for employees to carry out work of a particular kind, or

   (ii) for employees to carry out work of a particular kind in the place where the employee was employed by the employer,

  have ceased or diminished or are expected to cease or diminish.'

2.5 This is a broad definition that covers a myriad of situations. One of the most common misconceptions about redundancy is that it only arises where the employer is in financial trouble or struggling to provide work. In Kingwell and ors v Elizabeth Bradley Designs Ltd EAT 0661/02 Mr Justice Burton addressed the confusion thus: 'It appears to us that there is a fundamental misunderstanding about the question of redundancy. Redundancy does not only arise where there is a poor financial situation at the employer's... It does not only arise where there is a diminution of work in the hands of an employer... It can occur where there is a successful employer with plenty of work, but who, perfectly sensibly as far as commerce and economics is concerned, decides to reorganise his business because he concludes that he is overstaffed. Thus, even with the same amount of work and the same amount of income, the decision is taken that [a] lesser number of employees are required to perform the same functions. That too is a redundancy situation.'

That said, not every business reorganisation will lead to redundancies. Where, for example, an employer decides that its aims may be achieved by redeploying employees or by dismissing them and immediately re-engaging them on different terms and conditions, the definition of redundancy in S.139(1) may not be met – see further 'Redundancy or reorganisation?' below. (Note, however, that the definition of redundancy for the purposes of collective consultation is wider, so even if such a reorganisation does not fall within the definition of redundancy under the ERA, it may nonetheless trigger the statutory consultation procedure – see Chapter 12.)

2.6 It is convenient for discussion to split the definition into three 'redundancy situations':

- closure of the business
- closure of the employee's workplace
- a diminishing need for employees to do the available work.

While these three basic descriptions are convenient for discussion, it is always important to have regard to the exact wording of S.139(1) as *a dismissal is not a redundancy unless it falls within that section.*

Temporary cessation and diminution

2.7 Section 139(6) provides that the word 'cease' in S.139(1) means either a temporary or a permanent cessation of the business and 'diminish' means either a temporary or a permanent diminution. Where a business is closed on a temporary basis, it is a question of fact for the tribunal whether the closure amounts to a 'cessation' of the business for the purposes of the redundancy scheme.

Two contrasting examples:

- **Gemmell v Darngavil Brickworks Ltd** 1967 ITR 20, ET: G was dismissed when his employer closed down the brickworks for machinery repairs. The closure lasted 13 weeks and G was unemployed for 11 of them before he found another job. This was a temporary cessation of the business which entitled him to a redundancy payment

- **Whitbread plc t/a Whitbread Berni Inns v Flattery and ors** EAT 287/94: F and others were dismissed when their employer closed the Berni Inn restaurant in which they worked. Four weeks later the business reopened as a brasserie and the employees claimed unfair dismissal. The EAT upheld the tribunal's finding that there was no redundancy situation because a four-week closure for refurbishment was not a temporary 'cessation' within the meaning of the statute. In the tribunal's view, S.139(1)(a), read with S.139(6), is 'restricted to situations where the business ceases for a significant period even if there is an intention in the future to open it, but not a situation where the operation is closed temporarily for refurbishment'. (The issue of whether the change in the type of restaurant amounted to a cessation of the old business is discussed below under 'Closure of business'.)

2.8 Associated employers

Section 139(2) states that, for the purposes of the statutory definition of redundancy, the 'business' of an employer may be treated as one with the business of any associated employer. Two employers are 'associated' if one is a company controlled (directly or indirectly) by the other (who may be a company, but does not have to be) – S.231(a) – or if both are companies controlled (directly or indirectly) by another employer (who again may be a company, but does not have to be) – S.231(b).

'Company' means a limited company – Merton London Borough Council v Gardiner 1981 ICR 186, CA. However, this requirement has been modified to permit overseas companies to come within the definition – Hancill v Marcon Engineering Ltd 1990 ICR 103, EAT – and, indeed, partnerships consisting of limited companies – Pinkney v Sandpiper Drilling Ltd and ors 1989 ICR 389, EAT.

2.9 There is some judicial dispute as to what is meant by 'control' in the context of S.231, which we discuss at greater length in IDS Employment Law Handbook, 'Continuity of Employment' (2001). In Secretary of State for Employment v Newbold and anor 1981 IRLR 305, EAT, the EAT held that 'control' means control of more than 50 per cent of the votes attaching to shares, and is not a question of how or by whom the enterprise is actually run on a 'de facto' basis. However, in Tice v Cartwright 1999 ICR 769, EAT, the EAT ruled that an employment tribunal had been correct to hold that a partnership of two brothers had indirect control of a company in which the brothers each had a 50 per cent share, so that the partnership and the company were associated employers within the meaning of S.231(a) ERA. The EAT considered that in the circumstances of that case, 'control' dealt with practical rather than theoretical matters, and the correct legal test was of 'de facto' control. As the question does not seem to have been decided definitively by the Court of Appeal, issues of control will need to be decided by reference to all the relevant case law, and to the facts in each individual case.

The practical effect of S.139(2) is that a group of companies may, if it so chooses, select employees for redundancy from any part of the group, whether or not there is a redundancy situation in each individual company. The group can be looked at as a whole when applying a redundancy selection procedure.

One further point to note: S.139(3) provides that, for the purposes of the redundancy scheme, schools maintained by a local authority may be treated as a single business. Thus, if there is a redundancy situation at any of them, all the local authority's maintained schools can be treated as if they were a group of associated companies. This applies whether the staff are employed by the local authority itself or by the governing body of the relevant school.

Lay-off and short-time   2.10

If an employee is laid off or kept on short-time, rather than dismissed, he or she has no entitlement to a redundancy payment under S.139. A claim for a redundancy payment may be made under the special provisions described in Chapter 4, however.

Redundancy or reorganisation?   2.11

Confusion can arise as to the difference between a 'redundancy' and a 'reorganisation'. Often employers are uncertain as to whether the changes they are planning to make to working structures simply amount to a reorganisation or will give rise to a redundancy situation, in which case a proper redundancy exercise must be undertaken and redundancy payments will need to be made.

However, redundancy and reorganisation are not necessarily mutually exclusive. 'Redundancy' is a technical, legal definition; while 'reorganisation' simply means a change in working structures, and has no specific legal meaning. As the EAT put it in Corus and Regal Hotels plc v Wilkinson EAT 0102/03: 'Each case involving consideration of the question whether a business reorganisation has resulted in a redundancy situation must be decided on its own particular facts. The mere fact of reorganisation is not in itself conclusive of redundancy or, conversely, of an absence of redundancy.' Thus, a particular reorganisation may involve making redundancies, if the definition of redundancy is met; or it may not – where, for example, work is redistributed more efficiently, but without the need for a reduction in the number of employees doing a particular kind of work. (Conversely, redundancy may occur without the business being reorganised at all.)

The remainder of this chapter thus concentrates on the statutory definition of **2.12** redundancy, and the kinds of scenario caught by it. However, it is worth highlighting the variety of *alternatives* to redundancy that employers may wish to consider, assuming they are in a position to choose. These measures or reorganisations short of redundancy may include, for example:

- redeployment (i.e. moving employees to different roles or areas of the business)
- 'laying off' employees (see Chapter 4)
- short-time working (see Chapter 4)

43

- restricting overtime

- cutting back on temporary staff/independent contractors, or using them more widely

- reducing business costs, such as by cutting non-essential business travel or finding more efficient ways of working

- monitoring absence more closely

- offering career breaks

- removing discretionary benefits

- changing employees' terms and conditions.

2.13 But it is vital, before any of these options is implemented, that careful consideration is given both to the terms and conditions of the affected employees' contracts, and to the implications of any changes to those contracts that the action taken may entail. For a detailed analysis of the implications of changing employment terms, and how to achieve this lawfully, see IDS Employment Law Handbook, 'Contracts of Employment' (2009), Chapter 6, 'Variation of contract'. For details of how to categorise dismissals that are consequent upon a reorganisation, but do not meet the definition of redundancy, see IDS Employment Law Handbook, 'Unfair Dismissal' (2010), Chapter 8, 'Some other substantial reason'.

2.14 Closure of business

Section 139(1)(a)(i) covers situations where the employer has ceased, or intends to cease, carrying on the business for the purposes of which the employee was employed. Complete closure of the business is the easiest sort of redundancy situation to recognise under this heading, but other changes affecting the business can also result in a redundancy situation.

2.15 Change in nature of business

Where an employer changes the type of business which is carried on at the workplace, this may be regarded as a closure of the old business but only if the employer has replaced the business with a new one that is completely different in nature. Whether a new business is sufficiently different in nature to amount to a cessation of the old business is a question of fact for the tribunal. For example, in Whitbread plc t/a Whitbread Berni Inns v Flattery and ors EAT 287/94 (discussed under 'Definition of "redundancy" – temporary cessation and diminution' above), the tribunal decided that the closure of a Berni Inn and the opening of a brasserie four weeks later was not a cessation of the old business because both were 'middle range restaurants'. The EAT upheld that finding. In Lewis v A Jones and Sons plc EAT 776/92, on the other hand, the shutting down of a family shoe shop that reopened over two months later as a fashion shoe shop targeting a much younger clientele did amount to a cessation of the old business. According to the tribunal, the new business was 'an entirely new venture targeting a different clientele and using a different approach'. The EAT dismissed the appeal.

A change in the way the business is run or the qualifications required of employees is not sufficient. In Kleboe v Ayr County Council 1972 ITR 201, NIRC, for example, K was an unregistered schoolteacher. Regulations were introduced that required all teachers to be registered, but K's application for registration was turned down and the Council dismissed him. K argued that the Council had given up the business of teaching by unregistered teachers, and this was therefore a redundancy situation. The NIRC disagreed, saying that the Council's business was simply teaching and that neither the business nor the requirement for employees to do it had ceased or diminished.

Transfer of undertakings   2.16

If the employer ceases to carry on a business because it has been transferred to a new owner, whether or not there is a potential redundancy situation will depend on whether the transfer is covered by the special rules contained in the Transfer of Undertakings (Protection of Employment) Regulations 2006 SI 2006/246 (TUPE). Where the transfer is not covered by TUPE, the common law will apply.

TUPE is fully explained in IDS Employment Law Handbook, 'Transfer of Undertakings' (2011), and the law is only summarised here:

- at common law the transfer of a business automatically terminates all existing contracts of employment. The reason for this is that by ceasing to carry on the business the employer commits a repudiatory breach of contract by putting it out of its power to continue employing the employees. The employees will then be able to claim constructive dismissal for redundancy

- where TUPE applies, the Regulations replace the common law rule. On a relevant transfer, employment contracts do not terminate. Instead, they automatically continue with the substitution of the transferee as employer. Thus, there is no dismissal and no redundancy situation.

There are only two exceptions to this rule, both of which are addressed in more **2.17** detail in Chapter 1 under 'Transfer of Undertakings Regulations'. The first is where there is an express dismissal before the transfer. In this case the dismissal takes effect (but liability for the dismissal will, in many instances, transfer to the new owner). The second exception is where the employee expressly objects to working for the transferee. In this case the employee's contract is terminated and TUPE does not apply. However, the employee will still be able to claim constructive dismissal against the transferor.

Note that even where TUPE does apply to those employees who are transferred, there may still be redundancies in respect of employees who are not included in the transfer. In Delaney v Profile Security Services Ltd and anor ET Case No.1805774/09, for example, D was employed by PSS Ltd as a part-time security guard, working on a site operated by TC Ltd. The contract was retendered in 2008. Part-time security guards were specifically excluded from the tender. PSS Ltd was not awarded the contract and it provided information under TUPE to the new contractors, SES Ltd, including details of D and another part-time employee. A tribunal held that PSS Ltd was liable to pay D a redundancy payment. This was a service provision change within the scope of TUPE, but immediately before that change there was a requirement by TC Ltd that part-time working was not to be included in the service provision. This meant that D was no longer assigned to the organised grouping of resources or employees that were subject to the transfer.

2.18 **Post-transfer dismissals.** While many dismissals made following a transfer will be transfer-related and be governed by TUPE, there may be occasions where they are properly attributable to an inherited redundancy situation, and not to the transfer itself. Such dismissals will be for reason of redundancy. In Hayes v Concorde Interiors (Europe) Ltd ET Case No.1202865/09, for example, H was employed by Cofely Ltd as a mobile maintenance engineer working on a contract held with Somerfield. Cofely Ltd decided not to continue with the contract and CIE Ltd was asked to provide reactive maintenance services for some of Somerfield's stores. During due diligence, CIE Ltd discovered that Cofely Ltd employed twice as many engineers as it believed were needed for the work. It concluded that there was a long-standing redundancy situation that had not been addressed. CIE Ltd accepted all of the engineers on the basis that the position would be reviewed after two months. At that point it established that the contract was running at a loss and some of the engineers, including H, were made redundant. A tribunal found that the reason for dismissal was the redundancy situation that Cofely Ltd had not addressed, and not the fact of the transfer.

2.19 **Proposed transfer.** In Downs v Landscape Institute ET Case No.2202349/09 an employment tribunal had to decide whether an archivist was dismissed as redundant in circumstances where, at the time of dismissal, it was proposed to transfer the entire archive to a new owner. However, the transfer never actually took place and the archive was mothballed. The employment tribunal decided that the dismissal could not amount to redundancy because, at the time, the Institute intended to transfer the archive to a new owner and envisaged it remaining available for consultation and continuing to be catalogued and organised. As the dismissal did not fall into any of the potentially fair reasons for dismissal, it was unfair, even though there was, shortly afterwards, a genuine redundancy situation.

Closure of workplace 2.20

Section 139(1)(a)(ii) deals with the situation where an employer simply closes down a particular workplace. An employee who works at that particular workplace will be redundant if that was 'the place where the employee was... employed'. Even if the employer starts up the business again at a different location – i.e. simply moves that part of the business rather than closing it down completely – the employee will still be redundant. In deciding whether an employee is entitled to a redundancy payment on the closure of a workplace, two issues have to be considered:

- where the employee was employed to work

- any offer of suitable alternative employment at another workplace. If the employee unreasonably refuses such an offer from the employer, he or she will not be entitled to a redundancy payment – see Chapter 3 for details.

Place of employment 2.21

There is usually no difficulty in establishing where employees are employed to work. In most cases, it is where they report each day to carry out their duties. And in the case of 'travelling' jobs, employees usually have a defined area – their 'patch' – in which their duties are to be carried out. Furthermore, most contracts of employment specify either one identifiable place or one identifiable area as the employee's place of employment. Thus, in the typical case, it will be clear whether the place where the employee was employed to work has been closed down or not.

The EAT decided in one case that a temporary change in location does not alter an employee's place of work, even if the original workplace later closes down. In Kentish Bus and Coach Co Ltd v Quarry EAT 287/92 a driver was based at the Southwark depot. The employer decided to close down that depot and, until another one opened in the Southwark area, Q was asked to work from Leyton. The EAT upheld a tribunal's decision that Southwark remained Q's place of work for redundancy purposes while he worked temporarily elsewhere. He became redundant when the employer decided not to renew the operation in Southwark and asked him to stay at Leyton on a permanent basis.

Mobility clauses. Establishing the place of employment has proved more 2.22 problematic, however, where a contract contains a mobility clause that allows the employer to change the employee's place of work. The confusion stemmed from the fact that there were originally two conflicting lines of authority on the correct test for determining the place of employment in these circumstances. Some decisions favoured the factual (sometimes called the geographical) test, which deems the place of employment to be the place where duties are actually

47

carried out, while others applied the contractual test, which deems it to be the place or places where employees can be required to work under their contracts.

For many years, the contractual test held sway. For example, in United Kingdom Atomic Energy Authority v Claydon 1974 ICR 128, NIRC, C was employed under a contract whereby he could be required to work at any UKAEA establishment. The employer closed the unit where C worked in Suffolk and offered him a transfer to Berkshire, but he refused to move and was dismissed. When he claimed a redundancy payment, the NIRC said that 'the place where [the employee] was... employed' meant any place where C could be required to work under his contract – i.e. any UKAEA establishment in Great Britain or overseas – and that, since there was work available, C was not redundant. Sir John Donaldson explained that: 'Many men and women are employed under contracts of employment which provide for transfers over a wide area. If work is short in one place but available elsewhere within the area, there will be no redundancy situation and the employer can dismiss without being liable to make any redundancy payment.'

2.23 However, the contractual test was always open to the criticism that it distorted the wording of the statute in that, instead of ascertaining the place where the employee was employed to work, it concentrated on the place where he or she *might* be required to work. The test was finally laid to rest by two decisions which made it clear that the contractual test should no longer be considered good law and that the factual test should be applied. In Bass Leisure Ltd v Thomas 1994 IRLR 104, EAT, T was employed by BL Ltd as a collector. She was based at the company's depot in Coventry and her work involved driving to a number of public houses to collect the takings from fruit machines. The employer shut down the Coventry depot and based T in Erdington, some 20 miles away. The extra travelling time disrupted T's domestic arrangements and she resigned and claimed a redundancy payment. T's contract contained two transfer clauses but the tribunal found that the employer could not rely on them because the conditions which were attached to them had not been satisfied. The tribunal held that T had been constructively dismissed and that she was entitled to a redundancy payment. The EAT upheld this finding on the ground that the place where T was employed was the Coventry depot and not the Coventry area. The mobility clause did not affect T's position because the employer had not complied with its terms. The EAT also held that T had not been offered suitable alternative employment.

While that was enough to dispose of T's case, the EAT nevertheless decided to address the issue of whether the test of the place of employment is factual or contractual. The EAT noted that the use of the word 'the' in 'the place where the employee was... employed' in S.139(1)(a)(ii) suggested that there was one identifiable 'place'. That place could, however, be widely defined in the contract to include a geographical area. Thus, for example, 'the place' where a steel erector is employed could be the area within which he can be required to attend at construction sites to perform his duties. The EAT also found considerable difficulty with any construction which treated 'the place where the employee was... employed' as any place the employee could be contractually bound to work. It reasoned that if a contract provides that an employee works at A, but could be moved on notice to B, then A must be the place of work until it changes to B. In the EAT's view, to hold that both A and B are the places of work would be contrary to the express wording of the contract. It concluded that the place where an employee was employed for redundancy purposes was a factual matter and one to be ascertained from the employee's fixed or changing place or places of work and any contractual terms evidencing this. Any contractual terms that make provision for the employee to be transferred to another place are irrelevant for these purposes.

The EAT's approach in the Thomas case was subsequently endorsed by the **2.24** Court of Appeal in High Table Ltd v Horst and ors 1998 ICR 409, CA. In that case H, J and B worked for a contract catering company, HT Ltd, as silver service waitresses. Their contracts specified that they would be assigned to a catering contract with a particular firm in the City of London as their normal place of work, but a mobility clause also provided that they could be transferred to other contracts if the needs of the business changed. In 1992 the company where H, J and B were located reduced its catering budget and informed HT Ltd that the catering contract would have to be scaled down accordingly. As a result, the roles of H, J, B and one other waitress were amalgamated into one post with longer working hours. H, J and B were not prepared to work the additional hours and so the post was given to the other waitress. H, J and B received redundancy payments, but they brought claims of unfair dismissal. The tribunal hearing focused on the question of whether HT Ltd had acted reasonably in terms of consultation and in seeking to redeploy the employees. The tribunal decided that the dismissals were fair. The EAT allowed the employees' appeal on the basis that there was a question mark over whether the dismissals had in fact been for redundancy. The EAT took the view that, because there was a mobility clause in the employees' contracts, it could be argued that there was no diminution in the requirement for employees at the place where the employees worked, since the place where they worked was the whole of HT Ltd's operations. The employer appealed to the Court of Appeal, which held that the EAT had erred. According to the Appeal Court, the 'place' where an employee is employed should be determined primarily by a consideration of the factual circumstances pertaining prior to the dismissal. It was clear that the place where the employees were employed in this particular case was the premises of the principal client for whom they were accustomed to work, and that the diminution in the needs of that client for the services of the employees meant that there was a redundancy situation at the employees' place of work for the purposes of S.139(1)(a)(ii).

49

In reaching its decision, the Court of Appeal specifically rejected the argument that the statute imposed a contractual test in respect of determining whether or not a redundancy situation arises. However, the Court acknowledged that, if the employee's work involved a change of location – as would be the case where the nature of the employee's work required him or her to go from place to place – then the contract of employment may be of assistance in determining the extent of the place where the employee was employed. But it cannot be right to let the contract be the sole determinant, regardless of where the employee actually worked. If an employee has worked in only one location during his or her employment, then there is no reason to widen the extent of the place where he or she was employed merely because of the existence of a mobility clause.

2.25 It follows from the Horst case that the contractual test for determining the place where the employee is employed for the purposes of S.139(1)(a) has now been laid to rest. This does not mean that the contract of employment is to be disregarded altogether, however. As was emphasised in both the Thomas and the Horst cases, the terms of the employee's contract may be of relevance under the factual test as one of the factors to be taken into account. For example, if an employee has worked at a particular site for the whole of his or her employment and is dismissed when that site is closed, then that will be a dismissal for redundancy regardless of the fact that the employer would have been entitled under the contract to move the employee to another site. But if the employee has been moved from place to place during the employment, the terms of a mobility clause may be of relevance in determining the place where the employee was in fact employed.

There are two other reasons why the existence of a mobility clause remains relevant. First, if the employer seeks to enforce the clause against the employee, it may be able to avoid making a redundancy payment, either by avoiding a dismissal in the first place or by establishing that the reason for dismissal was not redundancy but misconduct (i.e. the refusal to obey a lawful instruction to move to a different place of work). Secondly, it is possible that a tribunal may consider the existence of a mobility clause as relevant to the question of whether the redundant employee has refused an offer of reasonable alternative employment (see Chapter 3).

2.26 Care should be taken, however, to ensure that the wording of the mobility clause permits the employer's actions. In Smith and anor v Westside Day Nursery Ltd ET Case No.1802542/09 WDN Ltd operated four nurseries in Hull, and the claimants worked in one of them. Their contracts of employment specified that they 'may be required to work at other locations' and the staff handbook, which neither claimant was ever given, provided that employees might be required to relocate on a permanent basis. In early 2009, WDN Ltd decided to close the nursery in which the claimants worked, as the numbers of children attending had declined, and informed employees that they would be relocated to one of the other nurseries. The claimants maintained that the offer of alternative work was not suitable for them in view of the increased travelling. A tribunal upheld their claims for a redundancy payment, on the basis that they had not been told where to report for work once the nursery closed, and were thus dismissed. In any event, the tribunal considered that the wording of the mobility clause was ineffective to enable WDN Ltd to transfer employees permanently. The contract described their nursery as their 'usual' place of work. A power to transfer temporarily, however, would have been consistent with the wording of the clause.

Territorial jurisdiction. The Court of Appeal's decision in High Table Ltd v **2.27** Horst and ors (above) was subsequently affirmed in the somewhat unusual case of Pitman v Foreign and Commonwealth Office 2003 ICR 699, EAT. P was an overseas security officer employed by the FCO under a contract which provided that he had to be prepared 'to serve anywhere in the United Kingdom or abroad'. In 1994 the FCO concluded that the number of overseas security officers should be reduced but that in some cases locally engaged security officers could be recruited to replace them. As a result, P was dismissed by reason of redundancy when his duties in New York were transferred to locally employed security officers. He brought a claim of unfair dismissal, arguing that there had not been a redundancy situation. In determining the claim in favour of the FCO, the employment tribunal first assumed that P was ordinarily working in Great Britain and that it therefore had jurisdiction to hear the claim under S.196 ERA. As a result, it concluded that P's place of work for the purposes of S.139 was within Great Britain, while his successor's place of work was New York. On appeal, the EAT held that the question of whether the tribunal has jurisdiction – and the determination in that context of whether somebody is ordinarily working abroad or in Great Britain – does not determine the question of where that person is employed for the purposes of S.139. Accordingly, the case was remitted to the tribunal to determine, inter alia, where the claimant was employed. (Note that S.196 was repealed in October 1999, leaving the ERA silent as to territorial jurisdiction. The question of territorial jurisdiction in *unfair dismissal* cases has since been governed primarily by the House of Lords' decision in Lawson v Serco Ltd and two other cases 2006 ICR 250, HL, and it is arguable that the principles established in that case apply to other claims, including claims for redundancy payments, under the ERA – see further Chapter 5 under 'Employees and excluded employees – overseas employment'. However, it would seem reasonable to assume that the general principle established in Pitman – that the question of whether there has been a redundancy is distinct from any question of jurisdiction – still applies even after the repeal of S.196.)

51

2.28 ## Transfer of undertakings

If the employer ceases to carry on business at a particular workplace because it has been transferred to a new owner, TUPE may come into play. This is discussed more fully under 'Closure of business – transfer of undertakings' above.

2.29 # Diminishing need for employees

Section 139(1)(b) states that there is a redundancy situation where the requirements of the business for employees to carry out work of a particular kind, or for employees to carry out work of a particular kind in the place where they are employed, have ceased or diminished. This covers three separate situations:

- where work of a particular kind has diminished, so that employees have become surplus to requirements

- where work has not diminished, but fewer employees are needed to do it, either because

  - the employees have been replaced by, for example, independent contractors or technology, or

  - because of a reorganisation which results in a more efficient use of labour.

2.30 It is the requirement for *employees* to do work of a particular kind which is significant. The fact that the work is constant, or even increasing, is irrelevant. If fewer employees are needed to do work of a particular kind, there is a redundancy situation – McCrea v Cullen and Davison Ltd 1988 IRLR 30, NICA. In Hand Tools Ltd v Maleham EAT 110/91 M was production manager for HT Ltd. Following a management buy-out, he took on the role of general manager. His functions included supervision of the shop-floor, although he also took on some sales activity work, which was not successful. He was eventually dismissed for redundancy. A tribunal ruled by a majority that there was no redundancy situation as the work which M had been required to do – i.e. supervision of the shop-floor – continued to be a necessary function of the company. On appeal, the EAT held that the tribunal had erred in treating the continuation of M's supervisory functions as the determining factor. The proper test in M's case was whether the requirement of the business for employees to carry out that particular kind of work had ceased or diminished, not whether there had been an end to or reduction in that kind of work. M had already conceded that the company could not sustain three executive employees where, before the buy-out, it had supported M working more or less on his own. By the proper definition of S.139(1)(b), M was redundant.

Note, however, that in cases of reorganisation where the overall number of employees remains the same or even increases, there may nevertheless be a redundancy situation where the requirements of the business for employees to carry out a *particular kind* of work have ceased or diminished, or are expected to do so. Such situations are discussed further below, under 'Less work available'.

The EAT has made it clear that there is no need under S.139(1)(b) for an employer to show an economic justification (or business case) for the decision to make redundancies. In Polyflor Ltd v Old EAT 0482/02 an employment tribunal held that there was no redundancy situation where an employee, having recently been placed in a new post, was dismissed and had his duties redistributed among four regional managers. Part of the tribunal's reasoning was that the employer's evidence fell well short of showing an economic need to cut costs or make the employee redundant. Overturning this decision on appeal, the EAT held that this was a clear redundancy situation since the dismissal was attributable to a diminution in the requirements for employees to do work of a particular kind. (Note, however, that the employer's motives may become relevant if it is alleged that the redundancy is a sham and that there is another, possibly discriminatory, reason for dismissal – see 'Reason for dismissal' below.) **2.31**

Part-time employees. In some circumstances, the diminution in the need for employees to carry out a particular kind of work may be minimal and the employer may only need to lose 'half a person'. This could be achieved by reducing an employee's hours, or by selecting a part-time employee for redundancy. It is important to note, however, that selecting someone who works part time for redundancy in preference to a full-time employee because of his or her part-time status may constitute a detriment for the purposes of the Part-time Workers (Prevention of Less Favourable Treatment) Regulations 2000 SI 2000/1551, unless that selection can be objectively justified. See further Chapter 8 under 'Automatically unfair dismissal – part-time and fixed-term employees'. **2.32**

Test of redundancy
2.33

The question of whether an employee is redundant within the meaning of S.139(1)(b) was for many years dogged by a controversy over the correct test for determining the work which the dismissed employee was employed to carry out. According to one approach – the 'function' test – it was necessary to focus on the work that the employee actually did and it made no difference that under his or her contract of employment he or she could in fact be required to do other work. According to the rival 'contract' test, however, it was necessary to focus on the work which the employee could be required to do under the contract of employment.

Thanks, however, to two decisions which took a bold and fresh look at S.139(1)(b), the whole contract/function controversy has been consigned to the dustbin of legal history. These two decisions established a test based directly on the statutory wording without any unnecessary gloss.

2.34 The first of these cases was Safeway Stores plc v Burrell 1997 ICR 523, EAT. In that case (the facts of which are given below under 'Less work available – redeployment') the EAT stated that the function/contract debate was based on a misreading of both the statute and previous authorities. Judge Peter Clark set out a simple three-stage test. A tribunal must decide: (i) was the employee dismissed? (ii) if so, had the requirements of the employer's business for employees to carry out work of a particular kind ceased or diminished, or were they expected to cease or diminish? (iii) if so, was the dismissal of the employee caused wholly or mainly by the cessation or diminution?

Judge Peter Clark stated that there are no grounds for importing into the statutory wording a requirement that there must be a diminishing need for employees to do the kind of work for which the *claimant* was employed. The only question to be asked when determining stage (ii) of the three-stage test is whether there was a diminution in the employer's requirement for *employees* (rather than the individual claimant) to carry out work of a particular kind. It is irrelevant at this stage to consider the terms of the applicant's contract. The terms of the contract are only relevant at stage (iii) when determining, as a matter of causation, whether the redundancy situation was the operative reason for the employee's dismissal.

2.35 The test set out in the Burrell case was widely acclaimed as bringing light and clarity to a previously dark and muddled area of redundancy law and was subsequently endorsed by the House of Lords in Murray and anor v Foyle Meats Ltd 1999 ICR 827, HL. In that case (the facts of which are also given below under 'Less work available – redeployment') Lord Irvine described the identical language used in the Northern Ireland equivalent of S.139(1) as 'simplicity itself'. The contract and function tests missed the point, he said, because the key word in S.139 was 'attributable' (in that the dismissal must be attributable to one of the three redundancy situations set out in the section – see 'Definition of "redundancy"' above) and there was no reason why the dismissal of an employee should not be attributable to a diminution in the employer's need for employees irrespective of the terms of the contract or the function which the employee performed. For Lord Irvine, S.139 asks two questions of fact. The first is whether there exists one or other of the various states of economic affairs mentioned in the section – e.g. whether the requirements of the business for employees to carry out work of a particular kind have ceased or diminished. The second question, which is one of causation, is whether the dismissal is wholly or mainly attributable to that state of affairs. Naturally, in the case of a dismissal of an employee who could have been employed elsewhere, or who was not carrying out work the requirement for which had ceased or diminished, it may be more difficult to establish that the dismissal was indeed attributable to the redundancy situation. But that is a question of fact, not law, for the tribunal to decide.

The advantage of the Burrell/Murray approach is that it removes the need to consider exactly what an employee can or cannot be required to do under his or her contract of employment and accords better with the wording of the statute. Another significant advantage is that it explains how a so-called 'bumping' dismissal – i.e. where an employee whose job is redundant is kept on at the expense of an employee in relation to whom no redundancy situation exists – can be a redundancy dismissal within the wording of the statute. Bumping redundancies are discussed under 'Reason for dismissal' below.

Having set out the test for redundancy, it is now necessary to look further at the different types of circumstances giving rise to a redundancy situation under S.139(1)(b).

Less work available
2.36

Where the number of employees needed has declined because the work required from those employees has declined, there is clearly a redundancy situation. In Short v PJ Hayman and Co Ltd EAT 0379/08, for example, the EAT upheld a tribunal's finding that the loss of a major contract which had provided 75 per cent of the work dealt with by the employer's insurance claims department gave rise to a redundancy situation, and that the dismissal of the claims manager was wholly or mainly attributable to the diminution in work.

But the situation is less clear cut where the business requires less work of a particular kind, but the number of employees remains the same overall. These difficult cases tend to fall into the following categories:

- reallocation of duties
- same work done under different terms and conditions
- same work done by different kind of employee
- work changes, but remains work of the same particular kind
- redeployment.

We examine these in turn.

Reallocation of duties. There is a conflict of authority on the question of whether a redundancy situation arises where a job disappears when an employer redistributes the same amount of work among the same number of employees. Two different approaches have been adopted: the 'requirements of the business' test and the 'jobs' test. The difference between these tests is best illustrated by an example: 2.37

- two individuals are employed as 'packer/stackers'. Following a reorganisation, the employer decides that he now requires one packer and one stacker. The overall requirements of the business are the same, in that the employer requires the same number of employees to do the same amount of work. The 'requirements of the business' test therefore suggests that there is no redundancy situation. The 'jobs' test, on the other hand, requires the tribunal to consider whether there has been a reduction in the requirement for employees to do work of a particular kind. If, therefore, packing/stacking can be categorised as 'work of a particular kind', then this will lead to the conclusion that the employees are redundant.

2.38   The leading authority for the 'requirements of the business' test is North Riding Garages Ltd v Butterwick 1967 ITR 229, Div Ct. In that case NRG Ltd took over the garage where B worked as workshop manager. The new management modified his duties to include estimating the cost of repairs. B was unable to cope with the new duties and was dismissed. The tribunal awarded him redundancy pay, because the requirement for a manager of the old type had ceased. This decision was reversed on appeal. The High Court held that the tribunal had applied the wrong test by looking at the allocation of duties between individuals, rather than the overall requirements of the business. The introduction of new methods may give rise to redundancy, but only if the new methods alter the nature of the work done. Mr Justice Widgery, giving judgment for the Court, said: 'For the purposes of [the ERA] an employee who remains in the same kind of work is expected to adapt himself to new methods and techniques... but if new methods alter the nature of the work required to be done it may follow that no requirement remains for employees to do work of the particular kind which has been superseded and that they are truly redundant... We think that the tribunal has fallen into error by applying the wrong test in that they have not looked at the overall requirements of the business but at the allocation of duties between individuals. It is irrelevant that the duties of the new manager are not identical with the duties formerly undertaken by the respondent if the overall requirements of the business are unchanged.'

Another example is Jones v Star Associated Holdings Ltd 1970 ITR 178, Div Ct, in which J was employed as manager of a bingo hall and a cinema. The employer promoted J's assistant by making her manageress of the bingo hall and demoted J by leaving him to run the cinema only (with a cut in pay). The High Court held that J was not redundant: there was no diminution in the requirements for work or for employees to do the work. (J might well, on the facts, have had grounds for an unfair dismissal claim, but that remedy had not been introduced at the time of his dismissal.)

2.39   In Frame It v Brown EAT 177/93 B was dismissed when her employer reallocated her duties among three other individuals in order to cut costs. She claimed unfair dismissal and the employer sought to rely on redundancy as the reason for the dismissal. The tribunal noted that the work B carried out had not diminished and the number of employees in the company remained virtually the same. It concluded that B was not redundant and held that the dismissal was unfair since the employer had failed to show a fair reason for dismissal. The employer appealed, arguing that it was irrelevant that the work previously carried out by B had not ceased: S.139(1)(b) required the tribunal to consider the needs of the business for employees to carry out work of a particular kind. The employer also argued that the tribunal had erred in finding that the overall number of employees in the company had remained the same. Referring to the two rival tests, the EAT expressed the view that the problem with the 'jobs' test is that it would hamper any reorganisation or reallocation of duties within a business enterprise. The EAT concluded that the tribunal had been entitled to consider the company's overall requirements for work of the type B carried out and that there was no reason to interfere with the tribunal's findings.

The main authority for the 'jobs' test is Murphy v Epsom College 1985 ICR 80, CA. In that case M was one of two plumbers but he also did some engineering work. Later M declined to perform the engineering tasks and the college decided to dismiss him and employ an engineer who would also undertake some plumbing. The evidence suggested that the college still needed two employees, one plumber and one who would do both plumbing and engineering work. On the 'requirements of the business' test, therefore, it appeared that there was no redundancy situation. Both the EAT and the Court of Appeal held, however, that M's dismissal was for redundancy: whereas before the business required a plumber who could do some engineering, now it required an engineer who could do some plumbing. The EAT justified its approach by reference to the wording of S.139, which defines redundancy as a diminishing need for 'employees to carry out work of a particular kind'. In this case, the employer no longer needed an employee to carry out work of the particular type done by M and he was, therefore, redundant. The Court of Appeal upheld this finding, saying that a reorganisation creating a substantial change in the kind of work required by the employer can result in redundancies even though his overall requirements for work or employees remain the same.

2.40 The Murphy decision is open to criticism in that the Court of Appeal did not take account of the earlier authorities when reaching its decision. Nevertheless, we would suggest that the 'jobs' test is entirely in line with the statutory wording, which speaks of a diminution in the requirements of the business 'for employees to carry out work of a particular kind'. It is significant that in Safeway Stores plc v Burrell 1997 ICR 523, EAT (see 'Test of redundancy' above), the EAT emphasised that the new test set out in that case was consistent with the decision in Murphy. As Judge Peter Clark put it: 'The employer originally had two plumbers, now it only required one. The employee was dismissed by reason of redundancy.'

The Murphy decision was also followed in British Broadcasting Corporation v Farnworth EAT 1000/97 where F, a radio producer, was replaced by a more experienced producer. The EAT upheld the tribunal's decision that her dismissal was for redundancy, stating that an employee is redundant when his or her particular specialism is no longer required, even if the employee is replaced by an employee with a different specialism so that the overall requirements of the business for employees have not diminished. Just as in the Murphy case a plumber who could do the work of a heating engineer was replaced by a heating engineer who could do plumbing, so in the instant case the post of 'Mark 1' producer had been replaced by that of 'Mark 2' producer. (The facts of the case are outlined in more detail below, under 'Same work done by different kind of employee'.)

2.41   The issue was revisited by the Court of Appeal in Shawkat v Nottingham City Hospital NHS Trust (No.2) 2002 ICR 7, CA. S worked exclusively as a thoracic surgeon for the Trust. However, the Trust decided to merge the cardiac and thoracic surgery departments in the hospital where S worked and subsequently informed S that he would be required to carry out both forms of surgery. He refused to carry out any cardiac surgery and was eventually dismissed. An employment tribunal found that S had been unfairly dismissed on the ground that the Trust had attempted to impose unreasonable duties on him that he had reasonably declined to carry out. However, the tribunal dismissed S's claim for a redundancy payment. It held that the Trust's requirement for employees to carry out thoracic surgery had not diminished and, therefore, there had been no diminution in the Trust's requirement for employees to perform 'work of a particular kind' within the meaning of S.139(1)(b)(i). Upholding this decision on appeal, the Court of Appeal confirmed that the correct approach is for a tribunal to decide, as a question of fact, whether the employer's need for employees to carry out work of a particular kind has diminished. It is, therefore, the kind of *work* that must be defined (such as, in the instant case, 'thoracic surgery') rather than the kind of *employee* (such as, in the instant case, '100 per cent thoracic surgeon'). Accordingly, although the effect of the Trust's reorganisation of the cardiac and thoracic departments changed the work that its employees in the thoracic department were required to carry out, since the Trust still needed the same amount of thoracic surgery being carried out, S was not redundant despite being asked to reduce the amount of thoracic surgery that he himself performed.

The Shawkat decision may appear, at first sight, to adopt a contrary position to that of the Court of Appeal in Murphy v Epsom College (above). However, the Court in Shawkat incorporated into its judgment Sir Denys Buckley's statement in Murphy that: 'Every case of reorganisation must, I think, depend ultimately on its particular facts. In each case it must be for the individual tribunal to decide whether the reorganisation and reallocation of functions within the staff is such as to change the particular kind of work which a particular employee, or successive employees, is or are required to carry out, and whether such change has had any, and if so what, effect on the employer's requirement for employees to carry out a particular kind of work.'

Murphy and Shawkat are, in fact, distinguishable. In Murphy the employer **2.42** required 'a different kind of tradesman... to perform functions and assume responsibilities in connection with the college's heating installations of a more extensive and more responsible kind than the functions which Mr Murphy was competent to perform' but who would also be able to assist with general plumbing work, meaning that the employer's need for plumbers was reduced from two to one. In Shawkat, on the other hand, while the employer's reorganisation changed the work that S personally was required to carry out, this change had no effect on the employer's requirement for employees to carry out a particular kind of work. Indeed, the EAT in Corus and Regal Hotels plc v Wilkinson EAT 0102/03 confirmed that there is no conflict between Murphy and Shawkat. The question of whether or not there is a diminution in the requirements of the business for employees to carry out a particular kind of work is a matter of fact for the tribunal to decide in each case.

Change in duties. A reallocation of duties may entail a fundamental change in **2.43** the duties of employees so that the work to be done after the reallocation is quite different from that done before. This may create a redundancy situation. In Robinson v British Island Airways Ltd 1978 ICR 304, EAT, the posts of 'Flight Operations Manager' (R's job) and 'General Manager Operations and Traffic' were abolished and a new job of 'Operations Manager' was created. Both holders of the existing jobs were considered unsuitable for the new one and they were dismissed. R claimed that his dismissal was unfair, but the EAT said that he was fairly dismissed because of redundancy. It based its judgment on the finding that the work in the new job was 'in a different league' (because it was far more important) from that in the old jobs. (Note that fewer employees were needed because two posts were replaced by one and the EAT could have found R to be redundant for this reason – although it did not.)

Same work done under different terms and conditions. The Court of Appeal **2.44** has held on a number of occasions that work and the requirement for employees to do it do not change simply because the work is carried out under different terms and conditions. Changes in terms and conditions are relevant to the fairness of a dismissal but they do not create a redundancy situation. In Chapman and ors v Goonvean and Rostowrack China Clay Co Ltd 1973 ICR 310, CA, the employer withdrew free transport to work because it was uneconomic and some employees lost their jobs because they could no longer get to work. The Court of Appeal held that there was no redundancy situation. The fact that the terms of employment had changed did not mean that the requirements for work and for employees to carry it out had changed, so that the statutory definition of redundancy was not satisfied. The result would have been different if the statute referred to the requirements for employees 'on the existing terms of employment' – but the statute does not contain these words. Lord Clyde put it well in Murray and anor v Foyle Meats Ltd 1999 ICR 827, HL, when he said: 'The contractual provisions which the employer may make with the employees are not necessarily a requirement of the business: they are rather a means whereby the requirements of the business in respect of the workforce may be met.'

2.45 A similar point was considered in Johnson v Nottinghamshire Combined Police Authority 1974 ICR 170, CA. There the employer introduced a double-shift system for two clerical workers at a police station, but the new hours did not suit them and they were dismissed and replaced by two different employees. They claimed redundancy payments, but the Court of Appeal held that the dismissals were not for redundancy. The same work still remained to be done by the same number of employees, the only difference being in the hours during which the work was to be done.

The point was emphasised again in Loy v Abbey National Financial and Investment Services plc 2006 SLT 761, Ct Sess (Outer House), where L argued that, following a takeover, certain aspects of his job were sufficiently different to indicate that his previous job had come to an end. Rejecting this contention, the Court re-emphasised that changes to an employee's terms and conditions, even changes that would entitle the employee to claim constructive dismissal, do not mean that the employee is redundant. The only test for redundancy is that found in Safeway Stores plc v Burrell 1997 ICR 523, EAT, and Murray and anor v Foyle Meats Ltd 1999 ICR 827, HL. Since, in the present case, the requirements for employees to do work of a particular kind had neither ceased nor diminished, L was not redundant. A similar conclusion was reached in Shawkat v Nottingham City Hospital NHS Trust (No.2) 2002 ICR 7, CA (discussed in full under 'Reallocation of duties' above), in which the Court of Appeal held that even though S had been unfairly dismissed on the ground that his employer had attempted to impose unreasonable duties on him that he had reasonably declined to carry out, he was not redundant because the Trust's requirements for employees to perform work of a particular kind had not diminished.

Two further examples:

- **Mitie Olscot Ltd v Henderson and ors** EAT 0016/04: the company tried to remedy its economic difficulties by seeking its employees' consent to a variation to their terms and conditions. When the employees refused, they were dismissed. The EAT upheld the tribunal's decision that the attempt to renegotiate the contracts, if successful, would not have resulted in job losses and that the real reason for the dismissals was the economic problems. This did not meet the definition of redundancy since the need for employees had not diminished

- **Martland and ors v Co-Operative Insurance Society Ltd** EAT 0220/07: the dismissal of the entire sales workforce, followed by an offer of re-engagement on new terms, was held to be for 'some other substantial reason' and not for redundancy. In the view of both the tribunal and the EAT, the work which was required both before and after the dismissal was 'selling' and neither changes in the method of performance nor a reduced level of contact with clients could justify an inference that the work was of a different kind.

A case that does not rest easily with the above authorities is McCafferty v **2.46** Rankin Park Club EAT 205/90. M was the manager of a social club and was responsible for day-to-day tasks, including the engagement and payment of casual staff. The club found itself in financial difficulty and decided to terminate M's existing employment and to offer him a job as bar manager. As bar manager he would still have been responsible for the day-to-day running of the club and for the engagement of casual staff but not for their payment. His salary would also have been reduced and he would have been responsible for his own national insurance and income tax contributions. In other respects his work would remain the same. M rejected the job and claimed unfair dismissal. The tribunal held that M had been dismissed for redundancy and the EAT upheld that decision.

With respect, it is difficult to see how the statutory definition of redundancy had been satisfied in this case. The evidence seems to show that the requirements of the business for a person to carry out the type of work which M had done previously had not diminished; all that had altered were some of the terms on which that type of work was to be carried out. The EAT did not refer to the Court of Appeal's judgment in either Chapman or Johnson and the decision must therefore be treated with some caution.

There are two situations where a change in the terms of employment can lead **2.47** to redundancy, however. These were recognised by the Court of Appeal in Johnson v Nottinghamshire Combined Police Authority (above). The first is where the change is caused by a redundancy situation. This can happen where a change in terms is accompanied by a reduction in the number of employees, as in:

- **Kykot v Smith Hartley Ltd** 1975 IRLR 372, QBD: two weavers working on the day-shift left and the employers decided to abolish the night-shift and transfer two weavers from the night-shift to the jobs vacated on the day-shift. They refused the transfer and were dismissed. A tribunal said that since there would have been no change in the work they did there was no redundancy. The High Court disagreed and pointed out that the reorganisation was caused by a general fall-off in trade and led to an overall reduction in the number of employees. This was enough to distinguish the case from the Johnson case (above) and the Court held that the dismissal of the night-shift workers was caused by redundancy

- **Dacorum Borough Council v Eldridge and Townsend** EAT 608/89: E and T were employed by the Council in the refuse collection department. As a result of the Local Government Act 1988 the Council was obliged to put its refuse collection service out to competitive tendering. The Council wished to submit a tender on behalf of the workforce and decided it would have to reduce the workforce and change working conditions. The changes entailed the ending of a working practice whereby employees worked substantially fewer hours than they were contractually obliged to do. Both E and T volunteered for redundancy but their requests were not accepted. They refused to accept the new terms and conditions and were dismissed. On the question of whether E and T were entitled to a redundancy payment the tribunal held that a redundancy situation had existed from the time the Council was statutorily obliged to put the services out to tender and the Council had failed to rebut the presumption of redundancy. E and T were therefore entitled to redundancy payments. The EAT held that the tribunal was entitled to come to that conclusion.

2.48 The second situation where a change in the terms and conditions of employment can lead to redundancy is where the nature of the changes means that the work could be described as being of a different kind. One question which sometimes arises is whether a change from the night-shift to the day-shift or vice versa is a change in the kind of work done. In Macfisheries Ltd v Findlay and ors 1985 ICR 160, EAT, the claimants worked night-shifts for domestic reasons and refused to change to day-shifts when the night-shift was terminated. They were dismissed and claimed redundancy payments. The tribunal held that the claimants' work on the night-shift was 'work of a particular kind' and that since the requirement for that work had ceased they were redundant. The EAT upheld this decision, saying that the tribunal had not assumed that working at night automatically made the work 'of a particular kind' – a view which would have been mistaken – but had looked at all the relevant factors such as the nature of the work done on the two shifts, the impact of night work on the claimants' personal and domestic lives, and the fact that they had a contractual right not to be compelled to change to day-working. (Note, however, that in Barnes v Gilmartin Associates EAT 825/97 another division of the EAT stated that it did not find the reasoning in Findlay 'altogether compelling'.) A different conclusion was reached in Maher v Photo Trade Processing Ltd EAT 451/83, where the EAT held that there was no redundancy situation when the night-shift workers were all offered work on the day-shift and where the work on the day-shift was substantially the same as on the night-shift. The business required the same number of employees for the same tasks but at different hours.

2.49 *Part-time to full-time work.* A similar question arises if an employer demands that a part-time worker becomes full time. One argument is that part-time work is 'work of a particular kind' and therefore if an employer requires fewer part-time workers there is a redundancy situation. An employment tribunal in

Brown v Dunlop Textiles Ltd 1967 ITR 531, ET, rejected that submission, however, as did the Court of Appeal in Johnson v Nottinghamshire Combined Police Authority (above). In Brown the tribunal did nonetheless find that there was a redundancy situation, because the employers needed fewer employees overall to do the work for which B had been employed. However, that decision would be unlikely to stand today, especially in light of the EAT's decision in Barnes v Gilmartin Associates (above). In that case a part-time secretary was sacked and replaced by a full-time secretary. A tribunal found that the employer had a requirement for a full-time secretary and could not afford to employ both a full-time and a part-time secretary. Accordingly, the post of part-time secretary was redundant. The EAT overruled the tribunal. Citing Johnson, the EAT held that it was bound to conclude that there was no diminution in the requirement for employees to carry out work of a particular kind – i.e. secretarial work. (The EAT went on to hold, however, that in the circumstances the dismissal was fair for some other substantial reason; namely, a business reorganisation.)

Of course, if a part-time employee is to be replaced by a full-time employee the nature of whose work will be of a different kind, there is a redundancy situation. Thus there was a redundancy situation where a part-time audiotypist was replaced by a full-time secretary whose duties were wider than audiotyping – Ellis v GA Property Services Ltd ET Case No.13453/89.

Reduced hours. Tribunals have, at times, struggled with the question of whether **2.50** there is a redundancy situation where, in response to a diminished level of work, the employer decides to reduce everyone's hours instead of making dismissals. In such circumstances, would someone who resigns and claims constructive dismissal, or who is dismissed for refusing to comply, be entitled to redundancy pay?

On one reading, the statutory definition appears to be met, in that the requirements of the business for employees to carry out work of a particular kind have diminished, and dismissals are the result. If the dismissal is a constructive dismissal, the reason for it is the reason for the employer's breach of contract that caused the employee to resign – Berriman v Delabole Slate Ltd 1985 ICR 546, CA – which, in these circumstances, would be redundancy.

The opposing view is that even though the level of work may have diminished, **2.51** there cannot be a redundancy situation where the employer does not seek to reduce the *number* of employees doing the work. Its requirements for employees to carry out that kind of work remain the same. On this reading, redundancy only occurs where the requirements of the business for *employees* doing the work have diminished, not where the requirements of the business for the amount of work to be done have diminished. This was the view taken by the EAT in Aylward and ors v Glamorgan Holiday Home Ltd t/a Glamorgan Holiday Hotel EAT 0167/02. In that case the claimants were employed by a company that provided respite care and holidays for elderly, disabled and disadvantaged people. The business consistently traded in profit for the ten months from March to December, but suffered losses in January and February. In March 2000, the company's accountant advised that it would need to take drastic action to avoid imminent insolvency, and the company decided to close the hotel for the months of January and February each year. Due to local authority requirements, it was unable to reduce staffing levels during the period the hotel was open, so instead the company proposed to change the employees' terms and conditions by reducing their weeks of paid work from 52 to 42 per annum. Nine out of the 29 permanent members of staff objected and were dismissed and replaced by new members of staff. A tribunal dismissed their claims for redundancy pay, and the EAT upheld this decision. It said: 'We are in no doubt that the tribunal decision in this case was correct, focusing as it did on the requirement for employees to do work of [a] particular kind rather than the amount of work to be done. The requirement for employees at this hotel had not altered. The number working there was to be the same before and after reorganisation. What occurred was a business reorganisation which involved a change in the terms and conditions and particularly the number of days that were to be worked by the same number of employees.'

A similar approach was adopted in Mitie Olscot Ltd v Henderson and ors (above), where the Appeal Tribunal accepted that the real reason for dismissal was 'some other reason' and not redundancy. Indeed, tribunals have long recognised the right of employers to dismiss employees who refuse to go along with a business reorganisation. While dismissals for refusal to agree to changes that the employer is contractually entitled to impose may constitute misconduct dismissals, dismissals of employees who refuse to accept a business reorganisation are generally pleaded as being for 'some other substantial reason of a kind such as to justify the dismissal of an employee holding the position which the employee held' (SOSR) – S.98(1)(b) ERA. For example, in Garside and Laycock Ltd v Booth EAT 0003/11 the EAT accepted that SOSR was established when an employee was dismissed for refusing to accept a pay cut that the employer had proposed as an alternative to compulsory redundancies. It was 'common ground' in that case that the dismissal did not fall within the category of redundancy. (For more examples of SOSR dismissals in the context of business reorganisations, see IDS Employment Law Handbook, 'Unfair Dismissal' (2010), Chapter 8.)

2.52 However, tribunals have not consistently followed the approach taken by the EAT in Aylward. Two contrasting cases:

- **Metcalfe v Fosse Environment Services Ltd** ET Case No.1805117/08: M, an office junior, went on maternity leave. Although she had worked for 14 hours a week, her maternity cover would work for only nine and a half hours a week. It became increasingly obvious that the work could be done within these hours and the employer, anxious to save costs, wrote to M proposing to reduce her hours to nine and a half a week on her return to work. M was unhappy with this and the employer agreed to pay her a redundancy payment, on the basis that her 14-hours-a-week job was no longer available. M claimed that she was unfairly dismissed and that her dismissal was discriminatory. A tribunal found that the reason for her dismissal was not redundancy. Although the requirement for office junior work had diminished, the employer's requirement for employees had not. It still needed an employee to do the work, but in fewer hours. The dismissal was for SOSR

- **Moore v Midas Precision Metalwork Ltd** ET Case No.1200536/09: a sheet metal worker was dismissed when he refused to accept a change to his terms and conditions of employment which meant that he would have been put on a three-day, rather than a five-day, week, with a corresponding reduction in pay. The employer had suffered badly as a result of a downturn in orders but it did not want to make staff redundant as it could not afford to make redundancy payments. It also wanted to try to keep all of the staff on to enable the company to trade effectively. The employees were consulted on the proposed change to a three-day working week but M refused to accept the new terms and was eventually dismissed for SOSR. However, the tribunal upheld M's claim for a redundancy payment, concluding that his dismissal was 'mainly attributable to the fact that the requirements of the business for employees such as himself to undertake sheet metalworking had diminished', albeit that the 'immediate cause' of dismissal was the ultimatum to accept the new terms and conditions of employment.

Some doubt has been cast on the reasoning in Aylward because the EAT based **2.53** its decision on a misreading of the ratio in Safeway Stores plc v Burrell 1997 ICR 523, EAT. As discussed under 'Diminishing need for employees – test for redundancy' above, the EAT in the Burrell case held that the correct test is whether there was a diminution in the employer's requirement for employees *generally* to carry out work of a particular kind, *not just the individual claimant*. The EAT in Burrell was not actually required to address the distinction between the amount of work to be carried out by employees and the number of employees needed to carry out that work, which was the issue in Aylward. Nevertheless, the EAT in Burrell stated clearly that 'it is necessary to look at the overall requirement for employees to do work of a particular kind; not at the amount of work to be done', and we would suggest that this is exactly what the EAT did in Aylward. It is not sufficient for the work to reduce, if the requirement for employees to carry out that particular kind of work does not.

However, if Aylward was incorrectly decided, it would mean that employers faced with a diminishing need for a particular kind of work to be carried out could not necessarily avoid making redundancies by unilaterally reducing the employees' hours, because employees in such circumstances could resign and claim constructive dismissal and be entitled to a redundancy payment. But the situation may be different where the employer *dismisses* the employees for refusing to accept the reduced hours and pay. It could be argued that such dismissals were for misconduct or 'some other substantial reason', not redundancy – although the tribunal in Moore, above, came to the opposite conclusion. (See also 'Reason for dismissal' below.)

2.54 **Same work done by different kind of employee.** There is no reduction in 'work of a particular kind' merely because there is a change in the kind of employee required to do it. In Vaux and Associated Breweries Ltd v Ward 1968 ITR 385, Div Ct, the employer dismissed a barmaid because it wanted somebody younger and more attractive. There was no change in the work to be done, so the Court said that dismissal was not by reason of redundancy. Similarly, in Pillinger v Manchester Area Health Authority 1979 IRLR 430, EAT, P, a scientific research officer, was dismissed because the work on which he was engaged would be done in future by a scientist of a lower grade. The EAT held that this was not redundancy: there was no change in the work to be done simply because it would be done by an employee of lower status (but compare British Broadcasting Corporation v Farnworth EAT 1000/97 below).

Two more examples of the same work being done by different employees:

- **Excel Technical Mouldings Ltd v Shaw** EAT 0267/02; 0524/02: E Ltd was headed by S, the General Manager, who had six managers working under him. A reorganisation resulted in a management triumvirate consisting of two of the subordinate managers and an external part-time consultant, plus the retention of five of the six subordinate management positions. S, however, was dismissed and his duties absorbed into the management team. A tribunal and the EAT both ruled that there was no redundancy. S had been carrying out managerial work, the need for which had not declined – the work of seven full-time managerial employees was still being carried out by seven employees after the reorganisation

- **Corus and Regal Hotels plc v Wilkinson** EAT 0102/03: CRH plc embarked on a restructuring exercise of its hotel business which involved the substitution of the post of general manager – held by W – with that of resident manager and the creation of a new position of area general manager. CRH plc contended that this restructuring rendered W redundant. An employment tribunal upheld W's complaint of unfair dismissal on the basis that the business requirements for employees to carry out W's work had not ceased or diminished even though the identity of the persons carrying out W's work had changed. The EAT approved that decision on appeal, ruling that the tribunal had not simply been influenced by the fact that the same number (or indeed more) employees were employed after the reorganisation than before it, but also, crucially, by the fact that they were doing the same work as before. W was therefore not redundant and his dismissal for that reason was unfair.

While status or qualifications *per se* cannot mark the work out as being of a **2.55** particular kind, the experience or greater competence of an employee may do so. In British Broadcasting Corporation v Farnworth EAT 1000/97 F was employed in the post of Radio Producer, 'Mark 1'. The BBC decided that the programme on which she worked needed a more senior producer. It therefore appointed a 'Mark 2' producer and dismissed F. A tribunal found that the reason for the dismissal was redundancy. It noted that the BBC required a wide range of producers of different experience and ability and the need for as many producers at the dismissed employee's level had diminished. The EAT pointed out that it is a question of fact for the tribunal to determine whether an employee's work is sufficiently specialised for him or her to be regarded as different from other comparable employees. It stressed that it is the work and not the person that is important, so that personal attributes are not relevant except in so far as they reflect upon the employee's ability to perform relevant tasks. Similarly, an employee's qualifications are irrelevant except in so far as they imply special skills, attributes or knowledge.

Work changes, but remains work of the same particular kind. There is no **2.56** redundancy situation if the new work is of the same kind as the old work. If the new work is of a different kind, however, there is a redundancy situation.

In Amos and ors v Max-Arc Ltd 1973 ICR 46, NIRC, the NIRC considered how such work was to be distinguished. The employer had decided to reorganise by subcontracting stainless steel work and expanding black metal work (which was less well paid). Some employees refused to do the black metal work and claimed redundancy payments. A tribunal held that all the work – both stainless steel and black metal – was 'sheet metal work' and was work of the same particular kind and that there was no diminution in the overall requirement for employees to do it. The NIRC decided that work of a particular kind meant work which is distinguished from other work of the same general kind by requiring special aptitudes, skill or knowledge: if steel work could be distinguished from metal work on those grounds, then a redundancy situation was created when the employer decided to subcontract it.

A redundancy situation was found to exist in Lambe v 186K Ltd 2005 ICR **2.57** 307, CA. There, L, an accountant, was employed as a corporate finance manager (CFM) specialising in mergers and acquisitions. In 2002 he was told by the head of corporate finance that if he wished to remain with the company he would have to change roles and move into the finance control department. The reason was that the employer wished to transfer another employee, P, from that department and put him into a newly created position of senior CFM. These proposed changes took place in the context of the company having recently deleted two other CFM positions. L turned down the new job on the ground that it was unsuitable and he was dismissed for redundancy. He contended that his dismissal was not by reason of redundancy, but his claim was rejected by a tribunal. He unsuccessfully appealed to the EAT and then to the Court of Appeal, which concluded that the tribunal's finding that there was a diminution in the company's need for CFMs, and in particular for a dedicated employee responsible for mergers and acquisitions, was fully supportable on the evidence. The company had clearly been undergoing a substantial downsizing. Moreover, P's new role was not merely to perform the job previously done by L but to deal with anticipated new business activities.

2.58 *Suitable alternative employment.* It is important to note that an offer of different work may be an offer of suitable alternative employment and if the employee unreasonably refuses to take up the offer he or she will not be entitled to a redundancy payment – see Chapter 3 for details. In Denton v Neepsend Ltd 1976 IRLR 164, ET, for example, the employer replaced a cold saw with an abrasive cutting machine. Although the purposes of the two tools were identical – cutting metal – the tribunal found that work on the new machine needed a much more sophisticated operational technique and was much more onerous because the machine worked at a higher speed. Work on the new machine was of a different particular kind and there was a redundancy situation. However, the tribunal went on to find that the offer of work on the new cutting machine was an offer of suitable alternative employment (although D had not acted unreasonably in rejecting it).

2.59 **Redeployment.** Problems have arisen where an employer seeks to redeploy an employee who appears to be redundant because the duties which he or she is actually performing have diminished. An employee's contract of employment may cover tasks that the employee does not actually perform and the question arises whether, if there is work available which an employee could be required under the contract to perform, that person can still be redundant. As has already been noted in the introduction to this section under 'Test of redundancy', there was a long-standing conflict between the 'function' test (under which there is a redundancy situation in respect of the employee if there is a diminution in the work which he or she actually did) and the 'contract' test (under which there is no redundancy unless there is a diminution in all work which the employee could be required to do under his or her contract of employment).

Until the late 1990s, the contract test was generally held to embody the correct approach. It was considered to derive from the case of Nelson v BBC 1977 ICR 649, CA, in which N worked as a producer in the BBC's Caribbean Service, but under his contract he could be required to work in any department the BBC wanted him to work in. When the BBC closed the Caribbean Service it offered N alternative work, but he turned it down and was dismissed. The BBC resisted his unfair dismissal claim on the narrow ground that there was an implied term in N's contract that he was employed only in the Caribbean Service and that he had become redundant when the Service disappeared. A tribunal accepted this argument and found a fair dismissal for redundancy. The EAT doubted the correctness of the BBC's argument, but said that even if there was not a redundancy there was still a fair dismissal for 'some other substantial reason'. The Court of Appeal overruled the tribunal and the EAT on the ground that the BBC's argument was wrong because N was not employed simply to work in the Caribbean Service but could be required to work anywhere. He was therefore not redundant on the ground that the work he was employed to do had diminished.

2.60 All this case decided was that the BBC failed to show that N was redundant on the very narrow ground on which it based its case. It did not argue that N was redundant because the BBC's requirement for employees to do work of a particular kind had diminished – and this argument, which would probably have succeeded, was never considered by the courts. But when the case subsequently returned to a different division of the Court of Appeal on another point in Nelson v BBC (No.2) 1980 ICR 110, CA, Lord Justice Brandon summarised the first Nelson case by stating that the employee 'was right in law in maintaining that, because the work which he was employed to do continued to exist, he was not redundant'. Although this statement of the contract test was strictly obiter and unsupported by further explanation, it was subsequently endorsed by the Court of Appeal in Cowen v Haden Ltd 1983 ICR 1, CA, and has been treated as binding authority by the EAT in a number of cases, including Pink v (1) White (2) White and Co (Earls Barton) Ltd 1985 IRLR 489, EAT.

Since then, however, as we have already seen, both the function and contract tests have been held to be unnecessary glosses on the wording of the statute and a new approach was put forward by the EAT in Safeway Stores plc v Burrell 1997 ICR 523, EAT. In that case B was employed by Safeway as a petrol filling station manager. As part of a restructuring exercise, the post of filling station manager was abolished and replaced with the post of filling station 'controller' – a lower-status job attracting a lower salary. B decided that he did not want to apply for the job of filling station controller and he was dismissed with a redundancy payment and pay in lieu of notice. He claimed that his dismissal was unfair. The employment tribunal decided, by a majority, that he had been unfairly dismissed because redundancy was not, in fact, the reason for his dismissal. The tribunal found that, under B's contract, Safeway could lawfully have called upon him to exercise many more functions and responsibilities than he actually did. However, the majority held that what mattered was the work that B was required to do in practice and concluded that the work he was actually doing was still being done, albeit by someone with a different job title. In their view, the requirements of Safeway for B to carry out work of a particular kind had not diminished and he had not been dismissed by reason of redundancy. The chairman of the tribunal, on the other hand, considered that it was the terms of B's contract that were decisive. In his view, the job that B was employed to do as a manager no longer existed and he was therefore redundant. Safeway appealed, arguing that the majority of the tribunal had applied the wrong test in deciding that there had been no redundancy.

2.61 The EAT held that both the majority of the tribunal and the tribunal chairman had adopted the wrong approach because both the function and contract tests were predicated on a misreading of the statutory provisions and previous authorities. The EAT stated that determining whether an employee has been dismissed for redundancy involved a simple three-stage test:

- was the employee dismissed?

- if so, had the requirements of the employer's business for employees to carry out work of a particular kind ceased or diminished, or were they expected to do so?

- if so, was the dismissal caused wholly or mainly by the cessation or diminution?

In deciding at the second stage whether there was a redundancy situation, the terms of the individual employee's contract of employment were irrelevant. The contract would only be relevant when enquiring whether the redundancy situation was the operative reason for the dismissal. The EAT pointed out that, even where a redundancy situation exists, if that does not cause the dismissal then there is no dismissal by reason of redundancy. Thus in the Nelson case, above, the employee was directed to transfer to another job as provided for by his contract. It was his refusal to do so, and not the redundancy situation, that was the operative cause of the dismissal.

2.62 The Burrell decision was subsequently endorsed by the House of Lords in Murray and anor v Foyle Meats Ltd 1999 ICR 827, HL. In that case M and D were employed by FM Ltd, which carried on business as livestock slaughterers in Northern Ireland. Under their contracts of employment M and D could be required to work elsewhere in the factory, such as the boning hall or the loading bay, and occasionally they did so. All the company's employees were engaged on the same terms. In 1995, following a downturn in business, the company needed to reduce the number of employees working in the slaughter hall by 35. M and D were among those selected and they were dismissed by reason of redundancy. Both employees complained of unfair dismissal. The tribunal found in favour of the company on the basis that the dismissals were by reason of redundancy as defined by statute in that the company's 'requirements for employees to carry out work of a particular kind' – i.e. work in the slaughter hall – had diminished. The Northern Ireland Court of Appeal upheld the tribunal's decision and M and D appealed to the House of Lords. The employees argued that the company's requirements for employees to carry out work of a particular kind related to those employees who were contractually employed to carry out work of a particular kind. As all the company's employees were engaged under the same terms, they were all contractually obliged to work in the slaughter hall. In the employees' view, therefore, the company should have included all their employees in the pool for selection for redundancy and should not have limited it to those actually working in the slaughter hall at the time. The House of Lords held that the tribunal had not erred in holding that the employees were dismissed for redundancy, notwithstanding that under their contracts of employment the employees could be required to work in any part of the employer's factory. The tribunal had been right to hold that the company's requirements for employees to carry out work of a particular kind had diminished within the meaning of the statutory definition of redundancy.

2.63 Lord Irvine, who gave the leading judgment, boiled the test down to two questions: the first is *whether the requirements of the business for employees to carry out work of a particular kind have diminished*. The second, which is one of causation, is *whether the dismissal is wholly or mainly attributable to that state of affairs*. Naturally, in the case of the dismissal of an employee who could have been employed elsewhere, or who was not carrying out work the requirement for which had diminished, it may be more difficult to establish that the dismissal was indeed attributable to the redundancy situation. But that is a question of fact, not law, for the tribunal to decide.

It follows from the Burrell and Murray decisions that, in cases involving employees who have flexibility clauses in their contracts, the question of whether the employee was dismissed for redundancy will focus on whether the redundancy situation was the reason for the employee's dismissal. If it was, then it will be irrelevant that, instead of dismissing the employee for redundancy, the employer could have required the employee to move to another kind of work. But where the employer does invoke a contractual right to redeploy the employee, it may be able to establish that the reason for the dismissal was the employee's misconduct in refusing to obey that lawful redeployment order, rather than any redundancy situation.

Fewer employees needed to do the work   2.64
Where the overall amount of work that needs to be done has not diminished, a redundancy situation may nevertheless arise where fewer employees are needed to do the work. This situation will typically arise where the employer has introduced technological changes to working practices that have the effect of requiring fewer employees to do the same amount of work. The situation may also arise where the employer uses independent contractors to perform part or all of the work needed to be done; or where the employer reorganises the work so that it can be done by fewer employees. We discuss these situations, in turn, below.

Technological advances. An obvious example of redundancy is where **2.65** employees' roles are rendered obsolete by technological advances. Thus in

---

71

Trevillion v Hospital of St John and St Elizabeth 1973 IRLR 176, NIRC, there was a redundancy situation where a stoker ran out of work when the last two of an original 12 solid fuel boilers were converted to oil.

In that case the work (stoking) disappeared altogether. However, new technology may mean that the work remains, but can be done by fewer employees. This also gives rise to a redundancy situation. Sir Hugh Griffiths gave an illustration in Scarth v Economic Forestry Ltd 1973 ICR 322, NIRC: 'Suppose a business has managed to produce a million cardboard boxes per year by the use of old machinery and ten men. It is intended to continue to produce a million cardboard boxes per year, but new machinery is bought which is capable of producing that number of boxes, but is satisfactorily operated by two men. The requirements of the business remain the same, namely the production of a million cardboard boxes per year; but the business no longer requires employees to produce those cardboard boxes in the numbers that it had previously done. So, eight employees become surplus to the requirements of the business... and when they are dismissed they are entitled to redundancy payments.'

2.66 A distinction must be made, however, between cases where the new technology results in fewer employees (a redundancy situation) and where the new technology is simply a new way of performing the same job (no redundancy). The important question here is whether the work remains of the *same particular kind* or whether the change in the manner of performance of the work is such that the job itself is different. The amount of retraining necessary for the employees to take on board the new technology may well be relevant here.

In Cresswell and ors v Board of Inland Revenue 1984 ICR 508, ChD, the High Court had to consider whether the Inland Revenue's introduction of a computerised system of clerical procedures to replace a manual clerical system amounted to a breach of contract. The employees argued that the change was such that they were being required to work under new contracts of employment. Mr Justice Walton, giving the judgment of the High Court, identified two key questions: what was the employee employed to do? And, was the job so altered as to fall outside the original job description? The High Court took the view that no employees had the absolute right to have the manner in which they carry out their employment maintained throughout their employment. Further, the Court thought that an employee is 'expected to adapt himself to new methods and techniques introduced in the course of his employment'. This latter point was subject to the duty of the employer to provide any necessary training or retraining. Commenting on the nature of the training which may be involved, the Court stated that it would be a question of fact whether the necessary training involves the acquisition of such esoteric skills that it is unreasonable to expect the employee to acquire them. However, in Walton J's opinion, 'in an age when the computer has forced its way into the schoolroom and where electronic games are played by schoolchildren in their own homes as a matter of everyday occurrence, it can hardly be considered that to ask an employee to acquire basic skills as to retrieving information from a computer or feeding such information into a computer is something in the slightest esoteric or even, nowadays, unusual'.

In the High Court's view, the job done by the employees was still the same after **2.67** computerisation, albeit that the methods of doing the job had changed. Consequently, the employer was not in breach of contract in requiring that the job be carried out by way of computerised, as opposed to manual, methods.

There may, however, be a trap for employees who accept a job change brought about by new technology and then find that they cannot cope. The following case illustrates the point:

- **Luckhurst v Kent Litho Ltd** EAT 302/76: L was a very experienced worker in black-and-white photographic printing. He agreed to convert to colour printing, but the quality of his work was never adequate and he was eventually dismissed after the black-and-white work dried up. The EAT held that this was a fair dismissal for capability reasons. L could have claimed a substantial redundancy payment when the changeover to colour took place, but he lost the right when he accepted reclassification and there was no longer a redundancy situation at the time of his dismissal.

Independent contractors. There may also be a redundancy situation where an **2.68** employer replaces employees with independent contractors. This is because the employer requires fewer *employees* – even though it may still need the same number of workers to do the work. In Bromby and Hoare Ltd v Evans and anor 1972 ICR 113, NIRC, the employer dismissed two decorators because their work could be done more efficiently by independent contractors. The NIRC said that this was a dismissal for redundancy.

A reorganisation bringing in outside contractors to do work previously done by employees does not have to be forced on the employer before it amounts to redundancy. As Lord McDonald said in Noble v House of Fraser (Stores) Ltd EAT 686/84: 'If an employer chooses to engage outside contractors instead of employees to do work of a particular kind he no longer requires employees to do it. That in our view clearly falls within the definition of redundancy.'

Note, however, that under the provisions governing service provision changes **2.69** in the Transfer of Undertakings (Protection of Employment) Regulations 2006 SI 2006/246, many 'contracting out' scenarios are covered by the Regulations, meaning that employees who formerly carried out the work will automatically transfer to the new contractor. For more details, see IDS Employment Law Handbook, 'Transfer of Undertakings' (2011), Chapter 1, under 'Service provision changes'.

2.70 Reorganisation of work. This is the third type of situation where there is a diminishing need for employees: the employer reorganises and redistributes the work so that it can be done by fewer employees. The leading cases are:

- **Sutton v Revlon Overseas Corporation Ltd** 1973 IRLR 173, NIRC: S was chief accountant. The employer reorganised, dismissed S as redundant and split the work he had previously done between three existing employees. There was no reduction in the work because business was increasing generally. S claimed that he was not redundant and that the dismissal was unfair. The NIRC held that S was redundant. Reorganisation enabled the existing work to be done by fewer employees and changes in job specifications eliminated the need for one employee, the chief accountant

- **Carry All Motors Ltd v Pennington** 1980 ICR 806, EAT: the employer decided that a transport depot was overstaffed because the work of the transport manager and the transport clerk (P) could be done by one person. The transport manager was retained but P was dismissed. A tribunal thought that this was not a statutory redundancy situation because there was no diminution in the work, and found P's dismissal unfair. The EAT held that the tribunal had applied the wrong test by concentrating on the requirements for work and ignoring the requirements of the business for employees to carry out the work. One less employee was needed so that P was redundant (and his dismissal was not unfair)

- **McCrea v Cullen and Davison Ltd** 1988 IRLR 30, NICA: M was the manager of CD Ltd. He went into hospital and his work was taken over by the company's managing director, who discovered that he could do both his own work and M's work. Accordingly, M was dismissed. The tribunal held that M was not redundant because the amount of management work had not diminished. The Northern Ireland Court of Appeal held, however, that M was dismissed for redundancy because the company needed fewer employees and the fact that the work had not diminished was irrelevant.

2.71 *Temporary understaffing.* In the Sutton case the NIRC added a refinement by saying that there would not be a redundancy situation if the business became temporarily understaffed through the shedding of employees during a reorganisation. This would mean that the requirement for the employees had not diminished. Two examples of temporary understaffing:

- **Harding v NUM** EAT 316/76: H was dismissed after a series of disputes with the NUM and his work was thereafter done on an ad hoc basis by the president. The NUM did not intend to replace him permanently until all claims H had brought against it had been disposed of. The EAT upheld a tribunal finding that H was not redundant: his work was only being done by an existing employee on a temporary basis until the coast was clear for the appointment of a permanent successor

74

- **O'Grady v Cookshop Supplies** ET Case No.31001/83: the employer was under pressure to stem losses in its shops. O'G, a full-time assistant, was abruptly dismissed to cut costs. However, the manageress found that she could not cope on her own, so a month later a full-time junior was engaged to replace O'G (at less pay). When O'G complained of unfair dismissal the employer pleaded redundancy. The tribunal decided that there had been no redundancy. All that had taken place was an unsuccessful experiment which showed that there had been no decrease in the requirement for employees to do O'G's work. (Even if there had been a redundancy, O'G's dismissal would have been unfair because she would have settled for lower pay or fewer hours if she had been consulted.)

However, this approach appears to conflict with S.139(6), which states that 'diminish' in S.139(1) means to diminish 'either permanently or temporarily and for whatever reason'. A better view, in line with the legislative definition, is that a temporary diminution in the requirement for employees *can* lead to redundancy dismissals – but it will be for employment tribunals to decide, on the facts, whether the definition is met (see Whitbread plc t/a Whitbread Berni Inns v Flattery and ors EAT 287/94, discussed above under 'Definition of redundancy – temporary cessation and diminution').

2.72 *Lack of capability.* If the dismissal is simply for reasons of economy – because the employer cannot afford to keep the employee on any longer – but the employer has made no decision to reorganise so as to reduce the number of employees, then the dismissal will not be for redundancy. In Hindle v Percival Boats Ltd 1969 ITR 86, CA, the employer dismissed H, a very capable woodworker, because he was uneconomically slow when working with fibreglass. The Court of Appeal (by a majority) held that this was not redundancy: it was a dismissal because of H's personal deficiencies. (Under the unfair dismissal legislation, not then introduced, it would have been a dismissal on the ground of capability.)

2.73 **Expected job losses.** Section 139(1)(b) states that there is a redundancy situation where the requirements of the business for employees to carry out work of a particular kind, or for employees to carry out work of a particular kind in the place where they are employed, have ceased or diminished *or are expected to cease or diminish*. Thus, an expectation that the need for employees will cease or diminish at some point in the future will amount to a redundancy situation in the same way as an actual cessation or diminution and any dismissals carried out as a result of that expectation will be for redundancy. In (1) Strathclyde Buses Ltd v Leonard and ors; (2) Ellum and ors v Strathclyde Buses Ltd EAT 507/97; 515/97 a tribunal held that the dismissal of employees following a merger was not for redundancy because, although the merger had created a redundancy situation, the tribunal was not satisfied that that situation applied to the dismissed employees. The tribunal accepted that it had been

75

known for some time that the employees' jobs would disappear once new technology had been installed, but it noted that that day was still a long way off. Moreover, the employer had had to bring in temporary workers to do much of the work formerly performed by the employees. The EAT overruled the tribunal and held that the employees were redundant. The tribunal had erred in focusing on the fact that temporary staff had been brought in, rather than on the fact that the dismissals occurred in the context of a merged company where redundancies were inevitable. The tribunal should have given more weight to the fact that the whole process of merging with another company involved an expectation of job losses and it was that which created the reason for the dismissals.

2.74 Reason for dismissal

Even if there is a redundancy situation a dismissed employee is only entitled to a redundancy payment if the dismissal was 'wholly or mainly' by reason of that redundancy – S.139(1). It has already been noted that a dismissed employee who is claiming a redundancy payment is presumed to have been dismissed by reason of redundancy – see 'Presumption of redundancy' above. If a party wishes to establish that there was no redundancy dismissal, that presumption must be rebutted either by proving that there is no redundancy situation or by showing that the dismissal was not wholly or mainly by reason of it.

In (1) McGibbon (2) McCoy v O.I.L. Ltd EAT 537/94 a company had to reduce its North Sea oil fleet from 14 vessels to 11 because of a downturn in business. A number of ratings were warned that redundancies would have to be made but were offered new contracts to do the same job on less favourable terms. Those who did not accept the terms were to be put into a redundancy pool out of which the eventual redundancies would be made according to a number of criteria. M was among the 40 ratings who were eventually dismissed for redundancy. The EAT was prepared to accept that there was a redundancy situation and that the employer's need for ratings had diminished. However, the EAT did not think that the tribunal had been entitled to hold that the actual dismissals – or that all of them – were attributable to redundancy. The reason for this was that the numbers did not add up: the number of ratings dismissed exceeded the number displaced by the removal of three vessels. One possible explanation for the dismissals was, as the ratings themselves claimed, that they were dismissed for refusing to accept the offer of new terms. The EAT held, therefore, that the company had failed to establish that the dismissals were by reason of redundancy.

2.75 Tribunals are only concerned with whether the reason for the dismissal was redundancy and not with the economic or commercial reason for the redundancy itself – James W Cook and Co (Wivenhoe) Ltd v Tipper and ors 1990 ICR 716, CA. In Moon and ors v Homeworthy Furniture (Northern) Ltd 1977 ICR 117,

EAT, H Ltd closed a factory on the ground that it was not economically viable. The employees sought to demonstrate that the factory was viable and the dismissals unfair, but the EAT ruled that there was no jurisdiction to consider the reasonableness of the decision to create a redundancy situation in the first place.

On the other hand, tribunals are entitled to examine the evidence available to determine what was the real or, if there was more than one, the principal reason for the decision to dismiss and to ensure the genuineness of a decision to dismiss for redundancy. Tribunals are not bound to accept the reason given for the dismissal, as the following case shows:

- **Hartwell Commercial Group Ltd v Brand and Jones** EAT 491/92; 506/92: B and J were employed as the managing director and accountant respectively in a company that formed part of the FS Group. When H plc took over the FS Group, the business was running at a loss. A report seen by W, the chief executive, recommended that B and J be made redundant but warned that, under a covenant entered into by the FS Group, the cost in enhanced redundancy payments would be £125,000. B and J were then criticised for their performance and soon afterwards both were dismissed for insubordination and poor performance. A tribunal found that W was not a truthful witness and that the dismissal letters were pretexts for the real reason, which was redundancy. The EAT upheld the decision, stating that where there is more than one possible reason for a dismissal the correct approach is to ask what was the real or primary reason. The test required the tribunal to consider all the available evidence and to bear in mind that a reason not communicated to the employees at the time could be a reason for dismissal.

There are several situations where difficulties may arise in determining whether the dismissal was by reason of redundancy. These are discussed in turn below.

Industrial action
2.76

Industrial action may force an employer to close the business or cut the workforce. The question has arisen whether the employees who took the action and thus, in a sense, caused the redundancy situation remain entitled to redundancy payments. As pointed out earlier, the reason for the redundancy situation is irrelevant to the question of whether a redundancy payment is due. It is the reason for the dismissal which counts. Therefore, if the employees were truly dismissed for redundancy they are entitled to redundancy payments. It is possible, however, that they were actually dismissed for taking part in the industrial action. This is a matter for the tribunal to decide on the evidence. Two illustrations:

- **Fenn v Mirror Group Newspapers Ltd** EAT 28/81: after a long history of unofficial action the company decided to dismiss the participants in one particular strike. It also closed down the magazine on which the strikers worked and made the rest of the staff redundant. The EAT held that the reason for the dismissal of the strikers was that they were a disruptive influence. Although they had caused other people to be made redundant, the reason for their dismissal was not redundancy

- **Sanders and ors v Ernest A Neale Ltd** 1974 ICR 565, NIRC: some employees took industrial action and the employer threatened to dismiss them unless they undertook to work normally. No such undertaking was given and the threat was carried out. The employer subsequently closed the factory and wound up the business altogether, giving redundancy payments to those employees who had not taken part in the industrial action. The NIRC said that there was clearly a redundancy situation, but it had not caused the dismissals of those taking industrial action.

2.77 In Webb and ors v Sundaw Products Ltd and Hall Foundries Ltd EAT 477/79 the EAT had to consider a lock-out by the employer, followed by closure of the business, when the employees refused to accept new terms and conditions of employment. It upheld the tribunal's finding that action meant to compel the acceptance of new terms was inconsistent with an intention to close the business, so that it was the refusal of the new terms that caused both the closure and the accompanying dismissals, and not the closure that caused the dismissals. It followed that the employees had not been dismissed because of redundancy.

Where an employer may have more than one motive in deciding to dismiss employees involved in industrial action, it is a question of fact which was the dominant or principal reason. In Baxter and ors v Limb Group of Companies 1994 IRLR 572, CA, the employees imposed an overtime ban after a long-running dispute with management over bonus payments. The employer warned them that the action might lead to their dismissal and when the employees refused to call it off they were summarily dismissed. Subsequently, the employer decided to dispense with directly employed labour and the work done by the dismissed employees was contracted out. A tribunal held that the employer's decision to contract the work out meant that there was a redundancy situation at the time of the dismissals and awarded the employees a redundancy payment. The EAT overturned this decision and a majority of the Court of Appeal also thought that the tribunal had erred. In Lord Justice Dillon's view, the test was quite simple – if the employer dismisses all the employees who refuse to call off industrial action and engages new employees, the reason for the dismissal is industrial action. In his opinion it made no difference to that reason that the employer chose to obtain the replacement workers as contract labour from another company, rather than directly employ new staff.

2.78 It is clear in the above case that there was a redundancy situation as soon as the employer made the decision not to replace the workforce with directly employed labour. The difficulty only arises in determining the real or principal reason for the dismissals. If the employer dismissed the employees simply because it could no longer tolerate industrial action from employees, that was the real reason and the employees were not redundant. If, on the other hand, the employer simply chose that moment to change the means by which labour was bought, and that was the dominant motive, then a redundancy situation would be the cause of the dismissals. The Court of Appeal concluded, on the facts of the case, that the industrial action was the principal cause of the dismissals.

(Note that where an employee is dismissed for taking part in industrial action, he or she may have the right to claim unfair dismissal under special provisions contained in the Trade Union and Labour Relations (Consolidation) Act 1992. An in-depth discussion of these provisions can be found in IDS Employment Law Handbook, 'Industrial Action' (2010), Chapter 8, 'Industrial action dismissals'.)

Concurrent reason for dismissal 2.79
If different reasons for dismissal are alleged, a tribunal may have to decide, on the balance of probabilities, which was the real, or main, reason for dismissal. Two examples:

- **Mac Fisheries Ltd v Willgloss** 1972 ITR 57, NIRC: W was a branch manager with some 40 years' service. The company said that it dismissed him because he was inefficient and cited four instances of this. But there was also evidence that 37 branches had been closed in the area as part of a rationalisation programme and that two other managers had been made redundant. A tribunal found that there were two reasons for the dismissal – redundancy and W's inefficiency. It decided that the company had not proved that inefficiency was the main reason for dismissal and awarded W a redundancy payment. The NIRC said that the tribunal was entitled to reach this conclusion

- **Jolly v Haynes and anor t/a Interlink Kings Lynn** ET Case No.1502403/10: J received a letter from her employer on 1 March 2010 giving notice that her employment would end on 27 August, and saying 'as you are now over the statutory retirement age we review your employment every six months'. J had received a similar letter the previous year and simply carried on working, so she expected the same to happen this time. However, on 25 April the employer informed all employees that the depot was to close and that they would all be laid off with effect from 3 September. J claimed a redundancy payment, but the employer maintained that her employment was terminated because of retirement. An employment tribunal found in J's favour. The employer met none of the requirements then in place for retirement dismissals under the ERA. Moreover, S.163 ERA provides that there is a presumption that an employee who claims a redundancy payment is dismissed for redundancy, and that it is for the employer to rebut that presumption. In this case the employer had failed to do so. J had not expected her employment to end on 27 August. She was sent the same letter of redundancy as all the other employees and she was paid to 3 September.

2.80 If the redundancy situation consists of a closure of a business or workplace and dismissals are left until the time of the closure, they are likely to be presumed to be because of redundancy. The date of dismissal will be a pointer to the reason. Some contrasting cases:

- **Marshall v Harland and Wolff Ltd and anor** 1972 ICR 101, NIRC: M had been on sick leave for about 18 months when the company decided to close his workplace. It sent him notice of dismissal and resisted his redundancy pay claim in part on the ground that he had been dismissed because of sickness, not redundancy. The NIRC held that the company had taken no action to dismiss M before the closure, although it could have done so. The fact that it left it until the closure indicated that the closure was the reason for dismissal – i.e. there was a redundancy situation

- **Guest v Wallis and Linnell Ltd (in liquidation)** EAT 636/80: G had been off sick for about ten months when the employer gave her 12 weeks' notice of dismissal because of her sickness. During the notice period the employer closed the factory where she had worked and all the employees were made redundant. The EAT held that closure of the factory did not act as a redundancy situation for G because she was already under notice of dismissal for sickness. The reason for her dismissal was sickness, and not redundancy

- **Curtis and anor v Worcestershire County Council** ET Case No.1304610/09: C and B were employed to work in a primary school. The school had difficulties and the Council decided it should close on 31 December 2008. By the time the decision was made C and B were both over normal retirement age and had been granted permission to remain in employment until 11 and 7 December 2008 respectively. In mid-2008 C and B both requested further extensions of their retirement dates. The Council advised the school that it should not grant an extension of their employment beyond 31 December 2008, in view of the school's closure. The school accordingly informed C and B that their employment would only be extended to 31 December, and that they would not be entitled to redundancy payments as their employment was terminating on the ground of retirement. The employment tribunal held that C and B were entitled to redundancy payments since, had their dismissals really been on the ground of retirement, the Council would have simply refused their request to have their employment extended. Redundancy was the main reason they were dismissed on 31 December.

2.81 *Misconduct.* Difficulties can arise where the employee's misconduct is a factor in the dismissal. In Watters v Thomas Kelly and Sons Ltd EAT 626/81 an elderly lady who ran the business closed it down, apparently because she thought closure was the only effective way of getting rid of W, of whom she was frightened because of his conduct. The EAT said that the reason for dismissal was the closure of the premises – i.e. a redundancy situation under S.139(1)(a). But it pointed out that S.140(1), which excludes the right to a redundancy payment in certain circumstances, might operate to reduce or eliminate the employee's entitlement in these circumstances – see Chapter 5 under 'Disqualification – misconduct'.

Change of reason for dismissal   2.82

In Waters v Stena Houlder Ltd EAT 145/94 W, an offshore rig electrician, was injured at work and off sick between April and September 1991. In May 1992 the injury troubled him again and he was off work from then onwards. In September the employer gave him ten and a half months' notice of redundancy but hoped to find him alternative employment before the notice expired. W went to great lengths to get himself fit but the company doctor said that, under the fitness guidelines operating in that industry, he was not fit enough for offshore work. Acting on this doctor's advice, the employer dismissed W for incapacity one week before he was due to receive his redundancy payment. A tribunal found that the employer had acted reasonably. W appealed. He relied on W Devis and Sons Ltd v Atkins 1977 ICR 662, HL, in which Viscount Dilhorne held that evidence of conduct which is discovered after a dismissal is irrelevant to the issue of whether the dismissal was reasonable. On the basis that subsequently discovered conduct could not have influenced an employer's decision to dismiss, his Lordship concluded that the reasonableness of a dismissal has to be determined in the light of facts known to the employer at the time of dismissal. Applying this reasoning, W argued that, once the employer had given him notice of dismissal for redundancy, the subsequent discovery of his incapacity did not permit it to substitute a different reason.

The EAT saw nothing in the authority which required it to hold that an employee could not be summarily dismissed, or dismissed with shorter notice, for conduct or incapacity which occurred during the original notice period. Since an employer would be entitled to dismiss summarily for vandalism, for example, while an employee was on notice for redundancy, the EAT could see no reason why the same should not apply if an employee became incapable of performing the contract. However, the EAT did consider that it was necessary for the tribunal to determine, as part of the reasonableness test, whether the employer had acted in good faith in bringing W's employment to an end in the way it did. As the tribunal had not expressly done this, the EAT remitted the case for that point to be determined.

81

2.83 Voluntary redundancy

Voluntary redundancy is a recognised category of dismissal for redundancy and normally presents no problems provided there is a genuine redundancy situation. Once an employer has made a decision that redundancies are needed, the fact that an employee agrees to, or volunteers for, redundancy does not mean that the contract is terminated by mutual consent. The employee is still considered to have been dismissed for redundancy – Burton, Allton and Johnson Ltd v Peck 1975 ICR 193, QBD.

2.84 **Voluntary redundancy or voluntary retirement?** A distinction must be drawn between voluntary redundancy and voluntary (early) retirement. In Birch and anor v University of Liverpool 1985 ICR 470, CA, the university offered an early retirement scheme but with a threat that enforced redundancies would be made if the scheme did not produce the required results. The Court of Appeal, reversing the tribunal's decision, held that there was no dismissal of those who opted for early retirement; their contracts were terminated by mutual consent. In Optare Group Ltd v Transport and General Workers' Union 2007 IRLR 931, EAT, on the other hand, three employees volunteered to leave their posts at the start of a redundancy exercise. Upholding the employment tribunal, the EAT held that these voluntary redundancies did amount to dismissal, and that it was immaterial that the employees, all of whom were close to retirement age, might have accepted a similar package even in the absence of a redundancy situation. However, the EAT noted that the result would have been different had there been evidence that the employees were anxious to leave and had expressed this wish independently of, or prior to, a redundancy situation arising.

If an employee is under notice of dismissal for redundancy and then agrees to take early retirement, he or she will still be considered to have been dismissed for the purposes of the redundancy scheme, provided there has been no express agreement to a withdrawal of the notice. In Gateshead Metropolitan Borough Council v Mills EAT 610/92 M was under notice for redundancy from his lecturing post. He applied, and was accepted, for early retirement. A tribunal found that M had been dismissed for redundancy and that he was entitled to a redundancy payment. The EAT held that the tribunal had been entitled to find that there had been a dismissal. The EAT did not accept the Council's argument that M's contract had been terminated by mutual consent when his application for retirement was accepted. Nor did the EAT accept that M's agreement to early retirement had the effect of impliedly withdrawing the notice. The EAT held that notice could not be withdrawn without M's consent. As the Council had failed to secure that consent, M was entitled to a redundancy payment.

2.85 Bumping

Selection criteria for redundancy are sometimes applied to a class of employees wider than the class to which the redundancy situation relates. This may mean

82

that employee A is dismissed and replaced by employee B, when it is really employee B's job that has become redundant. This is known as 'bumping' or 'transferred redundancy'. The leading case is:

- **W Gimber and Sons Ltd v Spurrett** 1967 ITR 308, Div Ct: S was a warehouse manager who was dismissed and replaced by a sales representative who had become surplus to requirements (and who was not replaced). The Divisional Court endorsed as sound in law the tribunal's view that: 'If there is a reduction in the requirements for employees in one section of an employer's business and an employee who becomes surplus or redundant is transferred to another section of that business, an employee who is displaced by the transfer of the first employee and is dismissed by reason of that displacement is dismissed by reason of redundancy.' The Court also held that the tribunal had been entitled to find that the employer had not displaced the presumption of redundancy.

But despite the above decision, for many years the lawfulness of bumping **2.86** redundancies remained in doubt. This was because, under what was known as the 'contract' test, an employee was only redundant if there was a diminution in the work which the *employee* could be required to do under his or her contract of employment – see 'Diminishing need for employees – test of redundancy' above. In a bumping situation, there is no diminution in the work on which the dismissed employee was employed. However, the more recent test of redundancy set out in Safeway Stores plc v Burrell 1997 ICR 523, EAT, and Murray and anor v Foyle Meats Ltd 1999 ICR 827, HL, places the emphasis on causation – i.e. was there a redundancy situation and, if so, was the employee's dismissal on account of that redundancy situation? Under this test, bumping dismissals are no longer problematic, although, as the House of Lords pointed out in Murray, where an employer dismisses an employee whose work was unaffected by any drop in demand it will naturally be more difficult to establish the necessary causal link between the redundancy situation and the dismissal. Tribunals will tend to look carefully at the reason for dismissal and if the predominant reason is, say, the unsuitability or conduct of the dismissed employee, then the reason for dismissal will not be redundancy. An example:

- **Leung and anor v Elements Oriental Buffet House Ltd** ET Case No.2101669/08: L and T, who were both in their fifties, were employed as chefs at a restaurant near Chester. In late 2007 or early 2008 their employer closed its restaurant in Southport, leaving the jobs of three men in their thirties redundant. L and T were dismissed as redundant with immediate effect and without consultation, in order to retain the younger men, who were paid at a lower rate than L and T. An employment tribunal upheld L and T's claims of unfair dismissal and age discrimination. The employees in Southport were significantly younger than the claimants, and the employer did not provide a satisfactory explanation as to why the claimants were bumped. The tribunal noted: 'Certainly and especially since this was a case of bumping, we wanted to hear far more than we did of the respondents' reasoning.'

2.87 The EAT placed a limitation on the scope of bumping in Babar Indian Restaurant v Rawat 1985 IRLR 57, EAT, by saying that bumping can only occur within one business, so that where an employer closed down one business and dismissed an employee in another business to make way for a transferred employee from the closed business the dismissal was not because of redundancy. The EAT applied the test of whether the two businesses could really be viewed as a 'single enterprise' or not. But they ignored S.139(2) ERA, which states that 'the business of the employer together with the business or businesses of his associated employers *shall be treated as one*' (our stress). (It made no difference to the result, however, since there was an alternative finding that if the dismissal was because of redundancy it was still unfair.)

Note that, in some cases, the reasonableness of a redundancy dismissal may depend upon whether the employer has properly considered and consulted on the possibility of bumping – Fulcrum Pharma (Europe) Ltd v Bonassera and anor, EAT 0198/10. This is discussed fully in the context of procedural fairness in Chapter 8 under 'Unreasonable redundancy'.

2.88 Chain of events leading to dismissal

Where a chain of events occurs that eventually results in an employee's dismissal it may be difficult to determine which event actually caused the dismissal. In Runnalls v Richards and Osborne Ltd and anor 1973 ICR 225, NIRC, for example, R, a long-distance lorry driver, was disqualified from driving. The employer looked around for other work and R was given work carrying materials on a lorry on private land. Later the employer decided to cease carrying materials in this way and R was dismissed. He claimed a redundancy payment. The NIRC held that the cause of the dismissal was R's disqualification from driving. There was no diminution in the requirements of the business for employees to carry out driving and therefore no redundancy situation.

2.89 Selection criteria and reason for dismissal

When an employer decides that a number of employees must go in a redundancy situation, it will have to apply selection criteria to decide which employees are to lose their jobs. In such circumstances redundancy will normally be the main reason for dismissal and the reasons for selection will be subsidiary reasons. So if employees are selected for redundancy on the basis of their attendance records, for example, the reason for dismissal will be redundancy and not absenteeism.

It is only in exceptional circumstances that a tribunal will hold otherwise. In Timex Corporation v Thomson 1981 IRLR 522, EAT, the employer put forward

T's incapability as a reason for his selection for redundancy. A tribunal found that incapability, not redundancy, was the real reason for dismissal. The EAT upheld the tribunal's decision and said that it was a matter of fact for the tribunal as to whether a redundancy situation was merely a pretext for a capability dismissal.

Expiry of limited-term contract 2.90

Statute expressly provides that there may be a dismissal for redundancy pay purposes if a contract is for a limited term and that contract terminates by virtue of the limiting event without being renewed under the same contract – S.136(1)(b). This covers fixed-term contracts, contracts made in contemplation of the performance of a specific task and contracts that terminate on the occurrence (or non-occurrence) of a particular event – S.235(2A) (see Chapter 1 under 'Expiry of limited-term contract').

If the reason for non-renewal is redundancy, this is treated as a dismissal by reason of redundancy. In Pfaffinger v City of Liverpool Community College and another case 1997 ICR 142, EAT, for example, the claimants were lecturers who had been employed for many years on a series of fixed-term contracts, each of which was for a single academic term. When the employer tried to renegotiate the terms of the contracts the claimants brought claims for redundancy payments. The EAT noted that the combined effect of the definition of 'dismissal' and the definition of a 'redundancy situation' is that, where an employee is employed on a succession of fixed-term contracts, the employee may be dismissed for redundancy on the expiration of each contract. The EAT concluded that the claimants were dismissed when their fixed-term contracts expired at the end of the academic term and that the reason for the dismissals was redundancy, in that the employer had no need for part-time lecturers to carry out the function of part-time lecturing during the vacation. (Note that the fact that the claimants may have had continuity of employment throughout the series of fixed-term contracts for other statutory purposes did not prevent the expiry of each fixed-term contract being by reason of redundancy. See Chapter 1 under 'Expiry of limited-term contract'.)

By contrast, in Shrewsbury and Telford Hospital NHS Trust v Lairikyengbam 2.91 2010 ICR 66, EAT, a locum consultant cardiologist who was employed on a series of fixed-term contracts was not dismissed for redundancy when his contract was not extended. There remained a requirement for the work of a consultant cardiologist on the expiry of L's contract: the position of locum consultant was essentially the same as the substantive consultant post for which L had unsuccessfully applied.

It makes no difference that the employee knows in advance that the contract is unlikely to be renewed because the work is diminishing. If the reason for non-renewal is a reduction in the need for employees to do work of a particular kind, then non-renewal is a dismissal for redundancy – Nottinghamshire County Council v Lee 1980 ICR 635, CA.

2.92 **Temporary cover.** The non-renewal of a temporary contract to cover for an absent employee – for example, one who is suffering long-term illness – does not fall within the definition of redundancy. If the absent employee later decides not to return, thus creating a job vacancy, and the temporary employee is not offered the post, dismissal is still not for redundancy but may be for 'some other substantial reason' (SOSR) – Whaite v Dumfries and Galloway Regional Council EAT 223/92.

Indeed, where an employee is engaged in order to cover for another employee who is, or will be, absent because of pregnancy, childbirth, adoption leave, additional paternity leave, or medical or maternity suspension, S.106(1) provides that his or her dismissal upon the resumption of work by the original employee will be treated as being for SOSR – S.106(1). However, S.106(1) will only apply where the employer informed the employee on his or her engagement, in clear and unambiguous language, that the employment would be terminated on the return of the permanent employee – Victoria and Albert Museum v Durrant 2011 IRLR 290, EAT. In that case, which concerned maternity leave cover, the EAT also observed, in passing, that where another reason for dismissal exists (such as redundancy), S.106 will not always displace that reason in favour of SOSR. That will only happen where there is no other reason for dismissal than to facilitate the return to work of the woman from maternity leave. For example, if an employee is 'bumped' out of a post so as to accommodate somebody whose post had disappeared, and the bumped employee is then given work covering for somebody on maternity leave and subsequently dismissed on her return, that employee might still be dismissed for redundancy.

2.93 **Expiry of apprenticeship.** There are some limited-term contracts which, by their very nature, cannot be renewed – for example, contracts of apprenticeship or training. In North East Coast Shiprepairers Ltd v Secretary of State for Employment 1978 ICR 755, EAT, an apprentice's contract expired and he was not offered further employment as a journeyman because there had been a diminution in the employer's requirements for journeymen in his trade. The EAT held that, while there was a redundancy situation, redundancy was not the reason for dismissal. The real reason was the expiry of the fixed term and the fact that an apprenticeship contract is a 'once in a lifetime agreement' which cannot be continued under the same contract when it comes to an end. Dismissal was bound to occur when the contract ended, whether or not there was a redundancy situation in the employer's business. It followed that the apprentice was not entitled to a statutory redundancy payment.

3 Alternative job offers

Offer and acceptance

Trial periods

Suitability and reasonableness

Death of employer or employee

Offers during maternity, adoption or paternity leave

There is no legal obligation on employers to search for suitable alternative **3.1** employment. However, the statutory redundancy payments scheme encourages them to offer alternative jobs to employees who have become redundant in their existing roles. On the one hand, failure to do so when alternative work is available may convert a dismissal for redundancy into an unfair dismissal – see Chapter 8 under 'Unreasonable redundancy – alternative employment'. On the other hand, an employer may avoid liability for a redundancy payment altogether if a redundant employee accepts an offer of alternative employment (subject to the employee's right to a four-week trial period), or if the employee unreasonably refuses an offer of suitable alternative employment.

Briefly, the statutory scheme works as follows: **3.2**

- the employee must be given notice of dismissal because of redundancy and the employer must make an offer of re-employment *before* the old employment ends. This may be an offer of the employee's old job back again – where for example, work has picked up after notice of redundancy has been given – or, more commonly, it may be an offer of a different job. The new job must start, or be due to start, either immediately the old job comes to an end or after an interval of not more than four weeks (give or take a weekend). (Note that there is one possible exception to the rule that an employee must have been given notice of dismissal, which is where the employee has been laid off or kept on short-time – see Chapter 4 under 'Eligibility for a redundancy payment')

- if the employee accepts the offer, he or she is treated as not having been dismissed and the question of a redundancy payment will not arise. This is subject to the employee's statutory right to a trial period of four weeks where the job is a different one, or where it is the same job but the terms and conditions are different. If the employee decides against the job and leaves during the trial period, he or she is treated as having been dismissed when the old job came to an end and as having refused an offer of new employment

- if the employee refuses an offer of new employment, he or she will lose the right to a redundancy payment if the offer constituted an offer of suitable employment and the refusal was unreasonable. He or she will still, however, be regarded as having been dismissed by reason of redundancy

- if the offer was for unsuitable employment, or if it was suitable but the employee's refusal of it was reasonable, then he or she will be entitled to a redundancy payment.

Note that this chapter is concerned with this statutory mechanism for offering alternative or renewed employment. The circumstances in which a failure to offer such employment can lead to a redundancy dismissal being rendered unfair or discriminatory are examined in more detail in Chapters 8 and 9.

3.3 Offer and acceptance

It is clear that an offer must be made in the case of a re-engagement in a new job, but an ambiguity in the statutory wording means that it is not absolutely clear whether an offer needs to be made in the case of a renewal of a contract on the same terms and conditions. S.138(1) of the Employment Rights Act 1996 (ERA) states:

> 'Where... an employee's contract of employment is renewed, or he is re-engaged under a new contract of employment in pursuance of an offer (whether in writing or not) made before the end of his employment under the previous contract... then, providing the new employment takes effect within four weeks of the end of the old contract, he will not be regarded as dismissed.'

3.4 It has been suggested that there should, in fact, have been a further comma after 'under a new contract of employment', as was the case in the Redundancy Payments Act 1965, which introduced the statutory scheme. The comma disappeared when the Employment Protection Act 1975 amended the scheme, and was not re-inserted when the RPA was consolidated into the Employment Protection (Consolidation) Act 1978. There followed two obiter opinions of the EAT in which the absence of that comma was interpreted as meaning that 'in pursuance of an offer' only applies to 're-engagement' – see SI (Systems and Instruments) Ltd v Grist and anor 1983 ICR 788, EAT, and Ebac Ltd v Wymer 1995 ICR 466, EAT. When the EP(C)A came to be consolidated into the ERA, a Parliamentary committee opted not to re-insert the comma, noting that, following Grist and Wymer, to do so would offend the principle that a consolidating statute should not change the law.

If the obiter views of the EAT are correct, then while an employer who fails to make an offer to *re-engage* an employee before the end of the previous contract will not be able to rely on S.138(1) to deny the employee a redundancy payment, an employer who fails to make an offer to *renew* in these circumstances will still be able to rely on S.138(1) (provided the renewal takes effect within four weeks of the ending of the old contract).

In our view, the distinction, if it exists, is best ignored in practice and employers **3.5** should assume that an offer is always necessary. There are three reasons for this:

- Section 141(1), which governs the situation where the employee either refuses the offer of re-employment or terminates the contract during the trial period, refers to an offer to renew or re-engage, indicating that an offer is required in either case for the purposes of this section

- there is no convincing or generally accepted definition of the difference between 'renewal' and 're-engagement'. One might think that 'renewal' meant the same job on the same terms, whereas 're-engagement' involved a different job on different terms. But this cannot be right because S.138(2) says that there must be a trial period where the contract is renewed on terms and conditions which differ (wholly or in part) from the corresponding provisions of the previous contract. The explanation may be that 'renewal' refers to the same job, which may be with different terms and conditions, such as a new workplace, while 're-engagement' means a different job, but this is not certain

- in any event, the employer will not be able to rely on an employee's unreasonable refusal of an offer in order to avoid liability for a redundancy payment unless it has actually made an offer – see S.141(1) and (2). Nor, it seems, will the employer be able to rely on the employee's unreasonable termination of the contract during the trial period unless an offer was made – see S.141(1) and (4).

In practice, most tribunals accept that an offer is necessary and do not try to distinguish between renewal and re-engagement.

Timing of offer
3.6

As pointed out above, the offer must be made *before* the ending of employment under the previous contract – Ss.138(1)(a) and 141(1). For an offer to be made it must be communicated to the employee. In Smith and anor v Brown Bayley Steels Ltd 1973 ITR 606, ET, the employer posted an offer of another job to S's house on 29 March. It arrived on 31 March. S's notice of dismissal for redundancy expired on 30 March and so the offer was made one day too late.

In any case, it is advisable not to leave an offer of alternative employment until the last minute, particularly if there has been a long notice period. The employee may prudently have found another job and the lateness of the offer may be a factor in deciding whether he or she acted reasonably in refusing it – see below under 'Suitability and reasonableness'.

3.7 The offer must be for new employment to start either immediately after the end of employment under the original contract or after an interval of not more than four weeks – Ss.138(1)(b) and 141(1). A weekend can be added on to the four weeks. Thus, if the employment ended on a Friday, Saturday or Sunday, the four weeks are calculated as if the employment had in fact ended on the following Monday – S.146(2).

An offer made before a notice of dismissal has been given is not a valid offer for these purposes. In McHugh v Hempsall Bulk Transport Ltd EAT 410/90 M worked as an HGV driver for HBT Ltd and was offered employment with the purchaser of its business, the offer to take effect on 1 January, the day of completion of the sale. M did not want to work for the transferee, R Ltd, and remained an employee of HBT Ltd, although his services were hired out to R Ltd. Two months later R Ltd said that it no longer required M's services and HBT Ltd, having no other employment to offer him, dismissed M on 9 February. Furthermore, it refused to give him a redundancy payment on the ground that he had been offered suitable alternative employment under the old S.94 EP(C)A (now repealed) on the transfer of the business. The EAT held that no offer of suitable alternative employment had been made to M because there was no offer which took effect either on termination of his employment or after an interval of not more than four weeks as required by S.141(1). It was necessary to consider the situation at the time M's contract was actually terminated and, at that time, there was no alternative employment on offer. He was therefore awarded a redundancy payment.

3.8 Contents of offer

The offer need not be in writing – Ss.138(1) and 141(1), but it must be made by the employer or by an associated employer – S.146(1). The associated company does not have to have any employees at the time the offer is made so a subsidiary or dormant sister company can make the offer for the purposes of the statutory scheme – Lucas and anor v Henry Johnson (Packers and Shippers Ltd) and anor 1986 ICR 384, EAT.

Two employers are 'associated' in this context if one is a company controlled by the other (who may be either a company or an individual) or if both are companies controlled by another employer (who again may be either a company or an individual) – S.231. 'Company' means a limited company and 'control' means control of more than 50 per cent of the votes attaching to shares. An offer of employment with another employer with whom the original employer has business dealings will not count unless the two employers are associated as defined – see, for example, Farquharson v Ross 1966 ITR 335, ET.

3.9 Although an offer need not be in writing, it is usually preferable that it is, particularly when the job offered is of a different kind, or on different terms and conditions, from that previously done by the employee. The onus is on the employer to show that an offer has been made, and if it cannot do so it cannot rely on the employee's refusal in order to avoid a redundancy payment – Kitching v Ward 1967 3 KIR 322, Div Ct. An offer in writing will be the most convincing evidence.

An offer should specify the material terms in sufficient detail to show where the new employment differs from the old. The statute does not actually say this, but the Divisional Court applied the general law of contract to reach this conclusion in Havenhand v Thomas Black Ltd 1968 1 WLR 1241, Div Ct. This was a case in which the provisions about notice and overtime were different under the new contract, but were not specified in the offer (which at that time had to be in writing). The Divisional Court ruled that the offer was inadequate and that H, despite having started employment under the new terms, was entitled to a redundancy payment because no valid offer of a new job had been made to him. Similarly, if the employer is offering an employee the choice between several different jobs, it should provide sufficient detail for the employee to clearly distinguish between them. A series of vague offers is no substitute for one precise offer – Curling and ors v Securicor Ltd 1992 IRLR 549, EAT.

3.10 This does not mean, however, that every 'i' must be dotted and every 't' crossed. In McKindley v William Hill (Scotland) Ltd 1985 IRLR 492, EAT, the Appeal Tribunal said: 'To be intelligible the agreement must embody important matters such as remuneration, status and job description.' It was not necessary for it to contain all the items that were required to be specified as written particulars of terms of employment under what is now S.1 ERA. Thus trivial omissions could be overlooked. In Kaye v Cooke's (Finsbury) Ltd 1974 ICR 65, NIRC, for instance, the NIRC thought that an offer was not invalidated simply because it did not refer to a 19p travel allowance.

Normally, however, an offer of alternative employment should make clear the financial prospects of a new job – Modern Injection Moulds Ltd v Price 1976 ICR 370, EAT, a point emphasised more recently in Fisher v Hoopoe Finance Ltd EAT 0043/05. In that case, HF Ltd, which was part of a group of companies, employed F as a new business manager and paid him approximately £40,000 per annum. At the same time as acquiring a new company – SF Ltd – the group decided to wind up HF Ltd, which ceased to trade. As a result, a redundancy situation arose in which F was in danger of dismissal. The employer kept F informed about the situation and drew his attention to a sales account manager vacancy within SF Ltd. It did not, however, give him details of the financial package, and F decided not to pursue it. He was therefore made redundant in April 2004. The following month, SF Ltd advertised the sales account manager position, offering a salary of £40,000 per annum. F brought a claim of unfair dismissal against HF Ltd, arguing that his employer's failure to provide him with financial information about the proposed alternative role had rendered his redundancy dismissal unfair. The tribunal rejected F's claim, concluding that since he had expressed no interest in the alternative job, there had been no need for the employer to make further enquiries of the vacancy at SF Ltd. Accordingly, HF Ltd had discharged its obligation to investigate and bring to F's attention any suitable alternative employment. The EAT, however, overturned this decision. In its view, the law should be that 'where there are one or more possibilities of suitable alternative employment available to an employee who is to be made redundant then the employer should normally inform the employee of the financial prospects of those positions'. The EAT accepted that it may not always be practicable for an employer to provide such information because the financial prospects of the positions in question might not have been determined. However, in this case, given the short period between F's dismissal and the advertisement of the sales account manager post, there was a 'clear indication' that HF Ltd either had the relevant financial information available to it when referring F to the vacancy, or could easily have obtained that information from SF Ltd. In view of this, the EAT held that the tribunal erred in concluding that HF Ltd had discharged its duty to bring suitable alternative employment to F's attention.

3.11 An alternative job offer must be recognisable as an offer of a new job and must be more than a general statement of intent to find alternative employment on the employer's part. In Byers v British United Trawlers (Aberdeen) Ltd SCOET S/738/81 B was a deck-hand on the trawler Pindaris. His employer wrote to him saying: 'It has... been decided to lay up Pindaris and offer alternative employment to the... crew in our Oil Rig Standby Fleet.' A tribunal held that this was not a valid offer. It did not state any of the essential terms and conditions and amounted to no more than a statement of intention to make an offer. A similar result occurred in Metanodic Engineers Ltd v Whitehouse EAT 695/78. There, W was a shop foreman who became redundant when the galvanising shop in which he worked closed down. He was then put onto other work, which consisted largely of painting the premises, although he never knew from one day to the next what he would be doing. The EAT held that there was nothing that could be fairly described as an offer, but only 'day-to-day acceptance by the employee of functional directions as to what he should do'.

An instruction to report for work at new premises on a specified date was held to be a valid offer by the House of Lords in McCreadie v Thomson and MacIntyre (Patternmakers) Ltd 1971 SLT 242, HL. The only difference between the new contract and the old was the change of workplace and that was adequately stated by specifying the new location address. Similarly, in Lonmet Engineering Ltd v Green 1972 ITR 86, NIRC, the employer posted a notice to say that it would be moving premises to Hemingfield. The notice contained two columns, one headed 'Coming to Hemingfield' and the other 'Not coming', and employees were invited to decide whether or not to move by putting their names in one of the two columns . The NIRC followed the McCreadie case in saying that this was a valid offer.

An offer must be for 'employment'. An offer of work on the condition that the **3.12** employee accepts self-employed status is not a valid alternative for these purposes – see, for example, Okuda v (1) Photostatic Copies (Southern) Ltd (2) Japan Office Equipment Ltd ET Case No.23253/92. Note also that where a collective offer is made to a number of employees and has to be accepted by all or none of them, the jobs must be suitable for all. If not, there will have been no offer of suitable alternative employment in respect of any of the employees – E and J Davies Transport Ltd v D Chattaway and ors 1972 ICR 267, NIRC.

Communication of offer **3.13**

An offer need not be made to each affected employee individually. In McCreadie v Thomson and MacIntyre (Patternmakers) Ltd 1971 SLT 242, HL, their Lordships stated that an offer posted on a noticeboard is valid 'so long as the offer is in writing, brought to the notice of the employee, capable of being understood by him and in fact read by him'. There was no doubt in McCreadie that the employee had read and understood the offer because he wrote a letter to one of the employer's directors refusing it. However, the offer must actually be seen and read by an employee. In Maxwell v Walter Howard Designs Ltd 1975 IRLR 77, ET, M was absent on sick leave when a notice containing an offer of work in new premises was put up on a noticeboard. Since he neither saw nor heard of the offer until after the employer had moved, a tribunal held that no offer had ever been made to him.

There is a trap here for employers. If an employee refuses to listen to an offer of another job, or simply says that he or she is not interested in receiving one, no valid offer will have been made if the employer takes the employee at his or her word. However, the employer cannot rely on the employee's unreasonable refusal of an offer of suitable alternative employment unless it has actually made an offer – so it will be left with liability for a redundancy payment. Two illustrations:

- **Simpson v Dickinson** 1972 ICR 474, NIRC: S, a shop assistant, became redundant when the shop changed hands. At an interview with the new owner, she made it clear that she was not interested in working for it or anybody else, but would instead take a holiday and then look for work in a hospital. Due to S's lack of interest, the employer never made her an offer. The NIRC held that because no offer had been made, she was entitled to a redundancy payment

- **Pearson v Stan Wharton Ltd** ET Case No.27715/85: P, a car salesman, worked for a company that ceased trading because of financial difficulties. The employer tried to offer him a similar job with an associated car leasing company, but P immediately indicated that he did not want to know

93

about it. The tribunal held that no offer had been made because P refused to hear it. In any case, it would not have been unreasonable for him to have refused it because of the general financial uncertainty surrounding the employer's enterprises.

3.14 Acceptance

If an employee accepts the alternative job on offer, he or she is treated as not having been dismissed from the previous contract – S.138(1). This is subject to the right to a trial period, for which see below. Just as an offer need not be in writing, there is no need for any particular formality over the employee's acceptance of the offer. An employee can accept an offer by simply turning up to work in the new job.

Note that S.138(1) – the provision concerning alternative job offers – applies only to the statutory redundancy scheme contained in Part XI of the ERA. It does not, therefore, prevent an employee from bringing an unfair dismissal claim under Part X of that Act. In Jones v Governing Body of Burdett Coutts School 1997 ICR 390, EAT, for example, J, a school caretaker, became redundant and accepted an offer of alternative employment as a site manager. While still employed as a site manager, he complained that he had been unfairly dismissed from his caretaker post. A tribunal rejected his claim on the ground that, by virtue of S.138(1), he was regarded as not having been dismissed from that post. The EAT overturned this decision, stating that S.138 was only concerned with the employer's liability to make a redundancy payment. The case was therefore remitted for the tribunal to reconsider J's unfair dismissal complaint.

3.15 Re-employment must be 'in pursuance of' offer

The statute refers to re-employment taking place 'in pursuance of an offer' made by the employer – S.138(1). If the terms and conditions of the new job turn out to be different in practice from those that were offered, the re-employment will not have been 'in pursuance' of the offer. As a result, the original dismissal for redundancy will stand. Two cases illustrate this:

- **Eaton v RKB (Furmston) Ltd** 1972 ICR 273, NIRC: E became redundant through the closure of his workplace. He accepted a move to new premises and his employer arranged to collect him near his home. After E had started the new job, the employer shifted the pick-up point to a mile further away from his home and he left and claimed a redundancy payment. The NIRC held that, because of the change in pick-up point, the new employment was on significantly different terms from those offered, so that re-employment had not been 'in pursuance' of the offer. E was therefore entitled to a redundancy payment

- **Clarke and ors v Wolsey Ltd** 1975 IRLR 154, ET: redundant hosiery department operatives were offered new jobs in the fashion knitwear department. The offer said that they would be working on a piece-rate system which would allow for average earnings of £27 per 40-hour week. After six months a typical operative was only earning around £14 per week. A tribunal held that the actual terms on which the operatives were re-employed had been significantly inferior to the terms offered, so that they were never genuinely employed under the offer. Thus, they were entitled to redundancy payments.

While the statutory trial period is limited to four weeks, this limitation does not apply when the employer fails to uphold the terms of the offer. However, the employee must still leave within a reasonable time, otherwise he or she may be taken to have agreed to a variation of those terms.

Trial periods   3.16

Three kinds of trial period might apply where a potentially redundant employee tries out a different job – a statutory trial period, a 'common law' trial period and a contractual trial period.

Statutory trial period   3.17
The statutory trial period is mandatory and always arises when the provisions of the new or renewed contract differ, wholly or in part, from the corresponding provisions of the previous contract as to the capacity and place in which the employee is employed and the other terms and conditions of employment – S.138(2)(a) ERA. The Divisional Court considered what is meant by this provision in Rose v Henry Trickett and Sons Ltd (No.2) 1971 ITR 211, Div Ct, and made three points:

- all differences count unless they are trivial or insignificant
- it is individual terms and conditions that must be looked at, not the whole contract as a package to be weighed against another contract as a package
- it is irrelevant that the new terms may be more favourable than the old terms.

If the contract is renewed on the same terms, there is no need for a trial period 3.18
and no statutory right to one. This most commonly happens where business picks up during the notice period and the employer decides that it need not make employees redundant after all.

The trial period begins when employment under the old contract ends, and it ends four weeks after the date on which the employee starts work under the new contract – S.138(3). (This is subject to a general proviso that the new contract must take effect not more than four weeks (give or take a weekend) after the old one ends – Ss.138(1) and 146(2).) 'Four weeks' in this context

95

means four consecutive calendar weeks. In Benton v Sanderson Kayser Ltd 1989 ICR 136, CA, B's trial period began on 22 December and the ensuing four calendar weeks included 11 days when the employer's premises were closed for Christmas. B argued that in such circumstances, 'four weeks' should be read as 'four working weeks', since otherwise an employee would have no proper chance of assessing the new job. The Court of Appeal rejected this contention, stating that the statute was quite unambiguous and that 'four weeks' could only mean 'four consecutive calendar weeks'.

3.19 **Termination or notice during the trial period.** The Act does not set down any method by which the employer or employee should terminate, or give notice to terminate, the trial period. Therefore, given that it takes place after the old contract of employment has ended, it is arguable that either party may terminate the trial period summarily, or give notice to terminate without having to observe any statutory notice requirements or any analogous requirements that may have existed under the old contract.

In any event, if the *employee* terminates – or gives notice to terminate – the new contract during the trial period, and the contract is then terminated, he or she will be treated as having been dismissed when the original contract came to an end and for the same reason that that contract ended, i.e. redundancy – S.138(2)(b)(i) and (4). The employee is also treated as having refused the offer of a new job. If the new job was suitable in relation to the employee and the employee acted unreasonably in leaving it, he or she will not be entitled to a redundancy payment – S.141(4). However, if the job was not suitable or, even if it was suitable, the employee was not unreasonable in leaving it, he or she will be entitled to a redundancy payment. 'Suitability' and 'reasonableness' are considered in the next section of this chapter. Note that if an employee indicates in writing during the trial period that he or she is not happy in the new job, but delays formally terminating the contract or giving notice until after the trial period has ended, he or she will not be treated as having been dismissed for redundancy – see, for example, Bodman v Hays Logistics UK ET Case No.1200619/02.

3.20 If the *employer* dismisses the employee or gives notice of dismissal during the trial period 'for a reason connected with or arising out of any difference between the renewed or new contract and the previous contract', then the employee is treated as having been dismissed when the original contract ended and for the same reason that that contract ended, i.e. redundancy– S.138(2)(b)(ii) and (4). The employee will then be entitled to a redundancy payment. 'A reason connected with or arising out of' any difference between the two contracts would certainly cover the employer deciding that the employee is incapable of doing the new job. For instance, in Bailey v Whitehead Bros (Wolverhampton) Ltd ET Case No.1317/82 a redundant works manager took a job as a librarian/ storekeeper with an extended trial period. Unfortunately, he was not physically capable of doing the new job and he was dismissed for this reason when the trial period ended. A tribunal decided that the dismissal arose out of a change to the new employment and that B was entitled to a redundancy payment because his old employment terminated.

In Hook v (1) Day (2) Freehall Hotels Ltd ET Case No.15806/78 H was employed as a maintenance worker at two hotels. One of them was sold and the new owner hired H as an odd-job man and relief barman. After three weeks – i.e. within the statutory trial period – the owner decided that he could do most of H's work himself and dismissed him. A tribunal held that H's dismissal arose out of a change to his new employment – in that he proved to be superfluous to requirements – and he was to be treated as having been dismissed for redundancy when his original contract ended. This case, like the Bailey case (above), was decided under the slightly different wording of S.84(6) of the Employment Protection (Consolidation) Act 1978 (which preceded S.138(2) ERA), and which talked about dismissal 'for a reason connected with or arising out of the change to the renewed, or new, employment'. However, given that the ERA was simply a consolidating Act and did not profess to make any substantial changes to the law, the case is probably still relevant.

3.21 Dismissal of the employee for another reason – e.g. misconduct – would not be 'for a reason connected with or arising out of' any difference between the two contracts, and would simply be an ordinary dismissal unconnected with the redundancy scheme. Such a dismissal would not have the artificial effect of reviving the employee's original dismissal for redundancy and he or she would not be entitled to a redundancy payment.

To summarise, if an employee is dismissed for redundancy but then enters a trial period in a new job:

- if he or she leaves or gives notice within the trial period, the employee will get a redundancy payment only if the job was unsuitable and/or he or she did not act unreasonably in leaving it

- if the employer dismisses the employee or gives notice within the trial period, the employee will get a redundancy payment unless the dismissal was for a new reason unconnected with the fact that he or she was on trial in a new job.

3.22 However, note that even if the employer dismisses the employee, or gives notice during the notice period, for a reason connected with or arising out of any difference between the renewed or new contract and the previous contract – thus entitling the employee to a redundancy payment – the employee will still have the right to bring an unfair dismissal claim in respect of the termination during the trial period. This is because, as we stated above, the statutory provisions about trial periods are contained in, and restricted to, part XI of the ERA, which covers the statutory redundancy scheme only. They have no

97

relevance to the unfair dismissal provisions contained in Part X of the Act. In Hempell v WH Smith and Sons Ltd 1986 ICR 365, EAT, H was made redundant and given a redundancy payment. She then had a trial period in a new job, but the employer decided that H was unsuitable and dismissed her within the trial period. Under the statutory redundancy scheme H was treated as having been dismissed for redundancy when her original contract ended. There was nothing she could claim over this because she did not contend that the original redundancy dismissal was unfair and she had already received a redundancy payment. However, the EAT held that H was entitled to bring an unfair dismissal claim over her dismissal during the trial period.

3.23 **Extension of trial period.** The parties may agree to a statutory trial period of longer than four weeks, but only in strictly limited circumstances: the extension must be to *retrain* the employee for employment in the new job – S.138(3). If the change in employment only consists of a change in workplace and the employee will be doing the same work, there is no need for retraining and the parties will be limited to the statutory four weeks.

An agreement for an extended trial period must:

- be in writing and be made before the employee starts work under the new contract
- specify the date on which the period of retraining will end
- specify the terms and conditions of employment that will apply to the employee after the end of the retraining period – S.138(6).

3.24 The EAT has held that an 'agreement' need not be a formal legal document or contract, but a unilateral document signed only by the employer will not do. To constitute an agreement, the employee must do something to indicate acceptance – e.g. by counter-signing the employer's letter – McKindley v William Hill (Scotland) Ltd 1985 IRLR 492, EAT.

If the statutory conditions for an extended trial period are not met, the employee will lose the entitlement to a statutory redundancy payment if he or she stays on beyond the normal four-week trial period. In Higton v Wiggins Teape Paper Ltd ET Case No.13814/86, for example, H's employer gave him an extended trial period of four months in a new job. There was a written document recording this but the tribunal doubted whether any other statutory requirements were met. Further, the document looked more like an offer than an agreement – it specified the length of the trial period but not the date on which it would end, and was silent on the terms and conditions that would apply to H after it ended. Also, the extended trial period did not seem to be for retraining, as H had no apparent need for this. However, what finally put paid to H's claim for a redundancy payment was that he did not give notice until after the four months had ended.

Further trial periods. The parties are not limited to one statutory trial period. **3.25**
Any number of trials in different jobs may take place. If they all prove abortive
and the employment is finally terminated, the employee is still deemed to have
been dismissed for redundancy when the original contract ended.

There is a six-month limitation period for a redundancy pay claim and that
time normally runs from the date of termination of employment. However, if
there has been a trial period, the limitation period runs from the end of the trial
period or, if there has been more than one trial period, the last trial period –
S.145(4)(a). This applies only for the purpose of calculating when the limitation
period for a claim starts.

Common law trial period

3.26

Employees may be entitled to a 'common law' trial period. This arises in
constructive dismissal cases where the employer, faced with a redundancy
situation, imposes new terms and conditions in breach of the employment
contract. If the imposed changes amount to a fundamental breach, the employee
has three choices: (i) terminate the contract and claim constructive dismissal;
(ii) accept the new terms, in which case there is an agreed variation of contract
and the question of a trial period does not arise; or (iii) continue working
(perhaps registering a protest) for a reasonable trial period. This is known as a
common law trial period. It may be longer than the statutory trial period of
four weeks, but not too much longer or the employee may be taken to have
accepted the new terms and conditions.

The question of a common law trial period does not arise if there is an express
termination by the employer and an offer of a new contract. Nor does it arise
if dismissal is through expiry of a fixed-term contract followed by re-employment
under a new contract. In such cases the employee is allowed the statutory four-
week trial period and no more. This is illustrated by Meek v (1) J Allen Rubber
Co Ltd (2) Secretary of State for Employment 1980 IRLR 21, EAT, where M
was dismissed following the closure of his workplace and offered another job
on a trial period to last not less than six months. M did not like the job and left
it after about seven months, leaving the employment altogether shortly
afterwards. He claimed a redundancy payment, arguing that the common law
trial period applied and that he had left within a reasonable time of the trial
period agreed with the employer. Upholding the tribunal's decision that M was
not entitled to a statutory redundancy payment, the EAT stated that he had
been expressly dismissed and had accepted an offer of alternative employment.
This meant that he was only entitled to the statutory four-week trial period.
Since he had not left within that period, M was to be treated as not having been
dismissed in the context of the statutory scheme. The extended trial period
agreed with the employer – which was not for the purposes of retraining – was
irrelevant to the statutory redundancy scheme.

3.27 The distinction between statutory and common law trial periods can be summarised as follows:

- where there has been an express dismissal, followed by re-employment under a new contract, the employee is entitled to the statutory four-week trial period only (unless he or she is retraining)

- where there is no express dismissal and the employer tries to deal with the redundancy situation by imposing new terms and conditions in breach of contract, the employee is allowed a reasonable period – the common law trial period – to make up his or her mind whether to accept the changed terms or to treat him or herself as constructively dismissed and leave. For example, in Bevan v CTC Coaches Ltd EAT 107/88 B was ordered to move his workplace from Monmouth to Cardiff. Some weeks later the employer proposed to remove paid travelling time from his hours and to make changes in transport provision. B resigned and claimed that he had been constructively dismissed. A tribunal held that he had accepted the employer's breach of contract by agreeing the move to Cardiff. The EAT, however, ruled that B was entitled to a common law trial period – which it described as 'thinking time' – after the employer's breach of contract in moving him to Cardiff. There had been further repudiations during the trial period and B was entitled to resign when he did. There had been a constructive dismissal.

3.28 One question that has arisen is whether an employee can claim both a common law and a statutory trial period. Two old cases that addressed this issue:

- **Air Canada v Lee** 1978 ICR 1202, EAT: L was a switchboard operator. The employer moved to new premises where the switchboard was in a basement. L tried out the new premises, did not like them and resigned two months later. The EAT held that the employer was in breach of contract by requiring L to move. She had a reasonable time at common law in which to make up her mind. As L had left within a reasonable time, she had been constructively dismissed, the reason for the dismissal being redundancy because her workplace had closed. The statutory trial period was irrelevant because it comes into play only when there has been an express dismissal. The only dismissal here was a constructive dismissal when L resigned, and once she had resigned there could be no further trial period

- **Turvey and ors v CW Cheyney and Son Ltd** 1979 ICR 341, EAT: when work in the employer's polishing department declined the employees, whose contracts did not oblige them to work anywhere else, were offered new jobs in other departments. They accepted the offer on a trial basis but left more than four weeks later having not liked the work. A tribunal rejected their claims for redundancy payments as they had exceeded the statutory trial period. However, the EAT held that where there is a breach of contract by the employer, the employee is entitled to a reasonable common law trial period for making up his or her mind whether to accept the new job or not. If the employee decides to take the job, he or she will then be entitled to a statutory trial period in addition to the common law trial period.

So far as a straightforward application of the common law rules is concerned, **3.29** the two cases produced the same result: in both, employees left after trying out the new jobs and the EAT held that they had been entitled to a reasonable trial period. But the Turvey case suggests that an employee is entitled to two trial periods – a 'reasonable' common law trial period plus the statutory four weeks. This is questionable as, once an employee has chosen to accept a variation of terms by staying in a new job for a reasonable time, the question of constructive dismissal should surely vanish. The employee has affirmed the new contract and so there is no dismissal which would trigger the right to a statutory trial period. Nevertheless, the Turvey case was cited with approval by the EAT in Kentish Bus and Coach Co Ltd v Quarry EAT 287/92. In that case Q worked as a bus driver based at the company's Southwark depot. When that depot closed the employer asked him to work at its Leyton depot until another depot was opened in Southwark. There was no mobility clause in Q's contract and the journey to Leyton took 1½ hours each way, but despite this Q agreed to give it a try. Five months later, he was asked whether he would stay permanently in Leyton and given two weeks to decide. Q was then dismissed for disobeying an instruction to work a late shift, but he claimed that the dismissal was really for redundancy. A tribunal found in his favour and awarded a redundancy payment. The EAT upheld this decision despite the long gap between closing the Southwark depot and Q's dismissal. He had acted reasonably in not deciding whether to accept the employer's breach until the new arrangement was offered on a permanent basis. In response to the employer's argument that the tribunal had failed to consider – or had misapplied – S.138, the EAT held that the trial period envisaged by that section had never started. Citing the Turvey case, it said that the statutory trial period does not come into operation until an employee has a reasonable amount of time to consider whether or not to accept the employer's repudiatory breach of contract.

According to the EAT in Optical Express Ltd v Williams 2008 ICR 1, EAT, a common law trial period cannot run concurrently with a statutory trial period. In that case W managed a dental and optical store for OE Ltd in Bolton, but his position became redundant when the company decided to close its dental service. OE Ltd offered W the position of manager at the Bolton optical store and at her current protected salary. As the contractual provisions differed from those of her previous contract, the four-week statutory trial period applied. During that period, W's solicitor wrote two letters outlining her concerns and reservations regarding suitability of the new role. Two weeks after the trial period ended W resigned, alleging that OE Ltd had committed a repudiatory breach of contract in eroding her position and status and in failing to answer her solicitor's letters, which entitled her to treat herself as constructively dismissed. She then claimed a statutory redundancy payment. Before the tribunal, OE Ltd disputed that W was entitled to the redundancy payment because she had unreasonably refused an offer of suitable alternative employment. In response, W argued that she had preserved her right to claim a statutory redundancy payment because her solicitor had terminated, or had given notice to terminate, the new contract during the statutory trial period, with the result that she was to be treated as having been dismissed for redundancy from the date that the original contract came to an end in accordance with S.138(4). The tribunal found that the letters neither gave notice to terminate nor did in fact terminate the new contract during the statutory trial period. Nevertheless, relying on Turvey and Lee, it held that there was a common law trial period which ran alongside the statutory procedure, meaning that W was entitled to a redundancy payment. Overturning this decision on appeal, the EAT held that where there was an express offer and acceptance of a S.138 contract of re-engagement, triggering a statutory trial period, it was impossible to suggest that a common law trial period ran alongside it. The tribunal had been wrong to rely on the decisions in Turvey and Lee in finding that a common law trial period applied when in neither case had a statutory trial period actually operated.

3.30 The application of the common law trial period also came under scrutiny in East Suffolk Local Health Services NHS Trust v Palmer 1997 ICR 425, EAT. There, P's employer decided to close the hospital where she worked and she accepted an offer to transfer to a new hospital. However, before commencing that employment, P realised that the travelling involved would be too difficult and told her employer that she would prefer redundancy. A tribunal upheld her claim for a redundancy payment. On appeal, the employer conceded that P would have been entitled to a redundancy payment had she declined the offer of alternative employment and been dismissed. She would also have been entitled to a redundancy payment had she commenced work at the new hospital and resigned during the statutory trial period. However, on the facts of the case, no formal dismissal had occurred; P had simply been warned that the hospital was to close. Since there was no dismissal, there could be no right to a redundancy payment. The EAT accepted that the tribunal had failed to identify a dismissal and allowed the appeal on that basis. However, it pointed out that it would, in principle, be open to the tribunal to find that an employee who accepts alternative employment but resigns before starting work under the new contract can claim a redundancy payment on the basis that there has been a constructive dismissal. In such circumstances, the employee is entitled to a period in which to decide whether to accept the new terms. The EAT therefore remitted the case to the tribunal to decide whether the proposed change in job location constituted a fundamental breach of contract which the employee had accepted.

In practice, the problems raised in the above cases may be avoided if the employer expressly terminates the old contract – thus effecting a dismissal – and offers a new job under a new contract. Then the employee will only be entitled to the statutory trial period and no question of a common law trial period will arise.

Contractual trial period
3.31

Nothing in case law or the ERA prevents an employer and employee from entering into a contractual arrangement whereby the employee undertakes an alternative role on a trial basis. In Inchcape Retail Ltd v Large EAT 0500/03 L was told that his role of parts manager at a car dealership was to become redundant, but that IR Ltd was keen to retain his services. It offered him the alternative role of operations manager in aftersales. L expressed doubts as to his suitability for the role, in response to which he and IR Ltd agreed a plan of action whereby he would do the role as a 'designate post' for six months while simultaneously undergoing a personal development plan to bring his skills into line with those needed to be operations manager. It was also agreed that if L did not develop those skills, the redundancy process would be restarted. During the six-month trial period, L did not receive the training he had expected and it became clear that he would not develop the necessary skills to do the job on a permanent basis. He sought to restart the redundancy process, but IR Ltd resisted, prompting him to resign and claim constructive dismissal.

The tribunal found that L had a contractual right for the redundancy process to be restarted and by failing to recognise this IR Ltd had acted in breach of contract, in response to which L had resigned. Upholding this decision on appeal, the EAT noted that the tribunal had not found that the statutory provisions were re-engaged when it became clear that the trial period was going to be unsuccessful. Rather, it found that IR Ltd had agreed to restart a redundancy process which included all possible outcomes, including the offer of alternative employment or dismissal with a payment equivalent to a statutory redundancy payment. In finding that the constructive dismissal was unfair, the tribunal had correctly taken the approach of assessing the suitability of offers of alternative employment.

Note that any contractual agreement for a trial period cannot waive an **3.32** employee's entitlement to a statutory trial period, since this would offend S.203 ERA, which renders void any provision of an agreement or contract which purports to waive or exclude an employee's rights under the Act.

Suitability and reasonableness
3.33

An employee will lose entitlement to a redundancy payment when he or she refuses the offer of an alternative job, or resigns, or gives notice during the trial period if:

- the job was identical to the old one or, if not identical, was 'suitable employment in relation to the employee', and

- refusal of the offer, or resignation during the trial period, was unreasonable – S.141(2)–(4) ERA.

The employer must show both that the job offered was suitable and that the employee's refusal of it was unreasonable – Jones and anor v Aston Cabinet Co Ltd 1973 ICR 292, NIRC. This means that an employer is expected to discuss an offer of alternative employment with the employee concerned since, if this is not done, the employer can only guess at the employee's reasons for refusing it.

3.34 This is an area in which case law is largely of illustrative rather than instructive value. There are two reasons for this. First, the two matters to be judged – 'suitability' and 'reasonableness' – are questions of fact for the tribunal. The words are ordinary English words with no special legal significance – for example, the EAT has rejected the contention that the 'reasonableness' of an employee's refusal of alternative employment should be judged in line with the 'range of reasonable responses' test used for determining whether or not a dismissal is unfair under S.98 ERA – Hudson v George Harrison Ltd EAT 0571/02. It follows that there is little scope for tribunals to misdirect themselves in law and appeals against their decisions are rarely successful, although see below on the need for tribunals to assess reasonableness from the subjective view of the employee.

Secondly, suitability is assessed objectively by the tribunal. However, there is also some subjectivity in this matter because it must assess whether the job offered is suitable 'in relation to the employee' concerned. In Chalmers v Northamptonshire Teaching Primary Care NHS Trust ET Case No.1902049/08, for example, the ward where C worked as a nurse was closed and she was offered an alternative role working in a hospice. She refused the job, maintaining that she was incapable of working in an environment where death was an inevitable outcome. The Trust refused to give C a redundancy payment, stating that she had unreasonably refused an offer of suitable alternative employment. In subsequent tribunal proceedings, it contended that it was ludicrous to suggest that a nurse with C's experience would be unable to cope with death. However, the tribunal held that she was entitled to a redundancy payment. C had spent most of her nursing career working in a rehabilitation ward and she did not have the 'psychological mindset' to work in a hospice. Further, when her father died seven years previously, she was absent for a year and had bereavement counselling. The tribunal accepted that C had a degree of emotional fragility when it came to dealing with death which could be exacerbated in the context of a hospice. Accordingly, the role was not suitable for her.

3.35 The reasonableness or unreasonableness of a refusal also depends on factors personal to the employee and is assessed subjectively from his or her point of view at the time of the refusal – Executors of JF Everest v Cox 1980 ICR 415, EAT. Accordingly, a tribunal will fall into error if it substitutes its own view about the reasonableness of a refusal. In Bird v Stoke-on-Trent Primary Care Trust EAT 0074/11 B's post was at risk of redundancy due to restructuring and she was invited to apply for whatever posts were available. However, as her job was partly managerial and partly clinical, and the only jobs available were exclusively managerial, she did not apply. B was eventually made redundant but without being paid a contractual or statutory redundancy payment. A tribunal dismissed her subsequent claim for the payments on the basis that she had unreasonably refused offers of suitable alternative posts. However, the EAT overturned this decision. The tribunal had wrongly substituted its own view about the reasonableness of B's refusal rather than considering whether someone in her particular circumstances could reasonably have taken the view that she did. If she had taken one of the posts, for example, it would have meant moving from managing a team of physio- and occupational therapists to being managed within a team, with the result that she could no longer call herself manager within the NHS. Therefore, viewed subjectively, B's refusal was not an unreasonable position to take.

The need to assess reasonableness subjectively makes it difficult to extract general principles from the cases, as tribunals must always consider the employee's individual circumstances. An apparent minor change in terms and conditions of employment may affect employees very differently. Two examples:

- **Day v Premier Grocery Products Ltd** ET Case No.1500344/08: D's post became redundant when the employer closed down its plant in King's Lynn where he worked, and he was offered an alternative job in Wisbech. However, the new job would have required him to work 15 weekends each year, which he was unable to do because he was a Colour Sergeant in the Territorial Army and in order to maintain and further his career in the TA he was required to commit to 25 weekends a year. In his subsequent tribunal claim for a redundancy payment, D pointed out that the new contract would significantly affect his ability to continue with his TA career (he was just two years away from reaching the position of company sergeant major, an objective that had taken him 25 years to achieve), and argued that swapping his rostered weekends when necessary would have been a major problem. The tribunal held that D was entitled to the payment. Given his particular circumstances, namely his commitment to the TA, his refusal of the alternative job was reasonable

- **Goodwin v Total Security Services Ltd** ET Case No.1500931/09: G was posted by the employer to work as a security guard at Tesco in Saffron Walden. The store eventually decided that it no longer needed the employer's services and G's post became potentially redundant. The employer offered G alternative jobs in Great Dunmow, Bishops Stortford and London but he rejected all of them. In subsequent proceedings, the employer maintained that G had unreasonably refused the offers, and so was not entitled to receive a redundancy payment. The tribunal accepted that the jobs constituted suitable alternative employment – it was not uncommon for security officers to be moved about. However, G could not read or write and had difficulty with written signs, notices and timetables, so using public transport would have presented particular difficulties for him. Furthermore, he was unable to drive. Accordingly, G did not have the skills to respond to events that people with reading skills would take in their stride, and so he had not acted unreasonably in refusing the offers of alternative employment.

3.36 Given the difficulty in distilling general principles from the cases, all that we can do here is point out some of the factors that tribunals may take into account, repeating our warning that decisions cannot normally be taken as precedents applicable in other cases.

3.37 Interrelation of 'suitability' and 'reasonableness'

A tribunal will first consider whether the alternative job offered is suitable. Only if it is will it then go on to consider whether the employee was reasonable in rejecting it. Where a suitable job offer is made, the employee would be well advised to carefully consider and to respond to the offer before rejecting it. This is because the way in which an employee considers a suitable offer and responds (or does not respond) to it will be a relevant consideration in the overall assessment of reasonableness – Lincoln and Louth NHS Trust v Cowan EAT 895/99.

In practice, tribunals often treat 'suitability' as covering factors relating to the *nature* of the job on offer as they affect the particular employee – e.g. job content, status, terms and conditions, while 'reasonableness' will generally cover factors relating to the employee's *personal circumstances* – e.g. domestic problems, housing, health. Nevertheless, in Spencer and Griffin v Gloucestershire County Council 1985 IRLR 393, CA, the Court of Appeal said (obiter) that drawing too rigid a distinction between the issues of a job's suitability and the employee's reasonableness or unreasonableness in turning it down would lead to confusion. Some factors may be common to both aspects and tribunals are entitled to look at them in either context.

3.38 A case that illustrates this point is Cambridge and District Co-operative Society Ltd v Ruse 1993 IRLR 156, EAT. There, R was the manager of a butcher's shop until it closed down. He was then offered the position of butchery department manager in a supermarket. However, R did not like the new position, feeling that he had suffered a loss of status. He was to some extent under the store manager's control, did not have his own key, and no longer had responsibility for banking money. The tribunal held that the post constituted suitable alternative employment but that R's perceived loss of status made it reasonable for him to refuse that offer. The employer appealed to the EAT on the ground that once an objective finding of suitability had been made, the employee could not rely on his or her subjective perception of that employment to refuse the offer. If the offer was suitable, R could only rely on factors extraneous to the job, such as personal factors affecting him. The EAT rejected this argument as there was nothing in S.141(2)–(3) which restricted an employee's reasons to factors unconnected with the employment itself. Accordingly, as a matter of law, it was possible for an employee to reasonably refuse an objectively suitable offer of alternative employment on the ground of his or her personal perception of the job.

Rather helpfully, the EAT considered the interrelationship between suitability and reasonableness once more in Commission for Healthcare Audit and Inspection v Ward EAT 0579/07. W's role was to be deleted in a reorganisation and she was offered a new job which she rejected because, in her view, it would have seen the size of her department reduced by 75 per cent; her budget would have been halved; and the future job prospects were not as good. She claimed a redundancy payment, which the Commission resisted on the basis that she had unreasonably refused suitable alternative employment. The tribunal found that, since the new job did not involve a loss of status nor impact adversely on her future job prospects, the employment was suitable, though it did recognise that suitability was marginal, a factor that it took into account in finding that W's refusal of the offer was reasonable. On appeal, the Commission argued that the tribunal could not take into account suitability of the new post when determining whether the refusal was unreasonable. Rejecting this contention, the EAT confirmed that there is no requirement for suitability and reasonableness to be considered in isolation. Simply put, a tribunal is entitled to have regard to the issue of suitability when considering the question of reasonableness.

The upshot of Ward is that, where a new job is overwhelmingly suitable for the **3.39** employee, it may be less of a challenge for the employer to demonstrate that the employee's refusal is unreasonable than it would be if, for instance, suitability is only marginal.

We now consider the following factors that tribunals have taken into account in assessing suitability and reasonableness:

- job content and status
- pay, including fringe benefits
- hours
- workplace
- job prospects
- timing of offer.

It should be noted that the willingness of an employee to undertake a trial period is *not* evidence that he or she considers it suitable. To determine otherwise would undermine the very reason for providing a statutory trial period in the first place – Laing v Thistle Hotels plc 2003 SLT 37, Ct Sess.

3.40 **Job content and status**
The fact that an employee's pay is preserved in a new job will not be sufficient to make the job suitable. A drop in status will most likely make a job unsuitable, even if earnings are maintained. In Taylor v Kent County Council 1969 ITR 294, Div Ct, a long-serving headmaster was offered a job as a schoolteacher. The Divisional Court held that this was like asking a director to work as a navvy and that the job was manifestly unsuitable. However, an employer should not refrain from offering alternative employment if the only job available involves a loss of status. In Green v GA Transport Ltd (t/a Allens Transport Services) EAT 306/79 the employer failed to offer an operations manager at risk of redundancy the position of HGV driver where there was evidence that he would have accepted it. The employer's failure to offer G the alternative job demonstrated that it had not acted reasonably in treating redundancy as a sufficient reason for dismissing him. However, contrast this decision with Barratt Construction Ltd v Dalrymple 1984 IRLR 385, EAT, where it was held that if a relatively senior employee is prepared to accept a lesser position instead of being made redundant, he or she ought to make this clear to the employer. Although Green and Dalrymple appear to represent conflicting authorities on the question of whether the employer should offer a lower status job, there are important differences between the two cases. The employee in Green had done the lower status job in the past, and there was evidence that he would have accepted it as an alternative position had it been offered. These factors, which strongly suggest that the alternative job was suitable, were not present in the Dalrymple case.

The importance of status is further illustrated by the following cases:

- Harris v E Turner and Sons (Joinery) Ltd 1973 ICR 31, NIRC: H was a joiner who was promoted to apprentice instructor, a position which carried with it staff status and higher pay. After six years the employer discontinued the joinery apprenticeship scheme and offered H alternative employment, on the same pay, as a bench hand in the joinery production shop. H refused the offer and sought a redundancy payment. A tribunal held that because H was a skilled joiner, this was a suitable offer which he had unreasonably refused. On appeal, the NIRC held that employment is not necessarily suitable simply because the employee has the skills necessary to perform it. For example, an offer of employment as a teller would not be suitable for a bank general manager. The tribunal had misdirected itself by not giving enough weight to the instructional content of H's work and to the status that went with it, which made the alternative work offered to him unsuitable

- **Marsden v Cambridge County Council** ET Case No.1500819/02: M was employed as a field social worker by the Council. She had reached the grade of senior practitioner prior to it being phased out in 1998, and was paid on a management band. The Council opted to withdraw social worker assistance from the service for which M worked, and she was offered alternative employment as a social worker (rather than as a senior social worker), with her pay protected for three years. In determining that she had not unreasonably refused an offer of alternative employment, an employment tribunal found that she was entitled to treat the offer as a demotion and to be concerned by the loss of her 'senior' status.

By way of contrast, in Browning v White Knight Products Ltd ET Case **3.41** No.3100413/98 a quality control technician's refusal to accept alternative work as a machine operator, on the ground that he had originally been employed as a machine operator and did not want to take a retrograde step in status, was held to be unreasonable. The tribunal was influenced by the fact that part of B's job as a quality control technician had been to stand in for machine operators on a routine basis while they took breaks.

Loss of job content may make a new job unsuitable where, for example, it fails to utilise the employee's skills. In Koch v Hoverlloyd Ltd ET Case No.428/82 the terms and conditions of K's new job were better, but the range of duties was much narrower and she estimated that she had lost two thirds of the content of her previous job. That made the job unsuitable and K's resignation during the trial period not unreasonable. A similar conclusion was reached in Morgan v Global Solutions Ltd ET Case No.2407066/04. There, M, a senior custody officer at Preston Crown Court, had her role made redundant and was offered the same position at Accrington Magistrates Court. Though her terms and conditions were identical, she had fewer supervisory responsibilities and spent much of her working day completing crossword puzzles. The tribunal held that, given the high regard M had for job satisfaction, it was not unreasonable of her to refuse the offer of alternative employment.

Conversely, extra job content may make it reasonable for an employee to reject **3.42** an offer of alternative employment. In Patchett v Buck and Hickman Ltd ET Case No.34883/81, for example, a redundant stock record clerk was given a 10 per cent rise and switched to a new job requiring more flexibility. A tribunal thought that her resignation was not unreasonable – but she was 60 years old, and it would have taken a different attitude had she been younger.

A substantial change in job content may also make it reasonable for an employee to refuse an offer of alternative employment. In Horsley v British Fuels Ltd ET Case No.57257/95, for example, an employee's 24 years of experience and extensive contacts in the wholesale side of the employer's business were factors taken into account by a tribunal in holding that he had reasonably refused an

109

offer of suitable alternative employment in industrial sales. The employee was entitled to refuse the change in career direction after so many years.

3.43 Pay and other benefits

Any significant drop in earnings is likely to make a job unsuitable. It is not only basic pay that counts but the whole package on offer, including the opportunity to earn overtime and bonuses – Kennedy v Werneth Ring Mills Ltd 1977 ICR 206, EAT. In Carron Co v Robertson 1967 ITR 484, Ct Sess, the Court of Session said that fringe benefits such as staff status, sick pay and holiday entitlement were elements in considering the suitability of a job.

In Grainger v White ET Case No.1168/85 the manageress of a hairdressing salon, who had 40 years' experience in the industry, was offered alternative employment as an assistant in a sports shop on the same pay. Among other things, the tribunal held that, while her pay was to remain unchanged, G would have lost the tips which she had received as a hairdresser. This made the offer unsuitable.

3.44 Employees offered lower-paid roles are sometimes given 'pay protection' for a specified period. However, such protection, particularly if it is for a limited time, will not necessarily mean that an employee had acted unreasonably in refusing an offer. In Marsden v Cambridge County Council (above), one of the factors which influenced the tribunal's decision that M had reasonably refused an offer of suitable alternative employment was that her pay would be frozen for three years, and then reduced to a lower grade. However, that decision can be contrasted with Wiseman v Central Lancashire Primary Care Trust ET Case No.2408405/08, where W worked as patient service manager, a Band 7 post. Following a merger and consequent restructuring process, her post became redundant and she was offered the alternative job of programme support officer, a Band 6 post. Although W's pay was set to reduce under the proposal, it would have been protected for two years. She refused the offer on the ground that her pension would be affected and she was set to retire in three year's time. The Trust refused to give W a redundancy payment, saying that she had unreasonably refused an offer of suitable alternative employment. A tribunal agreed. W's anticipated retirement date was only two months beyond the date when her pay protection would have ceased and so the loss in salary and its impact on her pension was negligible.

Redundancies are often made when an employer's business is facing hard times. Uncertainty over its ability to continue paying wages may also be a relevant factor in considering suitability or the reasonableness of a refusal to accept suitable alternative work. In GD Systems Ltd v Woods EAT 470/91 W worked for a small company as a computer programmer. On 31 March he was given one month's notice of termination. He had little work to do and on 24 April he was denied access to the employer's premises. Various offers of alternative employment were made to him orally but W refused them. A tribunal decided that his refusal was reasonable because there was no guarantee that his salary would be paid. His March salary had not been processed until May and he had brought a Wages Act claim (now a claim under Part II of the ERA) in respect of his April salary. The EAT upheld the tribunal's findings.

Working hours

3.45

A change in shift patterns will be a relevant factor for tribunals to consider. In Morrison and Poole v Cramic Engineering Co Ltd 1966 ITR 404, ET, the employer closed a night-shift and offered the employees work on a double day-shift (at less pay). The tribunal appreciated the difficulty that long-serving night-shift workers would have in reacclimatising to day work and found the offer unsuitable. Similarly, a change in the number of hours worked may be relevant. In O'Connor v Montrose Canned Foods Ltd 1966 ITR 171, ET, for example, a maintenance fitter was required to work a 40-hour week plus 14 hours of overtime. He was made redundant and offered new employment with no overtime. The offer was held to be unsuitable.

As mentioned above, the question of reasonableness is to be judged from a subjective rather than objective standpoint. As a result, family and caring considerations can be extremely relevant. Two contrasting illustrations:

- **Saggers v East Gloucestershire NHS Trust** ET Case No.18145/96: S's part-time clerical post became redundant and she refused an offer of alternative employment because it involved some work on Fridays. One of the reasons she took her original job was that it left her free on Fridays, when she had a long-standing commitment to visit an elderly neighbour. A tribunal held that S had unreasonably refused suitable alternative employment. There was no reason why she could not have fitted her neighbourly duties around work on Fridays, or rearranged them for another day of the week

- **Weston v A Welcome House Ltd** ET Case No.2301444/00: W worked in a care home from 7.30 pm to 7.30 am. AWH Ltd announced that the care home would close and offered her employment at another of its homes which was a 20-minute drive from her house. However, she would have to work until 8 am. W refused the offer – she needed to finish at 7.30 am to see her daughter off to school. A tribunal held that the offer of alternative employment was suitable but, considering the importance that W placed on seeing her daughter off to school, she had not unreasonably refused.

Change of workplace

3.46

In Chapter 2 under 'Closure of workplace – place of employment' we discuss the impact of a contractual mobility clause on the question of whether a redundancy situation has arisen. In this section, we proceed on the basis that no such clause exists (or, if it does, that it has not been invoked). The question then is whether a change of workplace might make an alternative job offer unsuitable, or enable the employee to reasonably refuse the offer if it is suitable.

A mere change of workplace is unlikely to make a job unsuitable if the nature of the job itself is unchanged. Rather, if an employee turns down an offer of identical work following relocation, his or her reasonableness will generally be in issue. In Payler v Douglas Wemyss LLP ET Case No.3501678/10, for example, the employer had its main office in Leicester, but for many years it also had an office in Loughborough. P had worked as a fee earner in the Loughborough office for 15 years until the employer decided to close it and begin consulting with staff on relocating to Leicester. P was offered an increased salary to offset her extra travelling costs, as well as the ability to work from home two days a week. However, she refused the offer and claimed a redundancy payment. A tribunal found that the employer had tried to counter every objection that P had raised to the move – it had even offered to pay for a dog-walking service. In refusing even to countenance the offer of suitable alternative employment, P had acted unreasonably.

3.47 The question of reasonableness will depend very much on the personal circumstances of the employee, since a change of workplace may affect employees differently. To illustrate this point, here are two cases decided by the same tribunal on the same day:

- **MacGregor v William Tawse Ltd** 1967 ITR 198, ET: M, who worked in the civil engineering and contracting industry, was offered work at a site in the Hebrides from which he would only get home one weekend every six weeks. He refused the offer. A tribunal held that the work was suitable – a degree of mobility was to be expected in the industry – and M's refusal was unreasonable

- **MacCallum v William Tawse Ltd** 1967 ITR 199, ET: M received an identical offer to that in the above case. However, he had a wife and five children, two of whom were in poor health, and his wife could not cope with prolonged periods of caring for the family alone. The tribunal held that while the work was suitable, M's special domestic circumstances made his refusal of the offer reasonable.

Generally, significant extra travelling time and cost will make a refusal to relocate reasonable. In Gibbs v Gardner ET Case No.2540/86 an employer closed its shop in Paddington and offered G identical work at another shop in Radlett. This would have increased his daily travelling time by nearly two hours and cost him an extra £17 per week. The tribunal held that G's refusal was reasonable. Similarly, in Landry v Wedlake Saint Solicitors ET Case No.3300098/10 L worked as a legal secretary near her home in Hertfordshire until the employer closed that office and relocated to London. She was offered a job in London but, after visiting the office and finding that her travelling time would be 2 hours and 15 minutes, L declined the offer. The employer claimed that L had unreasonably refused a suitable alternative post and had therefore forfeited the right to a redundancy payment. The tribunal disagreed. The employer had failed to show that L had made an unreasonable decision in rejecting the London job offer. She had made a lifestyle choice in refusing to commute to London: she was 57 years old – an age when many people are looking for ways to reduce time spent at, or going to and from, work.

An employer may offer to reimburse any increase in fares or the move may be **3.48** a minor one involving little or no extra cost. Even so, an employee with special domestic circumstances could still be acting reasonably in refusing to move. Two illustrations:

- **Cahill v (1) Keith Prowse and Co Ltd (2) Cecil Roy Ltd** ET Case No.33490/76: a change of premises in Central London meant that C would have to switch from a few minutes' walk to work to a half-hour bus ride. C suffered from claustrophobia and could not use public transport. Furthermore, she had a small son at home. A tribunal held that her refusal was not unreasonable

- **Charlwood v KPK (Sheet Metal) Ltd** ET Case No.22786/78: the employer moved only four miles and offered C enhanced benefits. But the four miles meant significant extra travelling because of traffic conditions and caused domestic problems for C, who was a widower with daughters aged 12 and 16. The tribunal held that his refusal was not unreasonable.

However, employees will not always succeed, even where large distances are involved. In Gotch and Partners v Guest 1966 ITR 65, ET, an architect was offered a move from Bournemouth to Bristol at an increased salary and with a contribution to his removal expenses. A tribunal thought that this was a suitable offer and that his refusal was unreasonable. And in Little v Beare and Son Ltd EAT 130/80 a warehouseman refused a move that would have increased his daily travelling from 32 to 72 miles. A tribunal found his refusal unreasonable: it thought that the travelling was not excessive for Greater London, and noted that the employer had provided L with a van to assist with his journey. The EAT refused to interfere because no point of law was involved.

The nature of an industry is also a factor to be taken into account. In Thompson **3.49** v Moroc Construction Ltd COET 1463/36 T worked as a van driver for a construction company at sites around 15 minutes' drive from his home. When work dried up at these sites he was offered new employment involving an extra 12 hours' travelling time (which would be paid) but he refused. The tribunal thought that it was usual in the construction industry to travel to distant sites, and that T's refusal was therefore unreasonable. However, in McGurrell v Garrett and Campbell Ltd ET Case No.32273/83 M, a printer, worked in Kingston, which was around 15 minutes by car from his home, and he was

113

offered an equivalent job in Central London when the Kingston premises closed. This would have meant an hour's journey each way by underground, which M disliked, and he refused. The employer argued that this was unreasonable because an hour or so each way was par for the course for London commuters. The tribunal, however, held that what others were willing to do was irrelevant. The move would have introduced an unacceptable feature into M's daily life and it was not unreasonable for him to refuse.

An employee may have personal objections to new premises, in which case a refusal to move may be reasonable if the objections are justifiable. In Flannery v Tetley Walker Ltd ET Case No.27541/79, for example, a redundant barmaid refused a move to a pub which was known to be frequented by rowdy customers and where the police were often called in. A tribunal found her refusal reasonable. And in Bates v North West Anglia Healthcare Trust ET Case No.1901514/98 B, a school nurse, lived and worked in King's Lynn where she was a 'pillar of the community' and knew all the families with whom she worked. A tribunal held that she had reasonably refused a move to a town about half an hour away – she felt isolated in strange territory and her pre-existing disposition to depression was exacerbated. In Fuller v Stephanie Bowman (Sales) Ltd 1977 IRLR 87, ET, on the other hand, F refused a move to new premises because they would be shared with a sex shop. The tribunal said that this could be a reasonable objection in some circumstances but, having visited the premises, it decided that F was being over-sensitive and that her refusal was unreasonable.

3.50 Job prospects

If the new employment on offer is only temporary, with no guarantee for the future, that may make it unsuitable even if the terms and conditions are otherwise identical. In Ireland v Fairfield-Rowan Ltd 1966 ITR 191, ET, for example, the employer offered to renew I's contract, but only for two months and with no certainty as to what would happen after that. A tribunal thought that I's refusal was reasonable. However, in Morganite Crucible Ltd v Street 1972 ICR 110, NIRC, an offer of work which the employee expected to last only 12–18 months was described by the NIRC as an offer of 'regular' rather than 'temporary' re-employment. It overruled a tribunal and held that the employee's refusal was unreasonable.

The fact that new employment is only temporary may, on the other hand, be the one factor that makes it suitable. In Dutton v Hawker Siddeley Aviation Ltd 1978 ICR 1057, EAT, D, a wood machinist, was asked to move temporarily to another department to train as a capstan operator. His pay and conditions would be unchanged and this was deemed a purely temporary move until work picked up in his original department. It was held that in the circumstances this was an offer of suitable alternative employment and D's refusal was unreasonable.

114

Reasonable suspicion that a job offer is not genuine may also justify an **3.51** employee's refusal. In Woodcock v J and G Meakin Ltd 1968 ITR 164, ET, a written job offer was made to W. However, the same job – and only one was available – was simultaneously offered to another employee. There was also evidence that the job had already been filled by a third employee. A tribunal thought that W's refusal of the offer was reasonable because he had grounds for believing that no job was in fact available. Similarly, in Page v Thorn Lighting Ltd ET Case No.66259/93 a redundant employee believed that an alternative job had been 'manufactured' for him so that he would not leave and work for a competitor. He raised concerns about the genuineness of the job with his employer but received no reply. P left at the end of the trial period and a tribunal held that he did not act unreasonably in rejecting the offer.

Timing of offer   **3.52**
The timing of an offer of re-employment may be a relevant factor in considering reasonableness. In Bryan v George Wimpey and Co Ltd 1968 ITR 28, ET, an offer was not made until the evening before B's notice expired and after he had prudently found another job. His refusal was held to be reasonable. The facts were similar in Thomas Wragg and Sons Ltd v Wood 1976 ICR 313, EAT, in which the Appeal Tribunal held that the lateness of an offer was a relevant, but not decisive, factor. However, when combined with the employee's worries about future redundancies in the industry and the fact that he had found another job, it did make his refusal reasonable in this case.

In Gregory v Hanning Ltd ET Case No.1900771/98 H Ltd, a small company in the mining industry, gave notice of redundancy to all employees but made clear that it hoped to rescind some of the notices if the industry picked up. Towards the end of his notice period, G was told that his employment could continue and that, to the best of the employer's knowledge, there was no further risk to his job. However, G rejected the offer as he had secured employment elsewhere. A tribunal rejected H Ltd's argument that G was not entitled to a redundancy payment because he had unreasonably rejected its offer of re-employment, pointing out that he had endured two months of uncertainty and that the future of H Ltd remained in doubt. G's new employer appeared to be a much more stable company and most people in G's position would have acted as he did.

Option to accept redundancy payment   **3.53**
It seems that if the offer of suitable alternative work also contains an option to accept a redundancy payment, then an employee who chooses the payment will not have unreasonably refused the offer of work. In Armstrong v NATS LTD ET Case No.2701583/09 A, who was at risk of redundancy, had been given a letter stating that if suitable alternative work could not be found, or if he did not want to be considered for any alternatives, then his employment would terminate, leaving him entitled to benefit from the employer's redeployment

115

and redundancy agreement. A interpreted this as an offer to choose between redeployment and a redundancy package. He refused the offer of work and was given notice of termination, but the employer refused to give him a redundancy payment, stating that he had unreasonably refused an offer of suitable alternative employment. A tribunal held that the offer was indeed suitable, but that the letter A had received provided him with an option, and in choosing the redundancy payment he did not unreasonably refuse an offer of alternative employment. He was therefore entitled to a statutory redundancy payment.

3.54 **Constructive dismissal**

In Sennitt v Fysons Conveyors Ltd EAT 297/93 the EAT held that an offer of alternative employment cannot, as a matter of law, be suitable if it could give the employee grounds for claiming constructive dismissal. S and others were dismissed by administrative receivers on the day that FC Ltd was due to complete the purchase of the employer's business. Immediately after the dismissals, the employees were offered new employment by the purchasers, but on less favourable terms regarding pay and fringe benefits. Also, the guaranteed hours were shorter – FC Ltd considered that the generous terms of employment given by the previous employer probably contributed to the downfall of the business. S refused the offer and claimed a redundancy payment. The EAT held that S had not received a suitable offer in law, as he had grounds for claiming constructive dismissal by FC Ltd. In reaching this conclusion, it relied on Reg 5(5) of the Transfer of Undertakings (Protection of Employment) Regulations 1981 SI 1981/1794 (now Reg 4(11) of the Transfer of Undertakings (Protection of Employment) Regulations 2006 SI 2006/246), which preserves an employee's right to treat him or herself as constructively dismissed if, on a transfer, changes are made to the working conditions that amount to a fundamental breach of contract. As there was no suitable offer in law, there was no need to consider whether S had acted reasonably in refusing it and he was entitled to a redundancy payment.

This case is open to criticism because it is not specifically justified by any part of the ERA, and runs counter to the rest of the statutory redundancy scheme provisions. It suggests that where, on a transfer, a redundant employee is offered conditions of employment which are sufficiently detrimental to give rise to a claim of constructive dismissal, a claim for a redundancy payment will automatically succeed. The usual defence open to an employer that the employee unreasonably refused the offer is not available in these circumstances. However, if S's claim had been for unfair dismissal, then the employer's reasons for seeking a change to terms and conditions would have been a relevant factor going to fairness of the dismissal and, on the facts of the above case, the employer might have succeeded.

Time off to look for work   3.55

If a tribunal finds that a redundant employee has unreasonably refused an offer of suitable employment, he or she is not entitled to a redundancy payment. However, the employee is still treated as having been dismissed by reason of redundancy, and so retains the statutory right under S.52 ERA to time off during the notice period to look for work or to make arrangements for training – see Chapter 11 for details.

Death of employer or employee   3.56

Slightly different rules apply where an individual employer, or the employee, dies. These rules, contained in Ss.174 and 176 ERA, are discussed below.

Death of employer   3.57

The death of an individual employer operates to terminate a contract of employment at common law. To reinforce the point, S.136(5) ERA states that the death of an individual employer is to be treated as a dismissal of his or her employees for the purposes of the statutory redundancy scheme. The business passes to the deceased employer's personal representatives, who may or may not have the power to continue running the business, depending on the terms of the will. If there is no such express or implied power in the will, the personal representatives may only keep the business running until it can be sold as a going concern.

The policy behind the legislation is to encourage continued employment and under the ERA personal representatives can offer to renew or re-engage employees as in any other redundancy situation. Indeed, S.174 has much the same effect as the normal scheme. If the employee accepts an offer of continued employment with the personal representatives, he or she is treated as not having been dismissed and consequently as not being entitled to a redundancy payment. If the terms of the offer differ from those under the old employment, the normal trial period will apply. If the offer is suitable and the employee unreasonably refuses it or leaves unreasonably during the trial period, he or she loses any right to a redundancy payment. The only differences between the normal scheme and the provisions of S.174 are that the new employment must begin within eight weeks (not four) of the old job finishing and the offer of new employment need not, for obvious reasons, be made before the previous employment came to an end.

Where no offer of renewal or re-engagement is forthcoming, it follows from **3.58** S.136(5) that the employee may claim a redundancy payment from the deceased employer's estate.

The mere substitution of personal representatives as the employer does not count as a significant difference in terms and no account is to be taken of such

117

substitution in assessing the reasonableness or otherwise of the employee's refusal of a job – S.174(4).

3.59 It may not always be easy to tell whether there has been an offer of renewal or re-engagement when employees simply carry on working in the business for a period after the death of an employer. In Ranger v Brown and ors 1978 ICR 603, EAT, the Appeal Tribunal held that tribunals should not infer the existence of an offer and acceptance in such circumstances. Instead, they should look to see whether there was any express or implied agreement, having regard to the length of time involved and the circumstances of the case generally.

It is possible for an employee to become his or her own employer on the death of the original employer. In Rowley, Holmes and Co v Barber and anor 1977 ICR 387, EAT, a sole trader left his business to his employee, who was also his sole executor. The employee was not professionally qualified and could not carry on the business himself, so he sold it and reverted to being an employee of the business. The EAT held that during the interval between the employer's death and the sale of the business, the employee was acting in two capacities – one as executor and the other as employee. Hence he was employing himself with the consequence that there was no break in the continuity of his employment.

3.60 **Domestic servants.** In the case of domestic servants in a private household, the personal representative is deemed to be the person to whom management of the household has passed in consequence of the employer's death – S.174(6). Typically, this may be a surviving spouse, who need not necessarily be an executor or personal representative. But this does not apply if the new head of the household is a purchaser for value. A house buyer does not incur any liability for redundancy payments to the domestic staff.

3.61 **Do the Transfer of Undertakings Regulations apply?** As a general rule, the Transfer of Undertakings (Protection of Employment) Regulations 2006 SI 2006/246 (TUPE) will apply to the transfer of a business from one employer to another, so that contracts of employment are not terminated and transfer automatically to the new employer. The contracts continue as though they had always been made with the new employer, who 'inherits' all the liabilities and duties in connection with the employment relationship transferred.

However, the question arises as to whether the Regulations apply to the transfer of a deceased employer's business to his personal representatives. There is a strong argument against the application of TUPE in this situation as the wording of Reg 4(1) provides only for the automatic transfer of contracts 'which would otherwise have been terminated by the transfer'. The contracts of the deceased employer's business would not otherwise have been terminated by the transfer, because they have already been terminated by the employer's death. This point is reinforced by S.136(5) ERA, which provides that the death shall operate as a dismissal. On this analysis, the Regulations do not apply and S.174 comes into play instead.

The main argument to the contrary was inspired by Reg 3(2) of the now-   **3.62** repealed Transfer of Undertakings (Protection of Employment) Regulations 1981 SI 1981/1794, which provided that a transfer could be effected 'by operation of law'. This was drafted as a 'catch-all' provision and would seem to involve some sort of automatic legal process applying to effect a legal transfer from one person to another. Thus, the automatic succession from a deceased sole trader to his personal representatives for the purpose of administering the estate could perhaps be considered a transfer by operation of law. It was accepted by an employment tribunal in Fitch v Secretary of State for Employment and ors ET Case No.24292/84 that an executor who runs a sole proprietor's business in an identical fashion after the latter's death would be subject to TUPE. However, there are difficulties with this analysis. First, it means that S.174 is superfluous. Secondly, it would have the effect of compelling the personal representatives to continue employment, a situation which might be at odds with their powers (or conflict with their duties) under the Administration of Estates Act 1925. The situation might also be problematic where, for example, the deceased employer's estate is bankrupt and has to be wound up. Most crucially, when the 2006 TUPE Regulations were drafted, the reference in Reg 3(2) to a transfer being effected 'by operation of law' was removed, as the growth in case law from the European Court of Justice had made a 'catch-all' provision unnecessary. Since there has been no indication from the ECJ that the EU Acquired Rights Directive (No.2001/23), which the Regulations implement, applies upon the death of an individual employer, the effect of removing this wording seems to fatally undermine the argument that TUPE applies on the death of an individual employer.

Nevertheless, until there is an authoritative ruling on this point, uncertainty over whether TUPE applies in these circumstances will continue. The issue becomes most significant when considering the position of employees who are not offered renewal or re-engagement by the personal representatives. If the Regulations were to apply, such employees would automatically have their contracts continued, at least for a time, which would probably be preferable to compensation for the loss of employment. If, as seems likely, the Regulations do not apply, the death of an employer would take effect as a dismissal and the employees' only remedy would be a claim for a redundancy payment against the deceased's estate.

Note that, where the business is continued by the personal representatives and later sold as a going concern, TUPE will apply to that later transfer.

119

3.63 Death of employee

If an employee who is under notice for redundancy dies after receiving an offer of re-employment, there is a further modification to the normal scheme. Three situations are covered:

- an offer has been made to the employee, but the employee dies before having made up his or her mind whether to accept or reject it. The employee is treated as if he or she had refused the offer. If the offer was suitable and it would have been unreasonable for the employee to have refused it, the deceased employee's estate will not be entitled to a redundancy payment – S.176(3)

- the employee accepts an offer of re-employment, but dies during the trial period without having given notice to terminate the trial. The estate will not be entitled to a redundancy payment if the new employment was suitable and it would have been unreasonable for the employee to terminate the trial – S.176(4)(a)

- the employee has given notice to terminate the trial during the trial period, but dies before the notice expires. He or she is treated as if the notice had expired and the contract had been terminated at the date of death. Again, the estate will not be entitled to a redundancy payment if the employment was suitable and the employee acted unreasonably in giving notice – S.176(4)(b).

3.64 An employee may have died intestate with the effect that there are no personal representatives to claim on behalf of the estate. If so, the tribunal may appoint an 'appropriate person' as an ad hoc personal representative for the purpose of carrying on tribunal proceedings – S.206(4) and (5). This may be somebody, such as a union representative, who had been authorised by the employee before death to act in connection with the proceedings. Alternatively, it may be the surviving spouse, parent, child or sibling of the deceased employee.

3.65 Offers during maternity, adoption or paternity leave

Regulation 10(1) of the Maternity and Parental Leave Regulations 1999 SI 1999/3312 (MPL Regulations) contains special provisions that apply where, during an employee's maternity leave, it is not practicable by reason of redundancy for her employer to continue employing her under her existing contract of employment. Almost identical provisions relating to employees on adoption and additional paternity leave are to be found in Reg 23 of the Paternity and Adoption Leave Regulations 2002 SI 2002/2788 (PAL Regulations), and Reg 28 of the Additional Paternity Leave Regulations 2010 SI 2010/1055 (APL Regulations) respectively.

In these circumstances, where there is a suitable available vacancy, the employee is *entitled* to be offered such a vacancy with the employer, his successor or an associated employer before employment ceases under the employee's existing contract – Reg 10(2) MPL Regulations, Reg 23(2) PAL Regulations and Reg 28(2) APL Regulations. Note that the APL Regulations uses the term 'suitable *alternative* vacancy' rather than 'suitable *available* vacancy'. However, we respectfully suggest – given that the rest of the clause is almost identical in formulation to the corresponding clauses in the MPL and PAL Regulations – that nothing turns on this difference in wording, and that the clause should purposively be construed as referring to a 'suitable available vacancy'.

The new contract must take effect immediately on termination of the previous **3.66** contract and must be such that:

- the work to be done is of a kind which is both suitable in relation to the employee and appropriate for him or her to do in the circumstances, and

- its provisions as to the capacity and place in which the employee is to be employed, and as to the other terms and conditions of employment, are not substantially less favourable to the employee than if he or she had continued to be employed under the previous contract – Reg 10(3) MPL Regulations, Reg 23(3) PAL Regulations and Reg 28(3) APL Regulations.

For a vacancy to constitute a 'suitable available vacancy' it must satisfy *both* limbs of the test – i.e. it must be suitable and appropriate for the employee to do *and* not be on substantially less favourable terms than his or her previous position – Simpson v Endsleigh Insurance Services Ltd 2011 ICR 75, EAT. It is for the employer to decide whether a vacancy is suitable, taking into account the claimant's personal circumstances and work experience, given that there was no requirement for the claimant to engage in that process – Simpson v Endsleigh Insurance Services Ltd.

If a suitable available vacancy exists (i.e. a vacancy that is suitable, appropriate **3.67** and not substantially less favourable than the employee's previous job) and the employer fails to offer it to the employee, the dismissal will be automatically unfair under S.99 ERA if the reason or principal reason for the dismissal is redundancy – for more detail, see Chapter 8 under 'Automatic unfair redundancy – family-friendly cases'. If, however, the employer does offer such a vacancy and the employee unreasonably refuses it, his or her dismissal will almost certainly be fair and the employee will lose the right to a redundancy payment – S.141 ERA.

If there is no suitable available vacancy, the employment (and the maternity, adoption or additional paternity leave period) will come to an end by reason of redundancy. However, the employee will be entitled to his or her notice period

121

and to a written statement of the reasons for the dismissal (S.92(4) ERA). The employee will also be entitled to a redundancy payment (statutory or contractual) provided that he or she has sufficient qualifying service.

3.68 For a more detailed discussion of redundancy during maternity leave (and, by extension, adoption leave and additional paternity leave), see IDS Employment Law Handbook, 'Maternity and Parental Rights' (2009), Chapter 4, under 'Redundancy during maternity leave'.

4 Lay-off and short-time

Overview of statutory scheme

Duration of lay-off or short-time

Notices and counter-notices

Employee's resignation

Eligibility for redundancy payment

Death of employee or employer

In most cases an employee can only claim a redundancy payment if he or she **4.1** has been dismissed for redundancy – see Chapter 1. This chapter is concerned with the one exception to that rule. Chapter III of Part XI of the Employment Rights Act 1996 (ERA) sets out a scheme that allows an employee who has been laid off or put on short-time to claim a redundancy payment provided that he or she complies meticulously with the statutory procedure. An employee may be laid off or put on short-time where, for example, the employer temporarily closes its operation because of a depleted order book or lack of supplies.

This scheme does not apply if the employee has been dismissed – S.151 ERA. Furthermore, it is not necessary for the employee to be redundant within the statutory definition, but only that he or she should have been laid off or put on short-time for the requisite period.

Overview of statutory scheme   4.2

The provisions of the ERA governing lay-offs and short-time working are no less complicated than their predecessors in the Employment Protection (Consolidation) Act 1978, which were described as 'labyrinthine' by Lord McDonald in Kenneth MacRae and Co Ltd v Dawson 1984 IRLR 5, EAT. He went on to say that 'the provisions... have been the despair of all who have been concerned with the interpretation of industrial legislation since the scheme of statutory entitlement to a redundancy payment was introduced in 1965'. Therefore, before considering the scheme in detail, it may be useful to set out a brief overview of it.

4.3 The basic features of the scheme are as follows:

- the employee must have been laid off or kept on short-time either for four or more consecutive weeks, or for a total of six weeks (no more than three being consecutive) in any period of 13 weeks – S.148(2) ERA

- in order to receive a redundancy payment, the employee must give the employer a written notice of intention to claim (NIC). This notice must be given within four weeks of the last of the weeks of lay-off or short-time on which the claim is based – S.148 ERA

- if the employer wishes to contest liability, then it must serve a written counter-notice to that effect within seven days of service of the employee's NIC – S.149 ERA

- if the employer has served, and not withdrawn, a valid counter-notice, then the employee must apply to a tribunal to decide the matter – S.149. Provided that the employee has fully complied with the requirements of the scheme, an employer can only defeat a claim at this stage if, at the date of service of the NIC, a period of at least 13 weeks of normal working could reasonably be expected to begin within the next four weeks – S.152 ERA

- finally, the employee must terminate his or her contract of employment by giving either one week's notice or contractual notice – whichever is the longer – S.150(1)–(2). This notice must be given within three weeks of the employer's failure to give, or the withdrawal of, a counter-notice; or, if the case has been contested, within three weeks of the employee being notified of the tribunal's decision – S.150(3) ERA.

This chapter looks at each of these elements in detail.

4.4 Definition of lay-off

For the purposes of the statutory scheme, a week of lay-off occurs when an employee, whose contractual remuneration depends on his or her being provided by the employer with work of the kind which he or she is employed to do, is not provided with such work, with the result that he or she is not entitled to any remuneration for that week – S.147(1) ERA. The employer 'provides' work if it offers the employee work within the terms of the contract of employment – Spinpress Ltd v Turner 1986 ICR 433, EAT. If the employee's remuneration does not depend upon his or her being provided with work, the lay-off provisions do not apply – see further 'Contractual right to withhold pay if no work available' below.

An employee will not be treated as being laid off if he or she was not available for work anyway – e.g. because of sickness. In Johnson v Knowsley Caravans Ltd ET Case No.5071/74, for example, the rest of the workforce was laid off during J's sickness absence, but the employment tribunal held that sickness, not lay-off, was the reason that J had no work.

Equally, an employee will not be regarded as laid off if the reason for not **4.5** working is that he or she has frustrated the employer's attempts to offer work that is available. In Coombs v Total Security South West ET Case No.1402601/06, for example, a client told the employer that it no longer wanted C, a security guard, to work at its premises owing to his unreliability. Having left, C made no serious attempt to contact the employer about alternative work, and although the employer wrote two letters to him about the availability of other work, C did not receive them as he had not provided details of his current address. In these circumstances, the tribunal rejected C's claim for a redundancy payment, commenting that 'a worker cannot invoke the lay-off provisions simply by going to ground, staying out of contact, and then claiming that the respondent never actually offered work so there was no work to do. You cannot (metaphorically) lie in bed and switch the telephone off and claim you are laid off.'

Definition of short-time working   4.6
A week of short-time working occurs if there is a diminution in the work provided by the employer and, as a result, the remuneration for any week is less than half a 'week's pay' as defined by Chapter II of Part XIV of the ERA – S.147(2). Short-time working is often described as a form of partial lay-off and can occur where the employer maintains its operation on a reduced scale, e.g. on two out of five days, in order to eke out what little work is available. The method of calculating a week's pay and the definition of a 'week' are explained in IDS Employment Law Handbook, 'Wages' (2011), Chapter 10.

Contractual right to withhold pay if no work available   4.7
The statutory scheme only applies where the employee's pay is dependent upon his or her being provided with work to do by the employer – i.e. the employer must have a contractual right to withhold remuneration if there is no work. In Cornwall Aluminium Windows Co Ltd v Dawidiuk EAT 1405/96 D was laid off in June 1996 after 17 years. After being away from work for six weeks, he resigned. The employer offered to take him back but D claimed that he had been dismissed and was entitled to a redundancy payment. The employer argued that the statutory provisions on lay-off applied. D's contract simply provided that 'your wage is £108 per week'. The EAT upheld a tribunal's decision that D was entitled to be paid during the period in which he remained an employee but was not being provided with work by the employer and that the lay-off provisions did not therefore apply.

Similarly, in Powell Duffryn Wagon Co Ltd and anor v House and ors 1974 ICR 123, NIRC, the employer repaired railway wagons and guaranteed its employees a minimum weekly wage, whether or not work was available.

125

Business dried up when British Rail staff prevented wagons from reaching the employer's repair shops and, having no work to do, H and his fellow employees were laid off without pay. Upholding the tribunal, the NIRC held that there was no statutory lay-off because the employees were entitled to a guaranteed minimum salary.

4.8 Note, however, that statutory guarantee payments made by an employer under Part III of the ERA (Ss.28–35) do not prevent an employee claiming to have been laid off or placed on short-time working, as such payments do not constitute remuneration to which the employee is entitled under the contract. If a lay-off lasts long enough, the employer may be obliged to pay both guarantee payments and a redundancy payment in respect of the lay-off. In Spencer v Purdy and anor t/a Kelco ET Case No.67371/95, for example, S's employment was terminated when the factory where she worked closed down. P made an offer of alternative employment which involved S working at home, but she refused and was consequently denied a redundancy payment. The tribunal held that S was entitled to a redundancy payment as, in its view, P did not make an offer of suitable alternative work. P was also ordered to make a guarantee payment to S in respect of one workless day. (Guarantee payments are discussed in IDS Employment Law Handbook, 'Wages', Chapter 6.)

4.9 **Piece workers and time workers.** Piece workers, whose remuneration varies according to the amount of work done, come under the statutory scheme, as do employees whose contractual terms either expressly or impliedly allow the employer to lay them off or introduce short-time work. Such terms may be found in the contract itself, be incorporated into the contract by virtue of a collective agreement, or be implied by custom and practice.

It has been suggested that time workers whose remuneration does not vary according to the amount of work done are not covered. However, under S.147(1) it is the *payment* of remuneration, not the *amount* of remuneration, that must be dependent on the provision of work. Thus, in our view, a time worker who is contractually entitled to a fixed salary, irrespective of how much work he or she does, will still be covered by the scheme if he or she can nonetheless be laid-off without pay where there is no work available. The decision in Powell Duffryn Wagon Co Ltd and anor v House and ors (above) would seem to support this view but ultimately, of course, whether or not an employer has a right to lay off is a question of fact to be decided by the tribunal in each case.

4.10 **Lay-off in breach of contract.** As we have seen, the right to lay off must be permitted by the contract of employment. If an employer lays off an employee or puts him or her on short-time without having an express or implied contractual right to do so, this will be a fundamental breach of contract leaving the employee entitled to resign and claim constructive dismissal (assuming the one-year qualifying service requirement is met). If the reason for dismissal was

126

redundancy, which is likely in a lay-off situation, the employee may also claim a redundancy payment in the normal way (provided that he or she has at least two years' continuous service), thereby avoiding the intricacies of claiming a redundancy payment by way of the lay-off and short-time provisions – Waine v R Oliver (Plant Hire) Ltd 1977 IRLR 434, EAT. He or she can also claim that the dismissal was unfair. A term permitting lay-off will only be implied into a contract if there exists for that employment a custom of laying off that is 'reasonable, certain and notorious' and is such that 'no workman could be supposed to have entered into service without looking to it as part of the contract' – Bond v Cav Ltd and anor 1983 IRLR 360, QBD. In Stevenson and anor v Good Stuff Ltd EAT 572/94 two part-time sales assistants were laid off despite the fact that a right to lay-off was not provided for in their contracts of employment. They resigned and claimed that they had been constructively dismissed. The EAT ruled that they were each entitled to a redundancy payment. There had been a decline in trade which reduced the employer's requirements for employees to perform work of a particular kind. That led to the lay-off and was the reason for the constructive dismissal.

Note that an employee who has been laid off or kept on short-time in breach of contract may elect to keep the contract going and claim any shortfall in wages under the protection of wages provisions contained in Part II of the ERA.

Unreasonable lay-offs. In A Dakri and Co Ltd v Tiffen and ors 1981 ICR 256, **4.11** EAT, the Appeal Tribunal held that there is an implied contractual term that any lay-off will only be for a 'reasonable' period and that, in the circumstances of the case, a lay-off lasting more than four weeks was a fundamental breach of contract entitling the employee to claim constructive dismissal by reason of redundancy. However, that case was called into question by the later decision of Kenneth MacRae and Co Ltd v Dawson 1984 IRLR 5, EAT, where the Appeal Tribunal held that a contractual right to lay off indefinitely is not normally subject to any test of reasonableness. The employer cannot be regarded as in breach of contract simply by virtue of the passage of time. The EAT went on to say that if an employee thinks that he or she has been laid off for too long, the remedy is to follow the statutory procedure for claiming a redundancy payment based on lay-off. The notion of an unreasonable lay-off still survives, however: the employment tribunal in Langford v DE Ware t/a Georgian Design Associates ET Case No.39477/95, for example, found that an employer who had been contractually entitled to lay off employees was entitled to do so only for a reasonable period not exceeding four weeks. Thus, an employee who resigned after a 16-week lay-off had been constructively dismissed and was entitled to a redundancy payment.

For the circumstances in which terms may be implied into contracts of employment see IDS Employment Law Handbook, 'Contracts of Employment' (2009), Chapter 2.

127

4.12 Duration of lay-off or short-time

The statutory scheme comes into play when either:

- the employee has been laid off or kept on short-time for four or more consecutive weeks – S.148(2)(a) ERA, or

- the employee has been laid off or kept on short-time for a total of six or more weeks in a period of 13 weeks. No more than three of the weeks can have been consecutive – S.148(2)(b).

For these purposes, it does not matter whether the weeks relied upon by the employee are weeks of lay-off, short-time, or a combination of the two – S.154(a) ERA. A 'week' for these purposes is a week ending with a Saturday, unless the employee's pay is calculated weekly by reference to a week ending with a day other than Saturday, in which case it means a week ending with that other day – S.235(1).

4.13 The stipulation in S.148(2)(b) that not more than three of the weeks claimed for should be consecutive may be important in the context of the time limit for making a claim. An employee must give a notice of intention to claim (NIC) not later than four weeks from the end of the last of the weeks of lay-off or short-time on which the claim is based – S.148(2). Suppose that in the course of a 13-week period an employee:

- is laid off for four weeks

- works again for four weeks

- is laid off again for three weeks

- works again for two weeks.

By the end of those 13 weeks it will be too late for the employee to claim a redundancy payment. He or she cannot rely on S.148(2)(b) by adding the four-week lay-off to the three-week lay-off and saying that the claim is within four weeks of the end of the latter. This is because the first period of lay-off was of more than three consecutive weeks. The claim should have been made within four weeks of the end of the first period of lay-off.

4.14 An employee who has not been laid off or kept on short-time for the full qualifying period may not present an NIC – see 'Notices and counter-notices' below – and any such notice that is presented will be invalid. In Allinson v Drew Simmons Engineering Ltd 1985 ICR 488, EAT, A was placed on short-time working on 26 September. On 20 October he gave notice that he intended to claim a redundancy payment. The EAT held that this notice, served before A had been on short-time for a full four weeks, was invalid and his claim for a redundancy payment failed.

128

Strikes and lock-outs 4.15

An employee cannot rely on any week of lay-off or short-time that occurs wholly or mainly as a result of a strike or lock-out – S.154(b) ERA. Note that the employee does not have to be a participant in the strike or lock-out, and the strike or lock-out need not be in the trade or industry in which he or she is employed. Indeed, the strike or lock-out need not even take place in Great Britain. The only requirement is that it should be the main cause of lay-off or short-time.

'Lock-out' and 'strike' are defined in S.235(4) and (5) ERA. These definitions are restricted to action taken to compel the other side to accept or reject terms and conditions of or affecting employment. Political or sympathy strikes do not count in this context. Furthermore, lay-offs or short-time working caused by industrial action short of a strike – such as a work-to-rule – are not excluded from the scope of the statutory scheme.

Tribunals have come to different conclusions about when a lay-off is deemed 4.16 attributable to a strike or lock-out. Here are two cases concerning the famous 1984 miners' strike:

- **Ward v SH Ward and Co Ltd** ET Case No.9977/85: W, a hotel waitress in Barnsley, was laid off following a serious downturn in business during the miners' strike. An employment tribunal held that the lay-off was mainly caused by the strike. Although W would otherwise have qualified for a redundancy payment, the weeks of lay-off could not be counted

- **Cooke v Hayden Nilos Conflow Ltd** ET Case No.13049/85: C was laid off during the miners' strike by HNC Ltd, which manufactured mining equipment. An employment tribunal found that there had been a 43 per cent reduction in business within the United Kingdom, but that export sales were unaffected. It was still possible for the employer to carry on with its business – even though it had a sound economic reason for the lay-off. In the tribunal's view, it had not been established that C's lay-off was mainly attributable to the strike.

Notices and counter-notices 4.17

A central feature of the lay-off and short-time scheme is the strict requirement for a notice of intention to claim (NIC) from the employee and – if the claim is to be opposed – a counter-notice from the employer. Notice is given by an employee to an employer if it is delivered to the employer or posted to it at the employee's workplace. Alternatively, the NIC may be given to a person designated by the employer, or left for such a person at a designated place, or posted to that person at a designated address – S.179(2) ERA. Counter-notice is given by an employer to an employee if it is delivered to the employee, left for the employee at his or her usual or last-known place of residence, or posted to the employee there – S.179(1).

If a notice is 'left' for a person at a place as specified above, it is presumed to have been received by that person on the day on which it was left there, unless the contrary is proved – S.179(4) ERA. As far as a notice sent through the post is concerned, S.7 of the Interpretation Act 1978 comes into play. This provides that, where an Act authorises a document to be served by post, then service is deemed to be effected at the time when the letter would be delivered in the ordinary course of post unless the contrary is proved. When posting a notice, it is advisable to obtain some proof of posting, but there is no requirement to send documents by registered post or recorded delivery. It should be remembered that the time limits for giving notices cannot be extended, even if the notices are lost in the post.

4.18 Notice of intention to claim

The employee's NIC must be given in writing. It need not be in specific terms but must indicate the employee's intention to claim a redundancy payment in respect of lay-off or short-time. The NIC must be served not earlier than the last of the days of lay-off or short-time relied upon and not later than four weeks starting with that date – S.148(2) ERA. Employment tribunals have no discretion to extend this latter time limit for any reason. However, if an employee sends the employer an NIC which is premature or defective in some way, he or she can cure the defect by sending another one, provided that this is done within the four-week time limit.

4.19 Employer's counter-notice

The employer's counter-notice must also be in writing. It must be given to the employee within seven days of service of the employee's NIC and must state, as a minimum, that the employer intends to contest any liability for a redundancy payment – S.149(a) ERA. As with the employee's NIC, the time limit cannot be extended for any reason.

The employer's counter-notice need not set out the details of the grounds upon which a redundancy payment is opposed. However, it must state that the employer intends to contest liability for a redundancy payment. In Fabar Construction Ltd v Race and anor 1979 ICR 529, EAT, the employer sent a letter that simply stated: 'We confirm our offer made to you on Friday, April 21, 1978, to commence work at our Chowdene site on Monday, April 24, 1978.' The EAT held that this was not a valid counter-notice because it did not indicate an intention to contest liability for a redundancy payment. Similarly, in Bradley v International Quality Control Laboratories Ltd ET Case No.9657/84 the employer sent a letter indicating its expectation of substantial work coming in and then said: 'Please consider this letter as a counter-notice under the redundancy payments scheme.' An employment tribunal held that this was inadequate.

The employer may withdraw a counter-notice by giving a subsequent notice of **4.20** withdrawal in writing. There is no time limit for this. If the employer does not do so, the question of the employee's eligibility for a redundancy payment must be decided by a tribunal – S.149 ERA. The only ground upon which the employer can defeat a claim at this stage is discussed under 'Eligibility for redundancy payment – employer's defence to contested claim'.

Employee's resignation   4.21

Once an employee has served a valid NIC, the final thing that he or she must do to secure a redundancy payment – subject to any defence raised by the employer – is resign by giving notice – S.150(1) ERA. An employee will not be entitled to a redundancy payment if his or her contract of employment still exists. However, if the employee decides to terminate the contract and take a redundancy payment, continuity of employment will be broken in the event that he or she resumes work with the same employer. Note, however, that the employee's resignation is not a constructive dismissal. This scheme does not apply to employees who are dismissed (whether constructively or otherwise) – S.151 ERA – as they could then simply rely on the fact of that dismissal to claim a redundancy payment (or compensation for unfair dismissal).

The employee must give one week's notice, or full contractual notice if the contract stipulates a longer period – S.150(2) ERA. A week's notice means a full week's notice. In Homson v FMS (Farm Products) Ltd 1967 ITR 326, ET, the employee gave notice on a Monday to terminate her employment the following Saturday. Her claim failed because this was not a full seven days' notice. Notice to terminate on a Saturday must be given on the previous Saturday to amount to a week's notice. Similarly, in Broadhurst v Brockhouse ET Case No.21734/86 the employee gave notice on a Monday to terminate his contract on pay-day (Friday). The tribunal held that for the notice to be valid it should have been given on the preceding pay-day. And in Hurdley v Fretwell and ors ET Case No.23337/95 H had already been laid off for nearly two months when, having obtained new employment, he served notice that he was applying for a redundancy payment as a result of the lay-off. However, he did not allow one week between leaving and starting his new employment and so the tribunal concluded that he was not entitled to a redundancy payment.

But provided sufficient notice is given, the form of the notice would appear to **4.22** be less prescriptive. In Walmsley v C and R Ferguson Ltd 1989 SLT 258, Ct Sess (Inner House), for example, W wrote to his employer saying: 'If you do not wish to do any of the above… then I am left with no option but to resign and instigate... tribunal proceedings against you. I look forward to hearing from you within seven days.' In subsequent proceedings, W admitted that he had not intended to give one week's notice because he did not know that this was necessary. The tribunal, however, construed the reference to 'seven days' as constituting a week's notice. The EAT overruled this, but the Court of Session restored the tribunal's original decision notwithstanding A's admission, holding that it was possible to read W's letter as giving one week's notice and that the tribunal had been entitled to read it in this way. The legal effect of the language used was important, not the intention of the writer. Furthermore, W was a workman not familiar with the statute.

The employee's notice to terminate need not be in writing. In Fabar Construction Ltd v Race and anor 1979 ICR 529, EAT, an oral offer to give a week's notice coupled with a request for the employee's P45 was held to be adequate notice.

4.23 The timing of service of the employee's notice to terminate is crucial since the time limits cannot be extended and a failure to serve the notice within the applicable time limit will deprive the employee of entitlement to a redundancy payment – S.150(1). There are three circumstances to consider:

- the employer does not serve a counter-notice within seven days of service of the NIC. The time limit here is three weeks after the end of those seven days – S.150(3)(a) ERA. This covers both the situation where the employer does not serve a counter-notice at all and where one is served late. It will also apply when the employer's counter-notice is invalid because it does not state the employer's intention to contest liability for a redundancy payment. This is treated as the equivalent of not giving a counter-notice at all, so that the same time limit applies – see, for example, Vennard v Deal 1969 ITR 315, ET

- the employer gives a counter-notice within the seven-day time limit, but withdraws it by a subsequent notice in writing. The time limit here is three weeks after service of the notice of withdrawal – S.150(3)(b) ERA. There is no time limit for service of an employer's notice of withdrawal

- the employer gives a counter-notice within the seven-day time limit and does not withdraw it. This means that the case must go to a tribunal. The time limit here is three weeks after notification to the employee of the tribunal's decision – S.150(3)(c) ERA. This means that an employee in a contested case does not have to resign until a tribunal has decided that he or she is eligible for a redundancy payment. But there is a catch, in that the three-week time limit applies even if the employer appeals – S.150(4). This means that if an employer's appeal is successful, the employee may be both out of a job (through having resigned within three weeks of the tribunal's decision) and unable to claim a redundancy payment.

Note that these are the *latest* dates on which an employee's notice to terminate **4.24**
may be given. It does not matter how early notice is given, provided that the
employee is still employed at the date of service of the NIC and can show the
requisite period of lay-off or short-time. In Armstrong and ors v Barber and
Nicholls Ltd ET Case No.21247/75 A was laid off on 7 February. She served
an NIC on 15 June and the employer did not serve a counter-notice. A gave
notice of termination on 15 August – which was outside the time limit. However,
she remained laid off and then served a second NIC on 20 August. Once again,
the employer did not serve a counter-notice and A's notice of termination was
held to have been presented in time – it did not matter that it predated the
valid NIC.

Eligibility for redundancy payment **4.25**

If the employer does not serve a counter-notice, or serves one and then
withdraws it, then, provided that the employee has followed the statutory
procedure and the lay-off or short-time was not mainly caused by a strike or
lock-out, the employee will be eligible for a redundancy payment just as if he
or she had been dismissed for redundancy, and subject to the same qualifying
conditions set out in Chapter 5. For these purposes, the period of qualifying
service is calculated up to the last day of the weeks of lay-off or short-time on
which the employee is relying – S.153 ERA.

Employer's defence to contested claim **4.26**
If the employee has followed the statutory procedure and the employer has
served a counter-notice, the issue must be decided by a tribunal. At this stage,
only one defence is available to an employer under a counter-notice. This is
that, at the date of service of the employee's NIC, it was reasonably expected
that the employee would, not later than four weeks after that date, enter into a
period of employment with the same employer of at least 13 continuous weeks
during which he or she would not be laid off or kept on short-time for any
week – S.152(1) ERA. Note that the relevant date is the *date of service of the
employee's NIC*: it will not necessarily help the employer if business has picked
up and there is plenty of work available at the *date of the tribunal hearing*,
which may be several months after the date of service of the NIC.

This defence is only available to an employer if it has served a valid counter-
notice. In Reid v Arthur Young and Son EAT 714/82 R served an NIC on the
employer after he was laid off. The employer wrote back to R saying that his job
was still available, but the EAT held that this did not constitute a valid counter-
notice. Consequently, the statutory defence was not open to the employer.

The employer's defence will fail automatically if the employee continues to be **4.27**
laid off or kept on short-time during each of the four weeks after the date of

133

service of the NIC – S.152(2) ERA. The only exception will be if the lay-off or short-time is wholly or mainly attributable to a strike or lock-out – S.154.

The criterion for establishing the employer's defence is what was reasonably to be expected at the date of service of the employee's NIC. In Dixon and ors v John Watson Fabrications Ltd ET Case No.315/75 D entered a period of 13 weeks' continuous employment two days after service of his NIC. An employment tribunal commented that this would not necessarily be conclusive. However, on the facts there was a reasonable expectation of continuing work at the date of service of the NIC, so D's claim for a redundancy payment failed.

4.28 This can be contrasted with Spencer v Thomas B Ramsden and Co (Bradford) Ltd ET Case No.1800743/98. There, S was laid off from 8 January to 10 February, when she was telephoned at home and told to return to work the following day. During the conversation, S was told that she would be working for two weeks, after which the situation would be reviewed. She served an NIC on 11 February; the employer served a counter-notice on 12 February, saying that within the next four weeks it expected to be in a position to give her continuous employment for at least the next 13 weeks. S worked from 11 February and remained in continuous full-time employment up to the date of the hearing – a period of approximately ten weeks. The employment tribunal found that, on the date that S served her NIC, there was no reasonable expectation that she would, within four weeks, enter into a period of employment of at least 13 weeks during which she would not be laid off. The tribunal based its decision on the fact that, on 11 February, the employer had told S that she would be working for two weeks after which time the situation would be reviewed. In the tribunal's view, on 11 February there was only a reasonable expectation of two weeks' work for S.

The 'period of employment' that the employee is expected to enter must refer to employment under the same contract of employment – Neepsend Steel and Tool Corporation Ltd v Vaughan 1972 ICR 278, NIRC. In that case, N, a skilled form tool grinder, was laid off but then offered less skilled work. This was at lower pay and involved night-shifts, which N had not previously worked. The NIRC held that this would not have been employment under the contract from which he was laid off and the employer had therefore failed to make out the statutory defence.

4.29 The statutory procedure under Ss.147–154 ERA can only be used to claim *statutory* redundancy pay. The employer may also operate a contractual scheme that offers an enhanced redundancy payment, but most contractual schemes will only apply when there has been a dismissal for redundancy. Therefore, they are unlikely to come into play when an employee has been laid off or kept on short-time.

Alternative work   4.30

There is a question-mark over whether an employer can defeat a claim under the lay-off and short-time scheme by making an offer of suitable alternative work under S.141 ERA – see Chapter 3. S.82(5) of the Employment Protection (Consolidation) Act 1978, the predecessor to S.141(2) ERA, provided that an employee who unreasonably refused an offer of suitable alternative work would not be entitled to a redundancy payment 'by reason of his dismissal'. These words led the employment tribunal in Cluett v Rawlings Builders (Canford Cliffs) Ltd ET Case No.31618/86 to conclude that the question of alternative job offers only arose where there had been a dismissal for redundancy. It had no relevance to a redundancy claim based on lay-off or short-time.

In Reid v Arthur Young and Son EAT 714/82 the EAT made the same point and laid great emphasis on the reference to a dismissal in S.82(5) EP(C)A. However, S.141(2) ERA makes no specific reference to a dismissal, providing merely that an employee who unreasonably refuses an offer of suitable alternative work will not be entitled to a redundancy payment. This suggests that once a tribunal has ruled that the employee is eligible under the scheme, and the employee then gives notice of termination, it may be open to the employer to oppose a redundancy payment on the basis that an offer of suitable alternative employment had been made in accordance with S.141. However, the 1996 Act was intended merely as a consolidating Act and did not profess to make any changes to the substantive law. As a result, the courts and tribunals are likely to treat any putative changes with considerable caution.

Death of employee or employer   4.31

There are special rules contained in Ss.175 and 176 ERA dealing with the effect of the death of the employee or employer on a claim for redundancy pay based on lay-off or short-time.

Death of employee   4.32

If an employee dies after serving an NIC but before he or she has given notice to terminate the contract and he or she is still within the period allowed for a notice to terminate, the requirement for a notice to terminate disappears – S.176(6)(a) ERA. This means that the deceased employee's estate may still claim a redundancy payment, subject to any statutory defence raised by the employer.

If an employee dies within seven days of serving an NIC, the employer is treated as having served a counter-notice even if he has not in fact done so – S.176(6)(b) ERA. The employer may then contest any tribunal proceedings.

135

4.33 Death of employer

Death of the employer is only relevant in the case of a personal employer, as opposed to the normal case of a corporate employer. If an employee is laid off or kept on short-time for one or more weeks before the death of the employer but has not yet served an NIC, and he or she is then taken on by the deceased employer's personal representative(s) but laid off or put on short-time again for one or more weeks, the week in which the employer died and the week in which the employee was taken on by the personal representative(s) are treated as consecutive weeks – S.175(2) ERA. This means that any weeks which elapse between death of the employer and re-employment by the personal representative(s) are disregarded for the purposes of accruing weeks of lay-off or short-time.

If the employee has served an NIC and the employer dies within four weeks of service and the employee has either not given any notice of termination, or has given notice but it has not yet expired, then the position depends upon whether the employee is re-employed by the employer's personal representative(s) within four weeks of the date of service of the NIC. If he or she is not re-employed, the statutory scheme operates as if the employer had not died and the employee had terminated the contract by giving the notice required under the scheme (see 'Employee's resignation' above). However, the personal representative(s) cannot use the employer's statutory defence under S.152 in these circumstances, and they cannot serve a counter-notice – S.175(3) and (4).

4.34 If the employee is re-employed in these circumstances, and was laid off or kept on short-time by the deceased employer for one or more weeks between service of the NIC and re-employment by the personal representative(s), and he or she is laid off or kept on short-time for at least one week following the start of employment with the personal representative(s), then the statutory scheme operates as if all the weeks of lay-off or short-time were consecutive and in the same employment – S.175(5). The time limit for service of the employee's notice to terminate is extended by any weeks between the death of the employer and the date of re-employment.

Note that the death of a personal employer operates so as to terminate a contract of employment – S.136(5). If an employee is not re-employed by the personal representative(s), he or she will have a claim for a redundancy payment, provided the failure to re-employ was due to redundancy – S.139(4). This will apply whether or not he or she was laid off or kept on short-time. The provisions are discussed in Chapter 1 under 'Dismissal by operation of law'.

5 Qualifications and exclusions

Employees and excluded employees

Qualifying service

Disqualification

Contracting out

This chapter deals with the qualifications to and exclusions from the right to a **5.1** statutory redundancy payment. Exclusions from the right to claim unfair dismissal, whether by reason of redundancy or otherwise, are dealt with in IDS Employment Law Handbook, 'Unfair Dismissal' (2010), Chapter 2.

The statutory redundancy pay scheme, which is set out in Part XI of the Employment Rights Act 1996 (ERA), applies only to employees – i.e. those working under a contract of employment or apprenticeship – Ss.135 and 230. But not all employees are entitled to redundancy payments when made redundant, since:

- certain categories of employment are specifically excluded

- only employees with sufficient qualifying service can claim

- employees who would otherwise qualify may become disqualified because of personal factors: failure to work out notice, misconduct, or unreasonable refusal of suitable alternative employment can all (in certain circumstances) lead to disqualification

- employees may have been collectively contracted out of the statutory redundancy scheme

- an employee may have failed to claim a redundancy payment within the statutory time limit.

Note that S.209 ERA gives the Secretary of State wide powers to vary or revoke **5.2** these exclusions or to create new ones by order.

In addition, certain exclusions from the right to claim a redundancy payment may arise under general law owing to:

- illegality in the contract, or

- state or diplomatic immunity.

These general law exclusions are large topics in themselves and are outside the scope of this Handbook. They are, however, dealt with in other IDS Employment

---

137

Law Handbooks: see 'Contracts of Employment' (2009), Chapter 4, for a discussion of illegality, and 'Employment Tribunal Practice and Procedure' (2006), Chapter 1, for state and diplomatic immunity.

5.3 Employees and excluded employees

Normally, only employees will be entitled to redundancy payments. 'Employee' is defined as 'an individual who has entered into or works under (or, where the employment has ceased, worked under) a contract of employment' – S.230(1) ERA. 'Contract of employment' is, in turn, defined as 'a contract of service or apprenticeship, whether express or implied, and (if it is express) whether oral or in writing' – S.230(2).

Whether or not a person is an 'employee' for the purposes of qualifying for employment rights protection is ultimately a question of fact for the court or tribunal. Employment status is discussed in depth in IDS Employment Law Handbook, 'Contracts of Employment' (2009), Chapter 1, under 'Who is an employee?'.

5.4 The limitation of the statutory scheme to employees means that certain categories of worker are not covered because they do not work under contracts of employment. These are:

- independent contractors and the self-employed (including many casual workers)
- office holders (subject to exceptions – see below)
- partners (i.e. individuals carrying on a business in common with a view to profit – Cowell v Quilter Goodison Co Ltd and anor 1989 IRLR 392, CA).

5.5 Agency workers

There has been much uncertainty in recent years over whether or not – in the absence of contractual documentation granting employment status – agency workers (i.e. workers supplied to an 'end user' by an employment business) can be classed as 'employees' of either the end-user or the employment business.

To a certain extent, this uncertainty has been resolved by recent authorities. In James v Greenwich London Borough Council 2008 ICR 545, CA, the Court of Appeal held that a tribunal will only be entitled to imply an employment contract between an agency worker and an end-user where it is necessary to do so to give business reality to the situation. In the view of the Court, there will be no such necessity where agency arrangements are genuine and accurately represent the relationship between the parties. Similarly, in Consistent Group Ltd v Kalwak and ors 2008 IRLR 505, CA, the Court of Appeal held that, where an express term in the contract between an agency worker and an employment business describes the former as self-employed, a contract of employment cannot be implied in direct contradiction unless it is necessary to do so. However, Kalwak should now be read in light of Autoclenz Ltd v Belcher 2011 ICR 1157, SC (a case concerning the employment status of alleged independent contractors), where the Supreme Court held that it is not necessary for a court to find that the parties had a common intention to misrepresent the true nature of their respective obligations before it is allowed to disregard contractual terms. It is sufficient that those terms do not represent the true agreement between the parties. Nevertheless, few agency workers will be able to establish that they are 'employees' of either the end-user or the employment business for the purposes of S.230 and thus have the right to claim redundancy pay.

Note that from 1 October 2011, agency workers with at least 12 weeks' **5.6** continuous employment in the same role will be entitled to the same basic working and employment conditions that they would have been entitled to had they been directly recruited by the hirer. However, Reg 6(2) and (3) of the Agency Workers Regulations 2010 SI 2010/93 specifically excludes any payment referable to the worker's redundancy.

Office holders   5.7

Some workers who are not employees may become eligible for redundancy payments by virtue of regulations made by the Secretary of State under Ss.171 and 172 ERA. The Redundancy Payments Office Holders Regulations 1965 SI 1965/2007 extended the statutory scheme to certain holders of public offices who do not rank as employees. These are clerks of the peace, justices' clerks, British Airports Authority police, rent officers and immigration medical inspectors. (Note that registrars of births, marriages and deaths are also covered by the Regulations, but with effect from 1 December 2007 such registrars ceased to be office holders and became employees of the relevant local authority – S.69 Statistics and Registration Service Act 2007.)

Under the Redundancy Payments Termination of Employment Regulations 1965 SI 1965/2022, chief constables and chief or assistant chief fire officers may be treated as employees eligible for redundancy payments in certain circumstances following the reorganisation of police forces and fire brigades.

Some public servants are 'employees' as defined but are excluded from the **5.8** redundancy scheme because they are regarded as being analogous to Crown servants (see below) and are protected under a separate scheme. By virtue of S.159 ERA, any employee who is treated as an office holder for the purposes of the Superannuation Act 1965 or as a civil servant for pension purposes has no right to a redundancy payment.

139

5.9 Crown servants, etc

Whether Crown servants – such as members of the Civil Service – can be said to have contracts of employment is unclear. However, the question is largely academic in this context since Crown servants have their own redundancy pay scheme and are excluded from the statutory scheme – Ss.159 and 191. Disputes about entitlement under Civil Service schemes may be referred to an employment tribunal – S.177. It should be noted that although the Trade Union Reform and Employment Rights Act 1993 extended a number of employment rights to parliamentary staff – who have never been regarded as employees – and paved the way for similar provisions in respect of members of the armed forces, these rights do not include a statutory right to a redundancy payment – see Ss.192, 194 and 195 ERA. These workers, therefore, have to rely on the severance terms forming part of their terms of engagement.

National Health Service employees were formerly excluded from the statutory scheme, but that exclusion was repealed on 1 April 1991 by S.66(2) of the National Health Service and Community Care Act 1990.

5.10 Employees of overseas Governments

Employees of the Government of any overseas territory are excluded from the statutory redundancy scheme – S.160. An overseas territory is any territory or country outside the United Kingdom – S.160(3).

5.11 Domestic servants

Domestic servants who are close relatives of their employers are excluded from the statutory scheme – S.161. This covers cases where the employer is parent, grandparent, step-parent, child, grandchild, step-child, sibling, half-brother or half-sister of the employee. Otherwise a domestic servant in a private household can claim a redundancy payment in the normal way as if the household were a business carried on by the employer.

5.12 Share fishermen and women

Share fishermen and women are excluded from the redundancy scheme (and from many other statutory rights under the ERA). A share fisherman or woman is one 'remunerated only by a share in the profits or gross earnings of the vessel' on which he or she is employed – S.199(2). In Goodeve v Gilsons 1985 ICR 401, CA, the Court of Appeal held that a fisherman was not excluded when he was remunerated by a share in the profits of the *fleet* of vessels in which he was employed.

5.13 Overseas employment

It used to be the case that an employee was not entitled to a redundancy payment if he or she was working outside Great Britain on the 'relevant date' (usually the date on which the dismissal took effect – see Chapter 6 under

140

'Statutory redundancy pay scheme – relevant date and calculation date' for further details) unless under his or her contract of employment he or she ordinarily worked in Great Britain – S.196(6) ERA. However, this provision was repealed by the Employment Relations Act 1999.

The ERA is now silent on the entitlement of overseas employees to redundancy payments. Guidance can be found, however, in the House of Lords' decision in Lawson v Serco Ltd and two other cases 2006 ICR 250, HL. There, their Lordships stated that the statutory right to claim unfair dismissal under the ERA now covers 'employment in Great Britain', and that in general an employee would be able to claim unfair dismissal if he or she were working in Great Britain at the time he or she was dismissed. In addition, employees working and based abroad may in exceptional circumstances be entitled to claim unfair dismissal, even though they are not employed in Great Britain at the time of dismissal, provided their employment has sufficiently strong connections with Great Britain and British employment law. It is arguable, by extension, that employees who are able to satisfy the Lawson test on the relevant date should be entitled to a redundancy payment under the ERA. For a detailed discussion of the Lawson test, see IDS Employment Law Handbook, 'Unfair Dismissal' (2010), Chapter 2, under 'Exclusions from right to claim – working abroad'.

Power to extend rights
5.14

Note that S.23 of the Employment Relations Act 1999 gives the Secretary of State power to extend the scope of existing employment rights, including the right to a redundancy payment, to a wider category of individuals than just 'employees'. The Act itself does not identify the intended beneficiaries of this provision but the Explanatory Notes to the Act state that the Government is committed to ensuring that 'all workers other than the genuinely self-employed enjoy the minimum standards of protection that the legislation is intended to provide, and that none are excluded simply because of technicalities relating to the type of contract or other arrangement under which they are engaged' (para 232). No regulations have yet been made under this provision.

In addition, as noted above, S.209 ERA gives the Secretary of State wide powers to vary or revoke exclusions or to create new ones by order.

Qualifying service
5.15

An employee needs to show two years' continuous employment in order to qualify for a redundancy payment – S.155. In general, continuity will remain unbroken as long as the contract of employment governs the whole or part of consecutive weeks – S.212. However, some breaks in employment count as periods of continuous employment despite the fact that there is no contract of employment in existence. In addition, some breaks in employment do not break

141

continuity even though they do not count as periods of continuous employment. See IDS Employment Law Handbook, 'Continuity of Employment' (2001), Chapters 2 and 3, for further details.

5.16 Two years' service at 'relevant date'

For continuity purposes, two years means two calendar years, each of 12 calendar months – S.210(2). It should be noted that this is not the same as 104 weeks, since four weeks are not the same thing as a calendar month and 52 weeks fall just short of a calendar year. So an employee who started employment on 5 January 2009 will have accrued one month's continuous service by 4 February 2009. If his or her employment is terminated on 2 January 2011 he or she will have worked for 23 (complete) calendar months. As a result, he or she will be two days short of showing two years' continuous employment for the purpose of qualifying for a redundancy payment.

It used to be the case under S.211(2) that any period of continuous employment before the employee's 18th birthday did not count for redundancy purposes. However, that provision was repealed with effect from 1 October 2006 by the Employment Equality (Age) Regulations 2006 SI 2006/1031 (which were themselves repealed on 1 October 2010 and 6 April 2011 and replaced by provisions in the Equality Act 2010) – see 'Disqualification – removal of age restrictions' below. Therefore, an employee made redundant today may count weeks of employment under the age of 18 as part of his or her total period of continuous employment. This is the case even if those weeks preceded the change in the law because the period of continuous employment must be calculated according to the rules in force on the 'relevant date' – normally the date on which employment comes to an end (S.145).

5.17

Although the 'relevant date' is normally the date on which employment comes to an end, if the employer has dismissed without notice or with less than the minimum statutory notice laid down in S.86(1), then the relevant date is the date on which the proper statutory notice would have expired had the employer given it on the date the employee was dismissed – S.145(5). In such circumstances there may be an interval of up to 12 weeks – the maximum statutory notice – between the termination of employment and the relevant date. S.213(3) provides that that interval counts as a period of continuous employment for the purpose of determining the employee's entitlement to a redundancy payment. See Chapter 6 under 'Statutory redundancy pay scheme – relevant date and calculation date' for further details.

5.18 Overseas working

Section 215(2) provides that weeks during the whole or part of which an employee was employed outside Great Britain do not count in calculating his or her period of employment for the purposes of the redundancy scheme, unless the employee remained an employed earner for national insurance purposes.

The test is whether the relevant NI contributions were payable, not whether they were actually paid. The Department for Work and Pensions will advise should there be any doubt as to whether an employee meets this condition.

A week of overseas employment that does not count under this provision does not break continuity of employment, however – S.215(3). Instead, the start of a period of continuous employment is deemed to be postponed by seven days for each week that does not count – S.211(3).

The above provisions do not apply to mariners employed on British ships who **5.19** are ordinarily resident in Great Britain – S.215(6). In their case, overseas weeks do count whether or not NI contributions were payable.

Receipt of redundancy payment   5.20
In general terms, receipt of a redundancy payment breaks continuity of employment for the purposes of the statutory redundancy scheme – S.214. However, such a payment does not break continuity of employment for any other purpose. This means that employees start counting again as far as future entitlement to redundancy payment is concerned (and will need to wait another two years before becoming so entitled) but not for other purposes, such as claiming unfair dismissal (as long as continuity has otherwise been preserved).

Section 214 has limited application in practice because payment of a redundancy payment will usually only occur as a result of a dismissal for redundancy. In such circumstances, an employee's employment will normally have come to an end altogether, so the question of future continuity will not ordinarily arise. One situation in which S.214 might apply is if an employee is dismissed for redundancy but business then picks up unexpectedly and within four weeks of dismissal he or she is given the old job back. It appears from S.138(1) that the employee may then be treated as not having been dismissed at all, thus preserving continuity of employment during the interval between 'dismissal' and re-employment (see S.213(2)). In such circumstances S.214 would break continuity for the purposes of the redundancy scheme. The employee does not have to pay back the redundancy payment, but does lose the accrued service if he or she should be made redundant again. S.138(1), and alternative job offers generally, are discussed in Chapter 3.

Genuine statutory redundancy payment. For the purposes of S.214 it is **5.21** irrelevant whether the redundancy payment was paid in respect of dismissal, lay-off or short-time – S.214(2). S.214(5) provides that a redundancy payment is treated as having been paid if:

- the whole of the payment has been paid to the employee by the employer, or

- a tribunal has determined liability and found that the employer must pay part (but not all) of the redundancy payment and the employer has paid that

143

part. This will happen when claims are brought under Ss.140(3) or 143 (see 'Disqualification – misconduct' below), or

- the Secretary of State has paid a sum to the employee in respect of the redundancy payment under S.167 – i.e. where the employer is insolvent.

5.22 In order for S.214 to break continuity for redundancy purposes, the employer must have been liable to pay a redundancy payment under the legislation. A 'redundancy' payment made when in fact there is no statutory liability to make it – because, for example, the employee has not been genuinely dismissed by reason of redundancy – does not break continuity of employment for the purposes of S.214 – Rowan v Machinery Installations (South Wales) Ltd 1981 ICR 386, EAT. Thus, if there is a transfer of an undertaking under the Transfer of Undertakings (Protection of Employment) Regulations 2006 SI 2006/246 (TUPE) from one employer to another, continuity of employment will not be broken even if a 'redundancy payment' was made. This is because if TUPE applies there is no dismissal and so no liability to make a statutory redundancy payment. In Senior Heat Treatment Ltd v Bell and ors 1997 IRLR 614, EAT, some employees received severance packages from the transferor in return for 'opting out' of a transfer of the business. However, before the date of the transfer the employees entered into contracts of employment with the transferee to take effect immediately after the transfer. When the transferee dismissed them less than two years later, the issue was whether they had sufficient continuity to claim redundancy payments. The EAT decided that they did, commenting that not every severance payment breaks continuity under S.214. In this case TUPE applied, which meant there was no dismissal on the transfer and so no right to a statutory redundancy payment. The employees had simply received a voluntary severance payment from the transferor. They clearly had no objection to the transfer since they had in fact agreed to go and work for the transferee. For further analysis of this case, see IDS Employment Law Handbook, 'Transfer of Undertakings' (2011), Chapter 2, under 'Objecting to the transfer – meaning of "objection"'.

5.23 **Payments made by Secretary of State.** Where an employee is dismissed by an insolvent company by reason of redundancy and an employer is unable to make a redundancy payment, the Secretary of State will make a payment out of the National Insurance Fund under S.167 ERA – see Chapter 7. By virtue of S.214(5)(c), continuity of employment is broken where such a payment is made.

In the following case, the Court of Appeal had to decide whether a payment by the Secretary of State had, by virtue of S.214, broken continuity, or whether continuity had not been broken because the Secretary of State had not been liable to make the payment in the first place:

144

- **Lassman and ors v Secretary of State for Trade and Industry and anor** 2000 ICR 1109, CA: L and some other employees were employed by R Ltd, which became insolvent. On 29 March 1988 T Ltd signed an option agreement to purchase R Ltd and two days later the employees were dismissed for redundancy. However, they accepted jobs with T Ltd to commence on the next working day. The then legal position led the Secretary of State for Trade and Industry to conclude that the employees were not protected by TUPE, and in June 1988 the employees received redundancy payments from him in respect of their 'dismissals' by R Ltd. However, owing to a subsequent decision of the House of Lords, it became clear that the employees had, in fact, transferred automatically to T Ltd under TUPE and had thus not been dismissed by R Ltd. Matters came to a head some years later, when T Ltd also became insolvent and the employees were dismissed by that company. They claimed a payment from the Secretary of State based on their period of employment with R Ltd as well as with T Ltd. In their view, since TUPE had applied to the 1988 transaction, the Secretary of State had not been liable to make the payments in respect of their 'dismissals' by R Ltd, meaning that S.214 had not broken continuity for redundancy purposes. The Court of Appeal observed that S.167 does not actually require an employee to be entitled to a redundancy payment for that payment to be valid. Rather, it requires the Secretary of State to be satisfied that the employee is so entitled, which is a subjective test, not an objective one. The question to be decided, therefore, was whether the Secretary of State had been satisfied that the payment should be made, not whether he had been entitled to reach the decision he did. On that basis, the Court held that the Secretary of State had properly concluded (on the basis of the law as it stood at the time) that the employees' contracts of employment had not transferred under TUPE, and that consequently they had been entitled to redundancy payments. This meant that continuity had been broken by S.214.

Reinstatement and re-engagement. Regulations made under S.219 ERA – the **5.24** Employment Protection (Continuity of Employment) Regulations 1996 SI 1996/3147 – provide that where an employee is reinstated or re-engaged in consequence of any act to which the Regulations apply, and the employee repays in full the amount of the redundancy payment, S.214 does not apply and that employee's continuity is preserved.

The actions to which the Regulations apply are:

- a claim made in accordance with a designated 'dismissal procedures agreement' under which employees are collectively contracted out of their statutory protection against unfair dismissal – see S.110 ERA (such agreements are rare)

- the presentation of a 'relevant complaint of dismissal' to a tribunal

- intervention by an Acas conciliation officer under S.18 of the Employment Tribunals Act 1996 to settle a case – see IDS Employment Law Handbook, 'Employment Tribunal Practice and Procedure' (2006), Chapter 9, under 'Acas conciliation'

- entry into a 'relevant compromise contract' – see IDS Employment Law Handbook, 'Employment Tribunal Practice and Procedure' (2006), Chapter 9, under 'Compromise agreements'

- an agreement to submit an unfair dismissal dispute to Acas arbitration in accordance with an Acas scheme approved by the Secretary of State – see S.212A of the Trade Union and Labour Relations (Consolidation) Act 1992

- a decision arising out of the use of one of the statutory disciplinary and dismissal procedures (DDPs) or statutory grievance procedures (GPs) contained in Schedule 2 to the Employment Act 2002 (e.g. a successful appeal against dismissal under a DDP). Note that, subject to certain transitional provisions, the DDPs and GPs were repealed on 6 April 2009 – see IDS Employment Law Supplement, 'Disciplinary and Grievance Procedures' (2009)

- a decision arising out of the 'statutory duty to consider procedure' contained in Schedule 6 to the Employment Equality (Age) Regulations 2006 SI 2006/1031 (under this procedure, the employee has a right to request to continue working beyond his or her intended retirement date). Note that, subject to transitional provisions, the statutory duty to consider procedure was repealed with effect from 6 April 2011 – see IDS Employment Law Supplement, 'Age Discrimination' (2006).

5.25 Change of employer

Continuity of employment normally applies only to employment with a single employer – S.218(1). However, there are a number of exceptions where employment with one employer can be carried forward and added to employment with a successor employer. A change of employer will not break continuity of employment in the following circumstances:

- there is a transfer of a business or undertaking – Transfer of Undertakings (Protection of Employment) Regulations 2006 SI 2006/246 / S.218(2)

- an employer who is a 'body corporate' is substituted by statute for another body corporate – S.218(3)

- the employer dies and the employee continues working for the employer's personal representatives or trustees – S.218(4)

- there is a change in the composition of an employer partnership or trust – S.218(5)

- there is a transfer of employment between associated employers – S.218(6)

- an employee of the governing body of a school maintained by a local authority is taken into the employment of the authority – S.218(7) and (11)

- health service employees are undergoing professional medical or dental training which involves their being employed by different health service employers – S.218(8)–(10).

Local government service. The Redundancy Payments (Continuity of **5.26** Employment in Local Government, etc) (Modification) Order 1999 SI 1999/2277 provides a further statutory exception for employees in local government service or in other related sectors. The effect of the Order is that virtually the whole of the local government service is to be treated as a single employer for the purposes of the redundancy scheme. If a local government employee is made redundant, his or her period of continuous employment is calculated by reference to his or her length of service in local government as a whole, rather than simply the length of service with the particular authority that has made the redundancy. This applies only in the context of the redundancy scheme. So, if an employee works for five and a half years for John O'Groats Council and then moves to Land's End Council and is made redundant after six months, he or she will be entitled to a redundancy payment based on six years' service. But he or she will not have the one year's service needed to bring an unfair dismissal claim against Land's End.

'Local government service' covers over 100 institutions in Great Britain, all of which are listed in the Order. Only service that falls strictly within the scope of the Order counts. In West Midlands Residuary Body v Deebank 1990 ICR 349, CA, D's local government service was interrupted by a period of ten months during which he had been compulsorily transferred to a regional water authority, which had taken over functions previously exercised by Birmingham City Council, D's employer. Water authorities (as they then were) are not listed in the Order. However, the Order does apply to 'any other body... established by or under any enactment for the purpose of exercising the functions of' a local government authority and D argued that this wording fitted the water authority. The Court of Appeal disagreed. It decided that in this context 'functions' meant 'current functions' and that the statutory wording only applied to bodies that carried out the current functions of local authorities as contractors or agents. It did not apply to a body established to take over completely the functions of a local authority. In any case, so many specific institutions are listed in the Order that it was surprising that water authorities should not have been listed if it had been intended to include them. D's continuity of employment was therefore broken by his spell with the water authority.

5.27 Similarly, in Scales v Suffolk Careers Ltd ET Case No.1501080/97 S began working in the careers service of various local authorities in 1992. In 1996 he began working for Suffolk Careers Ltd, which had won the contract to supply the careers service on behalf of Suffolk County Council. His employment terminated on 31 March 1997. S claimed his service was continuous from 1992 by virtue of the Order. Although Suffolk Careers Ltd was not named in the Order, it had applied to be included and its application was being processed. The tribunal dismissed S's claim. It said that the statutory framework had to be strictly applied, and unless an employer is named in the Order, employees cannot benefit.

(Note that both of these cases were in fact decided under the Redundancy Payments (Local Government) (Modification) Order 1983 SI 1983/1160, which preceded the 1999 Regulations. The principle established in the cases is, however, equally applicable to the later Regulations.)

5.28 **National Health Service.** As we have seen above, S.218(8) specifically provides that professional training undertaken with different health service employers does not break continuity. In addition, the Redundancy Payments (National Health Service) (Modification) Order 1993 SI 1993/3167 provides that the entire National Health Service is treated as a single employer for redundancy purposes. The employers covered are listed in Schedule 1 to the Order.

5.29 ### Renewal or re-engagement
As discussed above (under 'Receipt of redundancy payment'), if an employee is dismissed for redundancy but then re-employed after not more than four weeks, he or she will be treated as not having been dismissed at all – S.138(1) (see Chapter 3, 'Alternative job offers', for full details of the conditions which must be satisfied before S.138 applies). By virtue of S.213(2), the interval between dismissal and re-employment in such a case counts as a period of continuous employment, although continuity will still be broken under S.214 if the employee has received a redundancy payment.

When an employee is deemed to have been dismissed by the death of his or her employer the ERA allows an interval of eight weeks for him or her to be re-employed by the deceased's personal representative. The employee will then be regarded as not having been dismissed and the interval will count as a period of continuous employment – Ss.174(2) and 213(2).

5.30 # Disqualification

An employee who would otherwise be entitled to a redundancy payment may be or become disqualified by factors that are personal to him or her. For example, entitlement to redundancy pay may be affected if an employee who has been given notice of redundancy wishes to leave before his or her notice expires. This is dealt with in Chapter 1 under 'Dismissal by employer – leaving before notice expires'. Another form of disqualification, covered in Chapter 3, is the unreasonable refusal of an offer of suitable alternative employment.

In this chapter we consider the employee's misconduct as a special factor which may bar his or her right to a redundancy payment. We then go on to explain the special treatment of strikes, as a form of industrial misconduct, that take place after notice of redundancy has been given.

Note that a number of age-based disqualifying factors contained in the ERA **5.31** were removed by the (now repealed) Employment Equality (Age) Regulations 2006 SI 2006/1031. These were:

- lower and upper age limits (18 and 65) on the right to claim redundancy payments (Ss.211(2) and 156 ERA)

- an exclusion from the right to a redundancy payment in certain circumstances where the employee was also entitled to claim a pension (S.158).

However, as noted above, the two-year qualifying period for claiming a redundancy payment remains in place (despite its potentially indirectly discriminatory effect upon younger workers).

Misconduct **5.32**

Section 140(1) ERA provides that an employee loses the right to a redundancy payment if his or her conduct is such that the employer is entitled to dismiss without notice – i.e. if the employee is guilty of gross misconduct – and the employer does dismiss in one of the following ways:

- without notice, or

- with shorter notice than required by contract or statute, or

- by giving full (or more than full) notice accompanied by a written statement that the employer would, because of the employee's conduct, have been entitled to dismiss without notice. (Note that the employer does not have to provide such a written statement when it gives no notice or shorter notice – apparently even if short by just one day.)

This is a rather puzzling provision. As stated in the introduction to this chapter, **5.33** a dismissed employee is only entitled to a redundancy payment if he or she is dismissed because of redundancy. So, if the employee is dismissed for gross misconduct, it stands to reason that he or she will not be in a position to claim a redundancy payment. Quite simply, the principal reason for the dismissal will be the misconduct, not redundancy. At first glance, then, S.140(1) appears redundant in itself.

However, it seems that S.140(1) will be applicable where the employee is given notice for redundancy but is then dismissed for gross misconduct in the prescribed manner (i.e. the employer gives no notice, short notice or provides a written statement when giving full notice). Note that in these circumstances, S.140(2) and (3) provides limited exceptions to the operation of S.140(1) – see under 'Misconduct during notice period' below.

5.34 Another point worth making is that, strictly speaking, S.140 does not actually require an employee to be dismissed by reason of gross misconduct. It merely requires that the employer be *entitled* to dismiss by reason of gross misconduct. So, it appears that S.140(1) will apply where the employer in fact dismisses for redundancy but is entitled to dismiss for gross misconduct (of which the employer may not be aware at the time of dismissal). The employee will then be disqualified from receiving a redundancy payment if he or she has been dismissed in a prescribed manner under S.140. In X v Y Ltd 1969 ITR 204, ET, X was dismissed summarily, with pay in lieu of notice, because of redundancy. It was then discovered that he had been guilty of misconduct which would have entitled the employer to dismiss him summarily. The tribunal held that the employer had been entitled to dismiss X summarily because of his conduct, although it did not do so because it was unaware of it at the time. Since it had (fortuitously) dismissed without notice, X was not entitled to a redundancy payment. This type of situation is unlikely to occur very often since an employer that, unaware of an employee's gross misconduct, dismisses him or her by reason of redundancy is likely to dismiss with full notice and will not send an accompanying written statement precisely because it is unaware of the misconduct. It seems odd that an employer can profit from its failure to give sufficient notice whereas an employer who dismisses with full notice loses the benefit of this provision if it has not sent an accompanying statement. However, on a strict interpretation of S.140(1), this appears to be the case.

Section 140(1) may also apply where it is unclear whether the reason for dismissal is redundancy or misconduct. In these circumstances, S.163 means that it is likely that the employee will be presumed to have been dismissed by reason of redundancy. However, the employer may be able to rely on S.140(1) to counter this presumption provided it has dismissed in the prescribed manner.

5.35 The main policy reason behind S.140 appears to be that an employee guilty of gross misconduct has repudiated the contract of employment and rendered it voidable at the option of the employer, leaving him or herself vulnerable to dismissal without notice. Consequently, if that employee happens to be coincidentally redundant, there should be no entitlement to a redundancy payment. It should be noted that when statutory redundancy rights were first introduced by the Redundancy Payments Act 1965, it might well have suited the employer to contend that a dismissal was for some reason other than redundancy because there was then no statutory right for employees to claim unfair dismissal. If, however, the employer runs that argument today, it risks a finding of unfair dismissal that could well be more costly than a redundancy payment.

Objective test. The test under S.140(1) is an objective one – the employer must **5.36** be factually entitled to dismiss summarily. This means that the employee's misconduct must be gross misconduct – i.e. misconduct amounting to a repudiatory breach of contract warranting dismissal without notice. It is for the employer to prove that the employee was in fact guilty of the misconduct in question. This contrasts with the test for unfair dismissal, which is whether the employer acted reasonably in deciding to dismiss, and it is important not to confuse the two issues. In Bonner v H Gilbert Ltd 1989 IRLR 475, EAT, a tribunal decided that an employee was not entitled to a redundancy payment because his employer had an honest belief in his guilt, had reasonable grounds for that belief, and had carried out reasonable investigations. The EAT held that the tribunal should have asked whether the employer had shown that the employee had been guilty of a fundamental breach of contract, not whether it reasonably believed that he had committed misconduct.

Misconduct during notice period. As explained above, S.140(1) removes the **5.37** entitlement of an employee guilty of gross misconduct to a redundancy payment, provided the employer dismisses in a prescribed manner. However, there is an exception in the case of an employee who is already under statutory or contractual notice of redundancy and who is then dismissed for misconduct during 'the obligatory period of notice' in one of the ways described in S.140(1) – S.140(5)(a). S.140(3) provides that in such a case (provided the employee is not dismissed for taking part in a strike – see below) the tribunal has a discretion to order the employer to make an appropriate payment to the employee if it thinks it just and equitable to do so. That payment may be either a full redundancy payment or whatever portion of it that the tribunal thinks fit – S.140(4).

The policy behind this would appear to be that where an employee's claim to a redundancy payment has already crystallised (because he or she has already been given notice of dismissal for redundancy) then he or she should not necessarily lose the right to claim at least some of it if dismissed for some other reason in his or her final days of employment. It should be noted that under S.140(3) the employee is not technically entitled to any redundancy payment unless he or she refers the question to an employment tribunal. However, if it appears that there are circumstances which might justify the tribunal awarding some or all of the redundancy pay to the employee, it is clearly open to the employer to make an appropriate payment to the employee to save the time and expense of going to tribunal.

The 'obligatory period of notice' is the period of notice required by statute or **5.38** contract (whichever is longer) and ends on the date the employer's notice expires – S.136(4). Since the obligatory period is likely to differ from one employee to the next, it follows that some employees will forfeit their redundancy pay while others will not, even if they are given the same amount of notice. For example, if an employer gives 12 weeks' notice of redundancies as representing the maximum statutory notice, then the obligatory period will be the whole of the 12 weeks for an employee (A) with 12 years' service, who is statutorily entitled to 12 weeks' notice. But only the last two weeks of the notice period will be the obligatory period for an employee (B) with only two years' service because he or she will be statutorily entitled to only two weeks' notice (assuming there is no differing contractual right to notice). Therefore, if B is dismissed summarily for gross misconduct during the eighth week of his or her actual notice period, S.140(1) will apply to exclude his or her entitlement to a redundancy payment, and the S.140(3) exception will not apply so the tribunal will have no discretion to award redundancy pay even if the circumstances would otherwise appear to warrant it. However, if A were dismissed at the same time in identical circumstances, the S.140(3) exception would apply, and the tribunal's discretion to award a payment would crystallise.

The tribunal's discretion under S.140(3) is a wide one and is to award what it considers 'just and equitable' in the circumstances, up to the full amount of the potential statutory redundancy payment. In Lignacite Products Ltd v Krollman 1979 IRLR 22, EAT, K was summarily dismissed for stealing shortly before the expiry of his redundancy notice. The EAT refused to interfere with a tribunal's award of 60 per cent of K's statutory redundancy pay, although it thought that the award was high. The tribunal had looked at the relevant factors, including K's length of service (24 years), and the EAT could not substitute its own decision.

5.39 Other factors that tribunals may consider are the seriousness of the misconduct, the employee's previous record, whether the misconduct was a one-off offence and whether the employee has lost other benefits besides the statutory redundancy payment. In Danson v Capper Pipe Service Co (Western) Ltd ET Case No.8142/82, for example, an employee who had been given notice of redundancy was dismissed for refusing to obey an order. The tribunal thought that he should have been warned that he was endangering his redundancy payment. It also took account of the employee's previous trouble-free record and made an award of 50 per cent of his statutory entitlement. Some other examples:

- **Fenton v Samuel Webster and Wilsons Ltd** ET Case No.8298/85: F, who had been accepted for voluntary redundancy, stole a number of crates of drinks during his notice period. He was summarily dismissed and forfeited ex gratia severance payments of £9,258. The tribunal awarded 35 per cent of his redundancy payment

- **Peirson v Courtaulds Ltd** ET Case No.21015/79: P stole scrap material from his employer during the notice period. The total value was over £500 and the tribunal thought that he had been stealing systematically for over six months. Nothing was awarded

- **Phelps v Butler (1843) Ltd** ET Case No.51066/96: P was dismissed for redundancy in April 1996. He agreed with his employer that he would remain on 'garden leave' until 30 April, and would receive a redundancy payment. The employer then discovered that P had been diverting customers to a competing firm with which he had obtained work. The employer stopped the cheque for redundancy pay and notified P that his employment was terminated with immediate effect on 30 April, the last day of his employment under the earlier agreement. A tribunal found that by virtue of S.140(1) P had forfeited his right to a redundancy payment. However, it also found that the employer had given notice to P within the obligatory period and that it was just and equitable under S.140(3) to award P one half of his redundancy payment. It took into account P's distress at his redundancy, which he felt to be unjustified; P's failure to make personal gain from his disloyalty; and the fact that the incidents involving the diversion of customers had since been put right.

In a more recent case – Knox v Biotechnology and Biological Services EAT **5.40** 0066/06 – where S.140 was briefly considered, the EAT stated that a tribunal might also consider whether the employer adopted the course of action that it did as a device to seek to bring itself within the provisions of S.140 so as to avoid making a redundancy payment.

Strike during notice period. S.140(1) does not apply if an employee who has **5.41** been given notice of redundancy is dismissed for taking part in a strike during the obligatory notice period (see above) in circumstances which entitle the employer to treat the contract of employment as terminable without notice – S.140(2). Where this provision applies, the employee's right to a redundancy payment will be unaffected by participation in the strike.

Unlike S.140(3), S.140(2) is not dependent upon the tribunal's discretion, and the employee automatically retains his or her right to redundancy pay, provided the conditions under S.140(2) are satisfied. However, the position becomes more complicated if the employer serves a written notice of extension requesting the employee to extend the notice period by the number of working days lost because of the strike (see below).

Section 140(2) only applies when the employee participates in a strike and not **5.42** when he or she participates in any other type of industrial action (although industrial action short of a strike could fall under S.140(3) – a provision discussed immediately above). 'Strike' in this context means a strike about terms and conditions of employment – S.235(5). Participation in a strike about

153

something other than terms and conditions does not count for the purposes of S.140(2) (although, again, it could fall under S.140(3)). In addition, the ERA is explicit that taking part in the strike must constitute a repudiatory breach of contract, although it is hard to conceive of circumstances when such action would not do so. The ERA does not appear to impose a requirement that the strike be official (or protected) and it appears that unofficial (and unprotected) strike action would also fall under S.140(2) – see IDS Employment Law Handbook, 'Industrial Action' (2010), Chapter 8, for a description of the different types of industrial action.

The following case suggests that S.140(2) only applies when an employee *goes* on strike after having been given notice of redundancy – it does not operate if an employee is dismissed for redundancy when already on strike, which continues after the notice has been given:

- **Simmons v Hoover Ltd** 1977 ICR 61, EAT: 150 employees, including S, had been on strike for some two and a half months when the employer sent them letters giving one week's notice of redundancy. The strike was settled a few weeks later and the other employees returned to work, but S had found another job and claimed a redundancy payment instead. The EAT held that striking was a repudiatory breach of contract entitling the employer to dismiss S without notice. He was barred, therefore, from any entitlement to a redundancy payment by virtue of S.140(1) (then S.2(2) of the Redundancy Payments Act 1965), and S.140(2) (then S.10 RPA) did not apply.

5.43 However, it is arguable that this interpretation of S.140(2) is contrary to the wording of the provision, which refers to the employee 'tak[ing] part' in a strike after having been given notice of redundancy, not 'going on' strike at that time. Interestingly, S.143(1) – which governs extension of the notice period after a strike (see below) – specifically applies to the situation where the employee 'begins to take part in a strike' after notice of termination has been given.

5.44 **Extension of notice period after strike.** We have seen above that if an employee goes on strike during the obligatory period of notice, his or her right to a redundancy payment is unaffected, and that this is not dependent upon the tribunal's discretion. But the employer does have another option in these circumstances: namely, requiring the employee to make up the working days lost due to the strike by working through an extended notice period as a prerequisite to the employer agreeing to pay a redundancy payment.

Section 143 contains the rather complicated statutory scheme that regulates this option. Briefly, if an employee goes on strike when under notice of dismissal for redundancy, the employer may serve a written notice of extension requesting him or her to extend the notice period by the number of working days lost because of the strike – S.143(1). 'Notice period' in this context means the notice given by the employer, and is not limited to the obligatory period. The employer's written notice must:

- indicate the employer's reasons for making the request, and

- state that the employer will contest liability to make a redundancy payment if the employee does not comply with the request, unless the employer is satisfied that the employee could not comply with the request – e.g. because of sickness or injury – or that it was not reasonable in the circumstances for the employee to comply with it – S.143(2).

If the employee complies with the notice, then the notice of termination is **5.45** deemed to have effect as if the period specified had been extended by the period set out in the employer's written request and the employee will be entitled to a redundancy payment calculated as at that date. If the employee only partially complies, by coming to work on one or more but not all of the days within that period, the notice period is then treated as continuing up to the last day on which the employee turns up to work – S.143(7)–(8). The employee is then entitled to redundancy pay calculated as at that date.

If the employee does not comply with the employer's request – for example, by not turning up for work on any of the days requested – he or she will lose entitlement to a redundancy payment (unless the employer agrees to pay one anyway – S.143(4)) and must apply to a tribunal for an 'appropriate payment'. The tribunal may then award a redundancy payment in whole or in part if it is satisfied that the employee was unable to comply with the employer's request or that it was reasonable for the employee not to comply with it – S.143(3)–(6). The amount of the award is a matter for the tribunal's discretion.

Lay-off and short-time
5.46

Note that S.140(2) and (3) also apply as exceptions to S.140(1) where an employee who has given a notice of intention to claim a lay-off or short-time redundancy payment under S.148 is then dismissed for taking part in a strike or for misconduct after the service of the notice. But once the employee is dismissed, he or she is then barred from claiming lay-off or short-time redundancy – S.151. Any claim for a redundancy payment would have to be based on the express dismissal by the employer and would be dependent upon one of the exceptions to S.140(1) applying (i.e. S.140(2) or (3)). Lay-off and short-time redundancies are discussed in Chapter 4.

Contracting out
5.47

The general rule is that any provision attempting to exclude an employee's rights under the statutory redundancy scheme or to preclude his or her right to claim a redundancy payment in a tribunal is void – S.203(1) ERA. Note that, unlike many employment rights, it is not possible to use a compromise agreement or an agreement reached under the auspices of an Acas conciliation officer to exclude the right to a redundancy payment.

Section 197 used to allow a fixed-term employee to sign a written agreement waiving his or her right to a statutory redundancy payment upon the expiry and non-renewal of a contract for a fixed term of two years or more. However, this provision has now been repealed and, subject to transitional provisions relating to fixed-term contracts, it is now only possible for employees to 'opt out' of the redundancy payments scheme by way of collective agreement combined with an exemption order.

5.48 Fixed-term contracts
Since the repeal of S.197 ERA by the Fixed-term Employees (Prevention of Less Favourable Treatment) Regulations 2002 SI 2002/2034, any waivers inserted into contracts agreed, renewed or extended after the Regulations came into effect on 1 October 2002 will be invalid, and fixed-term employees whose contracts expire and are not renewed by reason of redundancy will have a right to a statutory redundancy payment if they have been continuously employed for two years or more.

These provisions mean that, subject to the transitional provisions below, fixed-term employees cannot be excluded from the statutory redundancy scheme. It is important to note, however, that fixed-term employees may be excluded from *contractual schemes* if such exclusion can be objectively justified – see IDS Employment Law Supplement, 'Fixed-term Work' (2003), Chapter 2, under 'Employer's reasons and objective justification'.

5.49 Transitional provisions. The repeal of S.197 was not retroactive, however. Transitional provisions contained in para 5 of Schedule 2 to the Regulations state that any existing waiver shall have effect where the 'relevant date' under S.145 ERA (see 'Qualifying service – two years' service at "relevant date"' above) falls on or after 1 October 2002, and both of the following conditions are satisfied:

- the contract was entered into before 1 October 2002 and has not been renewed since or, where there have been one or more renewals, the only or most recent renewal was agreed before that date, and

- the agreement to exclude any right to a redundancy payment was entered into and took effect before 1 October 2002.

Obviously, with the effluxion of time these transitional provisions have become increasingly irrelevant and the vast majority of fixed-term employees with two or more years of continuous employment are now covered by the statutory scheme.

Collective contracting out   5.50

Under S.157 ERA unions and employers may enter into a collective agreement whereby employees are, in defined circumstances, entitled to severance payments on the termination of employment. If the Secretary of State is satisfied with the scheme, he or she may issue an exemption order stating that the statutory redundancy scheme will not apply to the employees covered by the collective agreement.

It is a condition for making an exemption order that the collective agreement specifies that disputes under a contracted-out redundancy scheme should be referable to an employment tribunal – S.157(4). The tribunal will then have to apply the terms of the contracted-out scheme instead of those of the statutory scheme. An agreement between an employer and a union will not displace the statutory scheme unless it is the subject of an exemption order. In Godridge v Yorkshire Imperial Metals Ltd 1968 ITR 30, ET, there was an agreement between union and management that purported to displace some of the statutory provisions about alternative job offers in a redundancy situation. The tribunal held that the agreement was invalid because it had not been made the subject of an exemption order. Because of this it applied the provisions of the statutory scheme.

The Secretary of State may revoke an exemption order by making a subsequent **5.51** order – S.157(5). He or she may do this on the application of all or any of the parties to the agreement or without any application having been made. The Secretary of State is not, however, obliged to revoke an exemption order even if all the parties to it ask him or her to do so.

6 Redundancy payments

Statutory redundancy pay scheme

Enhanced redundancy pay

Age discrimination

Non-payment

An employer must pay a redundancy payment to an employee who is dismissed **6.1** by reason of redundancy, or is eligible for a redundancy payment by reason of being laid off or kept on short-time – S.135 Employment Rights Act 1996 (ERA). This rule is subject to some exclusions and qualifying conditions, which we discuss in Chapter 5.

In this chapter we look at the method of calculation for payments under the statutory redundancy scheme, and consider entitlements that may arise under an employer's enhanced redundancy pay scheme. We also examine the impact that the age discrimination legislation has had on redundancy pay.

Statutory redundancy pay scheme
6.2

According to the Government, the statutory redundancy pay scheme, which was originally introduced in 1965, exists to ensure that employees who are made redundant receive at least a statutory minimum severance payment that recognises the degree of their past commitment to the employer's business, and to promote labour market flexibility by easing the process of job transition. The current scheme governing statutory redundancy payments is set out in Part XI of the ERA.

Formula for calculating statutory redundancy pay
6.3

The amount of statutory redundancy pay an employee is entitled to depends on his or her age, length of service and pay. The employee is entitled to:

- one and a half weeks' pay for each complete year of service after reaching the age of 41

- one week's pay for each complete year of service between the ages of 22 and 40 inclusive, and

- half a week's pay for each complete year of service below the age of 22 – S.162(2) ERA.

159

The maximum length of service that may be taken into account in a redundancy pay claim is 20 years – S.162(3), a year being a period of 12 complete calendar months – S.210(2)(b). The total amount of a week's pay is also subject to a statutory maximum – S.227. S.34 of the Employment Relations Act 1999 provides that the statutory maximum limit for a week's pay is set by the Secretary of State each September by reference to the Retail Price Index. The current limit is £400 (with effect from 1 February 2011) – see the Employment Rights (Increase of Limits) Order 2010 SI 2010/2926. It follows that the absolute maximum statutory redundancy payment an employee can hope to receive is currently £12,000, i.e. (£400 x 1½) x 20.

6.4 A tribunal may award a reduced statutory redundancy payment if:

- the employee under notice of dismissal for redundancy has served a counter-notice on the employer to terminate the contract on a date earlier than the expiry of the employer's notice and the employer has served a further notice requiring the employee to work out the whole of the notice period, and the employee has refused to do so – S.142 (see Chapter 1 under 'Dismissal by employer – leaving before notice expires')

- the employee has been dismissed for misconduct while under notice of dismissal for redundancy or after giving notice of intention to claim redundancy arising from a lay-off or short-time situation – S.140(3) and (4) (see Chapter 5 under 'Disqualification – misconduct')

- an employee who has been on strike fails to comply with an extension notice properly issued by the employer in respect of the days lost because of strike action – S.143 (see Chapter 5 under 'Disqualification – misconduct').

Some employees may, because of statutory provisions, be paid by a person other than their employer. In such a case the person responsible for paying the remuneration is treated as the employer for most purposes of the statutory redundancy scheme – S.173. This will apply, for example, to a teacher who is employed by a school's board of governors but paid by the Local Authority. The governors hire and fire but the authority will be responsible for redundancy payments.

6.5 Age discrimination
Given the statutory redundancy payment scheme's reliance on age-based factors, the Government reviewed the scheme prior to the coming into force of the Employment Equality (Age) Regulations 2006 SI 2006/246 on 1 October 2006. In its *Coming of Age* consultation document, published in July 2005, it expressed an intention to remove the three age bands for calculating redundancy payments set out in S.162(2) ERA (see above). In the end, however, the Government decided to retain these bands. It considered there to be three groups benefiting from payments under the scheme – younger, prime age and

older workers – which each represent a distinct economic category. At one end of the spectrum, younger workers tend not to be out of work for long and only experience a small drop in pay when switching jobs. Older workers, on the other hand, face difficulties in finding new jobs, experience a substantial fall in pay if they do find new employment, and are much more likely to become long-term unemployed. As a result, the Government felt that the practice of applying different 'multipliers' to different age bands so as to give greater financial assistance to older workers in a redundancy context is justified.

The Government similarly decided to retain the two-year qualifying period for claiming a redundancy payment, despite its indirectly discriminatory effect upon younger workers (see further Chapter 5 under 'Qualifying service'). The statutory redundancy pay scheme has thus largely survived with its age-based criteria intact.

However, the following age-based aspects of the statutory redundancy scheme **6.6** were repealed with effect from 1 October 2006:

- the lower and upper limits on the right to claim redundancy payments (previously 18 and 65) in Ss.211(2) and 156 ERA. So, for example, employees aged 65 and over who are made redundant are entitled to a redundancy payment

- the 'taper' provision in S.162(4) and (5) ERA under which an employee's redundancy payment was reduced by 1/12th for every month of service over the age of 64, and

- Section 158 ERA, which excluded the right to a redundancy payment in certain circumstances where the employee was also entitled to claim a pension (together with S.162(8) ERA and the Redundancy Payments (Pensions) Regulations 1965 SI 1965/1932 made under that provision).

(Note that the Age Discrimination Regulations were repealed and replaced by the Equality Act 2010 in October 2010. However, no substantive changes were made to the law on age discrimination, or redundancy, by the new Act.)

Relevant date and calculation date **6.7**

In order to work out an employee's statutory redundancy entitlement, it is necessary to ascertain two key dates: the 'relevant date' and the 'calculation date'.

Relevant date. The relevant date is the date by reference to which: **6.8**

- an employee's entitlement to a redundancy payment is established (i.e. whether the employee has two years' continuous service – see Chapter 5 under 'Qualifying service'; is not otherwise disqualified from receiving such payment as a result, for example, of gross misconduct – see Chapter 5 under

161

'Disqualification'; and is not the subject of an exemption order issued under S.157 – see Chapter 5 under 'Contracting out')

- the amount of that payment is calculated under S.162 (and S.168 in respect of a claim from the Secretary of State)

- the six-month time limit for making a claim begins to run (see Chapter 10 under 'Statutory redundancy payments – time limits'), and

- the current statutory maximum week's pay is ascertained – see Article 4(2)(m) of the Employment Rights (Increase of Limits) Order 2010 SI 2010/2926.

6.9 The relevant date is generally the effective date of termination of the contract of employment, that is:

- where the contract is terminated by notice (by either the employer or the employee), the date on which that notice expires – S.145(2)(a)

- where the dismissal is without notice, the date on which the termination takes effect – S.145(2)(b)

- where the employment is under a limited-term contract which terminates by virtue of the limiting event without being renewed under the same contract, the date on which the termination takes effect – S.145(2)(c).

6.10 There are three cases where the relevant date will differ – either for all or some purposes – from the effective date of termination of the contract:

- where the employee is treated as dismissed under S.136(3) (where he or she has given notice to leave earlier than the expiry of the employer's notice – see Chapter 1 under 'Dismissal by employer – leaving before notice expires'), in which case the relevant date is the date on which the employee's notice expires – S.145(3)

- where the employee has accepted an offer of alternative employment and leaves during the trial period (or a subsequent trial period for another alternative job), the relevant date is the date of termination of the original contract – S.145(4)(b). However, the six-month time limit for claiming a redundancy payment will run from the effective date of termination of the most recent contract – S.145(4)(a)

- where the contract is terminated by the employer either with no notice or insufficient notice, the relevant date for the purposes of assessing the employee's qualifying service in relation to S.155 (period of continuous employment) and S.162(1) (the calculation of the amount of redundancy pay due) is the date on which the proper statutory notice under S.86 would have expired had it been given – S.145(5). Prior to the Employment Relations Act 1999, this later date was also the relevant date for the purpose of ascertaining the level of the maximum week's pay. However, this no longer seems to be the case. Note that the relevant date can be extended by the period of the statutory minimum notice due even if the employee has waived his or her right to notice and accepted pay in lieu – Staffordshire County Council v Secretary of State for Employment and another case 1989 ICR 664, CA.

Where an employee has been laid off or put on short-time, the relevant date is **6.11** the last day of the last week of the lay-off or short-time relied upon – S.153.

If an employee dies during the notice period, the contract of employment is treated as having expired by notice terminating on the date of the employee's death – S.176(1). If the employee dies after the contract has been terminated, but S.145(5) applies to postpone the date of termination to the end of the statutory notice period and this later date has not yet been reached, then the contract is also treated as having been ended by notice expiring on the date of the employee's death – S.176(2).

Calculation date. The 'calculation date' is the second key date in the statutory **6.12** redundancy pay scheme. This, the date on which an employee's 'week's pay' is calculated, is:

- where the employee was dismissed with no notice, or with less than the minimum statutory notice, the date on which the contract of employment ends – S.226(5)(b)

- in all other cases, the date on which notice would have been given by the employer in order to comply with the minimum notice requirements under S.86, working backwards from the relevant date – S.226(5)(c) and (6). (In other words, the date x weeks before the relevant date, where x weeks is the minimum statutory notice required.) This includes cases where the contract has been terminated by the giving of contractual notice which is longer than that required under the statute.

Where an employee has been laid off or put on short-time, the calculation date **6.13** is the day immediately preceding the lay-off or short-time relied upon – S.226(4).

Where a pay increase is awarded after the calculation date, the redundancy payment is calculated on the lower wage in force at the calculation date. This is so even if the pay increase is expressed as being back-dated to a date prior to the calculation date – see, for example, Jones v Cammell Laird Shipbuilders Ltd ET Case No.34115/84; or there is an implied contractual term that this will be the case – Leyland Vehicles Ltd v Reston and ors 1981 ICR 403, EAT.

Examples of relevant dates and calculation dates. Taking an employee who **6.14** has been in employment for six years and eleven months:

- if on 7 March she is given eight weeks' contractual notice of dismissal for redundancy, the relevant date by reference to which her age, length of service and statutory maximum week's pay will be calculated will be the effective date of termination of her contract – i.e. 2 May. The calculation date on which her week's pay will be measured is six weeks (her statutory notice period) before the expiry of her contract – i.e. 21 March. If on 22 March she received a pay rise, her statutory redundancy payment will be calculated by reference to her wage prior to the increase

- if on 7 March she is given only one week's notice of dismissal for redundancy, her calculation date is the date on which that notice expires – i.e. 14 March. Her relevant date for the purposes of calculating her length of service and the amount of her redundancy entitlement is the date on which her statutory period of notice would have expired – i.e. 18 April. She will therefore have seven years' continuous service and, if she turned 42 before this date, she will be entitled to one and a half weeks' pay in respect of her final year. The maximum week's pay applicable will be the rate in force on 14 March

- if on 7 March she is dismissed for redundancy without any notice, the relevant date will again be that date on which proper notice under S.86 would have expired – i.e. 18 April, while the calculation date will be 7 March, the date her contract terminated. The same is true if she is constructively dismissed for redundancy on 7 March and leaves without notice

- if on 7 March her fixed-term contract expires and she leaves because of redundancy her calculation date will be six weeks before 7 March – i.e. 24 January. Her relevant date will be 7 March and the maximum week's pay in force on that day will apply.

6.15 Variations before calculation date. The amount of a week's pay is assessed at the calculation date, subject to the statutory maximum in force at the relevant date. If an employee accepts a genuine variation in wage just before the calculation date, this is the wage upon which the redundancy pay will be calculated. In Valentine v Great Lever Spinning Co 1966 ITR 71, ET, an employee with 49 years' service who was warned about impending redundancy agreed to transfer to a lower-paid job and was made redundant after three months. A tribunal based his redundancy payment on the lower-paid job in which he was engaged at the calculation date. Similarly, in Webb v Taylor ET Case No.6976/85 a tribunal found that an employee who stayed in part-time employment on a temporary basis rather than being made redundant from her full-time job should have her redundancy pay calculated on the basis of her part-time wage.

Generally, however, a tribunal will, wherever possible, avoid finding that a period of lower-paid work puts an employee at a disadvantage when it comes to redundancy payments. It distinguishes between a temporary expedient and a contractual variation – only the latter will result in calculation at the lower rate. Two examples:

- **Nelson and ors v Ryley and Co (Shipping) Ltd (in liquidation) and anor** ET Case Nos.24061–63/84: employees were put on 'emergency' short-time work which, in the event, lasted for over two years before they were made redundant. The tribunal calculated their redundancy pay on the basis of their full-time salary, ruling that their contractual wages had not been varied

- **Friend v PMA Holdings Ltd** 1976 ICR 330, EAT: upholsterers' hours were cut during the three-day week caused by the miners' strike in early 1974 and were not increased before they were made redundant some months later. The EAT ruled that the employees had not agreed to a variation of their original contract and that their redundancy payments should be based on their wages under the original contract.

Where an employee's hours and wages have been increased shortly before the **6.16** calculation date, a tribunal will be more inclined to see a contractual variation. In Hart v John Blundells Ltd ET Case No.04341/84, for example, the claimant had worked full time during the last three months of her employment, having worked part time for the previous nine years. Her hours had originally been increased on a temporary basis when her manager went on holiday and had remained that way as a result of an injury he had sustained. The tribunal awarded her a redundancy payment based on her full-time wage, ruling that her contractual hours had been varied until such time as the manager was fit to return to work.

The practice of calculating redundancy pay on the basis of an employee's 'terminal pay' – i.e. his or her salary at the time he or she ceased to work for the employer – has been criticised on the basis that it discriminates unfairly against women, since more women than men reduce their hours in order to bring up a family. In Barry v Midland Bank plc 1999 ICR 859, HL, B had been employed by Midland Bank plc as a full-time clerk from 1979 to 1990, when she left in order to have a baby. She returned to work on a part-time basis until she accepted voluntary redundancy in 1993. Her severance payment under a contractual redundancy scheme (which reflected the calculation method adopted by the provisions of the ERA) was calculated on the basis of her part-time salary. B complained to a tribunal that the failure to take account of her 11 years' full-time service amounted to a breach of Article 119 of the EC Treaty (now Article 157 of the Treaty on the Functioning of the European Union) and the Equal Pay Act 1970 (now the Equality Act 2010). The House of Lords found that the scheme was not indirectly discriminatory against women even though it made no allowance for employees whose hours of work fluctuated. Their Lordships took account of the fact that the primary objective of the scheme was to provide support for lost income during the period following redundancy – not to remunerate for past service.

Some indirect support for the Barry decision may be found in the ECJ's ruling **6.17** in Grau-Hupka v Bremen 1994 ECR 1-5535, ECJ. In that case the ECJ ruled

165

that the EC Social Security Directive (No.79/7) does not require that a pension scheme compensate a woman for the 'lost years' while she was not working for family reasons.

6.18 Week's pay

Once the relevant date and the calculation date have been established, the next step is to calculate the employee's 'week's pay'. The rules governing the calculation of a week's pay are set out in Chapter II of Part XIV of the ERA, and vary depending on whether the employee can be said to have a set number of 'normal working hours' and whether he or she is a shift-worker or a piece-worker, or simply paid a set wage for a given number of hours. Basically, a week's pay is the contractual remuneration for working the normal working hours in a week. What constitutes a week's pay is covered in detail in IDS Employment Law Handbook, 'Wages' (2011), Chapter 10.

6.19 Tax treatment of statutory redundancy pay

Statutory redundancy payments are calculated on the basis of gross pay, and there are no deductions for income tax and national insurance – S.309(1) Income Tax (Earnings and Pensions) Act 2003 (ITEPA).

Note, however, that while statutory redundancy payments made under the ERA are specifically exempted from general earnings under S.62 ITEPA by virtue of S.309, such payments do fall within S.401 ITEPA and are chargeable to tax under that section on any amount exceeding £30,000 – see S.403. The maximum statutory redundancy payment (from 1 February 2011) is £12,000. Therefore, unless the value of other taxable elements of a termination package causes the £30,000 limit to be exceeded, statutory redundancy payments will usually be exempted in full.

6.20 Written statement

Unless the exact amount of the redundancy payment has been determined by a tribunal, the employer must provide the employee with a written statement indicating how the amount has been calculated – S.165(1) ERA. An employer who fails to provide the statement without reasonable excuse is guilty of a criminal offence, and liable on summary conviction to a fine not exceeding level 1 on the standard scale (currently £200) – S.165(2). While the level of the financial penalty may not act as a deterrent for non-compliance with S.165(1), providing a breakdown of the sums paid to the employee in respect of his or her entitlement to a redundancy payment will provide proof that the employer has discharged his obligation in this respect, thus preventing an employee from subsequently arguing that no redundancy payment has been made.

In the event that the employer has failed to provide a written statement, the employee can give written notice requiring him to provide it within a given period (which must be at least one week from the date the notice was given) –

S.165(3). Failure to comply with the notice without reasonable excuse is an offence punishable on summary conviction by a fine not exceeding level 3 on the standard scale (currently £1,000) – S.165(4).

Enhanced redundancy pay 6.21

Many employees are entitled upon redundancy to contractual payments in excess of the statutory payments made under S.162 ERA. These are commonly referred to as 'enhanced' redundancy payments.

Like the statutory scheme, an employer's enhanced redundancy scheme might use multipliers based on an employee's age and/or length of service, and thereby advantage older and long-serving employees. Provisions in the Equality Act 2010 (which replaced similar provisions in the Employment Equality (Age) Regulations 2006 SI 2006/246 with effect from 1 October 2010) specifically provide that this is allowed, as long as the enhanced scheme is modelled on the statutory scheme – see 'Age discrimination – enhanced scheme modelled on statutory scheme' below. This means that a scheme that has age-related elements and does *not* mirror the statutory scheme will be age discriminatory, unless the employer can show that it is objectively justified as a proportionate means of achieving a legitimate aim – see 'Age discrimination – enhanced scheme not modelled on statutory scheme' below.

Entitlement to enhanced redundancy pay 6.22

An employee's contract of employment or written statement of particulars may contain an express term that entitles him or her to a payment on redundancy that is in excess of the statutory redundancy payment. Alternatively, a term to that effect may be implied by virtue of the parties' conduct or by the custom or practice of a particular employer.

Often, enhanced redundancy payment schemes are contained in staff handbooks or collective agreements. Whatever the source of the terms relating to enhanced payments, an employee will only be able to enforce those terms if he or she can show that they have been incorporated into the individual contract of employment. Incorporation may be express (e.g. where the individual employment contract states that certain of its terms are regulated by, for example, a collective agreement) or implied (e.g. where there is a clear custom that terms of collective agreements are incorporated into the contract). For a detailed discussion of the general principles in relation to incorporated terms, see IDS Employment Law Handbook, 'Contracts of Employment' (2009), Chapter 2, under 'Incorporated terms'.

Express incorporation. In Keeley v Fosroc International Ltd 2006 IRLR 961, 6.23 CA, the Court of Appeal noted that provision for redundancy is a widely accepted – and important – feature of an employee's overall remuneration

167

package, and as such is 'particularly apt for incorporation' into an individual's contract of employment, even if couched in terms of information or explanation, or expressed in discretionary terms. So, for example, if an employee's employment is expressly made subject to the terms of a collective agreement or a staff manual which itself sets out the terms of the policy, then the policy will be incorporated into the employee's contract of employment. However, the Court of Appeal noted that it does not necessarily follow, in the event that another document has been expressly incorporated into a contract of employment, that *all* its terms will be incorporated and therefore amount to legally enforceable rights.

In Keeley, the employee's contract of employment consisted of a written 'statement of employment terms', which expressly incorporated the company's staff handbook by reference. The handbook dealt with various matters, such as annual leave, equal opportunities, grievances, parental leave, maternity rights and retirement, and also contained five pages setting out the company's redundancy policy. As regards compensation, that policy provided: 'Those employees with two or more years' continuous service are entitled to receive an enhanced redundancy payment from the company, which is paid tax free to a limit of £30,000.' The provision did not explain how the payment should be calculated, but did state that the details would be 'discussed during both collective and individual consultation'.

6.24 In July 2004 the employee was made redundant and claimed that the company was in breach of contract in failing to make him an enhanced redundancy payment. The High Court held that, although the relevant provision of the staff handbook used the word 'entitled', few of the other provisions in the redundancy section had the character of contractual terms because they were statements of principle or procedure. Accordingly, the enhanced redundancy payment provision, in its context, did not denote any contractual right. The Court of Appeal overturned this decision, holding that there were a number of factors which pointed strongly to the provision being contractual in nature; namely, the wording of the provision described the employee as being entitled to the payment; the provision was included in a section of the staff handbook headed 'Employee benefits and rights', which set out other entitlements such as the right to annual leave, parental leave and paternity leave; and the redundancy section itself also provided for entitlements – such as the right to paid time off to look for new work and the right to appeal against dismissal – which were distinct from the procedural, aspirational or discretionary elements of the section and amounted to 'close supporting context for concluding that statements of entitlement in that section were intended to have contractual effect'. The fact that the method of calculation of the payment was not specified – it was expressed to be decided on a case-by-case basis – did not prevent it from being an enforceable contractual right.

168

The Keeley case was followed in Harlow v Artemis International Corporation Ltd 2008 IRLR 629, QBD, where H's employment contract stated that 'all other terms and conditions are as detailed in the staff handbook as issued to you and subject to its most recent update'. The staff handbook had originally been a hard copy manual distributed to all staff but had later been replaced by a number of policies (including an enhanced redundancy policy) stored in electronic form on AIC Ltd's intranet. The High Court held that the enhanced redundancy policy contained in a part of the staff handbook which also dealt with matters such as holiday and sickness leave was apt for incorporation into an employee's contract as an express term. The Court noted that the Court of Appeal in Keeley had identified two significant factors to take into account when determining the nature of a provision: first, the importance of the provision in the overall bargain; and second, its precise wording. The High Court had no doubt that the redundancy provisions would be of importance in the overall bargain, as part of the remuneration package. It noted that not all handbook provisions will be contractual – some are merely 'declarations of an aspiration'. However, that was not the case here – the calculation method of the redundancy payment was clearly stipulated and there was provision in the policy itself for time off work to look for new employment. Furthermore, the policy was included in a section of the handbook dealing with entitlements – such as annual leave and sick leave – which must have been contractual.

The fact that AIC Ltd appeared to have varied its practice in making **6.25** redundancy payments to other employees did not affect H's rights to his redundancy terms contained in the published policy in force at the time of his redundancy. The High Court cited the cases of Solectron Scotland Ltd v Roper and ors 2004 IRLR 4, EAT, and Jones v Associated Tunnelling Co Ltd 1981 IRLR 477, EAT, in support of the proposition that where an employer purports unilaterally to change the terms of a contract that do not immediately impinge on the employee (and changes in redundancy terms do not impinge on an employee until he or she is in fact made redundant), the fact that an employee continues to work knowing that the employer is asserting that a change has been effected does not mean that the employee can be taken to have accepted the variation.

Similarly, the fact that other employees have rarely taken up the option of a redundancy enhancement does not meant that it ceases to be a contractual right. In Arkley v Sea Fish Industry Authority EAT 0505/09 the EAT held that a redundancy policy was couched in mandatory – not discretionary – terms, with the result that a provision providing for ten years' enhanced pension benefits to redundant employees was a contractual right. Clause 1 of the policy provided that 'compensation in accordance with the scheme will be payable' and clause 2(e) referred to staff 'entitlement' to immediate payment of pension benefits. The EAT, relying on the Supreme Court's guidance in Chartbrook Ltd v Persimmon Homes Ltd 2009 1 AC 1101, SC, on the construction of

169

contractual terms, noted that the proper construction of A's contract was what a reasonable person, having all the background knowledge available to the parties, would have understood the language in the contract to mean. Applying that test, the EAT held that the reasonable person would have concluded that redundant staff in A's position would be offered ten years' enhanced pension benefits. This conclusion was reinforced by the employer's custom and practice of offering redundant employees the enhancement – although this option was rarely taken up – and the fact that it had not sought to amend the policy. It therefore followed that A had a reasonable expectation that he would be offered the enhancement when made redundant and that the employer's unilateral withdrawal of that option amounted to a breach of contract.

6.26 **Implied incorporation.** The main route by which redundancy terms are implied into employment contracts is where they are regularly (but not necessarily universally) adopted in a particular trade or industry or by a particular employer – commonly referred to as 'custom and practice'. The traditional requirement for implication via this route is that the custom in question must be 'reasonable, notorious and certain'. This means that the policy's terms must be fair and not arbitrary or capricious, must be generally established and well known, and must be clear cut. The onus of proving that redundancy terms have been impliedly incorporated falls on the employee. Any claim for an enhanced payment is likely to fail if the employee cannot adduce sufficient evidence of the custom or practice he or she is relying upon. Essentially, the custom or practice has to be so clear and obvious that, in effect, the parties knew they had to adhere to it and did not consider it necessary to set it out expressly – see Stenhouse and ors v First Edinburgh Ltd EAT 0017/04.

Probably the most important factor in determining whether an implied right to enhanced payments has arisen is whether a clear and certain policy of making such payments has been *communicated* to employees. If that has not happened, it is difficult to see how they can have a reasonable expectation that they will receive enhanced payments if made redundant, and it is equally difficult to see how the redundancy policy could be regarded as being sufficiently 'notorious' in the sense of being well known.

6.27 The facts of Albion Automotive Ltd v Walker and ors 2002 EWCA Civ 946, CA, provide a useful example of how, in practice, courts and tribunals approach the issue of whether employees have acquired an implied contractual entitlement to enhanced redundancy payments. There, the Court of Appeal held that an employment tribunal had correctly concluded that there was such an entitlement, in view of the following findings of fact:

- the redundancy terms, when first applied, had been the outcome of high profile negotiations

- it was likely that the terms had been approved by the employer's parent company

- the terms had subsequently been applied to further redundancy exercises with little or no consultation with the parent company

- the availability of the enhanced terms had been drawn to the attention of all the employees in writing at the time of each redundancy exercise

- the policy had been followed for an extensive period of time and had affected 750 employees, amounting to three quarters of the workforce

- the policy had been followed for six redundancy exercises and had been intended to be applied in two others

- payment of the enhanced terms had been virtually automatic from the employer's point of view, and

- all employees had a reasonable expectation that enhanced payments would be made.

In Harlow v Artemis International Corporation Ltd 2008 IRLR 629, QBD, the **6.28** High Court allowed H's claim for enhanced redundancy pay on the basis that the enhanced redundancy policy was apt to be incorporated into his employment contract as an express term (see under 'Express incorporation' above). It nonetheless went on to consider whether an entitlement to enhanced redundancy pay could alternatively have been implied by custom and practice. Following the Albion case, it considered the following facts to be significant: that the policy was published and readily available on the company website; that the company had paid enhanced redundancy payments for many years; and that the policy was dealt with in the same section as other contractual terms. Furthermore, employees had a reasonable expectation that enhanced payments would be made to them and, indeed, most other employees facing redundancy were compensated in accordance with the policy. These factors all supported a finding that entitlement to an enhanced redundancy payment could be implied by custom and practice.

By way of contrast, in Quinn and ors v Calder Industrial Materials Ltd 1996 IRLR 126, EAT, the Appeal Tribunal held that redundant employees had no implied contractual right to enhanced redundancy payments. The employer's policy of making such payments was not incorporated into any agreement, and details of the policy had never been communicated to the employees. Although the policy had been followed in every case over a period of years, the payment remained discretionary. The EAT similarly held that the claimant was not entitled to an enhanced payment on her redundancy in Pellowe v Pendragon plc EAT 804/98. In that case, the employer had for 20 years given redundant employees a payment greater than their statutory redundancy pay. However, the chart for calculating the amount was contained in a management manual

171

that was not publicised to staff. Following a transfer of the business, the new employer made the claimant redundant but only gave him statutory redundancy pay. The EAT upheld the tribunal's decision that the claimant had not acquired a contractual right, through custom and practice, to the enhanced payment. It had not been made known to staff that they would receive enhanced payments and so the term could not be said to be notorious.

6.29 Occasionally, reliance on custom and practice works the other way round, in that the employer seeks to show that a custom or practice has displaced the employee's apparent contractual right to enhanced payments. Such an argument was advanced – albeit unsuccessfully – by the employer in Solectron Scotland Ltd v Roper 2004 IRLR 4, EAT, as a defence to employees' seeking to enforce enhanced redundancy terms. The EAT, upholding a tribunal's decision, ruled that, on the evidence presented, no custom or practice had come into being by which the employees' contractual entitlement had been removed. The practice relied upon was not certain (since different terms were applied in respect of each redundancy exercise carried out), reasonable (since it depended on the whim of the employer), or notorious (since there was no consistent application of any of the terms). The EAT observed that it was doubtful, in any case, whether a custom could ever vary existing contractual rights. But even if it could, the practice in question would have to be a very long-established one.

An employer may find it easier to rely on custom and practice to impose *conditions* on entitlement to enhanced redundancy pay, rather than to displace the right entirely. In Garratt v Mirror Group Newspapers Ltd 2011 ICR 880, CA, the Court of Appeal held that a term was implied by custom and practice to the effect that redundant employees would only be entitled to an enhanced redundancy payment if they signed a compromise agreement. All redundant employees since 1993 had complied with this requirement and it was common knowledge among the current workforce that this was company policy. However, when G was made redundant in 2006 he refused to sign a compromise agreement and was not paid an enhanced redundancy payment. The Court rejected his argument that the position had changed when a collective agreement, which had been reached in 2002, was incorporated into his contract of employment in 2005. The Court noted that the collective agreement clarified the manner of calculation of redundancy payments but made no mention of the compromise agreement condition. The Court further noted that the evidence was that the requirement for a compromise agreement was 'taken as read' when the collective agreement was negotiated, and gave the view that a term to that effect could be implied by the 'officious bystander' test. Accordingly, it could not be suggested that the agreement was intended to change the practice of requiring a compromise agreement, nor that it had this unintended effect.

The facts in the Garratt case provide a clear example of when a term may be **6.30** implied into a contract of employment through custom and practice to the benefit of the employer. However, it is generally preferable for employers to ensure that there is an express term in the contract, thereby avoiding any uncertainty in the matter. As the Court of Appeal pointed out in Garratt, the employer could have put the issue 'beyond argument' by publicising to the workforce that an enhanced redundancy payment would only be paid if the outgoing employee signed a compromise agreement.

Avoiding payments by dismissing for a reason other than redundancy. In **6.31** Jenvey v Australian Broadcasting Corporation 2003 ICR 79, QBD, an employee who had already been earmarked for redundancy was dismissed for asserting a statutory right. He brought a claim before the High Court, seeking damages representing the enhanced redundancy payment that he did not receive. The High Court held that had the employee not been dismissed for asserting a statutory right (an automatically unfair reason for dismissal), he would have been dismissed on the same date by reason of redundancy because his full-time position would have ended. The High Court judge – Mr Justice Elias – decided that in these circumstances a term should be implied into the employee's contract to the effect that, where an employer has decided to dismiss the employee by reason of redundancy, and where any other reason for dismissal would have the effect of depriving him or her of enhanced redundancy benefits, the employer would not dismiss him or her for any reason other than redundancy without good cause. In this case, where the employee was dismissed for an automatically unfair reason after it had been resolved to dismiss him for redundancy, he was entitled to recover damages for breach of contract as compensation for the loss of the enhanced benefits.

Tax treatment of enhanced redundancy pay
6.32
As a general rule, payments under enhanced redundancy pay schemes are not subject to income tax, as they do not represent emoluments paid in return for services rendered by the employee by virtue of his or her employment – see Mairs (HM Inspector of Taxes) v Haughey 1993 IRLR 551, HL. However, to the extent that they exceed £30,000 they are treated as employment income and are therefore chargeable under S.403 of the Income Tax (Earnings and Pensions) Act 2003. For a detailed discussion of the tax treatment of termination payments, see IDS Employment Law Handbook, 'Employment Tribunal Practice and Procedure' (2006), Chapter 9, under 'Taxation of termination payments'.

Age discrimination
6.33

As we explained under 'Statutory redundancy pay scheme – age discrimination' above, the Government retained a number of age-based features of the statutory redundancy scheme after the Employment Equality (Age) Regulations 2006

173

SI 2006/246 came into force. In particular, it retained the three age bands for calculating redundancy payments set out in S.162(2) ERA – see 'Statutory redundancy pay scheme – formula for calculating statutory redundancy pay' above. The Government was of the view that the practice of applying different multipliers to different age bands so as to give greater financial assistance to older workers in a redundancy context is justified.

However, the situation is somewhat different when it comes to enhanced contractual payments. Enhanced payment schemes can be divided into two groups: enhanced schemes modelled on the statutory scheme, and enhanced schemes not modelled on the statutory scheme, and different considerations apply depending on the type of scheme involved.

6.34 **Enhanced scheme modelled on statutory scheme**
An employee's enhanced redundancy entitlement is often calculated with reference to his or her age and/or length of service – both, on the face of it, age discriminatory criteria. However, when drafting the Employment Equality (Age) Regulations 2006 SI 2006/246 ('the Age Regulations'), the Government decided to include an exemption allowing employers, in certain circumstances, to continue with this practice. In this regard, Reg 33 of the Age Regulations set out an 'approved' scheme under which employers can still make enhanced redundancy payments that vary according to the employee's age, without needing to show objective justification. This scheme, which is now contained in para 13 of Schedule 9 to the Equality Act 2010 (EqA), closely mirrors the statutory redundancy scheme, which we discussed under 'Statutory redundancy pay scheme' above.

Under para 13(3) of Schedule 9, enhanced payments can be made to the following types of 'qualifying employee':

- an employee who is entitled to a statutory redundancy payment

- an employee who would have been entitled to a statutory redundancy payment if he or she had attained the requisite two years' qualifying service, or

- an employee who agrees to the termination of his or her employment where, if he or she had been dismissed, he or she would have fallen into one of the above two categories – for example, an employee who takes voluntary redundancy.

6.35 The redundancy payment made to a qualifying employee must be calculated in accordance with the statutory scheme. However, the employer may then enhance the amount paid by doing any or all of the following:

- ignoring the limit on a week's pay provided for by S.227 ERA, to which statutory redundancy payments are subject. The employer can apply its

174

own limit on a week's pay above that contained in statute, or can base redundancy payments on employees' actual pay

- applying a multiplier to the amount of statutory redundancy pay allowed for each year of employment. So, for example, a year's service under the age of 22 might attract a week's pay under the enhanced scheme instead of half a week's pay under the statutory scheme. If it does, applying the same multiplier, a year's service between the ages of 22 and 40 *must* attract two weeks' pay instead of one, and a year's service over the age of 41 *must* attract three weeks' pay instead of one and a half

- applying a multiplier to the total amount of the payment – para 13(5).

This exception is extremely limited, and most enhanced redundancy payment schemes will fall outside its scope.

Enhanced scheme not modelled on statutory scheme   6.36
An employer who uses a method to calculate the amount of enhanced redundancy pay that diverges from the requirements set out in para 13 of Schedule 9 to the EqA (see 'Enhanced scheme modelled on statutory scheme' above) but still contains age-related criteria will have to objectively justify the scheme if challenged on age discrimination grounds. We examine justification in this context below.

Note that para 10 of Schedule 9 (previously Reg 32(1) of the Age Regulations) allows employers to provide benefits based on employees' length of service. However, this exception does *not* apply to any benefit awarded to an employee by virtue of his or her ceasing to work for the employer, and thus does not cover enhanced redundancy payments, as para 10(7) (previously Reg 32(7)) makes clear. Therefore, enhanced redundancy schemes based on the indirectly discriminatory criterion of length of service (without also incorporating the age bands used by the statutory scheme) will fall foul of the legislation unless they can be objectively justified.

Of course, the safest course of action for an employer with an enhanced 6.37 redundancy scheme falling outside para 13 of Schedule 9 to the EqA is to amend it. However, if the scheme is contractual, renegotiating it might prove both difficult and expensive. For information about changing employees' terms and conditions, see IDS Employment Law Handbook, 'Contracts of Employment' (2009), Chapter 6.

Objective justification. As mentioned above, there is a 'justification defence' 6.38 available to employers facing claims of direct or indirect age discrimination in relation to their enhanced redundancy schemes. However, the Government stated in the *Coming of Age* consultation document that 'the test of objective justification will not be an easy one to satisfy... treating people differently on

175

grounds of age will be possible but only exceptionally and for good reasons'. In order to benefit from the defence, the employer must show:

- in a direct discrimination claim, that the less favourable treatment meted out to the claimant on the ground of his or her age was a proportionate means of achieving a legitimate aim

- in an indirect discrimination claim, that the provision, criterion or practice which placed persons of the claimant's age group at a disadvantage was a proportionate means of achieving a legitimate aim – Ss.13(1) and (2) and 19 EqA (previously Reg 3(1)(a) and (b) of the Age Regulations).

6.39 In the consultation document, the Government suggested that one possible legitimate aim of an age-discriminatory scheme could be to encourage and reward loyalty among its workforce. In MacCulloch v Imperial Chemical Industries plc 2008 ICR 1334, EAT, M was made redundant by ICI in October 2006. She was 36 years of age and had been employed by the company for seven years. ICI's redundancy policy, in use for 35 years, provided that upon dismissal by reason of redundancy an employee was entitled to 'a severance payment comprising a percentage or number of weeks of qualifying pay based on age and the period of employment by ICI'. The method of calculating the exact payment differed depending on whether an employee's length of service was more or less than ten years. An employee with more than ten years' service who had reached the age of 50 would receive 175 per cent of qualifying pay. Once the employee reached the age of 57, the rate of pay the employee was entitled to began to diminish until, at the age of 61 years and 11 months, he or she would only be entitled to 50 per cent of qualifying pay. ICI's explanation for the generous payments between ages 50 and 57, provided the employee had worked for it for at least ten years, was that it became more difficult to obtain employment as a person grew older. The reason for the diminishing rate from the age of 57 onwards was that employees at that point would be in the position to have the maximum pension under the company's final salary scheme.

M claimed that the scheme unlawfully discriminated against her on the ground of her age, as she would have been entitled to a higher redundancy payment had she been older and/or had longer service. A tribunal, however, accepted that encouraging and rewarding loyalty is a legitimate aim. Furthermore, it was legitimate to try to protect older employees by giving them a larger financial payment, as they were more vulnerable on losing their job than younger employees. The tribunal also accepted the employer's submission that it had to respect the contractual entitlements and legitimate expectations of its existing workforce (the company had actually consulted on changes to the scheme as a result of the Age Regulations, but the majority of employees had opted to keep the status quo); and that the scheme's generous payments encouraged good industrial relations, a further legitimate aim. Turning to the issue of proportionality, the tribunal noted the following: the scheme applied to the entire workforce and had been successfully in place for 35 years; it avoided the need for compulsory redundancies; it helped manage change in a changing world; and the ten-year length of service cap was reasonable in rewarding loyalty. The tribunal also had regard to the costs involved in setting up an alternative scheme, and the contractual promises made. Given all this, the tribunal found that M's treatment under the scheme had been objectively justified, and hence dismissed her claim. However, the EAT allowed M's appeal on this point and remitted the case to the same tribunal to weigh the reasonable needs of the undertaking with the discriminatory effect on the individual.

In remitting the claim, the EAT held that while the tribunal had identified **6.40** certain legitimate aims of the scheme, it had not properly determined if the measures adopted were proportionate ways of achieving those aims. The principal features that the tribunal appeared to consider were the generosity and general acceptance of the scheme. In the EAT's view, while these features may well be relevant in helping to achieve the aims of the scheme, they did not deal at all with the issue of whether the difference in treatment was justified. Nor was there any recognition of the degree of difference in payment made to M and the chosen comparator, and an assessment as to whether this was reasonably necessary to achieve the scheme's objective. While refusing to rule out the possibility that a scheme such as ICI's may be justified, the EAT concluded that the analysis needed to reach that conclusion was lacking from the tribunal's decision. Mr Justice Elias, then President of the EAT, gave his views on the circumstances that might give rise to objective justification. He endorsed the employer's objective of rewarding loyalty as the reason for linking payments to length of service. He also approved the tribunal's findings that encouraging turnover and creating opportunities for junior staff are, in principle, capable of being legitimate aims that might be furthered by increasing payments for older workers; and that it could be legitimate to pay more to older workers as they are particularly vulnerable in the job market. In Elias P's view, the tribunal had been entitled to draw on its own experience in this respect rather than looking to the employer for evidence of the obstacles faced by older workers.

On remission, the tribunal held that the scheme was proportionate and dismissed M's claim. It noted that there was 'considerable judicial support' for the idea that older people do not find work as easily as younger people. Moreover, ICI had acknowledged the potentially discriminatory impact of the scheme and had tried to change it. However, a 'flatter' scheme was not acceptable to the workforce, many of whom presumably welcomed the potential financial safety net that the scheme could provide them in later life. The tribunal further found that changing the scheme to make it less discriminatory would have been detrimental to the legitimate aims of maintaining a contented workforce and promoting good industrial relations.

6.41 The same enhanced redundancy scheme as that in MacCulloch came up for consideration again in Clark v Terra Nitrogen (UK) Ltd ET Case No.2504785/08 but from the perspective of a man of 61 years of age who had been employed by the company for 37 years. When C was made redundant, his payment under the enhanced scheme was 55.9 per cent of qualifying pay. C claimed that the reduction in his payment amounted to age discrimination. The tribunal noted that the aims of the scheme were to recognise loyalty and service to the company. It was also an incentive to encourage employees to take up voluntary redundancy and thereby reduce the number of compulsory redundancies. In relation to those employees aged between 50 and 57, the aim was specifically to help those who might find it difficult because of their age to obtain alternative employment. With those employees aged 57 and over, the tribunal was satisfied that the aim of the scheme was to put redundant employees on the same footing as those who worked on to retirement. This was not only to prevent a windfall but also to prevent retained employees from being resentful. The company's aims were to achieve financial equality not only between employees who had been made redundant but also between redundant employees and retained employees. The tribunal was therefore satisfied that the company's aims were legitimate. In considering whether the aims were proportionate to the discriminatory effect on C, the tribunal had regard to the actual effect on C and weighed that against the business needs. It took account of the fact that the scheme was generous and had been accepted by the workforce as it had operated successfully in the past. Moreover, the trade unions were happy for the scheme to continue following the coming into force of the Age Regulations. The tribunal also noted that C was, in effect, losing only 11 months' employment with the company compared with someone aged 50, who would potentially be losing 12 years' employment. In these circumstances, the tribunal was satisfied that the company's aims were proportionate to the discriminatory impact on C and therefore dismissed his age discrimination claim.

In Galt and ors v National Starch and Chemical Ltd ET Case Nos.2101804/07 an employer was able to show that its enhanced redundancy scheme had a legitimate aim. On this occasion, however, it fell at the proportionality hurdle. The facts were as follows. The employer decided to close its Warrington site and entered into discussions with the recognised trade union. As part of a package of measures, the workforce was offered enhanced redundancy terms – employees would receive a payment of three weeks' gross pay for each year of service under 40 years of age, and four weeks' gross pay for each year after that age. G and a number of other redundant employees claimed that the enhanced scheme treated them less favourably than employees who were older, as some or all of the years that they were entitled to count for the purposes of the relevant calculation were worked when they were under 40. The tribunal held that G and his colleagues had been unlawfully discriminated against contrary to the Age Regulations. It accepted that the employer had a legitimate aim: 'The company clearly feared that, unless acceptable proposals were made to the employees in question, there was a possibility of industrial unrest. The purpose of offering the enhanced redundancy terms was to avoid such unrest and bring about an orderly and satisfactory closure of the Warrington site.' However, in the view of the tribunal majority, the less favourable treatment of the claimants was not a proportionate means of achieving that aim, as the claimants' treatment did not actually contribute to the pursuit of the legitimate aim. Paying different amounts of redundancy pay according to employees' ages did not actually ensure that the closure of the site would occur without the feared industrial unrest. It followed that there had been unlawful discrimination.

Preventing a windfall as a legitimate aim. While preventing employees **6.42** receiving a windfall is a *potential* legitimate aim, the tribunal's decision in Ormerod v Cummins Engine Co Ltd ET Case No.2508268/09 illustrates that an employer needs to put forward a clear case as to what the windfall might be. A failure to do so is likely to lead a tribunal to conclude that the aim of avoiding a windfall is not a legitimate one in the particular circumstances. Moreover, to be in a position to be able to demonstrate proportionality in such cases, an employer will need to put forward sufficient evidence showing how an employee would be better off with the windfall.

The main facts of the case were as follows. O, who had been employed since 1974, was made redundant in 2008 at the age of 63. A collective agreement contained specific redundancy terms with employees aged between 51 and 64 years of age receiving a redundancy payment of four weeks' pay for each completed year of service. O's enhanced redundancy payment would have been £38,733, but the employer decided that, in view of the economic situation, all redundancy payments would be capped at the level of the gross earnings that would have been received had employees remained in employment until the normal retirement age of 65. This meant that O's payment was capped at £24,461 and then further reduced by his notice payment to £17,497. O claimed that he had been unlawfully discriminated against contrary to the Age Regulations and the tribunal upheld his claim. It found that O had been less favourably treated on the ground of his age as he had not received the full contractual entitlement to four weeks' pay for each completed year of service because he was approaching retirement. This amounted to both direct and indirect age discrimination.

Turning to the question of justification, the tribunal noted that avoiding a **6.43** windfall was a potential legitimate aim. However, it found that in the instant case the employer's aim to avoid a windfall was not legitimate due, in part, to the fact that the employer had made no attempt to advance a clear case as to what that windfall was. Indeed, the employer had not shown that O would, in fact, have received a windfall at all. O gave evidence that his redundancy and early receipt of pension would result in a £5,000 reduction in his pension lump

179

sum and a £1,000 annual reduction in his pension, amounting to an actuarial loss of over £20,000. O's redundancy and early drawing of his pension had also deprived him of various other benefits; for example, the loss of the chance to work on and enhance his pension, the loss of the opportunity to work any overtime in 2009 and 2010, and the loss of any potential bonuses.

On the question of proportionality, the tribunal held that the employer had failed to show that its actions would in any event be proportionate as 'no effort had been made... actuarially or in any other way to calculate precisely how [O] would have been better off in receiving the enhanced payment up to the cap' rather than working to retirement age with the opportunity to receive various benefits as referred to above. It had not provided the tribunal with any evidence as to O's pension entitlement, how it related to or compared with his enhanced redundancy entitlement, or the impact of the other financial provisions. In these circumstances, the tribunal held that it was not possible to conclude that the capping of O's redundancy payment was proportionate.

6.44 Many enhanced redundancy schemes contain 'tapering' provisions that provide for a reduction in the amount of redundancy pay the closer the employee gets to retirement age. The legitimate aim generally relied upon by employers in these circumstances is that older employees would otherwise enjoy a windfall from a redundancy in circumstances where they are shortly to retire. However, whether tapering is a proportionate means of achieving that aim will depend on the facts of the case. In Loxley v BAE Systems Land Systems (Munitions and Ordnance) Ltd 2008 ICR 1348, EAT, L brought a claim of direct age discrimination based on BAE's redundancy scheme, which gave an entitlement to a redundancy payment based mainly on length of service. However, only those under 60 were so entitled, and those aged between 57 and 60 had their payments reduced according to tapering provisions. L was 61 at the time he agreed to take redundancy and was not entitled to the contractual redundancy payment. The rationale for excluding those over 60 was that, until 1996, employees were required to retire at 60 and could do so on a full pension. The tapering requirements and the exclusion of over-60s were designed to prevent those close to retirement from receiving a windfall in the event that they were made redundant. In 1996 the retirement age was raised to 65, although until 1 April 2006 employees could still take their pension at 60 without incurring a penalty to their accrued benefits. A tribunal rejected L's claim, finding that the scheme was justified by the need to prevent employees close to retirement receiving a windfall. The tribunal also thought that the fact that the scheme had been agreed in consultation with trade unions went some way to support the contention that it was justified. L appealed to the EAT.

Mr Justice Elias, then President of the EAT, concluded that the tribunal's analysis had been defective. The tribunal had mistakenly focused on related changes to the pension scheme, rather than the redundancy scheme, and so did

180

not properly engage with the justification issue. Commenting on the aims of the scheme at issue, he held that excluding an employee entitled to immediate pension benefits from a redundancy scheme altogether, or reducing the benefits paid under it, may be justified, but that a tribunal would need to thoroughly assess the impact on the employee. Remitting the case, he stated that it might be that L's pension entitlement, even if taken earlier than he would otherwise have wished, would be far more valuable than any redundancy entitlement. However, although the tribunal appeared to have had a lot of financial information about the various benefits, it had failed to analyse that information. The EAT warned that the fact that a scheme is collectively agreed does not guarantee that it will be justified.

Loxley was referred to in Kraft Foods UK Ltd v Hastie 2010 ICR 1355, EAT, **6.45** where the Appeal Tribunal considered whether an enhanced redundancy scheme that capped payments at the amount the employee would have earned had he or she continued in employment until normal retirement age indirectly discriminated against a 63-year old employee on the ground of his age. H had taken voluntary redundancy and then brought a claim of indirect age discrimination after his redundancy pay was capped at £76,560 – the amount he would have earned had he remained in work until the normal retirement age of 65, and which was £14,000 less than he would have received without the cap. The EAT held that since the purpose of the scheme was to compensate employees for the loss of the expectation of remaining in employment, imposing a cap to prevent an employee receiving a 'windfall' that was more than he or she could have earned until retirement was a proportionate means of achieving a legitimate aim and was therefore justified. Mr Justice Underhill, President of the EAT, stated that he would have reached the decision on justification without reference to previous authority, but that he drew 'strong support' for his conclusion on objective justification from obiter (i.e. non-binding) comments made by Mr Justice Elias (his predecessor as President of the EAT) in Loxley to the effect that age-related provisions in contractual redundancy schemes properly directed at the prevention of a windfall are justifiable.

However, employers should not assume that the tapering of benefits will invariably be justified. In MacCulloch v Imperial Chemical Industries plc 2008 ICR 1334, EAT, the tribunal at first instance commented that the tapering provision in ICI's redundancy policy, which reduced payments to employees between the ages of 57 and 62, was not a proportionate means of achieving a legitimate aim. The taper may have been justified when many of the employees were members of the final salary pension scheme – and thus would receive their maximum pension entitlement – but that was no longer the case as the final salary scheme had been closed. This part of the decision was not appealed. Employers should therefore seek to ensure that any cap (or taper) is clearly

181

aimed at preventing a windfall to the employee and that it strikes the correct balance between the needs of the business and any discriminatory effect on the employee.

6.46 Non-payment

Any issues relating to an employee's right to a payment on redundancy or the exact amount of the redundancy payment fall within the jurisdiction of the employment tribunal – S.163(1). Furthermore, an employee may be able to bring an action in the civil courts where he or she alleges non-payment of a redundancy payment – and therefore breach of contract – under a contractual scheme. For general information on how to bring claims in an employment tribunal and the procedural requirements involved – such as time limits and compensation limits – see Chapter 10, 'Enforcement', and IDS Employment Law Handbook, 'Employment Tribunal Practice and Procedure' (2006). An employer's inability to pay in the context of insolvency is discussed in Chapter 7.

Note that S.7 of the Employment Act 2008 introduced a new power for employment tribunals to award additional financial loss to employees who have brought a successful claim for a redundancy payment where that loss is attributable to the employer's non-payment – see S.163(5) ERA. The amount that a tribunal can award under this head must be 'appropriate in all the circumstances'. This power does not apply to claims presented to employment tribunals before 6 April 2009 – see para 5 of Part 1 of the Schedule to the Employment Act 2008 (Commencement No.1, Transitional Provisions and Savings) Order 2008 SI 2008/3232.

7 Payments from National Insurance Fund

As a social protection measure, all EU Member States are required to offer a **7.1** guarantee – albeit a limited one – to employees whose employer becomes insolvent. In this regard, Article 3 of the EU Insolvency Directive No.2008/94 (originally No.80/987) imposes a general obligation on Member States to 'take the measures necessary to ensure that guarantee institutions guarantee... payment of employees' outstanding claims resulting from contracts of employment or employment relationships, including, where provided for by national law, severance pay on termination of employment relationships'. In fact, well before the coming into force of the original Directive, UK legislation already provided for payments such as outstanding holiday pay, arrears of salary or wages (up to a certain limit), pay in lieu of notice and statutory redundancy payments to be made out of a central fund to employees left high and dry by the insolvency of their employer.

This chapter is concerned with the recovery of redundancy payments pursuant to this State guarantee. But, as we shall see, the circumstances in which such recovery can be made extend beyond where the employer is shown to be insolvent. The relevant UK statutory provisions also require a payment to be made out of a central fund where an intransigent employer refuses to pay up despite it being clear that a statutory redundancy payment is payable.

Entitlement to payment   7.2

Section 166 of the Employment Rights Act 1996 (ERA) contains a scheme whereby an employee may apply to the Department for Business, Innovation and Skills (BIS) for a redundancy payment out of what was originally called 'the Redundancy Fund' and is now called the National Insurance Fund (NIF).

The statutory provisions in effect require two conditions to be satisfied. First, the employee must show that the employer is liable to pay him or her an *'employer's payment'*. This is defined in S.166(2) ERA as:

• a statutory redundancy payment

183

- a payment owing under an Acas-conciliated settlement or a compromise agreement that was made in respect of a claim to a statutory redundancy payment, or

- a termination payment under an agreement to which an exemption order applies under S.157 (see Chapter 5 under 'Contracting out').

7.3 In this chapter we are exclusively concerned with recovery of statutory redundancy payments. It goes without saying that, for such a payment to be payable, the employee must have been made redundant as defined by the ERA – see Chapter 2 for details.

The second requirement is that the employee can show that one or other of the following two situations applies:

- he or she has taken all reasonable steps – short of legal proceedings – to recover the payment from the employer and the employer has refused or failed to pay, or has only made partial payment – S.166(1)(a), or

- the employer is insolvent as defined and the whole or part of the payment remains unpaid – S.166(1)(b).

Both of these situations are analysed in detail below.

7.4 Employer's refusal to pay

As mentioned above, one of the two situations that may trigger entitlement to a payment from the NIF is where an 'employer's payment' (which, as we have seen, includes a statutory redundancy payment) has not been paid by the employer despite the fact that the employee has taken all reasonable steps to recover the payment from the employer. S.166(1)(a) ERA provides that the employee may apply to the Secretary of State (for which read BIS) for a payment from the NIF where '[he or she] has taken all reasonable steps, other than legal proceedings, to recover the payment from the employer and the employer has refused or failed to pay it, or has paid part of it and has refused or failed to pay the balance'.

For these purposes, the phrase 'legal proceedings' does not include employment tribunal proceedings, but does include proceedings to enforce an employment tribunal's decision – S.166(4) ERA. An employee is not therefore expected to take enforcement proceedings in the county court before being able to apply to the Secretary of State – but will be expected to bring a claim for a redundancy payment before a tribunal if there is any reasonable basis for doubting whether a statutory redundancy payment is, in fact, payable. This might be so, for example, if it is unclear whether or not the employee has been dismissed for redundancy, or whether the claimant in question is an 'employee' working under a contract of employment as opposed to an independent contractor. It may also be the case if there is a legitimate dispute about whether the employee

184

has sufficient continuous service (currently two years) to be eligible for a statutory redundancy payment. However, whenever liability on the employer to pay a redundancy payment is clear cut, the cases suggest that the Secretary of State is not entitled to require the employee to commence tribunal proceedings against the employer before applying for a payment out of the NIF – see, for example, Jeffrey v Grey 1967 2 ITR 335, ET.

The question of whether an employee had taken 'all reasonable steps' to recover **7.5** a payment before applying to the Secretary of State came up in some of the very first cases decided under the redundancy provisions. For example, in Williams v Black 1967 ITR 317, ET, the employer had disappeared and apparently left the country, making it impossible for the employee to serve a tribunal claim on him. The tribunal felt that it could not decide on the merits of the employee's claim but it did decide how much he would have been entitled to so that he could apply to the Secretary of State for payment out of what was then the Redundancy Fund. In the circumstances, the employee was found to have taken all the steps he could reasonably take.

In Jeffrey v Grey (above) the employer admitted liability but simply said that he was unable to pay. The tribunal said that the commencement of tribunal proceedings was not a necessary step to recover payment in these circumstances because they could not help the employee to get money from the employer.

In general, the importance of S.166(1)(a) is that, unlike other payments **7.6** potentially payable from the NIF (such as holiday pay and payment in lieu of notice), it enables an employee to claim an 'employer's payment' even if the employer is not insolvent. It is often the case that an employer is unable or refuses to pay a redundancy payment in circumstances where, despite all appearances to the contrary, the employer is not actually 'insolvent' as defined by the relevant legislative provisions. And sometimes a payment is refused for no other reason than the employer's intransigence. In either case, provided the employee can satisfy the precondition of having taken all reasonable steps to recover the payment, he or she can look to BIS to recover the payment from the NIF.

Employer's insolvency

7.7

The second situation that triggers an employee's entitlement to claim a statutory redundancy payment from the NIF is where the employer is 'insolvent' as statutorily defined – S.166(1)(b).

Individual employers. By virtue of S.166(6) ERA, an *individual* employer is **7.8** insolvent in this context if:

- he has been adjudged bankrupt or has made a composition or arrangement with his creditors (in England and Wales), or sequestration of his estate has been awarded or he has executed a trust deed for his creditors or has entered into a composition contract (in Scotland), or

- he has died and his estate falls to be administered in accordance with an order under S.421 of the Insolvency Act 1986 (in England and Wales), or he has died and a judicial factor appointed under S.11A of the Judicial Factors (Scotland) Act 1889 is required by that section to divide his insolvent estate among his creditors (in Scotland).

7.9 **Corporate insolvency.** Where the employer is a *company*, then under S.166(7) ERA that company is insolvent if:

- a winding-up order or an administration order has been made, or a resolution for voluntary winding up has been passed, in respect of the company

- the company is in administration for the purposes of the Insolvency Act 1986

- a receiver or (in England and Wales only) a manager of the company's undertaking is duly appointed, or (in England and Wales only) possession has been taken of any company property by or on behalf of the holders of any debentures secured by a floating charge on that property, or

- a voluntary arrangement proposed in the case of the company for the purposes of Part I of the Insolvency Act 1986 has been approved.

It is important to note that a company will not be regarded as insolvent simply because it has ceased trading, cannot pay its debts or has otherwise fallen into some kind of financial difficulty. In Pollard and ors v Teako (Swiss) Ltd 1967 ITR 357, ET, a landlord sent in bailiffs to take possession of a company's premises. The business closed with no prospect of reopening and the sale of stock and furniture was insufficient to pay off the arrears of rent. The company, however, was not insolvent as defined. No steps were taken to put it into liquidation because there were no remaining assets to realise. The same principle has been confirmed by subsequent cases – see, for example, Secretary of State for Trade and Industry v Key and ors EAT 1356/01.

7.10 In Secretary of State for Trade and Industry v Walden and anor 2000 IRLR 168, EAT – a case concerning a claim for payment of arrears of pay from the NIF – the EAT ruled that an employment tribunal had erred in assuming that some kind of insolvency procedure must have occurred to explain the dissolution of a company that had got into financial difficulties. The EAT emphasised that the relevant statutory provisions set out an exhaustive list of events amounting to insolvency. The onus is firmly on the claimant seeking to make a claim against the Secretary of State to adduce direct evidence of one of those events. Absence of proof that one of the events has occurred is fatal to the claim. The EAT pointed out that documentary proof of the fact that one of the specified types of insolvency procedure has been commenced is obtainable from Companies House.

The limitations discussed above could be a major drawback for employees were it not for the fact that, in respect of statutory redundancy payments and the other type of 'employer's payment' defined by S.166(2) ERA, an employee is entitled to make a claim to BIS under S.166(1)(a) if he or she has taken all reasonable steps to recover the payment in question from the employer (see under 'Employer's refusal to pay' above). In other words, whereas the absence of insolvency proceedings is fatal to other types of claim potentially payable out of the NIF, this need not be the case where the relevant claim concerns a statutory redundancy payment.

Partnerships. Where the employer is a limited liability partnership (LLP), the 7.11 partnership is judged to be insolvent under S.166(8) ERA if:

- a winding-up order, administration order or a determination for a voluntary winding-up has been made with respect to the partnership

- a receiver or (in England and Wales only) a manager of the undertaking of the partnership has been appointed or (in England and Wales only) possession has been taken by or on behalf of the holders of any debenture secured by a floating charge of any of the partnership's property comprised in or subject to the charge, or

- a voluntary arrangement proposed in relation to the partnership has been approved under Part I of the Insolvency Act 1986.

It would seem that any other type of partnership can only be insolvent for the 7.12 purposes of S.166(1)(b) if each and every partner is insolvent. In Secretary of State for Trade and Industry v Forde 1997 ICR 231, EAT, the Appeal Tribunal ruled that, for an employer comprising a partnership to be regarded as 'insolvent', it is necessary that each and every one of the individual partners has been adjudged personally bankrupt. The EAT reached this decision on the basis that an employee who is employed by a partnership as a whole (as distinct from employment by an individual partner in a personal capacity) must show that his or her 'employer' (i.e. the partnership) is insolvent in order to secure entitlement to payments by the Secretary of State from the NIF. In the EAT's view, a partnership as a whole cannot be insolvent, since it 'is not an entity which can be or would be adjudged bankrupt'. However, it is arguable that the Appeal Tribunal overlooked the provisions of Part V of the Insolvency Act 1986, which allow 'unregistered companies' to be compulsorily wound up. For this purpose, the Insolvent Partnerships Order 1994 SI 1994/2421 expressly includes a partnership in the definition of 'unregistered company' and makes provision for the partnership as a whole to be wound up as insolvent. It is not necessary under the 1994 Order for each partner to be individually insolvent, since the partnership is regarded as an entity in itself.

Types of insolvency procedure. A detailed analysis of the various insolvency 7.13 procedures that apply to individual, corporate and partnership insolvency is

187

beyond the scope of this Handbook. However, the topic is outlined in IDS Employment Law Handbook, 'Transfer of Undertakings' (2011), Chapter 6, 'Transfer of insolvent companies', in the section on 'Types of insolvency procedures'.

7.14 Qualification

In order to rely on the provisions for payment from the NIF, the claimant must show that he or she is entitled to a redundancy payment, which means, in the case of a statutory redundancy payment, that he or she must have completed two years' continuous service. This is so even if the employee is claiming under a contractual scheme covered by an exemption order – irrespective of whether that scheme contains any requirement for two years' service – S.167(2) ERA. In such a case, however, the period of continuous employment must be calculated in accordance with the provisions of the contracted-out scheme and not with those of the ERA. (See Chapter 5 under 'Contracting out' for a more detailed discussion of contracted-out schemes.)

The claimant must also be an 'employee' as defined by S.230 ERA. This means that he or she must be working or have worked under a 'contract of employment' (i.e. a contract of service or apprenticeship) – see Chapter 5 under 'Employees and excluded employees'. In practice, most of the case law generated by the statutory provisions for payments from the NIF concerns the issue of whether or not the claimants have employee status. BIS will decline to make such payments if, in the view of its officials, there is a question mark over the employment status of the claimant. In such cases, claimants often end up challenging the refusal of the Secretary of State to make a payment by taking tribunal proceedings – see, for example, Secretary of State for Trade and Industry v Bottrill 1999 ICR 592, CA, and Nesbitt and anor v Secretary of State for Trade and Industry 2007 IRLR 847, EAT.

7.15 A rare form of disqualification is where the claimant's contract has become *frustrated* by the time of the insolvency. This occurred in Collins v Secretary of State for Trade and Industry EAT 1460/99, where the claimant had, as a result of an injury to his hand, been off work for a considerable amount of time. At the beginning of 1999, the managing director offered him the choice of remaining on the books or taking a redundancy payment. Since he thought he might eventually be fit to return to work, he opted for the former. However, a couple of months later the company went into receivership and the claimant at that point sought a redundancy payment from the Secretary of State. This was rejected on the ground that the claimant's contract had, by the time of the redundancy, come to be frustrated by his inability to work over a protracted period. An employment tribunal ruled in favour of the Secretary of State and, on appeal, the EAT upheld the tribunal's decision. Owing to the fact that the contract had been frustrated, the claimant was not employed under a contract of employment at the relevant date. In so concluding, the EAT rejected the claimant's contention that, in a situation where both parties regard the employment as continuing, it was not open to a tribunal to conclude that the contract had in fact been terminated by frustration.

Procedure   7.16

When an employer fails to pay the statutory redundancy payment or is insolvent, the employee may apply to the Secretary of State for a redundancy payment – S.166(1) ERA. He or she may, of course, apply to an employment tribunal first. A tribunal decided in Barcza v Potomac Restaurants Ltd (in liquidation) 1968 ITR 234, ET, that it had jurisdiction to hear a redundancy payment claim when the employing company was in liquidation and the employee had made no application to the (then) Department of Employment for payment out of the (then) Redundancy Fund.

Although there is no specific time limit for making an application to the Secretary of State, it should be noted that S.166(1) stipulates that an employee can only claim payment out of the NIF if his or her employer is 'liable to pay' an employer's payment. Where the particular payment in question is a statutory redundancy payment, the employer can only be said to be liable to pay if, within six months of the 'relevant date' (i.e. the date of termination of employment) the employee takes one or more of the steps listed in S.164(1) regarded as necessary to establish his or her right to claim a payment. The relevant steps are:

- the employee makes a written claim for the payment to the employer – S.164(1)(b)

- the question as to the employee's right to, or the amount of, the payment has been referred to an employment tribunal – S.164(1)(c). (Note that a claim is 'referred to a tribunal' when it is physically received at the tribunal office, not when it is posted – Secretary of State for Employment v Banks and ors 1983 ICR 48, EAT), or

- the employee presents a claim of unfair dismissal to a tribunal under S.111 – S.164(1)(d).

These steps are discussed in detail in Chapter 10 under 'Statutory redundancy   7.17 payments – time limits'. So long as the employee has a 'live' claim against the employer triggered by having taken one of the necessary steps within the applicable time limit, the employee is entitled to apply to the Secretary of State for payment from the NIF in the event that the employer is insolvent or has simply refused to pay up.

The Secretary of State is only liable for a statutory redundancy payment that an employer is liable to make. An employee is not entitled to a statutory redundancy payment from his or her employer if he or she fails to take one or more of the

189

steps listed in S.164(1) within the prescribed time limits. In those circumstances, since the employer is not liable to make the redundancy payment, the Secretary of State is under no liability to make it either – see Crawford v (1) Secretary of State for Employment (2) Colmore Depot 1995 IRLR 523, EAT. In that case, C failed to apply for a redundancy payment when his employer's business, which was in receivership, was sold. This was because all the parties assumed that there had been a transfer under the Transfer of Undertakings (Protection of Employment) Regulations 2006 SI 2006/246 (TUPE). Over a year later it became clear that there had not been a transfer. C applied to the Secretary of State for a redundancy payment but was refused on the ground that his claim was out of time. The EAT agreed. It rejected C's claim that it should consider the spirit and intention of the legislation and that time should only begin to run against C when it became clear that there had been no transfer. The EAT recommended that employees of companies that become insolvent make provisional claims for a redundancy payment from the employer and the Secretary of State promptly to cover themselves in the event that the insolvent undertaking is not transferred to a third party under TUPE.

7.18 Information from employer

The Secretary of State may require the employer to provide such information and documents as he or she needs to determine the employee's entitlement – S.169(1) ERA. Failure to comply without reasonable excuse is a summary offence punishable by a fine not exceeding level 3 on the standard scale – S.169(2). Deliberately or recklessly providing false information is an offence punishable by a fine or imprisonment or both – S.169(3) and (4).

7.19 References to tribunals

The Secretary of State is not bound to pay up on an application by an employee under S.166. He or she may challenge the employee's entitlement or the amount of the payment claimed or both before an employment tribunal – S.170(1). Even if there has been an earlier tribunal hearing that has awarded a redundancy payment to the employee, the Secretary of State, if dissatisfied with the claim, may require the case to be reheard on its merits – Secretary of State for Employment v Banks and ors 1983 ICR 48, EAT. This somewhat surprising decision shows that the Secretary of State is not bound by an earlier tribunal's determination against the employer as to the employee's entitlement to a redundancy payment. So, for example, a prior decision as to an employee's sufficiency of continuous service in respect of entitlement to a redundancy payment can be 'unpicked' by the Secretary of State if he or she has cause to argue that that decision was wrong.

Similarly, if the employee disputes the Secretary of State's refusal to make a payment, the employee may refer the question to a tribunal by virtue of S.170(1). If the employee does so, he or she is not obliged to join the employer as a party to the proceedings but may proceed solely against the Department – Jones v Secretary of State for Employment 1982 ICR 389, EAT.

Finally, it should be noted that in Smith v Secretary of State for Trade and **7.20** Industry 2000 ICR 69, EAT, the Appeal Tribunal doubted whether an employment tribunal, in cases brought against the Secretary of State, was a suitably 'independent and impartial tribunal' within the meaning of Article 6(1) of the European Convention on Human Rights. This was because the tribunals were then run by the Secretary of State under the auspices of the Department of Trade and Industry. However, in Scanfuture UK Ltd and anor v Secretary of State for Trade and Industry 2001 ICR 1096, EAT, the Appeal Tribunal accepted that procedural changes that had subsequently been made to the powers of the Secretary of State in respect of lay members removed the concern that employment tribunals were not an appropriate adjudicator of disputes concerning payments from the NIF. Although lay members are still appointed by the Secretary of State, the process now involves an element of open competition, and lay members cannot be removed from office without substantial judicial involvement. A suitable framework is therefore in place to provide the necessary protection against any improper interference and influence, so that no reasonable and well-informed observer could have justifiable grounds for doubting the impartiality or independence of an employment tribunal appointed under the current system.

Since the Scanfuture decision, further changes have been made and the employment tribunal service is now under the umbrella of the Ministry of Justice, thus distancing it even further from the Department currently responsible for administering the NIF, namely BIS.

Amount of payment   7.21

If the employee is claiming a statutory redundancy payment, then the amount to be paid from the NIF is a redundancy payment computed in the usual way, less anything that has actually been paid by the employer – S.168(1)(a) ERA. If the employee is claiming a sum owing under an Acas-conciliated settlement or a compromise agreement, the amount to be paid is either the amount owing under the agreement or the amount of any redundancy payment that the employer would have been liable to pay but for the agreement, whichever is the lesser amount – S.168(1)(aa).

Things are somewhat more complicated if the employee is claiming under a redundancy scheme covered by an exemption order made pursuant to S.157 ERA. This provision – which deals with rare instances where trade unions and employers have jointly agreed to operate a redundancy scheme that stands in the place of the statutory provisions for redundancy payments – is discussed in Chapter 5 under 'Contracting out'. Where a payment is to be made from the

NIF in respect of a scheme covered by an exemption order, it is necessary to compute both the amount due under the scheme and the amount that would have been due under the statutory redundancy scheme. In calculating the latter amount, however, the provisions of the exempted scheme relating to the computation of continuous employment and the determination of the 'relevant date' are deemed to override any conflicting statutory provisions – S.168(2) and (3). The amount thus computed is called the 'relevant redundancy payment'. What the employee is entitled to from the NIF is either the amount due under the contracted-out scheme or the 'relevant redundancy payment', whichever is the lesser – S.168(2).

7.22 Interest

Under the Employment Tribunals (Interest) Order 1990 SI 1990/479 simple interest at the prevailing rate per annum (currently 8 per cent) is payable on any compensation or monetary award made by an employment tribunal that remains unpaid 42 days after the date of a 'relevant decision' of the tribunal in which the sum payable has been specified. By virtue of Article 2(2) of the 1990 Order, a relevant decision requires a decision or order of the tribunal in which the precise amount of the payment has been specified or from which such amount is otherwise ascertainable solely by reference to the decision or order.

In light of the above, if an employer becomes liable to pay such interest on account of a failure to pay the redundancy payment as ordered by a tribunal, and the employee subsequently looks to the Secretary of State to make the payment from the NIF, the payment by the Secretary of State must include the interest that was owed by the employer. However, if the only relevant decision made by a tribunal is the decision requiring payment by the Secretary of State from the NIF – in other words, no prior relevant decision has been made against the employer – the Secretary of State will not be required to pay interest unless he or she him or herself fails to make payment within 42 days of the promulgation of the tribunal's decision – see Secretary of State for Employment v Reeves 1993 ICR 508, EAT.

7.23 Subrogation of rights and remedies by Secretary of State

Whenever a payment is made from the NIF, the employee's rights and remedies against the employer are transferred to and vest in the Secretary of State – S.167(3) ERA. Under the same provision, any decision of an employment tribunal ordering a redundancy payment to be paid by the employer to the employee will be treated as an order for the payment to be paid to the Secretary of State. If the Secretary of State is successful in recovering money from the employer, such money will then be paid back into the NIF – S.167(4).

8 Unfair redundancy

Redundancy is one of the potentially fair reasons for dismissal listed in **8.1** S.98(2)(c) of the Employment Rights Act 1996 (ERA). Given this, in many cases an employer's liability in respect of a redundancy dismissal will be fully discharged by the payment of statutory or, where appropriate, contractual redundancy pay. However, it remains open to an employee to argue that his or her 'redundancy' dismissal was unfair under the ERA for one of the following reasons:

- the dismissal was not by reason of redundancy, but was instead for a reason which is not potentially fair under S.98(1) or (2)

- although a redundancy situation existed, the employee was selected for redundancy for a prohibited reason, meaning that the dismissal was automatically unfair – S.105 and related provisions

- although a redundancy situation existed, and the employee was not selected for an automatically unfair reason, the dismissal was nevertheless unreasonable under S.98(4).

In addition, an employee might claim that the decision to select him or her for redundancy was an act of unlawful discrimination. Discriminatory redundancy selection is discussed in Chapter 9 under 'Discriminatory selection'.

Occasionally a redundancy dismissal can also amount to a breach of contract. **8.2** In Keable v Imagedata Group Ltd ET Case No.1806353/09, for example, K was employed under a contract of apprenticeship, but was dismissed by reason of redundancy nine months before his apprenticeship was due to end. His employer had decided that in view of its financial situation it could no longer afford to employ trainees. However, his contract of apprenticeship could be terminated only with good cause. An employment tribunal upheld K's claim of breach of contract. The employer had committed itself expressly to completing the apprenticeship and it would have been reasonably practicable to have kept him on, despite the difficult economic situation. Breach of contract claims are discussed in IDS Employment Law Handbook, 'Contracts of Employment' (2009), Chapter 7.

193

8.3 **Reason for dismissal**

Where an employee argues that his or her dismissal was not by reason of redundancy, but was instead for a reason which is not potentially fair under the ERA, the statutory presumption that a dismissal is for redundancy will not operate and it will fall to the employer to show the reason for dismissal.

For a dismissal to be by reason of redundancy, a redundancy situation must exist – see Chapter 2. However, it must be stressed that it is not for tribunals to investigate the reasons behind such situations. In Moon and ors v Homeworthy Furniture (Northern) Ltd 1977 ICR 117, EAT, H Ltd closed a factory on the ground that it was not economically viable. The employees sought to demonstrate that the factory was viable and the dismissals unfair, but the EAT ruled that there was no jurisdiction to consider the reasonableness of the decision to create a redundancy situation. That would be akin to considering the merits of an industrial dispute, the power to do which had been removed by the Trade Union and Labour Relations Act 1974.

8.4 In a number of decisions reached after Moon v Homeworthy, including Orr v Vaughan 1981 IRLR 63, EAT, and Ladbroke Courage Holidays Ltd v Asten 1981 IRLR 59, EAT, the Appeal Tribunal required the employer to show that the decision to make redundancies was based on proper information and consideration of the situation. This approach can be justified on the ground that the absence of such information and consideration throws into question whether the dismissals are by reason of redundancy at all. In the Ladbroke Courage Holidays case the EAT went so far as to suggest that the employer should be able to show a strong economic case for redundancies. However, this rests unhappily with the Court of Appeal's decisions in Hollister v National Farmers' Union 1979 ICR 542, CA, and James W Cook and Co (Wivenhoe) Ltd v Tipper and ors 1990 ICR 716, CA. In the Hollister case, the Court held that a good commercial reason was enough to justify the decision to make redundancies, and in Tipper it stressed that tribunals are not at liberty to investigate the commercial and economic reasons behind a decision to close. It did accept, however, that tribunals could question whether the decision to dismiss was genuinely on the ground of redundancy, and could therefore require that the decision to make redundancies was based on proper information. In short, a tribunal is entitled only to ask whether the decision to make redundancies was genuine, not whether it was wise.

8.5 **Retirement**

The now-repealed Schedule 6 to the Employment Equality (Age) Regulations 2006 SI 2006/1031 introduced a statutory procedure under which employers could compulsorily retire employees who had reached the 'normal retirement age' (NRA) for their position, or 65 if there was no NRA, without attracting

194

age discrimination or unfair dismissal liability. The Employment Equality (Repeal of Retirement Age Provisions) Regulations 2011 SI 2011/1069, which came into force on 6 April 2011, abolished this procedure, subject to transitional provisions under which the latest date on which a retirement dismissal could take effect was 5 April 2012. 'Retirement' is thus no longer one of the potentially fair reasons for dismissal under S.98 ERA. For further details of the now-repealed procedure, see IDS Employment Law Handbook, 'Unfair Dismissal' (2010), Chapter 9. For a discussion of age discrimination in a redundancy context, see Chapter 9 of this Handbook under 'Discriminatory selection – age discrimination'.

Automatically unfair redundancy 8.6

There has been a significant rise in recent years in the number of circumstances in which a dismissal will be held to be automatically unfair – i.e. unfair without any consideration of reasonableness under S.98(4) ERA. The relevant statutory provisions amend the substantive law of unfair dismissal and are designed to afford a greater degree of protection to certain categories of worker, or to those who carry out specific functions that are related to their employment. Most, but not all, of these provisions are contained in S.105 ERA.

From an employer's perspective, a dismissal that infringes one or more of these provisions can prove more costly than a 'standard' unfair dismissal, as in some cases the compensation cap normally applicable to such claims will be set aside. Furthermore, most of the provisions disapply the one-year qualifying period for unfair dismissal rights.

In most cases, a dismissal will be automatically unfair where the *reason or* **8.7** *principal reason* for it falls into one of the prescribed categories – for example, the employee was absent on jury service (S.98B), was a health and safety representative (S.100), or had asserted a statutory right (S.104). The automatically unfair redundancy provisions of S.105, however, are subtly different. They proceed on the basis that the reason or principal reason for dismissal was redundancy – a potentially fair, and thus not automatically unfair, reason for dismissal. They go on to provide that such a redundancy dismissal will nevertheless be automatically unfair where the employee was *selected* for redundancy for an automatically unfair reason.

Relevant provisions 8.8

In this section we provide a list of the statutory provisions governing automatically unfair redundancy selection. This is followed by a brief discussion of each of these provisions. Reference should also be had to IDS Employment Law Handbook, 'Unfair Dismissal' (2010), Chapters 10–13.

195

Section 105(1) ERA states that an employee who is dismissed shall be regarded as unfairly dismissed if:

- the reason (or, if more than one, the principal reason) for the dismissal is that the employee was redundant – S.105(1)(a), and

- it is shown that the circumstances constituting the redundancy applied equally to one or more other employees in the same undertaking who held positions similar to that held by the employee and who have not been dismissed by the employer – S.105(1)(b), and

- it is shown that 'any of subsections (2A) to (7N) applies' – S.105(1)(c).

8.9 Subsections (2A)–(7N) apply where the reason (or, if more than one reason, the principal reason) the employee was selected for redundancy was:

- a reason relating to *jury service* as specified in S.98B – S.105(2A)

- a *health and safety* reason as specified in S.100 – S.105(3)

- a reason relating to a shop worker's or betting worker's refusal to do *Sunday work* as specified in S.101 – S.105(4)

- a reason relating to the employee's rights under the *Working Time Regulations 1998 SI 1998/1833* as specified in S.101A – S.105(4A)

- a reason relating to the employee's role as an *occupational pension scheme trustee* as specified in S.102 – S.105(5)

- a reason relating to the employee's role as an *employee representative or candidate* for the purpose of collective redundancies or a transfer of an undertaking as specified in S.103 – S.105(6)

- that the employee made a *protected disclosure* as specified in S.103A – S.105(6A)

- a reason relating to the employee's *assertion of a statutory right* as specified in S.104 – S.105(7)

- a reason relating to the employee's rights under the *National Minimum Wage Act 1998* as specified in S.104A – S.105(7A)

- a reason relating to the employee's rights under the *Tax Credits Act 2002* as specified in S.104B – S.105(7B)

- a reason relating to the employee's *right to request flexible working* as specified in S.104C – S.105(7BA)

- a reason relating to the employee's *right to request study or training* as specified in S.104E – S.105(7BB) (subject to an exemption for employers with fewer than 250 employees)

- that the employee took *protected industrial action* within the meaning of S.238A of the Trade Union and Labour Relations (Consolidation) Act 1992 (TULR(C)A) – S.105(7C)

- a reason specified in Reg 28(3) or (6) of the *Transnational Information and Consultation of Employees Regulations 1999 SI 1999/3323* – S.105(7D)

- a reason specified in Reg 7(3) of the *Part-time Workers (Prevention of Less Favourable Treatment) Regulations 2000 SI 2000/1551* – S.105(7E)

- a reason specified in Reg 6(3) of the *Fixed-term Employees (Prevention of Less Favourable Treatment) Regulations 2002 SI 2002/2034* – S.105(7F)

- a reason specified in Reg 42(3) or (6) of the *European Public Limited-Liability Company Regulations 2004 SI 2004/2326* – S.105(7G) (note that these provisions were repealed on 1 October 2009 but re-enacted in European Public Limited-Liability Company (Employee Involvement) (Great Britain) Regulations 2009 SI 2009/2401 – see below)

- a reason specified in Reg 30(3) or (6) of the *Information and Consultation of Employees Regulations 2004 SI 2004/3426* – S.105(7H)

- a reason specified in paragraph 5(3) or (5) of the Schedule to the *Occupational and Personal Pension Schemes (Consultation by Employers and Miscellaneous Amendment) Regulations 2006 SI 2006/349* – S.105(7I)

- a reason specified in Reg 31(3) or (6) of the *European Cooperative Society (Involvement of Employees) Regulations 2006 SI 2006/2059* – S.105(7J)

- a reason specified in Reg 46(2) or 47(2) of the *Companies (Cross-Border Mergers) Regulations 2007 SI 2007/2974* – S.105(7K)

- a reason specified in Reg 29(3) or (6) of the *European Public Limited-Liability Company (Employee Involvement) (Great Britain) Regulations 2009 SI 2009/2401* – S.105(7L)

- a reason relating to a *trade union blacklist* prohibited under the Employment Relations Act 1999 (Blacklist) Regulations 2010 SI 2010/493 – S.105(7M)

- a reason specified in Reg 17(3) of the *Agency Workers Regulations 2010 SI 2010/93* – S.105(7N).

There are two further provisions not yet in force. These cover selection **8.10** for redundancy:

- for a reason relating to the automatic enrolment of jobholders into a pension scheme as specified in S.104D ERA – S.105(JA). The automatic enrolment scheme, contained in the Pensions Act 2008, is intended to be phased in from October 2012, and

197

- of employees under the age of 18 who have been dismissed for exercising, or proposing to exercise, their right to participate in education or training as specified in S.101B ERA – S.105(4B)). At the time of writing, a date for the coming into force of S.101B has not yet been appointed.

8.11 In addition to the protection afforded by S.105 ERA, Reg 20(2) of the Maternity and Parental Leave etc Regulations 1999 SI 1999/3312 (MPL Regulations), Reg 29(2) of the Paternity and Adoption Leave Regulations 2002 SI 2002/2788 (PAL Regulations), and Reg 34(2) of the Additional Paternity Leave Regulations 2010 SI 2010/1055 (APL Regulations) make it automatically unfair to select an employee for redundancy for reasons connected with pregnancy, maternity suspension, maternity leave, paternity leave, adoption leave, parental leave, dependant care leave or 'keeping in touch' days. Dismissal is also automatically unfair if the employee becomes redundant during or at the end of his or her maternity, paternity or adoption leave and the provisions relating to offers of suitable alternative employment are not complied with under Reg 10 MPL Regulations, Reg 23 PAL Regulations or Reg 28 APL Regulations – Reg 20(1) MPL Regulations; Reg 29(1) PAL Regulations; Reg 34(1) APL Regulations.

There are also two automatically unfair redundancy provisions contained in the TULR(C)A. These apply where the employee was selected for redundancy for a reason (or principal reason) relating to:

- his or her membership or non-membership of a trade union, or to his or her participation in trade union activities or use of trade union services – S.153 TULR(C)A, or

- trade union recognition or derecognition – para 162, Sch A1 TULR(C)A.

8.12 And finally, Reg 7(1) of the Transfer of Undertakings (Protection of Employment) Regulations 2006 SI 2006/246 (TUPE) provides that a dismissal (including a redundancy dismissal) will be automatically unfair where the sole or principal reason for the dismissal is:

- the transfer itself, or

- a reason connected with the transfer that is not an economic, technical or organisational reason entailing changes in the workforce.

8.13 **Qualifying periods.** Note that there is no qualifying period for any of the above claims of automatically unfair selection for redundancy, with the exception of claims under Reg 7(1) of TUPE, which requires that an employee has one year's continuous service at the date of dismissal.

8.14 **Exceptions.** The automatically unfair reasons for selection for redundancy listed above are virtually identical to the automatically unfair reasons for dismissal (for which see IDS Employment Law Handbook, 'Unfair Dismissal'

(2010), Chapter 10, under 'List of automatically unfair reasons'). There are three possible exceptions to this.

First, S.12 of the Employment Relations Act 1999 makes it automatically unfair to dismiss for a reason related to the statutory right to be accompanied at disciplinary or grievance hearings. However, it makes no provision for a selection for redundancy to be automatically unfair on this basis.

Secondly, dismissal because of a 'spent' conviction within the terms of the **8.15** Rehabilitation of Offenders Act 1974 is likely to be automatically unfair, unless the employee falls into a statutorily excluded category – see S.4(3)(b) of that Act. The Act makes no provision for a selection for redundancy to be automatically unfair on this basis, although it is arguable that it would be, so long as the spent conviction plays a material part in the employee's eventual dismissal. See IDS Employment Law Handbook, 'Unfair Dismissal' (2010), Chapter 6, under 'Criminal offences at work – spent convictions under the Rehabilitation of Offenders Act 1974'.

Finally, no *specific* provision is made to render selection for redundancy automatically unfair if the reason is connected with a transfer of an undertaking to which the Transfer of Undertakings (Protection of Employment) Regulations 2006 SI 2006/246 (TUPE) apply. However, a redundancy dismissal that is solely by reason of the transfer, or for a reason connected to the transfer that is not an 'economic, technical or organisational reason entailing changes in the workforce', will be automatically unfair under Reg 7(1) TUPE. But if the employer can establish that the reason for the selection and dismissal was an ETO reason, the dismissal will be potentially fair. See 'Transfer of undertakings' below for more extensive discussion of this issue.

Same undertaking and similar position   8.16
The provisions of S.105 ERA set out above are concerned with selection *from a group*, as one of the conditions for demonstrating automatic unfair dismissal is that the redundancy circumstances 'applied equally to one or more other employees in the same undertaking who held positions similar to that held by the employee and who have not been dismissed' – S.105(1)(b). As the EAT pointed out in MacAskill v John G McGregor (Stornoway) Ltd EAT 705/79, the effect of the wording of S.105 is that it does *not* apply to an employee who holds a unique position within an undertaking – although the dismissal of such an employee on the ground of redundancy may still be unfair under S.98(4) (similar reasoning would apply to redundancy dismissals under Reg 20(2) MPL Regulations 1999; Reg 29(2) PAL Regulations 2002; Reg 34(2) APL Regulations 2010; and under the TULR(C)A, which use identical wording to that used in S.105 ERA).

This means that an employee who claims that his or her selection for redundancy was for an automatically unfair reason will have to point to another individual employed in a similar position within the same undertaking who was not dismissed – see S.105(1)(b) ERA; Reg 20(2)(b) MPL Regulations; Reg 29(2)(b) PAL Regulations; Reg 34(2)(b) APL Regulations; and S.153(a) and para 162(a), Sch A1 TULR(C)A. In practice, the two issues of 'similar position' and 'same undertaking' are often blurred by tribunals, which simply refer to the pool of employees (holding similar positions in the same undertaking) from which the selection for redundancy was made.

8.17 **Employed in the same undertaking.** The question of whether an individual is employed in the same undertaking as others arises where an employer runs a number of plants or sites. The ERA does not define 'undertaking', which is a question of fact for the tribunal and may be overturned by the EAT only on the ground of perversity.

Where 'undertaking' is defined by agreement, this will generally be accepted. Where there is no agreement, tribunals have tended to define 'undertaking' fairly widely, as comparisons will in any case be limited to those holding 'similar positions' within that undertaking. Factors such as location, flexibility of labour and the type of skill used have all been held to be relevant. Furthermore, a range of employer activities may be covered if some degree of central direction exists. In Kapur v Shields 1976 ICR 26, QBD, Mr Justice Phillips said, in a different context, that 'some evidence of organisational unity, e.g. common accounting, management, purchasing arrangements, insurance, and so on' would suggest the existence of an undertaking. And in Oxley and ors v Tarmac Roadstone Holdings Ltd 1975 IRLR 100, ET, the fact that two plants shared a works manager was seen as important by the tribunal. Common management at some higher level was inevitable among plants owned by a single organisation. But at this low level, and coupled with a common bonus scheme, labour flexibility and similar work at both plants, it was seen as indicating a single undertaking.

8.18 **Employees holding similar positions.** 'Position' is defined in S.235(1) ERA by reference to an employee's status, the nature of the work he or she does, and his or her terms and conditions of employment. The decisions do not show any marked degree of consistency in determining whether employees hold similar positions and the question tribunals tend to ask themselves is the general one of whether a claimant was unfairly selected from a pool of employees, the pool sometimes being chosen without specific reference to either the undertaking concerned or the position of other employees. Two examples of decisions on 'position':

* **Powers and anor v A Clarke and Co (Smethwick) Ltd** 1981 IRLR 483, EAT: Class 1 drivers, who could drive articulated lorries as well as four-wheel vehicles, were, by reason of their skill, in a different 'position' from Class 3 drivers, who could drive only four-wheelers

- **Copeman and Sons Ltd v Harris** EAT 792/86: the selection of a 'picker' from only one department when there were pickers doing virtually identical jobs in another department who had less service than the employee dismissed was an unfair restriction of the pool.

The tribunal's decision in the Copeman case was overturned by the EAT on a **8.19** different point, but it refused to interfere with the tribunal's finding that the restriction of the pool to one department was unfair. The position of employees is a question of fact, and as such is for the tribunal to decide. The EAT can overturn a finding of fact on the basis that it is perverse – that no reasonable tribunal could have reached it on the evidence available – but it is usually reluctant to interfere in this way.

There are, however, a number of cases where the EAT has expressly disagreed with tribunals on the question of 'position'. In Wellworthy Ltd v Singh and ors EAT 79/88, for example, the EAT overruled a tribunal's decision that the restriction of the pool for redundancy selection to the department within which the redundancy situation arose was unfair. The tribunal had said that this restriction unfairly disadvantaged one group of employees, but the EAT pointed out that any criteria upon which a selection was based would disadvantage some employees.

The label attached to a particular job is not conclusive when it comes to **8.20** assessing the employee's position. Similar job titles may conceal real differences between the status of employees or the nature of the work they do. In Twidale v The Thomas Hill Engineering Co (Hull) Ltd ET Case No.21874/86, for example, an employee solely concerned with sales was termed a 'draughtsman' in common with those who were draughtsmen in the ordinary sense. He was found not to occupy the same position as the rest. The same tribunal also found that an employee treated by the company as being in a different position from the others was in reality in the same position as them.

Note that the Court of Appeal has stated that, when comparing the position of employees, regard should only be had to the relative positions of the redundant employees and that any protected activities should be disregarded, even if the employee concerned had a contractual right to undertake such activities – O'Dea v ISC Chemicals Ltd t/a Rhône-Poulenc Chemicals 1996 ICR 222, CA. This case, which concerned a trade union representative selected for redundancy, is discussed under 'Selection for trade union reasons' below.

Selection for a reason relating to jury service 8.21

Section 105(2A) provides that the selection of an employee for redundancy will be automatically unfair if the reason or principal reason for the selection was one of the following reasons set out in S.98B(1):

201

- he or she has been summoned to attend for jury service under the Juries Act 1974, the Coroners Act 1988, the Court of Session Act 1988 or the Criminal Procedure (Scotland) Act 1995, or

- he or she has been absent from work because he or she attended court in pursuance of being so summoned.

8.22 However, S.98B(1) will not protect the employee if the employer can show that:

- the circumstances were such that the employee's absence on jury service was likely to cause substantial injury to the employer's undertaking

- the employer brought those circumstances to the attention of the employee

- the employee refused or failed to apply to the appropriate officer to be excused from attending court or for the obligation to attend to be deferred, *and*

- the employee's refusal or failure was not reasonable – S.98B(2).

The 'appropriate officer' is defined in S.98B(3), but is usually also identified in the letter accompanying the summons for jury service.

8.23 ## Selection for health and safety reasons

Section 105(3) provides that the selection of an employee for redundancy will be automatically unfair if the reason or principal reason for the selection was one of the following reasons set out in S.100(1):

- that the employee carried out, or proposed to carry out, activities in connection with preventing or reducing risks to health and safety at work, having been designated by the employer to do so – S.100(1)(a)

- that the employee performed, or proposed to perform, the functions of a health and safety representative, or member of a safety committee, either in accordance with arrangements established by statute or after being recognised as such by the employer – S.100(1)(b)

- that the employee took part, or proposed to take part, in consultations with the employer in accordance with the Health and Safety (Consultation with Employees) Regulations 1996 SI 1996/1513, or in an election of employee safety representatives in accordance with those Regulations – S.100(1)(ba)

- that the employee brought to the employer's attention, by reasonable means, circumstances connected with his or her work which he or she reasonably believed were harmful or potentially harmful to health and safety. (This only applies where there is either no health and safety representative or committee, or it was not reasonably practicable for the employee to raise the matter by those means) – S.100(1)(c)

- that the employee left, proposed to leave, or (while the danger persisted) refused to return to, his or her place of work or any part of the place of work in circumstances of danger which he or she reasonably believed to be serious and imminent and which he or she could not reasonably be expected to avert – S.100(1)(d)

- that the employee took, or proposed to take, appropriate steps to protect him or herself or other persons from danger which he or she reasonably believed to be serious and imminent – S.100(1)(e). (The question of whether the steps an employee has taken, or proposed to take, were appropriate is to be judged by reference to all the circumstances, including, in particular, his or her knowledge and the facilities and advice available to him or her at the time – S.100(2). If the employer shows that it was, or would have been, so negligent for the employee to take the steps that he or she took, or proposed to take, that a reasonable employer might have dismissed him or her for taking those steps, or proposing to take them, then the dismissal will not be regarded as unfair – S.100(3)).

Note that the statutory maximum compensatory award (currently £68,400) **8.24** does not apply to a claim brought under S.105(3) – S.124(1A). Furthermore, if an employee is selected for redundancy for one of the first two reasons above, a minimum basic award of, currently, £5,000 applies – S.120(1).

In Smiths Industries Aerospace and Defence Systems v Rawlings 1996 IRLR 656, EAT, a health and safety representative was selected for redundancy on the basis of a points system relating to performance at work. He argued that his dismissal was connected with his health and safety activities and was accordingly unfair under S.105. A tribunal rejected the claim, holding that the employer's assessments had been carried out in good faith and that the employee's health and safety activities had not contributed in any material way to his selection for redundancy. The EAT upheld the decision. There was no evidence to suggest that the employee's selection was related to his activities as a health and safety representative. In particular, there was nothing to suggest that his absence from ordinary work duties in order to deal with health and safety matters or his insistence on compliance with health and safety requirements had caused the person carrying out the selection exercise to be biased against him.

In the following cases, however, the tribunal did find that the claimants had **8.25** been selected for redundancy for health and safety reasons:

- **Irish v Commercial Vehicle Auctions Ltd** ET Case No.2801157/08: I was one of three yard operatives. His role was to move vehicles and plant items to different parts of the site, and occasionally to collect customers' vehicles from their homes and deliver them to the site. In autumn 2007 CVA Ltd began to use an overflow site to store vehicles, and this could only be reached from the main site by using a public road. I became concerned that some of the vehicles he had to drive on the public road were not roadworthy. He raised his concerns with his employer. In February 2008, without any

203

prior warning, I was dismissed as redundant. The tribunal found that on the evidence the principal reason for I's dismissal was that he had made a protected disclosure, which tended to show that the health and safety of the public was endangered. (Note that this case was also brought under S.105(6A) – see 'Protected disclosures' below)

- **Flynn v Bunzl Vending Services Ltd** ET Case No.3301922/09: F worked for BVS Ltd cleaning, servicing and filling vending machines. She submitted a grievance, saying that she was required to lift large containers filled with milk, weighing around 14 kilos, to about chest height. BVS Ltd did not respond to her grievance and shortly afterwards she was selected for redundancy. A tribunal found that there was a strong connection between F lodging her grievance concerning the health and safety issue and her selection for redundancy, both because of the timescale and because BVS Ltd did not reply to her grievance even though she was raising an urgent health and safety issue.

8.26 Selection for refusing to work on Sundays

The ERA contains the provisions relating to Sunday trading that were previously contained in the Sunday Trading Act 1994 and the Betting, Gaming and Lotteries Act 1963 (as amended by Schedule 8 to the Deregulation and Contracting Out Act 1994). The purpose of these provisions is to safeguard the employment rights of shop and betting workers who object to working on Sunday. They also define the impact of such objections on the employment relationship and on unfair dismissal rights. Briefly, if a worker can bring him or herself within the definition of a 'protected' shop worker or betting worker or an 'opted-out' shop worker or betting worker, he or she will have the right to refuse to do Sunday work. In these circumstances, any agreement or provision of an employment contract will be unenforceable in so far as it requires the employee to work on a Sunday, and any dismissal for a refusal or threatened refusal to do Sunday work is deemed to be automatically unfair.

Section 105(4) ERA, read in conjunction with S.101, provides that it is automatically unfair to select an employee for redundancy if the principal reason for the selection is that:

- the employee was a protected shop worker or an opted-out shop worker, or a protected betting worker or an opted-out betting worker, and the sole or principal reason for the employee's selection for dismissal was that he or she refused (or proposed to refuse) to do shop work, or betting work, on Sunday or on a particular Sunday – S.101(1), or

- the employee was a shop worker or a betting worker and the sole or principal reason for which the employee was selected for dismissal was that he or she gave (or proposed to give) an opting-out notice to the employer – S.101(3).

The definitions of 'protected' shop and betting workers and 'opted-out' shop **8.27** and betting workers are central to the operation of this provision and are examined in detail below. Essentially, a protected worker is a worker who was already employed as a shop or betting worker (but not solely working on Sundays) when the Sunday trading provisions came into force, or a worker who cannot be contractually required to work on Sundays. An opted-out worker is a worker who has given his or her employer a written notice opting out of Sunday work.

Note that, in addition to the provisions in the ERA which relate to Sunday working, an employee selected for redundancy on the basis that he or she refused to work on Sundays could have a claim under the religion or belief provisions in the Equality Act 2010 (previously the Employment Equality (Religion or Belief) Regulations 2003 SI 2003/1660) – see IDS Employment Law Guide, 'The Equality Act 2010' and IDS Employment Law Handbook, 'Race and Religion Discrimination' (2004).

'Protected worker'. Under S.36 ERA an employee will be a protected shop or **8.28** betting worker if he or she meets one of two sets of criteria. The first set is as follows:

- the worker must have been in employment as a shop/betting worker on the day before the 'relevant commencement date' – S.36(2)(a). The relevant commencement date is 26 August 1994 for shop workers and 3 January 1995 for betting workers – the respective dates on which the Sunday Trading Act 1994 and Schedule 8 to the Deregulation and Contracting Out Act 1994 came into force

- on that day, he or she must not have been employed to work only on Sunday – S.36(2)(a)

- the worker must have been continuously employed during the period beginning with the day before the relevant commencement date and ending with the 'appropriate date' – S.36(2)(b). (The 'appropriate date' means the effective date of termination for the purposes of S.101 – S.101(4). For discussion of the 'effective date of termination' see IDS Employment Law Handbook, 'Contracts of Employment' (2009), Chapter 11), and

- he or she must have been a shop/betting worker throughout that period of continuous employment, or throughout every part of it during which the worker's relations with his or her employer were governed by a contract of employment (see below) – S.36(2)(c).

(Note that S.36(4) deems an employee to be a protected worker for the purposes **8.29** of S.36(2)(a), despite the fact that the employment relationship had ceased by the day before the relevant commencement date, if that employee's continuity of employment was preserved at the commencement date by virtue of S.212(3) or under S.219 (absence by reason of sickness, temporary cessation of work or arrangement or custom, or absence pending reinstatement/re-engagement of a dismissed employee); and, when the employment relationship ceased, that employee was a shop worker or betting worker and was not employed to work only on Sunday.)

Alternatively, a worker may be a protected worker if, under the terms of his or her contract, he or she is not and cannot be required to work on Sundays, and could not be required to do so even if Part IV of the ERA (which deals with Sunday working) were disregarded – S.36(3). This provision applies regardless of whether the employee was in employment at the relevant commencement date. An employer's right to require an employee to work on Sunday is clearly a question of construction of the relevant contract of employment.

8.30 'Shop worker' and 'shop work' are defined in S.232. A 'shop worker' means an employee who is or may be required under his or her contract of employment to do shop work – S.232(1). 'Shop work' is defined as work in or about a shop on a day on which the shop is open for the serving of customers – S.232(2). 'Shop' includes any premises where any retail trade or business is carried on – S.232(3). 'Retail trade or business' includes the business of a barber or hairdresser, the business of hiring goods other than for use in the course of a trade or business, and retail sales by auction, but does not include a catering business or the sale of programmes, catalogues, etc at theatres or other places of amusement – S.232(6). (See further IDS Employment Law Handbook, 'Unfair Dismissal' (2010), Chapter 10, under 'Dismissal for refusing to work on Sunday').

'Betting worker' and 'betting work' are defined in S.233. A 'betting worker' is defined as an employee who is required, or may be required, to do betting work under his or her contract of employment – S.233(1). 'Betting work' is defined as work at a track for a bookmaker, being work which consists of or includes dealing with betting transactions, and work in a licensed betting office at a time when the office is used for betting transactions – S.233(2).

8.31 '**Opted-out worker**'. An opted-out shop worker/betting worker is an employee who, under his or her contract of employment, is or may be required to work on Sunday, but is not employed to work only on Sunday, and who has given his or her employer a signed and dated 'opting-out' notice stating that he or she objects to working on Sunday. To satisfy the statutory requirements, opted-out workers must have been in continuous employment as a shop or betting worker during the period beginning with the day on which the opting-out notice was given and ending with the 'appropriate date' (i.e. the effective date of termination of the contract – see above) – Ss.40 and 41(1) ERA. Opted-out workers do not obtain the protection afforded by the Act until the expiry of three months after the opting-out notice was served – S.41(3), although this may be reduced to one month where the employer has failed to provide an explanatory statement of the worker's rights regarding Sunday working – S.42.

Loss of 'protected' or 'opted-out' status. Under S.36(5) a protected shop **8.32** worker or betting worker will lose that status if, on or after the commencement date, he or she gives the employer an 'opting-in notice' and, after giving that notice, makes an express agreement with the employer to do shop work or betting work on Sundays or on a particular Sunday. An 'opting-in notice' is a signed and dated notice in which a worker states that he or she wishes to work on Sunday or does not object to Sunday working – S.36(6).

Similarly, under S.41(2) an opted-out shop worker or betting worker loses that status if he or she gives the employer an opting-in notice after previously giving an opting-out notice, and then expressly agrees to do shop work or betting work on Sunday or a particular Sunday.

'Express agreement' is not defined in either case and would therefore seem to encompass verbal as well as written agreements. However, the opting-in notice must be in writing – S.36(6).

Working time cases   8.33

Section 105(4A), read in conjunction with S.101A, provides that it is automatically unfair to select an employee for redundancy on the ground that the employee:

- refused (or proposed to refuse) to comply with a requirement which the employer imposed (or proposed to impose) in contravention of the Working Time Regulations 1998 SI 1998/1833 – S.101A(1)(a)

- refused (or proposed to refuse) to forgo a right conferred by those Regulations – S.101A(1)(b)

- failed to sign a workforce agreement for the purposes of those Regulations, or to enter into, or agree to vary or extend, any other agreement with the employer that is provided for in those Regulations – S.101A(1)(c), or

- performed (or proposed to perform) any functions or activities as a workforce representative for the purposes of the Regulations or as a candidate in an election of workforce representatives – S.101A(1)(d).

Where the last of the above reasons applies, the minimum basic award of, currently, £5,000 applies – S.120(1).

Full details of the 1998 Regulations can be found in IDS Employment Law Handbook, 'Working Time' (2009).

207

8.34 **Selection of occupational pension scheme trustees**
Section 105(5) protects employees who act as trustees of relevant occupational pension schemes which relate to their employment. S.105(5), read in conjunction with S.102, provides that it is automatically unfair to select an employee for redundancy on the ground that he or she performed (or proposed to perform) any functions as such a trustee. Employees who are directors of a company that is a trustee are also protected – S.102(1A).

A 'relevant occupational pension scheme' means an occupational pension scheme (as defined in S.1 of the Pension Schemes Act 1993) established under a trust – S.102(2).

Where an employee brings a successful claim under S.105(5) the minimum basic award of, currently, £5,000 applies – S.120(1).

8.35 **Pension consultation dismissals.** The Occupational and Personal Pension Schemes (Consultation by Employers and Miscellaneous Amendment) Regulations 2006 SI 2006/349 require employers to engage in an information and consultation process with employee representatives when seeking to make changes to occupational or personal pension schemes. S.105(7I) provides that the selection of an employee for redundancy will be automatically unfair if the reason (or, if more than one, the principal reason) for his or her selection was one specified in para 5(3) or (5) of the Schedule to the Regulations. These reasons are that the employee:

- performed or proposed to perform the functions of a representative under the Regulations

- exercised, proposed to exercise, or made a request to exercise, the right to paid time off under paras 2 or 3 of the Schedule

- made, or proposed to make, a complaint to an employment tribunal to enforce a right or secure an entitlement under the Regulations. (It is immaterial whether the employee actually had the right or entitlement, or whether it was infringed, provided the claim to the right, and (if applicable) the claim that it had been infringed was made in good faith – para 5(6))

- complained, or proposed to complain, to the Pensions Regulator over failures to comply with requirements of the Regulations

- stood as a candidate in an election for employee representatives

- attempted to influence by lawful means the voting in elections for representatives

- voted in such an election

- expressed doubts about whether such an election was properly conducted.

In respect of the last four of these reasons, para 5(5)(h) specifies that it will also be automatically unfair to select an employee for redundancy for proposing to do, failing to do, or proposing to decline any of these things.

Selection of employee representatives

8.36

A number of legislative provisions require the election of employee representatives. While in many cases these will be pre-existing trade union representatives, given that the majority of the UK workforce is non-unionised, there are a large number of non-union representatives. Such employees enjoy an extensive level of protection from detriment or dismissal as a result of exercising their duties as representatives, and this is reflected in the protections against selection for redundancy found in S.105.

The collective redundancy consultation procedures in the TULR(C)A (see Chapter 12) and the Transfer of Undertakings (Protection of Employment) Regulations 2006 SI 2006/246 both provide for consultation with employee representatives, and S.105(6) ERA, read in conjunction with S.103, provides that it is automatically unfair to select an employee for redundancy if the principal reason for selection is that the employee:

- being an employee representative for the purposes of collective consultation on redundancy or transfer of undertakings, or a candidate in an election for such representatives, performed or proposed to perform any functions or activities as such an employee representative or candidate – S.103(1), or

- 'took part in an election of employee representatives'. This provision would seem to extend protection to employees selected for redundancy on the grounds that they voted in or organised an election of employee representatives – S.103(2).

Note that where an employee succeeds under S.105(6), the minimum basic award of, currently, £5,000 applies – S.120(1).

Protected disclosures

8.37

Section 105(6A), read in conjunction with S.103A, provides that it is automatically unfair to select an employee for redundancy on the ground that he or she has made a 'protected disclosure' within the meaning of Part IVA of the ERA.

Part IVA (Ss.43A–43L) was inserted into the ERA by the Public Interest Disclosure Act 1998 (PIDA). It provides protection for workers who disclose information about their employers on matters such as the commission of a criminal offence, failure to comply with a legal obligation, a miscarriage of justice, danger to health and safety, and damage to the environment. The worker making the disclosure must be acting in good faith and must have reasonable grounds for his or her belief. For further details of these provisions

209

see IDS Employment Law Handbook, 'Unfair Dismissal' (2010), Chapter 13, and IDS Employment Law Supplement, 'Whistleblowing at Work' (2004).

8.38 An example of selection for redundancy under this head:

- **Pattenden and anor v Medway Council** ET Case No.1101213/08 and others: the claimants, P and B, made protected disclosures in relation to a company which maintained the Council's housing stock. On 9 July 2007 the Council published restructuring proposals, and at about the same time the claimants' manager said that whistleblowers in the department might be subject to legal and disciplinary action. P and B were made redundant as a result of the restructuring on 15 January 2008. A tribunal upheld P's claim of automatic unfair dismissal. Although there was a genuine reorganisation, the people who had most significantly influenced it were those against whom the protected disclosures were made, and the evidence did not support the decision to select P for redundancy. The Council failed to prove that he was not made redundant because he had made protected disclosures. However, B had been made redundant for 'independent sound reasons'.

Note that certain health and safety cases may give rise to claims both under this head and under S.100(1)(c) – see, for example, Irish v Commercial Vehicle Auctions Ltd (discussed under 'Selection for health and safety reasons' above).

8.39 While the provisions introduced by the PIDA are aimed at encouraging 'whistleblowing', the broad term 'failure to comply with a legal obligation' is not qualified. It is therefore arguable that an employee who raises, in good faith, a complaint that his or her employer is not complying with its obligations under the contract of employment, and who is later selected for redundancy as a result of having made such a complaint, would be automatically unfairly dismissed – see Parkins v Sodexho Ltd 2002 IRLR 109, EAT; Cavendish Munro Professional Risks Management Ltd v Geduld 2010 ICR 325, EAT.

Note that the statutory maximum compensatory award, currently £68,400, does not apply to dismissals under S.105(6A) – S.124(1A).

8.40 **Selection for asserting a statutory right**
Section 105(7) provides that it is automatically unfair to select an employee for redundancy on one of the grounds specified in S.104(1). Those grounds are that the employee:

- brought proceedings against the employer to enforce a relevant statutory right, or

- alleged that the employer had infringed a relevant statutory right.

It is sufficient that the employee, without specifying the right, made it reasonably clear to the employer what the right claimed to have been infringed was – S.104(3).

It is specifically stated that it is immaterial whether or not the employee actually **8.41** has the right and whether or not it has been infringed – but the employee's complaint must have been made in good faith – S.104(2). For example, in *Philip Hodges and Co v Crush* EAT 1061/95 C reluctantly agreed to a pay cut as an alternative to dismissal when her employer found her work performance disappointing. C consulted a legally qualified friend and a law centre, and the latter wrote to the employer claiming that her reduction in pay was an unlawful deduction from her wages, contrary to what is now S.13 ERA. C was dismissed when she told her employer about the advice she had received. The tribunal upheld her claim that she had been dismissed for asserting a statutory right. The EAT upheld this finding. C had made her claim in good faith and it was irrelevant that her rights under S.13 had not in fact been infringed.

Relevant statutory rights. Section 104 does not apply to all statutory rights **8.42** but only to the 'relevant' rights referred to in S.104(4). The rights covered are as follows:

- the right to receive a written statement of employment particulars, a statement of changes to particulars or an itemised pay statement – Ss.1, 4 and 8 ERA

- protection of wages rights – Ss.13, 15, 18 and 21 ERA

- the right to a guarantee payment – S.28 ERA

- protection from detriment rights (jury service; health and safety; Sunday working; working time; trustees of occupational pension schemes; employee representatives; paid time off for study or training; protected disclosures; maternity, paternity and parental leave; time off for dependants; tax credits; flexible working; and study and training) – Ss.43M–47F ERA

- the right to time off for public duties – S.50 ERA

- the right of redundant employees to paid time off to look for work or arrange training – Ss.52 and 53 ERA

- the right to paid time off for ante-natal care – Ss.55 and 56 ERA

- the right to time off for dependants – S.57A ERA

- the right of pension scheme trustees to paid time off – Ss.58 and 59 ERA

- the right of employee representatives to paid time off – Ss.61 and 62 ERA

- the right to paid time off for a young person for study or training – Ss.63A and 63B ERA

- the right to make a request in relation to study and training, and have it properly considered by the employer – Ss.63D and 63F ERA

- the right to remuneration on suspension on medical grounds – S.64 ERA

- the right to alternative work and remuneration on maternity suspension – Ss.67 and 68 ERA

- the right to parental leave – S.76 ERA

- the right to have an application for flexible working properly considered – Ss.80G and 80H ERA

- the right to minimum notice – S.86 ERA

- the right to receive a written statement of reasons for dismissal – S.92 ERA

- the right not to be unfairly dismissed – S.94 ERA

- the right to a redundancy payment – S.135 ERA

- the right not to suffer unauthorised deductions from wages in respect of union subscriptions – S.68 TULR(C)A

- the right not to suffer unauthorised deductions from wages in respect of a union political fund – S.86 TULR(C)A

- the right not to be offered an inducement in relation to union membership or activities – S.145A TULR(C)A

- the right not to be offered an inducement in relation to collective bargaining – S.145B TULR(C)A

- the right not to be subjected to a detriment on grounds related to union membership or activities – S.146 TULR(C)A

- the right of union officials to paid time off for union duties – Ss.168 and 169 TULR(C)A

- the right of union learning representatives to paid time off for learning and training activities – Ss.168A and 169 TULR(C)A

- the right of union members to time off for union activities – S.170 TULR(C)A

- the rights conferred by the Working Time Regulations 1998 SI 1998/1833, the Merchant Shipping (Working Time: Inland Waterways) Regulations 2003 SI 2003/3049; the Fishing Vessels (Working Time: Sea-fishermen) Regulations 2004 SI 2004/1713 or the Cross-border Railway Services (Working Time) Regulations 2008 SI 2008/1660

- the rights conferred by the Transfer of Undertakings (Protection of Employment) Regulations 2006 SI 2006/246.

212

Dismissal for asserting a statutory right is discussed further in IDS Employment Law Handbook, 'Unfair Dismissal' (2010), Chapter 12.

National minimum wage 8.43

Section 105(7A), read in conjunction with S.104A, provides that it is automatically unfair to select an employee for redundancy on the ground that:

- any action was taken, or was proposed to be taken, by or on behalf of the employee with a view to enforcing, or otherwise securing the benefit of, a right to the national minimum wage (NMW) or other rights under the National Minimum Wage Act 1998

- the employer was prosecuted for an offence under the 1998 Act as a result of action taken by or on behalf of the employee to enforce a right under that Act, or

- the employee qualifies, or will or might qualify, for the NMW.

For full details on the National Minimum Wage Act 1998, see IDS Employment Law Handbook, 'Wages' (2011), Chapter 5.

Tax Credits Act 2002 8.44

Working tax credits are designed to top up the earnings of working people (employed and self-employed) on low incomes, including those who do not have children. They are made up of a number of elements depending on the circumstances of the worker concerned, including elements to support the costs of approved or registered childcare and to help working households in which someone has a disability. Payment of tax credits is made via the employer through normal pay except in respect of the childcare element, which is paid directly to the main carer.

Section 105(7B) ERA, read in conjunction with S.104B, provides that it is **8.45** automatically unfair to select an employee for redundancy on the ground that:

- any action was taken, or was proposed to be taken, by or on behalf of the employee with a view to enforcing, or otherwise securing the benefit of, a right conferred on the employee by regulations made under S.25 of the Tax Credits Act 2002

- a penalty was imposed on the employer, or proceedings were brought against it, under the Act as a result of action taken by or on behalf of the employee for the purpose of enforcing, or otherwise securing the benefit of, such a right, or

- the employee is entitled, or will or may be entitled, to working tax credit.

213

It is immaterial whether or not the employee has the right or whether or not it has been infringed, but the employee's claim to the right, and (if applicable) the claim that the right has been infringed, must be made in good faith – S.104B(2).

8.46 ## Flexible working

Under S.105(7BA), the selection of an employee for redundancy will be automatically unfair if the sole or principal reason was one of those specified in S.104C relating to the employee's statutory right to request flexible working. These are that the employee:

- made (or proposed to make) an application to work flexibly under S.80F

- exercised (or proposed to exercise) a right conferred on him or her under S.80G (such as the right to appeal, or the right to be accompanied to a meeting to discuss his or her request or appeal)

- brought proceedings against the employer under S.80H (alleging that the employer had failed to comply with the statutory procedure for hearing his or her request, or that a refusal of his or her request was based on incorrect facts), or

- alleged the existence of any circumstance which would constitute a ground for bringing such proceedings.

8.47 The statutory right to request flexible working is set out in Ss.80F – 80I ERA, read with the Flexible Working (Eligibility, Complaints and Remedies) Regulations 2002 SI 2002/3236 and the Flexible Working (Procedural Requirements) Regulations 2002 SI 2002/3207. For a full discussion of these provisions, see IDS Employment Law Handbook, 'Maternity and Parental Rights' (2009), Chapter 11.

8.48 ## Study and training

On 6 April 2010, the Government introduced a right for employees to request to undertake study and training. The rules governing the operation of this right are found in Ss.63D–63K ERA; the Employee Study and Training (Eligibility, Complaints and Remedies) Regulations 2010 SI 2010/156; and the Employee Study and Training (Procedural Requirements) Regulations 2010 SI 2010/155. S.104E ERA sets out the circumstances in which dismissal in relation to a request to undertake study and training will be automatically unfair and S.105(7BB) states that it will be automatically unfair to select an employee for redundancy for a reason specified in S.104E: namely, that the employee made (or proposed to make) an application for study and training; exercised or proposed to exercise a right under S.63F; brought proceedings under S.63I; or alleged the existence of any circumstances which would constitute a ground for bringing such proceedings.

214

The right to request to undertake study or training is very similar to the right to request flexible working that applies to carers of children under the age of 17 – see IDS Employment Law Handbook, 'Maternity and Parental Rights' (2009). An employee is not entitled to have his or her request granted, but merely to have it considered seriously and for rejections to be made on legitimate grounds. For more information on how the right to request study or training operates in practice, see IDS Employment Law Handbook, 'Unfair Dismissal' (2010), Chapter 10, under 'Dismissal relating to study and training'.

8.49 Initially, the Government intended to stagger the introduction of the right to request study and training. It was made available to employees of companies employing at least 250 employees on 6 April 2010, with the intention that the right would be extended to all employees from 6 April 2011. However, in an announcement made to coincide with the Budget speech on 23 March 2011, the Government indicated that the April 2011 extension would no longer go ahead. The right therefore continues to remain available only to those employed in undertakings with 250 or more employees.

Protected industrial action cases

8.50 Under S.238A TULR(C)A, a dismissal is automatically unfair if the principal reason for the dismissal is that the employee took official industrial action and the dismissal occurred:

- within the period of eight weeks beginning with the day on which the employee started to take industrial action

- after the end of the eight-week period, but the employee had ceased to take part in the industrial action before the end of that period, or

- after the end of the eight-week period, but the employer had not taken such procedural steps as would have been reasonable for the purposes of resolving the dispute – S.238A(2).

Section 105(7C) ERA provides that it is also automatically unfair to select an employee for redundancy in any of the above circumstances.

Full details of the protected industrial action provisions are contained in IDS Employment Law Handbook, 'Industrial Action' (2010), Chapter 8.

Part-time and fixed-term work

8.51 Both the Part-time Workers (Prevention of Less Favourable Treatment) Regulations 2000 SI 2000/1551 (PTW Regulations) and the Fixed-term Employees (Prevention of Less Favourable Treatment) Regulations 2002 SI 2002/2034 (FTE Regulations) contain provisions protecting employees from being dismissed for exercising rights under the Regulations.

215

8.52 Section 105(7E) and (7F) ERA states that an employee is automatically unfairly dismissed for redundancy where the reason for redundancy selection was one of the automatically unfair reasons for dismissal provided for in Reg 7 PTW Regulations and Reg 6 FTE Regulations. These reasons are similar in the two sets of Regulations, but not identical. In both sets the following reasons for dismissal are automatically unfair:

- the employee brought proceedings against the employer under the Regulations, or gave evidence or information in connection with such proceedings brought by any worker

- the employee requested a written statement of the reasons for his or her less favourable treatment

- the employee has otherwise done anything under the Regulations in relation to the employer or any other person

- the employee alleged that the employer had infringed his or her rights under the Regulations

- the employee had refused (or proposed to refuse) to forgo any of his or her rights under the Regulations

- the employer believes or suspects that the employee has done or intends to do any of these things.

8.53 In addition, the FTE Regulations provide that it will be automatically unfair to dismiss an employee where:

- he or she sought a written statement of the reasons for variation of a fixed-term contract

- he or she refused to sign a workforce agreement for the purposes of the FTE Regulations

- he or she performed or proposed to perform any functions or activities as a workforce representative or candidate for the FTE Regulations

- the employer believes or suspects that the employee has done or intends to do any of these things.

Note that while the PTW Regulations generally protect all workers, not just employees, it is only employees who are protected from unfair dismissal and unfair redundancy selection under Reg 7(1). Other workers must rely on the right not to be subjected to a detriment for one of the reasons listed above, contained in Reg 7(2).

8.54 Trade union blacklists

The Employment Relations Act 1999 (Blacklists) Regulations 2010 SI 2010/493 came into force on 2 March 2010 and introduced a further ground of automatically unfair dismissal, the detail of which is found in S.104F ERA. These Regulations are aimed at preventing the use of trade union 'blacklists' and to this end Reg 3 prohibits the compilation, use, selling or supply of a list which:

- contains details of persons who are or have been members of trade unions or persons who are taking part or have taken part in the activities of trade unions, and

- is compiled with a view to being used by employers or employment agencies for the purposes of discrimination in relation to recruitment or in relation to the treatment of workers.

8.55 Discrimination in this context does not refer to a breach of the Equality Act 2010, but to less favourable treatment on the grounds of trade union membership or trade union activities – Reg 3(3).

Regulation 4 sets out a number of exceptions to the general prohibition: where the person supplying a list does not and could not be expected to know that it is a prohibited list; where the list is compiled, used or supplied in order to expose a breach or possible breach of Reg 3; where the list is compiled, used, sold or supplied to recruit to a post that reasonably requires either trade union membership or knowledge of trade union matters; where the action relating to the list is required by law; or where the list is used or supplied in connection with legal proceedings.

8.56 Section 105(7M) ERA, read in conjunction with S.104F, provides that it is automatically unfair to select an employee for redundancy where the selection relates to a prohibited list and either:

- the employer contravenes Reg 3 in relation to that list, or

- the employer relies on information supplied by a person who contravenes Reg 3 in relation to that list, and knows or ought reasonably to know that the information relied on is supplied in contravention of Reg 3.

For more information on the blacklisting provisions, see IDS Employment Law Handbook, 'Unfair Dismissal' (2010), Chapter 10, under 'Dismissal relating to trade union blacklists'.

Agency workers
8.57 The Agency Workers Regulations 2010 SI 2010/93 (AW Regulations), which came into force on 1 October 2011, give temporary agency workers the right, after 12 weeks on the same assignment, to equal treatment in comparison with permanent workers as regards basic working conditions. New S.105(7N) ERA provides that the selection of an employee for redundancy will be automatically unfair if the reason (or, if more than one, the principal reason) for the selection was one specified in Reg 17(3) AW Regulations.

217

The reasons specified in Reg 17(3)(a) are that the agency worker:

- brought proceedings under the Regulations

- gave evidence or information in connection with such proceedings brought by any agency worker

- made a request under Reg 16 for a written statement (relating to the agency worker's basic working and employment conditions)

- otherwise did anything under the Regulations in relation to a temporary work agency, hirer, or any other person

- alleged that a temporary work agency or hirer has breached the Regulations (unless the allegation is both false and not made in good faith – Reg 17(4)), or

- refused (or proposed to refuse) to forgo a right conferred by the Regulations.

8.58 It will also be automatically unfair to select an agency worker for redundancy on the ground that the hirer or temporary work agency believes or suspects that the agency worker has done or intends to do any of the above – Reg 17(3)(b).

By their very nature the AW Regulations apply not just to agency workers who are employees but also to those who are workers. However, the right to claim automatically unfair dismissal under Reg 17(1) and the right to claim automatically unfair dismissal for being selected for redundancy under S.105(7N) ERA apply only to employees. Interestingly, S.105(7N) (unlike Reg 17(1)) does not actually specify that the *complainant* has to be an agency worker, leading to the possibility that an employee who is not an agency worker but stands up for the rights of an agency worker may claim automatic unfair dismissal if he or she is selected for redundancy on this basis, but not if he or she is simply dismissed (in which case he or she would have to establish that the employer's actions were unreasonable under S.98(4) in the usual way – see 'Unreasonable redundancy' below).

8.59 Collective labour laws

Recent years have seen the following legislation enacted to comply with European collective labour laws:

- the Transnational Information and Consultation of Employees Regulations 1999 SI 1999/3323

- the Information and Consultation of Employees Regulations 2004 SI 2004/3426

- the European Cooperative Society (Involvement of Employees) Regulations 2006 SI 2006/2059

- the Companies (Cross-border Mergers) Regulations 2007 SI 2007/2974

218

- the European Public Limited-Liability Company (Employee Involvement) (Great Britain) Regulations 2009 SI 2009/2401 (which replaced relevant provisions of the European Public Limited-Liability Company Regulations 2004 SI 2004/2326).

Each of these sets of Regulations envisages the election of employee representatives to sit on consultative bodies. In addition, they all provide protection from dismissal, both for employees sitting on such bodies and for employees exercising rights under the Regulations.

The various subsections of S.105 that relate to these Regulations operate to **8.60** extend the protection against dismissal found within the Regulations themselves to protection from selection for redundancy. The circumstances under which the Regulations render a dismissal unfair include:

- that the employee performed or proposed to perform the functions of a representative

- that the employee or a person acting on his behalf made or proposed to make a request to exercise an entitlement conferred on the employee by the Regulations

- that the employee voted in a ballot for representatives

- that the employee brought tribunal proceedings, or complained to the Central Arbitration Council or the EAT, in relation to rights conferred by the Regulations

- that the employee stood in an election for representatives

- that the employee sought to influence, by lawful means, an election held under the Regulations.

Family-friendly cases
8.61

The laws governing what is often referred to by the umbrella term 'family-friendly rights' include substantial protection against dismissal for a reason related to an employee taking his or her statutory entitlement to maternity leave, paternity leave, adoption leave, parental leave, or dependant care leave. The starting point is S.99 ERA, which provides that a dismissal will be automatically unfair if:

- the reason (or principal reason) for it is of a prescribed kind, or it takes place in prescribed circumstances, and

- the reason or circumstances relate to pregnancy, childbirth or maternity; ordinary, compulsory or additional maternity leave; ordinary or additional adoption leave; parental leave; ordinary or additional paternity leave; or dependant care leave (and may also relate to redundancy or other factors – S.99(3)).

8.62 'Prescribed' means prescribed by regulations and the relevant regulations for redundancy selection purposes are Reg 20(2) and (3) of the Maternity and Parental Leave etc. Regulations 1999 SI 1999/3312; Reg 29(2) and (3) of the Paternity and Adoption Leave Regulations 2002 SI 2002/2788 and Reg 34(2) and (3) of the Additional Paternity Leave Regulations 2010 SI 2010/1055. These provisions, which are all drafted in similar terms, effectively provide that it is automatically unfair to select an employee for redundancy for a reason connected with:

- the pregnancy of the employee

- the fact that the employee has given birth to a child (and the dismissal ends her maternity leave period)

- a relevant requirement or recommendation which gives rise to a maternity suspension within the meaning of S.66(2) ERA

- the fact that she or he took, sought to take or made use of the benefits of ordinary or additional maternity leave or additional paternity leave

- the fact that she or he failed to return after a period of ordinary or additional maternity leave, additional adoption leave or additional paternity leave where the employer did not notify her or him of the date on which the period in question would end and she or he reasonably believed that the period had not ended, or the employer gave her or him less than 28 days' notice of the date on which the period in question would end and it was not reasonably practicable for her or him to return on that date

- the fact that she or he considered undertaking, or refused to undertake, work on 'keep-in-touch' days during a period of maternity leave, adoption leave or additional paternity leave, within the meaning of Reg 12A MPL Regulations, Reg 21A PAL Regulations or Reg 26 APL Regulations

- the fact that she or he took or sought to take ordinary or additional adoption leave; ordinary paternity leave; parental leave; or time off to care for a dependant under S.57A ERA

- the fact that the employer believed that he or she was likely to take ordinary or additional adoption leave or additional paternity leave

- the fact that he or she declined to sign a workforce agreement for the purposes of the MPL Regulations, or

- the fact that the employee, being a representative of members of the workforce for the purposes of a workforce agreement on parental leave, or a candidate in an election in which any person elected will, on being elected, become such a representative, performed (or proposed to perform) any functions or activities as such a representative or candidate.

Suitable alternative employment. As is addressed in some detail in Chapter 3 **8.63** under 'Offers during maternity, adoption or parental leave', an employee who is made redundant while on maternity, adoption or additional paternity leave is entitled to be offered suitable alternative employment in preference to other employees – Reg 10 MPL Regulations, Reg 23 PAL Regulations, and Reg 28 APL Regulations. These subsections count as prescribing regulations for the purposes of S.99 ERA, meaning that a failure on the part of the employer to comply with these provisions will lead to a finding of automatically unfair dismissal.

Discrimination. Selection for redundancy or a failure to offer suitable **8.64** alternative work on the ground of an employee's maternity leave, etc may also give rise to a discrimination claim. See further Chapter 9 under 'Discriminatory selection – pregnancy and maternity leave'.

Selection for trade union reasons
8.65

Section 153 TULR(C)A deals with selection for redundancy on grounds related to trade union membership or activities. The section provides that it is automatically unfair to select an employee for redundancy for any of the reasons specified in S.152(1). Those reasons are that:

- the employee was, or proposed to become, a member of an independent trade union

- the employee had taken part, or proposed to take part, in the activities of an independent trade union at an appropriate time

- the employee had made use of, or proposed to make use of, trade union services at an appropriate time

- the employee had failed to accept an offer or inducement in relation to trade union membership or activities, or collective bargaining, made in contravention of the employee's rights under S.145A or S.145B TULR(C)A

- the employee was not a member of any trade union, or of a particular trade union, or of one of a number of particular trade unions, or had refused, or proposed to refuse, to become or remain a member.

An 'appropriate time' means a time outside the employee's working hours or within his or her working hours by arrangement with the employer – S.152(2).

Note that the minimum basic award of, currently, £5,000 applies in the case of a successful claim under S.153 – S.156 TULR(C)A.

An example of a successful claim under S.153:
8.66

- **Andrews v Chorley Borough Council** ET Case No.2412016/09: A worked for the Council, latterly as Markets Manager. He was a branch secretary of UNISON. As part of a restructure to effect cost savings the Council decided

221

to get rid of 17 posts, including A's, and replace them with fewer new posts. A was put into a pool with H, the Town Centre Manager. H was appointed to the new post of Town Centre and Markets Manager and A was given notice of redundancy. A appealed to a panel of local councillors, but the dismissing officer was not present and the tribunal found that the hearing was not sufficiently probing and rigorous. It held that A was unfairly dismissed because of his trade union activities. H was better fitted for the post of Town Centre and Markets Manager, but the Markets Coordinator post was still vacant and was not offered to A, and there had been no discussion with him of other suitable vacancies. A had caused problems for management, and the tribunal concluded on the balance of probabilities that the Council had decided that A should leave because of his trade union activities and had used the restructure to bring about that result. A was the only employee made compulsorily redundant.

8.67 Where employees spend a large proportion of their time on union activities, and a correspondingly small proportion on the work they are employed to do, they often score badly on the usual criteria applied for redundancy selection, such as quantity of work and work abilities. If employees are dismissed in these circumstances, it is often very difficult to determine the true reason for their selection. Was it the union activities or the work performance? It seems from the cases that where employers permit their officials to spend so much time on their union duties that their work suffers as a result, any selection of those officials for redundancy is likely to be automatically unfair. Two examples:

- **Dundon v GPT Ltd** 1995 IRLR 403, EAT: D, a union official, was employed as an accounts clerk in a large organisation. When he was appointed senior union representative, his employer gave him a less demanding job so that he could devote more time to his union duties. However, when it was found that D was spending most of his day on union matters, the employer agreed with him that he would spend only half the day on such duties. The arrangement soon lapsed and D went back to spending most of his day on union matters. A few years later, the employer needed to reduce its workforce and drew up selection criteria. It instructed its assessors that employees who were involved in union activities were to be assessed in the same way as other employees, with an allowance made for reasonable time off for union duties. D was selected for redundancy because his work output was so low and because of his bad timekeeping. A tribunal found that although D's union activities were relevant to his selection, they were not the main reason for it because the employer had not objected to those union activities. It held, therefore, that the dismissal was not automatically unfair under S.153. On appeal, the EAT overruled the tribunal on the ground that it had construed S.153 too narrowly: selection for trade union reasons included cases where there was no conscious or malicious selection on union grounds. In the EAT's view, D was selected for redundancy because he spent too much time on union activities – but he had carried out those activities at 'an appropriate time', since he had been given tacit permission to carry them out at the time he did. The EAT held that D had been automatically unfairly dismissed for trade union reasons

• **Robertson v Rolls Royce plc** ET Case No.321/94: R, who was employed as a fitter, was also a shop steward for the AEEU. He spent some 70 to 80 per cent of his time on trade union duties and he seemed to be free to engage in those activities at any time during his working shift. This affected his work in so far as he tended to be given the shorter and less complex jobs. When R asked for more complex work he was told that he would not be given it because there was no guarantee that he would be there to complete it. A redundancy situation arose and the employer was advised that it must not base its selection of employees on their union activities. R was made redundant and he complained that he had been selected for union reasons. A tribunal found that the employer had not carried out a reasonable assessment of R's abilities as he had been assessed according to the work he actually carried out rather than the work he was capable of doing. It held that the dismissal was unfair on this ground. Turning to S.153, the tribunal also concluded that R had been selected because he had engaged in trade union activities.

8.68 In Herbert v Air UK Engineering EAT 575/97, however, H, a workshop tradesman, spent three and a half hours a day on his shop steward duties. A redundancy situation arose in the workshop, with the result that either H or another employee would be made redundant. The employer adopted three selection criteria: qualifications, attendance record and length of service. H and the other employee scored equally on attendance and service but H was selected for redundancy because he was significantly outscored on qualifications. H argued unsuccessfully before a tribunal that his dismissal fell within S.153 because he had had no chance to gain the relevant qualifications because of the time spent on his trade union activities. The EAT upheld the tribunal's decision on appeal. Whereas in the Dundon case, above, the employee had been selected for redundancy because the employer felt he was spending too much time on his union activities, in the instant case the employee's dismissal was genuinely due to his lack of qualifications. The tribunal's finding that the employee did not gain the qualifications because of his union activities was not at all inconsistent with the finding that he was fairly dismissed because he lacked those qualifications. The EAT also rejected the argument that some sort of weighting factor should have been applied to the qualification criterion to allow for time spent on union activities. It might be possible to incorporate a weighting factor into a criterion based on employees' output, but it was not so easy to do so in the case of a qualification criterion. In any event, an employer must be entitled to regard qualifications for a skilled job as a high priority.

Important as trade union activities are, they could not be legitimately invoked to seek to compensate for lack of qualifications.

As discussed under 'Same undertaking and similar position' above, an employee claiming unfair selection for redundancy under S.153 must show that the redundancy situation applied equally to one or more employees who held positions similar to that held by the employee and who were not dismissed. 'Position' in relation to an employee is defined in S.235(1) ERA as meaning the following matters taken as a whole: his or her status as an employee, the nature of the work, and his or her terms and conditions of employment. Where an employee holds a unique position within an undertaking, a claim under this section is therefore unlikely to be successful. In such a case, the employee may have to rely for a remedy on the ordinary provisions for unfair dismissal.

8.69 In O'Dea v ISC Chemicals Ltd t/a Rhône-Poulenc Chemicals 1996 ICR 222, CA, O's contract specified that he was employed as a technical services operator (TSO), although for many years he had worked as a packaging operator to enable him to carry out his functions as the senior shop steward for the TGWU. By the time he was made redundant he was spending half his time on union activities. When the redundancy situation arose, O was encouraged to apply for other vacancies within the company but was told that he would be treated as an 'ordinary employee' for these purposes – i.e. he would only be considered for vacancies on the basis that, in future, he would not be involved in union activities. When he was dismissed, O claimed that he had been selected for redundancy on the ground of his union membership, contrary to S.153. A tribunal decided that the principal reason for O's dismissal was redundancy and not his union activities. Even if these activities had led to his being selected for redundancy, there was no other employee who held a position similar to his and who was retained in employment. The other TSOs who were retained did that job all the time and O was in a unique position vis-à-vis the other employees. Accordingly, an essential criterion of S.153 had not been made out. However, the tribunal did find the dismissal unfair on procedural grounds. O's appeal to the EAT was dismissed and he appealed to the Court of Appeal.

With regard to the definition of 'position', the Court of Appeal stated that, when comparing employees, consideration should only be given to the relative positions of the redundant employees and the trade union activities should be disregarded, even if the employee concerned had a contractual right to undertake such activities. If the time spent by a shop steward on union activities could put him or her in a position dissimilar to other employees, that would defeat the purpose of S.153, which is to protect employees carrying out such activities. Accordingly, it was an error of law for the tribunal to take account of O's union activities when considering whether his position was unique. However, the Court rejected O's argument that the tribunal should have ignored the fact that O was not actually working as a TSO to enable him to spend half his working day on union matters. The Court concluded that such an interpretation of 'position' was unacceptable because it would require a tribunal to ignore not only what O did as a shop steward but also what work he did as an employee, as well as the terms and conditions of employment. The tribunal should, therefore, have limited its consideration to O's status as a skilled manual worker, to the nature of his work as a packaging operator, and to his terms and conditions of employment as a TSO. On this basis, O had not shown that there were other employees who held similar positions to the one he held. His position was not comparable to that of the TSOs or even the packaging operators. Furthermore, the tribunal had not been satisfied that his selection for redundancy was for a trade union reason. O's appeal was dismissed.

It seems that S.153 is concerned only with dismissal of individual employees on account of what they have done or proposed to do. In Carrington and ors v Therm-A-Stor Ltd 1983 ICR 208, CA, redundancies were brought forward because the TGWU requested recognition and 'coincidentally' 20 union members were selected. S.153 was held to have no application because the reason for dismissal was the union's request for recognition, which had nothing to do with what individual employees had done or proposed to do. (Note, however, that such actions by an employer could be caught by the provisions on recognition – see below.) **8.70**

Although union activity is protected under S.153, industrial action is not. This means that employers, when selecting for redundancy, are allowed to take into account the fact that certain employees remained loyal during a strike while others did not – Cruickshank and ors v Hobbs 1977 ICR 725, EAT. In that case the EAT pointed out that selection on this basis might be particularly appropriate where the industrial action itself had 'caused or aggravated the redundancy'. The fairness of such dismissals would then depend on the issue of reasonableness. (Note, however, the limited protection available under S.105(7C) ERA for employees who take official industrial action – see 'Protected industrial action cases' above.)

Trade union dismissals are discussed in greater detail in IDS Employment Law Handbook, 'Trade Unions' (2000), Chapter 9.

Trade union recognition cases
8.71
The Employment Relations Act 1999 introduced statutory procedures for the recognition and derecognition of trade unions for collective bargaining. The provisions are contained in Schedule A1 to the TULR(C)A.

Among other things, these provide for protection from dismissal and selection for redundancy for reasons connected with trade union recognition. Para 162 of Schedule A1, read in conjunction with para 161(2), provides that it is automatically unfair to select an employee for redundancy for the sole or principal reason that the employee:

225

- acted with a view to obtaining or preventing recognition of a union (or unions) by the employer under the Schedule

- indicated that he or she supported or did not support recognition of a union (or unions) by the employer under the Schedule

- acted with a view to securing or preventing the ending of bargaining arrangements under the Schedule

- indicated that he or she supported or did not support the ending of bargaining arrangements under the Schedule

- influenced or sought to influence the way in which votes were to be cast by other workers in a ballot arranged under the Schedule

- influenced or sought to influence other workers to vote or to abstain from voting in such a ballot

- voted in such a ballot, or

- proposed to do, failed to do, or proposed to decline to do, any of the above.

However, the employee will not be protected if his or her act or omission was 'unreasonable' – S.161(3).

Trade union recognition is discussed in greater detail in IDS Employment Law Handbook, 'Trade Unions' (2000), Chapter 5.

8.72 Transfer of undertakings

Briefly, the Transfer of Undertakings (Protection of Employment) Regulations 2006 SI 2006/246 (TUPE) provide that where there is a 'relevant transfer' – for which, see IDS Employment Law Handbook, 'Transfer of Undertakings' (2011), Chapter 1 – the employment contracts of the employees employed in the undertaking are automatically transferred from the transferor to the transferee (Reg 4(1)), together with all the transferor's rights, powers, duties and liabilities in respect of such contracts (Reg 4(2)). As a result, on a relevant transfer, there is no *automatic* dismissal and no redundancy situation.

Where, however, there are express dismissals, Reg 7 provides that they will be automatically unfair where the reason for dismissal is the relevant transfer, or a reason connected with the transfer which is not an economic, technical or organisational (ETO) reason entailing changes in the workforce. If a dismissal is by reason of the transfer itself, there is no issue of the employer raising an ETO defence – the dismissal will be automatically unfair. All employees of both the transferor and the transferee are protected by this provision.

8.73 Where the reason for dismissal is an ETO reason, this only establishes that the dismissal was not automatically unfair – the reasonableness of the dismissal will still fall to be considered under S.98(4). In addition, Reg 7(3)(b) provides that, where there is an ETO reason, then the dismissal will be by reason of redundancy if S.98(2)(c) is satisfied (i.e. if the employee is redundant within the meaning of S.139 – see Chapter 2 of this Handbook). Otherwise, the dismissal will be potentially fair for 'some other substantial reason' within the meaning of S.98(1)(b).

Does redundancy constitute an ETO reason? Unfortunately, neither the **8.74** Regulations nor the EU Acquired Rights Directive (No.2001/23), which TUPE implements, provides an answer to the question of whether the classic redundancy situation involving a diminution in the requirement for employees can constitute an ETO reason. However, while the legislation does not offer a definition, there is a substantial body of case law on what amounts to an ETO reason (see IDS Employment Law Handbook, 'Transfer of Undertakings' (2011), Chapter 4, for more details).

If the transferee does not require the full complement of employees belonging to the transferor, the case law suggests that this would amount to an 'economic' or 'organisational' reason entailing changes in the workforce, so that Reg 7(1) would not apply to render the dismissals automatically unfair. Two examples:

- **Meikle v McPhail (Charleston Arms)** 1983 IRLR 351, EAT: McP took over the pub where M worked. M continued to be employed for a short time after the transfer but then McP realised that he had over-committed himself and M was therefore dismissed. The EAT accepted that the reason was an 'economic' one under what is now Reg 7(2), and went on to judge the dismissal fair under the ordinary reasonableness test set out in S.98(4)

- **Trafford v Sharpe and Fisher (Building Supplies) Ltd** 1994 IRLR 325, EAT: SF Ltd took over the builders supply merchants where T worked as an estimator. He also ran a department on how to adapt equipment for use by the disabled. SF Ltd soon realised that the business it had bought was substantially overstaffed and that it had to reduce the workforce in order to make the business viable. It did not want either an estimating service or a disabled equipment advisory service and T was made redundant. The EAT accepted that the employer had shown an 'economic, technical or organisational reason' for the dismissal. However, it upheld the finding that T had been unfairly dismissed under S.98(4) (for which, see 'Unreasonable redundancy' below) for lack of proper warning and consultation.

It is difficult to find any objection to the decisions in the above cases, which **8.75** both involved genuine redundancy situations. But the decision of the House of Lords in Litster and ors v Forth Dry Dock and Engineering Co Ltd (in receivership) and anor 1989 ICR 341, HL, demands that any dismissal occurring prior to the transfer be made on genuine ETO grounds. If there is any suggestion that they are part of a collusive bargain made between the transferee

227

and the transferor, then the pre-transfer dismissals will most likely be rendered automatically unfair by virtue of Reg 7(1).

In this context, it is also worth noting that a transferor employer cannot rely on the ETO reason of the transferee in order to carry out pre-transfer dismissals. In Hynd v Armstrong and ors 2007 IRLR 338, Ct Sess (Inner House), H, a corporate lawyer, was employed by Morison Bishop, a law firm with offices in Edinburgh and Glasgow, in its Glasgow office. The partners in the firm decided to dissolve the partnership with effect from 31 July 2002, with the intention of forming two new firms: an Edinburgh-based firm called Morisons and a Glasgow-based firm called Bishops. Since Bishops was to concentrate on property law and litigation, the Glasgow partners of Morison Bishop anticipated a reduced requirement for corporate lawyers. Acting with the authority of the other partners in the firm, they made H redundant on 31 July 2002 – the date on which the partnership dissolved. H claimed that his dismissal was automatically unfair under what is now Reg 7(1). The tribunal and the EAT held that Reg 7(1) did not apply, since B's reduced demand for corporate lawyers was an ETO reason. On appeal, the Court of Session examined the Acquired Rights Directive and held that the ETO defence has to be limited to dismissals for reasons which entail changes in the transferor's own workforce. H's appeal was therefore allowed.

8.76 Even if, as appears to be the case, genuine redundancies can constitute an ETO reason, it is nevertheless arguable that not all redundancies will invariably fall within Reg 7(2). This is because, for the reason for dismissal to constitute an ETO reason, the economic or organisational reason must 'entail' changes in the workforce. This equates with a requirement to show that the particular dismissal was 'necessary' at the time it was made. It is therefore open to tribunals to go behind the contention that there has been a diminution in the requirements of the business and ask themselves whether, in the circumstances, the dismissals achieved a proper commercial aim and whether the veracity of the employer's explanation for the need to reduce the numbers of the workforce has been undermined by subsequent events – see Swinnock v Grosvenor of Chester (Automotives) Ltd t/a Grosvenor Mazda (in liquidation) and ors EAT 189/93.

This contrasts with the position of redundancies in an ordinary context under S.139 ERA where tribunals are enjoined *not* to look behind the fact of the redundancy situation to question how this has arisen and whether other options apart from dismissal were viable – Moon and ors v Homeworthy Furniture (Northern) Ltd 1977 ICR 117, EAT. See further Chapter 2 under 'Reason for dismissal'.

8.77 Once the employer has surmounted the hurdle of showing an ETO reason for dismissal, the tribunal must decide whether in the circumstances (having regard to equity and the substantial merits of the case as well as the size and administrative resources of the business) the employer acted reasonably in treating the ETO reason as a sufficient reason for dismissal – S.98(4). Failure by a tribunal to take this step – by presuming that an ETO reason is sufficient by itself for concluding that the dismissal is fair – would be an error of law – McGrath v Rank Leisure Ltd 1985 ICR 527, EAT. The reasonableness test is applied in the usual way – see 'Unreasonable redundancy' below.

Breach of statutory dismissal procedures   8.78

Prior to their abolition in April 2009, employers wishing to make redundancy dismissals were required to follow the statutory dismissal and disciplinary procedures (DDPs) contained in the Employment Act 2002. A failure by an employer to follow a relevant DDP rendered the dismissal automatically unfair by virtue of S.98A(1) ERA and could lead to an increase in the compensatory award of up to 50 per cent. Conversely, where the non-completion of the DDP was attributable to the fault of the employee, compensation could be reduced by up to 50 per cent.

The DDPs, together with S.98A(1), were repealed on 6 April 2009. However, they continue to apply to disputes that arose prior to that date but are awaiting a tribunal hearing, as well as those that started before 6 April 2009 but continued after that date – see IDS Employment Law Supplement, 'Statutory Disciplinary and Grievance Procedures' (2009) for full details.

Unreasonable redundancy   8.79

Even if not automatically unfair, a redundancy dismissal may still be unreasonable (and therefore unfair) under the general unfair dismissal provisions contained in S.98(4) ERA. This states that 'the determination of the question whether the dismissal is fair or unfair (having regard to the reason shown by the employer) – (a) depends on whether in the circumstances (including the size and administrative resources of the employer's undertaking) the employer acted reasonably or unreasonably in treating it as a sufficient reason for dismissing the employee, and (b) shall be determined in accordance with equity and the substantial merits of the case'.

A dismissed employee may complain, for example, that he or she was unfairly selected for redundancy; that it was unreasonable for the employer to have dismissed him or her for redundancy where alternative work was available; or that the employer's redundancy procedure was defective – perhaps owing to a failure to consult.

In Williams and ors v Compair Maxam Ltd 1982 ICR 156, EAT, the Appeal 8.80 Tribunal laid down guidelines that a reasonable employer might be expected to follow in making redundancy dismissals. The EAT stressed, however, that in determining the question of reasonableness it was not for the tribunal to impose

229

its standards and decide whether the employer should have behaved differently. Instead it had to ask whether 'the dismissal lay within the range of conduct which a reasonable employer could have adopted'.

The factors suggested by the EAT in the Compair Maxam case that a reasonable employer might be expected to consider were:

- whether the selection criteria were objectively chosen and fairly applied
- whether employees were warned and consulted about the redundancy
- whether, if there was a union, the union's view was sought
- whether any alternative work was available.

8.81   In this section, we start by looking at the rules pertaining to procedural fairness in redundancy dismissals. We then look in detail at the issues a tribunal will consider when assessing the reasonableness or otherwise of a redundancy dismissal, including the unit to which any selection criteria were applied – usually referred to as the 'pool for selection'; the selection criteria themselves; the manner in which the criteria were applied; and the manner in which the redundancy dismissals were implemented.

8.82   **Procedural fairness and the ruling in 'Polkey'**
The House of Lords' ruling in Polkey v AE Dayton Services Ltd 1988 ICR 142, HL, substantially changed the law of unfair dismissal, its main impact being to firmly establish procedural fairness as an integral part of the reasonableness test now found in S.98(4) ERA. Their Lordships decided that a failure to follow correct procedures was likely to make an ensuing dismissal unfair unless, in exceptional cases, the employer could reasonably have concluded that doing so would have been 'utterly useless' or 'futile'. With regard to redundancy dismissals, this meant, in the words of Lord Bridge, that 'the employer will not normally act reasonably unless he warns and consults any employees affected or their representative, adopts a fair basis on which to select for redundancy and takes such steps as may be reasonable to avoid or minimise redundancy by deployment within his own organisation'.

The issue of procedural fairness in unfair dismissal cases was overhauled – temporarily – in 2004 with the advent of the statutory dismissal and disciplinary procedures (DDPs), which were contained in the Employment Act 2002. In terms of redundancy, two main changes were brought about by the statutory procedure regime. First, as we saw under 'Automatically unfair dismissal – breach of statutory dismissal procedures' above, procedural failures that infringed the minimum standards required by the DDPs led to a finding of automatically unfair dismissal under S.98A(1) ERA. Secondly – and more importantly for the purposes of 'ordinary' (as opposed to 'automatic') unfair dismissal – S.98A(2) stated that a failure by an employer to follow a procedure

230

other than an applicable statutory procedure in relation to the dismissal would not be regarded as by itself making the dismissal unfair if the employer could show, on the balance of probabilities, that it would have decided to dismiss the employee had that procedure been followed.

8.83 The effect of S.98A(2) was a 'Polkey reversal'. In other words, whenever a tribunal was minded to find that a dismissal was unfair for (non-statutory) procedural reasons alone, it was open to the employer to show that compliance with a fair procedure would, on the balance of probabilities, have made no difference. Sometimes it would simply not be possible for a tribunal to form a view of what might have been, in which case the employer would not have proved its case. But where the employer could satisfy the burden placed on it, and the procedural defects did not infringe the statutory dismissal procedures, the dismissal would be fair.

However, in April 2009 the statutory dispute resolution procedures, along with S.98A, were repealed in their entirety by the Employment Act 2008. As a result, the issue of procedural fairness in unfair dismissal cases is once more governed by Polkey. Thus, an employer cannot avoid a finding of unfair dismissal simply by arguing that 'although our procedure was defective, we would have dismissed him/her anyway'. Rather, a procedural failure renders a redundancy dismissal unfair under S.98(4), and the question of whether the employee would have been dismissed even if a fair procedure had been followed will be relevant only to the amount of compensation payable – see IDS Employment Law Handbook, 'Unfair Dismissal' (2010), Chapter 18, under 'Polkey reductions'. For example, in Arhin v Enfield Primary Care Trust 2010 EWCA Civ 1481, CA, the Court of Appeal upheld a tribunal's decision that, while the employee had been unfairly dismissed for redundancy as a result of being left out of a pool for competitive selection, she was not entitled to reinstatement, re-engagement or a compensatory award. Even if a competitive selection procedure had taken place, she had no chance of being retained or employed.

8.84 Note that when the statutory procedures were repealed, they were replaced by a revised Acas 'Code of Practice on Discipline and Grievance'. The Code's provisions are taken into account by tribunals in determining the procedural fairness of most dismissals and an unreasonable failure to observe the Code's requirements may lead to an increase (or reduction) in compensation. However, the Code does not apply to redundancies. Thus, for redundancies, the guiding principles of procedural fairness are those that applied pre-2004.

Contractually agreed procedures
8.85 Prior to its repeal in 1994, S.59(1)(b) of the Employment Protection (Consolidation) Act 1978 made redundancy dismissals in contravention of a customary arrangement or an agreed procedure automatically unfair. Today, if an employee is selected for redundancy in breach of a customary arrangement

231

or agreed procedure, a tribunal must determine whether that selection was fair or otherwise under the general reasonableness test set out in S.98(4) ERA.

Although an employer does not have to show that there were special reasons for departing from a customary arrangement or agreed procedure, in order to avoid an unfair dismissal finding it must show that it was reasonable for it to have done so. Thus, while there is no longer anything on the statute book that gives agreed procedures and customary arrangements a special protected status, an employer cannot simply ignore them.

8.86 Furthermore, where it can be shown that an agreed redundancy procedure was incorporated into an employee's contract of employment, a departure from that procedure may give rise to an action for wrongful dismissal based on the employer's breach of contract. The incorporation of collective agreements into contracts of employment is discussed in IDS Employment Law Handbook, 'Contracts of Employment' (2009), Chapter 2, under 'Incorporated terms'. Suffice it to say here that where an agreed procedure has been incorporated into the employee's contract and the employer dismisses in breach of that procedure, the normal remedy will be an award of damages for wrongful dismissal. However, in exceptional circumstances, the courts may be prepared to grant an interlocutory (temporary) injunction (called an interim interdict in Scotland) to restrain the breach pending a full trial of the issue – i.e. to prevent the employer dismissing in contravention of the agreed procedure until the case has come to court. Injunctions are subject to a number of principles. In particular, the courts will not normally order the continued employment of an individual in whom the employer no longer has trust and confidence.

In the following two cases employees were selected for redundancy in contravention of an agreed redundancy procedure and sought injunctions to restrain their dismissals until the case could come to trial. In each case the employers had departed from the LIFO ('last in, first out') criterion because they wanted to use additional criteria (see 'Selection criteria' below for discussion as to the lawfulness of LIFO as a criterion for selection). The crucial question for the courts was whether the employers had sufficient confidence in the abilities of the employees to do their jobs to delay dismissal until the issue could be fully tried. The courts came to different conclusions:

● **Alexander and ors v Standard Telephones and Cables plc** 1990 ICR 291, ChD: the High Court refused to grant an injunction. Although the employees to be made redundant were not untrustworthy or incompetent, in the employer's view they were less able to carry out their work than those employees to be retained. This meant that the employer did not have complete confidence in the employees selected. The Court also found that the relationship of employer and employee had in fact broken down in that the employer believed that it did not have any work for the selected employees to do

- **Anderson v Pringle of Scotland Ltd** 1998 IRLR 64, Ct Sess (Outer House): the Court of Session took a different view and granted A the injunction sought. The Court stated that it did not follow that, because the employer preferred to retain other employees, it no longer had trust and confidence in A. The position would have been different, however, if there had been any question of mistrust. The Court concluded that the balance of convenience favoured the preservation of the status quo.

While both courts accepted that an injunction could only be granted in circumstances where trust and confidence has not broken down, they took different views as to what inferences should be drawn from the fact that an employee has been selected for redundancy in the first place. It is easy to see the force in both arguments. Once employees have been assessed according to particular criteria, there is some substance to the view that the employer would have less confidence in those employees who scored lower than in those who scored higher. On the other hand, there is clearly strength in the Court of Session's argument that selection for redundancy does not mean that the employment relationship has necessarily broken down. The work performance of an employee who has been selected for redundancy is unlikely to be so unacceptable that it would destroy the confidence the employer had in the employee, otherwise the employer would have considered dismissal on other grounds. **8.87**

Voluntary redundancies **8.88**

An employer will not necessarily be acting unreasonably if it does not invite volunteers before making compulsory redundancies. In Lintin v Imagelinx UK Ltd ET Case No.2603643/08, for example, a tribunal found that an employer had acted within the range of reasonable responses in discounting making voluntary redundancies on efficiency grounds, given that it had kept an open mind during the consultation process.

Pool for selection **8.89**

In carrying out a redundancy exercise, an employer should begin by identifying the group of employees from which those who are to be made redundant will be drawn. This is the 'pool for selection' and it is to these employees that an employer will apply the chosen selection criteria to determine who will be made redundant. In assessing the fairness of dismissals, tribunals will first look to the pool from which the selection was made, since the application of otherwise fair selection criteria to the wrong group of employees is likely to result in an unfair dismissal. If an employer simply dismisses an employee without first considering the question of a pool, the dismissal is likely to be unfair – Taymech Ltd v Ryan EAT 663/94.

Of course, there will be some redundancy situations where, because of the complete closure of the workplace, business or unit, selection as such will not be necessary. For example, in Zeff v Lewis Day Transport plc EAT 0418/10 the EAT upheld a tribunal's finding that there was no question of selection, and thus no need for selection criteria to be applied, where the employer closed down its chauffeur desk. The manager and two controllers on the chauffeur desk were made redundant; two administrators who had previously been assigned to the chauffeur desk were moved to the car desk and continued the same jobs as before. Similarly, in Kirby v North Midland Construction plc ET Case No.2602999/08 a tribunal dismissed a claim by a construction engineer who was manager of the rail department that he had been unfairly selected for redundancy because he should have been put into a pool with four other managers, whose jobs he could do. The tribunal considered that the employer had not acted unreasonably in concluding that there were real differences between K's job and those of the other managers, and that as the whole of K's department was being closed it had good reasons for dealing with him separately.

8.90 **Range of pools available.** Where there is a customary arrangement or agreed procedure that specifies a particular selection pool, the employer will normally be expected to adhere to it unless the employer can show that it was reasonable to depart from it – Russell v London Borough of Haringey, Court of Appeal, 12.6.00. Where there is no customary arrangement or agreed procedure to be considered, employers have a good deal of flexibility in defining the pool from which they will select employees for dismissal – Thomas and Betts Manufacturing Ltd v Harding 1980 IRLR 255, CA. They need only show that they have applied their minds to the problem and acted from genuine motives. For example, sometimes it may be to an employer's advantage to draw the pool for selection as widely as possible. This will give it the flexibility to select less capable staff across a range of departments or job categories instead of losing valued employees from a more narrowly defined group. In other situations, it may be appropriate to draw the pool more narrowly. In Gilleard v Lupton Fawcett LLP ET Case No.1812129/09, for example, a solicitor's firm employed associate solicitors and assistant solicitors, the associate solicitors being more highly paid than the assistants. G was an associate solicitor. The firm decided to make redundancies among the associate solicitors since it was the more complex work that was drying up. The firm began consultations with the associate solicitors with a view to making them all redundant. They proposed taking a pay cut so that they would be no more expensive than the assistant solicitors, thus enabling the cuts to be made across both categories, but the firm said that the selection of the associates was on the basis of the nature of the available work. G and the other associates were dismissed as redundant, and a tribunal dismissed G's unfair dismissal claim. The firm had sound business reasons for making the selection in this way. Associate solicitors would at some point get frustrated with the low level of the work available; and if there were no assistant solicitors being trained up there would be no employees ready to be promoted to associate solicitors if the market picked up. Further, the loss of skills and experience involved in dismissing associate solicitors was not of concern since there was under-capacity among the firm's directors who did have those skills and experience.

However, in all cases, the tribunal must be satisfied that the employer acted **8.91** reasonably and, in considering whether this was so, the following factors may be relevant:

- whether other groups of employees are doing similar work to the group from which selections were made

- whether employees' jobs are interchangeable

- whether the employee's inclusion in the unit is consistent with his or her previous position

- whether the selection unit was agreed with any union.

A tribunal will judge the employer's choice of pool by asking itself whether it **8.92** fell within the range of reasonable responses available to an employer in the circumstances. As the EAT put it in Kvaerner Oil and Gas Ltd v Parker and ors EAT 0444/02, 'different people can quite legitimately have different views about what is or is not a fair response to a particular situation... In most situations there will be a band of potential responses to the particular problem and it may be that both of solutions X and Y will be well within that band.' This does not mean, however, that tribunals will uncritically accept an employer's reasoning for drawing the pool for selection in a particular way. Three examples:

- **Kvaerner Oil and Gas Ltd v Parker and ors** (above): the EAT upheld a tribunal's decision that an employer's pool for selection fell outside the range of reasonable responses. As a result of an internal reorganisation, KOG was split into two separate business units with their own management and budget structures. Both business units operated from the same site, and, in the months leading up to the claimants' redundancies, undertook mostly the same work. When redundancies became necessary, KOG confined the pool for selection to a single business unit. Four of the workers who were made redundant challenged this decision, claiming that KOG had artificially restricted the pool in order to get rid of employees who were on more expensive terms. The tribunal noted that the two business units were separately accounted for and managed. But it concluded that the claimants 'did not appreciate these organisation distinctions', as, so far as they were concerned, they were working in the same location doing very similar work. The EAT upheld the tribunal's decision that both business units should have been identified as the applicable pool. KOG had adopted too narrow an approach in giving undue weight to the different financial and management

235

structures of the two business units. A reasonable employer would have adopted a wider approach and would have brought into consideration other factors, such as, in particular, the interchangeableness of the work between the two units

- **Hendy Banks City Print Ltd v Fairbrother and ors** EAT 0691/04: the claimants worked for a printing company in its 'finishing' department. Their work involved many tasks, one of which was the use of a perfect-binding machine for which they had been specifically trained. In 2002, as a step in the implementation of a redundancy programme, the employer chose a pool comprising only those who worked on the perfect-binding machine. A tribunal ruled that the pool had been defined too narrowly, given that (i) the claimants were the most experienced workers and they undertook all aspects of finishing work; and (ii) they spent no more than one third of their time on the machine, with the other two thirds being spent doing the same work as other members of the finishing department. On appeal, the EAT rejected the employer's contention that the tribunal had wrongly substituted its view of the correct pool for that of the employer. The EAT accepted that the reasons given by the tribunal for coming to the conclusion that the selected pool was not a reasonable one were perfectly sound

- **Davies v JCB Transmission** ET Case No.2901458/08: JCB employed a number of workers on a contract which stated that they were on a temporary appointment of uncertain duration; that they were employed to cover peaks in demand; and that the contract would expire when demand reduced. By 2008 the company suffered a downturn in demand and decided to implement redundancies. It put all employees, permanent and those on the temporary contracts, into one pool for selection. However, a tribunal found that it was unreasonable to include the fixed-term employees in the same pool for selection as permanent employees. The fixed-term contracts were determinable upon the occurrence of a specific event – a downturn in demand – and JCB would not have faced a successful claim of treating the fixed-term employees less favourably by terminating their contracts because demand had reduced.

8.93 **Same work.** An employer will need to have justifiable reasons for excluding a particular group of employees from the selection pool where those in the excluded category do the same, or similar, work to those who are up for selection. Two examples:

- **British Steel plc (Seamless Tubes) v Robertson and ors** EAT 601/94: the employer excluded a group of craftsmen, described as 'multi-skilled', who had recently been trained in all the various skills required by the company but who had short service. Redundancies were actually made from a pool of long-serving mechanical maintenance engineers and electrical engineers on the basis of 'last in, first out'. The tribunal decided that the multi-skilled craftsmen should have been included in the pool for selection as they could undertake the work of those in the selected pool. The tribunal said that it could be fair in certain circumstances to exempt a group of craftsmen from redundancies, but in the present case it was unreasonable for the employer to have done so given that both groups did similar work. The EAT upheld this finding

- **Holland v C and G Concrete Ltd** ET Case No.2600735/09: H was employed as a concrete mixer driver and he delivered concrete four days a week and mortar one day a week. Another driver, X, was originally classed as a mortar mixer driver, but for the two years prior to his dismissal he had been a concrete mixer driver four days a week and a mortar mixer driver for only one day a week. Due to the effect of the recession on the construction industry, the company decided to make one mortar mixer driver and one concrete mixer driver redundant from the site where H and X worked. The company treated the two categories of driver as two separate pools. H was identified as the lowest scoring driver in the concrete mixer group and X was the lowest scoring driver in the mortar mixer group. Both were made redundant. A tribunal found that H had been unfairly dismissed. It considered it manifestly unfair to H for the employer to put X in the mortar mixer pool rather than the concrete mixer pool. If he had been properly allocated the concrete mixer pool, he would have scored lower than H, who would thus not have been selected for redundancy.

8.94 It may be unreasonable to exclude a group of employees doing similar work from the selection pool even where the employees in the pool would have to undertake some training before carrying out the work done by the excluded employees. In Thornley v JCT600 Ltd ET Case No.1800944/10 T was one of seven technicians employed by JCT600 Ltd in its specialist workshop. Five of the technicians, including T, worked on Ferrari and Maserati vehicles and two worked on Lotus vehicles. In October 2009 JCT600 Ltd decided to reduce the number of technicians by one and T was selected from among the five technicians working on Ferrari and Maserati cars. A tribunal held that he had been unfairly dismissed. JCT600 Ltd had acted unreasonably in excluding from the pool the two technicians working on Lotus cars. In a previous redundancy exercise the pool had consisted of all the technicians. There was no consideration at any stage of transferring one of the technicians working on Maserati and Ferrari cars to Lotus in the event that a Lotus technician was selected for redundancy, yet this would have only required ten days' training. In fact, all technicians worked on all of the cars from time to time. (Note that this case is also discussed under 'Mobility clauses' below.)

8.95 **Interchangeable jobs.** A fair pool for selection is not necessarily limited to those employees doing the same or similar work. Employers may be expected to include in the pool those employees whose work is interchangeable. In

237

Blundell Permoglaze Ltd v O'Hagen EAT 540/84, for example, a tribunal found a dismissal unfair because the pool from which the selection was made was unreasonably restricted. BP Ltd employed six employees in their warehouse, three of whom were drivers and three of whom were warehousemen. The drivers could perform the warehousemen's jobs but the reverse was not true. BP Ltd decided to get rid of one lorry and one employee. After unsuccessfully seeking a volunteer for redundancy from all six staff, it applied a LIFO test among the drivers alone. Had the test been applied to all six workers, O'H would not have been dismissed. The tribunal found the choice of pool for the selection unreasonable as the drivers could have, and had in the past, performed warehouse work, and the employer had originally sought a volunteer for redundancy among all six men. (The tribunal accepted that had the redundancy been needed from among the warehousemen, it would have been wrong to have included the drivers in the pool, since the warehousemen could not do the drivers' jobs.) Similarly, in Wright v Bluesky International Ltd ET Case No.1901774/09 W worked for BI Ltd as a marketing communication executive. In October 2008 she was promoted to the role of marketing manager, but was made redundant in May 2009 as BI Ltd considered that much of her role had disappeared because of budget cuts. A tribunal upheld her claim of unfair dismissal. BI Ltd acted unreasonably in simply identifying W's role as potentially redundant: her job was substantially interchangeable with that of the web marketing executive and should have been put in a wider pool covering the marketing department, to include that post.

However, in Lomond Motors Ltd v Clark EAT 0019/09 the EAT overturned a tribunal's decision that the pool should have included an extra person, on the ground that her role was not properly interchangeable with the others. C worked as a branch accountant for a car dealer. The dealer operated from two sites, one in Glasgow and one in Ayr. In 2006 it acquired two further sites, one in Edinburgh and one in Stirling, which were served by another branch accountant, G. G was given responsibility for the Edinburgh site, C was transferred to work at the Stirling site, and another employee became branch accountant for Glasgow and Ayr. By the end of 2007 it was decided that a single employee should cover both the Edinburgh and Stirling sites. C was selected for redundancy from a pool consisting of C and G, but not the branch accountant for Glasgow and Ayr. A tribunal found that the employer's determination of the pool was not reasonable, on the basis that it should have included the branch accountant for Glasgow and Ayr. However, the EAT disagreed, noting that the tribunal had found as a fact that that accountant did not have the requisite experience to cover the Stirling site and the jobs were therefore not properly interchangeable. While the pool might have included all three, the employer did not act unreasonably in deciding to have a pool of two.

8.96 **'Bumping'.** Job losses confined to one team can result in the dismissal of skilled and experienced staff who are of greater long-term value to the organisation than other individuals whose posts are not directly affected. One way round this problem is to define the pool for selection broadly so as to encompass a number of different teams or job titles. The lawfulness of such a course of action was confirmed by the House of Lords in Murray and anor v Foyle Meats Ltd 1999 ICR 827, HL (discussed in Chapter 2 under 'Diminishing need for employees'). In that case, their Lordships confirmed that there is no reason why a dismissal of an employee cannot be regarded as being 'attributable' to a diminution in the employer's need for employees to do work of a particular kind within the meaning of S.139 ERA (definition of redundancy), irrespective of the terms of the particular employee's contract or the function that he or she performs. This potentially allows so-called 'bumping' dismissals, whereby an employee, X, whose job is redundant, is redeployed to another job and the employee in that job, Y, is the one who is actually dismissed. Although Y's job may not be redundant, his or her dismissal is clearly attributable to redundancy in that it has been brought about by the diminished need for work of a particular kind, namely the work previously done by X.

The question arises whether bumping is merely an option available to an employer when determining how to define the appropriate pool or whether, to ensure fairness, the employer is obliged to consider bumping. Many of the cases on the subject turn on the issue of seniority. In Dial-a-Phone and anor v Butt EAT 0286/03 the EAT approved a finding that the employer should have considered the possibility of bumping a more junior employee. In that case, the EAT rejected the idea that it is always necessary for a senior employee to tell the employer that he or she is willing to accept a more junior role or a pay cut before the employer is obliged to consider the possibility.

8.97 In Lionel Leventhal Ltd v North EAT 0265/04 the EAT gave more detailed guidance on the circumstances in which an employer should consider bumping. A senior editor was selected for redundancy because he was the company's most expensive employee. A tribunal found his dismissal unfair, partly on the basis that the employer should have considered making a more junior employee redundant and offering his or her job to the claimant rather than merely assuming that the claimant would be unwilling to accept the resulting drop in salary. On appeal, the EAT was referred to case law, including the Court of Appeal's decision in Thomas and Betts Manufacturing Ltd v Harding 1980 IRLR 255, CA, which established that it can be unfair for an employer to fail to consider offering alternative employment to a potentially redundant employee, even in the absence of a vacancy. In the view of the EAT in Leventhal, whether or not such a failure is unfair is a question of fact for the tribunal, which should consider matters such as:

- whether or not there is a vacancy
- how different the two jobs are

239

- the difference in remuneration between them

- the relative length of service of the two employees

- the qualifications of the employee in danger of redundancy.

The EAT accepted that the tribunal had been entitled, on the facts, to hold that the employer's failure to take the initiative in considering the above matters rendered the claimant's dismissal unfair.

8.98 The factors set out in Leventhal were referred to with approval by another division of the EAT in Fulcrum Pharma (Europe) Ltd v Bonassera and anor EAT 0198/10. There B was recruited in January 2006 as a Human Resources Executive/Office Manager with responsibility for all HR matters and for managing a team of administrative staff. After a year, as a result of rapid growth in the business, B had given up her supervisory duties and become HR Manager. By mid-2008, C had joined as HR Executive, in a supporting role to B. In 2009, however, FP Ltd decided to reduce its HR function to one executive role, which was the role being carried out by C, intending to use an external consultancy for more complex HR issues. B was advised that her role was at risk of redundancy. B argued that both she and C should have been put at risk, and that C should have been made redundant because B had more experience and had performed both roles. FP Ltd maintained that C's role was not directly affected as it intended to continue to operate with an HR executive role. B was dismissed, and brought a claim for unfair dismissal. The tribunal, in holding that B had been unfairly dismissed, considered that as the human resources function was being reduced from two to one, the pool for selection should have been two, namely B and C.

FP Ltd appealed to the EAT, which agreed with the tribunal that FP Ltd had been wrong to conclude, without any further or meaningful consultation as to the size of the pool, that the pool was one person simply because it was the manager's role that had to go. However, the tribunal had erred in finding that the pool should necessarily have consisted of two employees without any further analysis. The facts that B had previously carried out C's role, and that C had 'acted up' during B's sick leave, were not by themselves sufficient to determine that both B and C should be in the pool. The tribunal should have considered the approach taken in the case authorities, such as the Leventhal case.

8.99 But it would be wrong to conclude on the basis of Leventhal that an employer *must* consider bumping to avoid a finding of unfair dismissal. Indeed, in another decision the EAT held that a tribunal had correctly concluded that a dismissal was not rendered unfair by an employer's failure to consider dismissing a well-established junior employee in order to retain a more highly experienced senior employee – Byrne v Arvin Meritor LVS (UK) Ltd EAT 239/02. These cases suggest that the duty to act reasonably does not impose an absolute obligation to consider bumping as an option but that, in particular circumstances, the failure to do so may fall outside the band of reasonable responses.

Previous experience in the role. In Fulcrum Pharma (Europe) Ltd v Bonassera **8.100** and anor (above) the EAT noted that the fact that the claimant had previously carried out a more junior role did not, by itself, determine that both roles should be included in the pool for selection. However, in Martin v Pepperl and Fuchs Ltd ET Case No.2410568/09 a tribunal considered that because M, a UK Sales Manager, had in the past done the role of Project Sales Manager, both roles should have been included in the pool. Evidence that a senior employee has previous experience in a more junior position may be relevant to whether or not 'bumping' should be considered, but this is a matter for the tribunal to decide on the facts of the case.

Multi-site redundancies. Difficulties can arise where a business is spread over **8.101** a number of different sites. Should the employer treat employees working at different sites as separate groups for the purpose of redundancy selection? Or should the sites be lumped together?

As noted above under 'Range of pools available', employers are allowed a certain degree of flexibility in determining the pool for selection. As a result, the make-up of the selection pool or pools in multi-site redundancy situations will vary, and much will depend upon the particular employer's business needs.

Take, for example, a nationwide employer with ten sites throughout the **8.102** country. In addition to other staff, it employs 10–20 sales staff at each site (150 in all). The employer proposes to make 50 of the sales staff redundant nationwide. Its preference is to treat each site as an entity in itself, so that a number of redundancies are made out of the pool of sales staff at each particular site. This approach may be entirely reasonable. The employer may have good business reasons for treating each site separately – perhaps it wants to avoid closing any sites, but needs to retain some sales staff at each site for it to function properly.

But it will all depend on the facts. In Highland Fish Farmers Ltd v Thorburn and anor EAT 1094/94, for example, the EAT upheld a tribunal's decision that an employer was acting unreasonably by treating employees working at different sites as separate groups for the purpose of redundancy selection. The employer in question needed to make eight employees redundant out of its total workforce of about 50, which was spread over a number of different fish-farming sites in North Scotland. It decided to dismiss all three employees at the Torridon site, closing it down completely, and selected the other five from various other sites. Two of these were from the Aird site, which was only 40 minutes away from Torridon and shared some facilities with the business there. A majority of the tribunal decided that the pool of selection was unfair as it was not open to a reasonable employer to consider the Torridon and Aird sites in isolation. The EAT refused to interfere with the finding as it was a question of fact for the tribunal.

8.103 In different circumstances, however, it may be reasonable for the employer to concentrate its selection upon a single site. In Clews and ors v Liverpool City Council EAT 463/93 the Council operated two security forces, the Static Force and the Mobile Force. It made several attempts to amalgamate the two but these were resisted by the relevant trade unions. When the decision to make all nine supervisors in the Static Force redundant became known, the plan caused a great deal of industrial unrest, leading to a three-day strike and wide-scale picketing. The tribunal rejected the employees' contention that the pool for selection should have comprised both forces. It decided that it would have been unreasonable to combine them for the purposes of a selection pool given the animosity between the two forces, which had deliberately been kept separate against the wishes of the employer, and the fact that the training of the Mobile supervisors was different from that of the Static supervisors. The EAT upheld this decision.

8.104 *Mobility clauses.* It could be argued that the existence of a mobility clause in an employee's contract of employment means that he or she could, or should, be included in a selection pool established in respect of a redundancy situation arising at a site to which he or she could be transferred; or, conversely, that he or she should be transferred out of a redundancy selection pool in reliance on such a clause. This argument was canvassed before the EAT in Lomond Motors Ltd v Clark EAT 0019/09 (see '"Bumping"' above). However, the EAT thought that there was 'considerable force' in the submission that mobility clauses are *not* relevant to an assessment of whether or not an employer has acted within the band of reasonableness in selecting the pool. As discussed in Chapter 2 under 'Closure of workplace – place of employment', a redundancy at the place where an employee in fact works is not rendered less genuine by the existence of a mobility clause which would have allowed the employer to send the employee elsewhere to work. The EAT in Lomond Motors extended this reasoning to the determination of the selection pool: 'It is not a question of considering what, historically, the position was... nor is it a matter of considering what, at some indefinite future date, the position might be. It is a matter of examining what actually is the position at the time of redundancy.' The tribunal had thus erred, to the extent that it was influenced in its decision as to the reasonableness of the employer's determination of the selection pool by the existence of a mobility clause in the claimant's contract of employment.

In Thornley v JCT600 Ltd ET Case No.1800944/10 (discussed under 'Same work' above) a tribunal considered that the likelihood that the Lotus operation was going to be relocated away from the main workshop did not justify the exclusion of the technicians working on Lotus cars from a pool for redundancy selection. T was one of seven technicians employed by JCT600 Ltd in its specialist workshop. Five of the technicians, including T, worked on Ferrari and Maserati vehicles and two worked on Lotus cars. In October 2009 JCT600 Ltd decided to reduce the number of technicians it employed by one and T was selected from among the five technicians working on Ferrari and Maserati cars as it was likely that the Lotus operation was going to be relocated away from the main workshop. The tribunal held that this was unfair dismissal. JCT600 Ltd acted unreasonably in excluding from the pool the two technicians working on Lotus cars.

Arguably, however, the existence of mobility clauses may be relevant where, in **8.105** practice, employees do regularly work between different sites. There may then be justification for including employees who are notionally based at different sites in one selection pool for redundancy purposes. For example, where an employer is intending to close down two out of ten sites, it would normally be reasonable for the redundancy selection to be concentrated on those two sites alone. However, where a particular type of employee – such as sales staff – move to a significant degree between sites in the course of their work, it may be reasonable for the sales staff to be selected from all ten sites for redundancy.

Pool for selection and collective consultation. It is worth noting here the **8.106** distinction between the pool for selection in a multi-site redundancy situation and the concept of 'establishment' under the collective consultation provisions contained in S.188 TULR(C)A (discussed in Chapter 12). The statutory duty to consult employee representatives arises under S.188(1) 'where an employer is proposing to dismiss as redundant 20 or more employees *at one establishment* within a period of 90 days or less' (our emphasis). The meaning of 'establishment' is critical here. An employer could contend that, where each site is treated as a separate pool for redundancy selection purposes, each should be regarded as a separate establishment for the purposes of S.188(1). Thus, even if it is proposing to make 20 or more employees redundant nationwide, fewer than 20 employees are being made redundant at each site and therefore the statutory duty to consult does not arise.

We discuss the meaning of 'establishment' in Chapter 12. Suffice it to say here that it is a legal concept defined by European and domestic case law that is entirely separate and distinct from the unfair dismissal provisions of the ERA, which give employers considerable latitude when choosing the pool for redundancy selection, provided they act within a range of reasonable responses. Take Mills and Allen Ltd v Bulwich EAT 154/99, for example, where the EAT held that members of a nationwide direct sales team, based in different offices, were a single team and therefore one 'establishment' for the purposes of S.188. That conclusion would have had no bearing on the appropriate pool for redundancy selection had the individual employees in that case brought unfair redundancy claims under the ERA.

8.107 **Selection criteria**
If the selection pool is reasonable, the tribunal will then consider the selection criteria applied by the employer to employees in the pool.

8.108 **Criteria should be clear.** It may well be unfair to score employees on a range of pre-advised selection criteria, and then to take into account additional factors of which the employees are unaware in deciding who to select for redundancy. In Watkins v Crouch t/a Temple Bird Solicitors EAT 0145/10 the selection criteria made known to the workforce were fee-earning ability, client-facing skills, knowledge of the firm's administrative procedures, availability for suitable work following any reorganisation, and adaptability. Each employee was given a mark against each criterion. W, a conveyancing secretary, and another employee were dismissed on the basis that they had the two lowest scores in the pool. However, W produced leaked documents to the tribunal which showed that the firm's receptionist, who was also in the pool, had scored lower than her but had not been selected for redundancy. The firm sought to justify the receptionist's retention on the ground that she was too valuable an employee to lose. It argued that how employees scored against the five criteria was only one part of the decision-making process, and that the workforce knew that other factors would be taken into account, including the overall requirements of the business. The EAT overturned a tribunal's decision that W had not been unfairly dismissed, on the basis that the tribunal had failed to address W's arguments. It remitted W's claim to a different tribunal, as it was possible that the tribunal would still have found W's selection to be fair if it had found that the firm had made it clear to the workforce that scoring was subject to its right to retain a particular employee if that was what the future of the practice required, and if the firm's assessment of the receptionist could not be said to be flawed. However, the EAT noted that if the 'overall requirements of the business' were to be taken into account in deciding whether employees should be made redundant, it could well be argued that this should have been one of the advertised selection criteria on which all employees were scored, although it added that so subjective a criterion might not satisfy the requirement for selection criteria to be objective (see below).

8.109 **Criteria must be objective.** In order to found reasonable dismissals, the selection criteria must be objective; not merely reflecting the personal opinion of the selector, but being verifiable by reference to data such as records of attendance, efficiency and length of service. Some examples of criteria that were found to be insufficiently objective:

- **Williams and ors v Compair Maxam Ltd** 1982 ICR 156, EAT: the retention of employees who, in the manager's opinion, 'would keep the company viable' was ruled to be entirely subjective and unreasonable and the resulting dismissals unfair

- **KGB Micros Ltd v Lewis** EAT 573/90: the selection of salesmen based on a 'cost savings' criterion – those who cost most in terms of overheads but who generated least revenue were selected – was not an appropriate yardstick by which to assess employees' performance. The employer had failed to undertake any real appraisal of the employees and its selection process completely lacked objectivity

- **Everitt v Sealine International Ltd** ET Case No.1313646/09: the selection of employees on the basis of 'commitment'. The tribunal considered that unless such a criterion is closely defined and measurable by agreed benchmarks it is subjective, and the fact that an employee forum had agreed the selection criteria did not make it any less so.

By contrast, 'employee trajectory and future potential' was found not to be too **8.110** subjective in Ganesan v Opera Solutions Ltd ET Case No.2203343/09.

In Howard v Siemens Energy Services ET Case No.2324423/08 an employment tribunal refused to criticise an employer for applying a selection criterion for redundancy purposes that reflected employees' adherence to the company's 'Values'. The tribunal found that the employer's use of the 'Values' – which were 'Accountable', 'Altogether' and 'Adaptable' – as a selection criterion was reasonable. However, the way in which adherence was assessed lacked objectivity and transparency. The 'Values' were a recent introduction and the tribunal found that the evidence showed that they had not been universally adopted within the company, nor had proper training been carried out on what they meant. Furthermore, there was no method of cross-checking or benchmarking different managers' assessments of the 'Values', which were necessarily subjective. Thus, there was no way of being certain that all managers applied the criterion in the same way. The claimant had therefore been unfairly selected for redundancy.

Extent of employer's discretion. Provided an employer's selection criteria are **8.111** objective, a tribunal should not subject them or their application to over-minute scrutiny – British Aerospace plc v Green and ors 1995 ICR 1006, CA. Essentially, the task for the tribunal is to satisfy itself that the method of selection was not inherently unfair and that it was applied in the particular case in a reasonable fashion. Thus, employers are given a wide discretion in their choice of selection criteria and the manner in which they apply them and tribunals will only be entitled to interfere in those cases which fall at the extreme edges of the reasonableness band.

Although this approach has been consistently approved by the higher courts for many years, the way in which tribunals deal with issues of fairness continues to provide fertile ground for appeals to the EAT. The outcome of these appeals shows that tribunals will rarely be justified in finding a dismissal unfair on the basis of the particular criteria adopted by the employer or the application of those criteria to the particular factual matrix. In Drake International Systems Ltd (t/a Drake Ports Distribution Services) v O'Hare EAT 0384/03; 0577/03, for example, the EAT held that a tribunal erred in criticising an employer for not excluding industrial injuries from absences taken into account for redundancy purposes. The tribunal had imposed its own view as to the reasonableness of selecting the particular claimant for redundancy. Similarly, in LTI Ltd v Radford EAT 164/00 the EAT held that a tribunal fell into error when it concerned itself with its own view of what selection criteria should have been applied rather than maintain focus on the employer's criteria. In that case, the employer had devised and applied a skills-based test under which those in the pool for selection had to perform a series of tasks within a set period for which they were assessed. The tribunal considered that this particular test not only disadvantaged the claimant but also failed to achieve the employer's stated aim of retaining those who had the most flexible skills. However, as the EAT observed, it was for the employer to decide how to make an assessment of skills. The tribunal's task was simply to consider whether a reasonable employer could have chosen the assessment method adopted in the particular case. Furthermore, in the absence of evidence that the skills test was an unfair measure of ability, the finding that the test had placed the claimant at a particular disadvantage indicated that the tribunal had wrongly focused on what was fair to the claimant and not on whether the employer had acted reasonably overall.

8.112 **Length of assessment period.** The length of the assessment period is likely to be important when it comes to determining the reasonableness of the application of selection criteria, as a short assessment period may not show the true picture. And employers will normally be expected to make allowances where an employee's assessment period is truncated by maternity leave, disability or other statutory absences, to ensure that he or she is scored fairly as against other employees. Two examples:

- **Eurocasters Ltd v Greene** EAT 475/88: the selection criteria (productivity, absenteeism, attitude to work and cooperation with requests to work extra hours) were applied over a period of two years, during one of which G had been absent on maternity leave. She scored badly and was made redundant without consideration of the fact that her record had been exemplary prior to her maternity leave. The EAT found that the dismissal was unfair, the reasonable selection criteria having been unfairly applied

- **Vij-Solanki v IDT Global Ltd** ET Case Nos.2203531/08 and another: V finished a period of maternity leave in March 2008, although she did not return to work until late April, having taken accrued holiday. In June 2008 the employer had to make redundancies and V was selected. A tribunal found that it was unreasonable for the employer to use only the period commencing January 2008 to assess those at risk, as V had been away from work for much of this time. The decision to limit her assessment period to 2.5 months was one which no reasonable employer could have reached. There were other options open to it which could have mitigated any unfairness (actual or perceived), including adding in a period of four months prior to V's maternity leave; simply scoring her on the six months prior to her maternity leave; or even taking a three-month assessment period for all staff from May to July 2008.

Protected activities and selection criteria. As we saw under 'Automatically 8.113 unfair redundancy' above, employees who carry out trade union and other activities are protected in that their dismissal will be automatically unfair if they are selected for redundancy on account of those activities. That does not mean, however, that such employees should receive special treatment in a redundancy selection exercise. Thus, in Smiths Industries Aerospace and Defence Systems v Rawlings 1996 IRLR 656, EAT, an employee who spent approximately one third of his working time on his duties as a health and safety representative was selected for redundancy under a system based on seven criteria related to performance. The employee argued that his dismissal was unfair because the employer had failed in the selection process to take account of the skills and qualities that were entailed in the performance of his health and safety functions. The EAT rejected that claim. It said that the protection afforded to such representatives in a redundancy exercise is neutral. That is, while they are entitled not to be discriminated against on the grounds of their health and safety activities, equally they are not entitled to be given more favourable treatment than their fellow employees in the pool for redundancy selection. Taking a representative's performance of health and safety duties into account when conducting a redundancy exercise would result in discrimination in that employee's favour.

Nor will the fact that the time spent on protected activities has hampered the employee's ability to match certain criteria necessarily assist the employee. In Herbert v Air UK Engineering EAT 575/97 a workshop tradesman who spent three and a half hours a day on his shop steward duties was selected for redundancy because he was less qualified than a colleague. The employee argued before a tribunal that his dismissal was unfair because he had had no chance to gain the relevant qualifications on account of the time spent on his trade union activities. The EAT upheld the tribunal's decision that the employee's dismissal was genuinely due to his lack of qualifications and was fair. The fact that the employee had not gained the qualifications because of his union activities made no difference. The EAT also rejected an argument that some sort of weighting factor should have been applied to the qualification criterion to allow for time spent on union activities. Whereas it might be possible to incorporate a weighting factor into a criterion based on employees' output, it was not so easy to do so in the case of a qualification criterion. In any event, an employer must be entitled to regard qualifications for a skilled job as a high priority. Important as trade union activities are, they could not be legitimately invoked to seek to compensate for lack of qualifications.

8.114 **Specific criteria.** Below, we discuss some of the more common criteria used by employers when selecting employees for redundancy. It should be pointed out, however, that the reasonableness of any particular criterion will always be a question of fact dependent on all the circumstances of the case.

8.115 *Last in, first out (LIFO).* LIFO was traditionally regarded as the easiest and the most obviously objective method of selection to administer and, until fairly recently, was the most common method used. However, its popularity has seen a steady decline owing to a number of factors: selection by service alone can have a detrimental impact on an employer's skills base; on average, women have shorter periods of service than men, meaning that the application of the criterion is potentially indirect sex discrimination; and, finally, the application of LIFO would appear to amount to indirect age discrimination (for more on this, see Chapter 9 under 'Discriminatory selection – age discrimination'). Practically speaking, any use of LIFO will now require objective justification in order to avoid contravening discrimination law.

Given this, the standing of the historical case of Westland Helicopters Ltd v Nott EAT 342/88 must be called into question. There, the EAT took the view that to ignore an employee's length of service, or to give it very little weight in the redundancy selection process, could be unreasonable for unfair dismissal purposes. The employer assessed employees for 'efficiency, proficiency and productivity', taking into account length of service only where scores were identical, and dismissed those with the lowest scores. The EAT suggested that a better policy would have been to add length of service to the calculations for all those employees whose scores were within the same bracket. These days, however, it is unlikely that a tribunal would find that an employer had acted outside the band of reasonable responses by failing to apply a potentially age discriminatory criterion.

8.116 *Performance, skill and knowledge.* It is very common for employers to select employees for redundancy on the basis of their performance at work. The potential stumbling block relates to how that performance is measured. For example, an organisation that sets employees targets and regularly reviews staff performance against those targets should have to hand objective and verifiable documentation on which to rank employees' performance. However, an employer that does not regularly monitor performance, and instead relies on the subjective opinion of the employee's manager at the time redundancy is considered, will be leaving itself open to the allegation that the criterion is either not objective or is not being applied in a fair manner.

Employers also need to ensure that employees are compared fairly. In Griffiths v GEA Denco Ltd ET Case No.1316291/09 G was a sales engineer, employed to sell GEA products. These were difficult to sell, as there was no existing client base or reputation, the products had not been designed for the UK market, and the exchange rate made the price high. When the company suffered a reduction in turnover G was placed in a pool with other sales engineers, who all sold Denco products, which did not suffer from the same problems. G was selected for redundancy because on the selection criteria, which included performance, he scored lowest. A tribunal found that in comparing G's performance with that of the other sales engineers the company was not comparing like with like. The difficulties in selling GEA products impacted on G's scores and meant that the application of the scoring process was not reasonable.

Nevertheless, it is reasonable, not to mention sensible, for an employer to try **8.117** to retain a workforce that is balanced in terms of ability. Hence an individual's skill and knowledge are reasonable considerations, provided they are assessed objectively. The precise choice of factors and their relative weighting will be determined according to the current and future needs of the business. In Dresser UK Ltd v Burnett EAT 112/86, for example, the EAT held that the employer had acted reasonably in selecting B for redundancy rather than a colleague, because B's background was in sales and he lacked the engineering experience required for the post.

Employers should, however, ensure that criteria are clearly defined from the outset. In Odhams-Sun Printers Ltd v Hampton and ors EAT 776/86 the employer's criterion was LIFO, subject to the retention of a 'balance of skills' in each department. The EAT agreed with the tribunal that this was vague and imprecise and therefore flawed. Similarly, selection on the basis of a nebulous criterion – such as 'attitude to the work' – will usually be unreasonable.

In Graham v ABF Ltd 1986 IRLR 90, EAT, 'quality of work, efficiency in **8.118** carrying it out and the attitude of the persons evaluated to their work' only narrowly passed the reasonableness test. G was selected for redundancy largely because of his attitude to the work allocated him – including obscene language and hostility – which had been the subject of complaint by colleagues and his manager. Although the EAT thought 'attitude to work' was 'dangerously ambiguous', it upheld the tribunal's finding that it was reasonable on the facts.

Flexibility. Employers may wish to retain employees who are willing and able **8.119** to be flexible in their approach to their job. However, employers should ensure that the criterion is necessary and can be applied in an objective manner and does not impact unfairly on particular employees. In Mole v Lamax Foods UK ET Case Nos.3303708/09 and others, for example, M's selection for redundancy was found to be unfair in that one of the five criteria used was 'flexible approach', defined as willingness to work at the head office for 2–3 days per week and willingness to travel through the United Kingdom and overseas. This was outside the range of reasonable responses because M was originally employed as home-based and was only required to come into the head office once or twice a week, whereas the other two employees in the pool were employed on contracts which stated that their normal place of work was the head office. Furthermore, M did not need to travel in her role as much as the other employees.

Note that a requirement to be flexible in terms of hours or travelling is potentially indirectly discriminatory against women, who are more likely to have childcare or caring responsibilities. It may also impact unfairly on disabled employees. Employers relying on such criteria would therefore need to be able to objectively justify their use to avoid a finding of unlawful discrimination under the Equality Act 2010 – see further Chapter 9.

8.120 *Disciplinary records.* Employers are naturally inclined to take into account matters such as an employee's disciplinary record when selecting for redundancy. Provided the record is objective and similar offences are given the same weight, the use of such a criterion is likely to be fair.

One question that has arisen in the context of dismissal for misconduct is whether, in deciding to dismiss, an employer can take account of expired disciplinary warnings. In Airbus UK Ltd v Webb 2008 ICR 561, CA, the Court of Appeal reviewed case law on this question and concluded that it did not support the proposition that the conduct which was the subject of an expired warning must be ignored for all purposes when making the decision to dismiss. The Court did, however, indicate that its decision should not be read as encouraging reliance on expired warnings as a matter of course. Rather, the effect of Webb is to confirm that the use of an expired warning is a matter to be considered as part of the overall question of the reasonableness of dismissal.

8.121 While, in the context of redundancy, the decision in Webb does not outright legitimise keeping expired warnings on file for the purposes of redundancy selection, it does confirm that there is no automatic or absolute bar on such use. However, it is likely that tribunals would consider it unfair for employers to take into account incidents that did not result in any disciplinary action being taken. In Meyer v Loftus Family Property ET Case No.3304813/09 M had been told that no disciplinary action was to be taken in relation to a particular incident, but that she would be dismissed if she repeated her actions. Although M submitted a grievance, this was not formally dealt with. A tribunal found that M was unfairly selected for redundancy because her employer took the incident into account in scoring her in respect of 'disciplinary record'.

8.122 *Attendance records.* It is generally unwise to make attendance the sole criterion for redundancy selection. But where it is used as a criterion, there are conflicting authorities as to whether employers are required to look into the reasons behind employees' absences. In Paine and Moore v Grundy (Teddington) Ltd 1981 IRLR 267, EAT, the Appeal Tribunal found a dismissal unfair because of the employer's failure to investigate the reasons for an employee's absence. In

Dooley v Leyland Vehicles Ltd, unreported 17.6.86, Court of Session (Inner House), on the other hand, the Court of Session held that it was reasonable for employers to ignore the reasons behind absences because it was often impracticable for employers to discover them.

Where an employer *is* aware of the reasons behind an employee's absence, it may be held to have acted unreasonably if it does not then take them into account. In O'Neill v DGF Ltd ET Case No.1302373/09, for example, O's selection for redundancy was unfair because, in calculating his score under the attendance criterion, the employer had included absences when O's wife, who was about to give birth, had been up all night suffering from stomach pains; when he had had to take his child to the dentist; and when his wife had again been ill all night and they had been unable to find a babysitter. All these absences potentially gave O a right to take time off work under S.57A ERA (time off for dependants). If these absences had been ignored – in the same way as absences relating to maternity and paternity rights were – O would not have been selected for redundancy. (Note that in this case the tribunal may have been swayed by the fact that O was not given an opportunity to challenge his scoring.)

8.123 In Byrne v Castrol (UK) Ltd EAT 429/96 the EAT denied that Paine and Moore v Grundy (Teddington) Ltd (above) established any inflexible rule that a tribunal will automatically fall into error if it fails to consider whether the employer, in using attendance as a criterion, has taken into account the reasons for the selected employee's absences. Whether or not the employer has done so is merely one of the factors that the tribunal may wish to consider in determining the fairness of a redundancy dismissal. There was also a danger, said the EAT, that employers might make subjective judgments as to the merits or demerits of the reasons given by individual employees for their non-attendance.

The period over which attendance is assessed may be a significant factor – see 'Length of assessment period', above. Although the question of what amounts to a reasonable period is a question of fact for the tribunal to decide in the particular case, the period should be substantial, particularly where long-serving employees are concerned. In Fleming v Leyland Vehicles Ltd ET Case No.S/1561/84 a tribunal criticised a six-month period as arbitrary and limited because it meant that an employee with 15 years' service was selected for redundancy while shorter-serving employees who had avoided sickness over the six-month period were retained. 18 months would have been a more suitable period.

8.124 Note that when using attendance as one of the selection criteria, employers must be mindful of discrimination law. Pregnancy-related absences should be discounted to avoid infringing the substantial legal rights afforded to pregnant workers – see Chapter 9 under 'Discriminatory selection – pregnancy and maternity leave', and IDS Employment Law Handbook, 'Maternity and Parental Rights' (2009), Chapter 13. In addition, where an employee's absences are caused by a disability, selection on the ground of his or her attendance record might amount to disability discrimination under the Equality Act 2010 – see Chapter 9 under 'Discriminatory selection – disability discrimination'.

8.125 *Health.* An employee's health (though not his or her disability) may be reasonably taken into account in the selection process. It may be reasonable to adopt criteria designed to retain the fittest workers – but employers should try to ensure that their facts are accurate so that they can make an informed decision rather than act on assumptions. Wherever possible, the employee should be consulted and the employer should consider offering him or her alternative employment. In Porter v Streets Transport Ltd EAT 274/86 the selection of P for redundancy on the ground that he suffered from a gastric ulcer was reasonable, but the EAT found that a failure to consult him had resulted in the employer's failure to offer him a vacant post and made the ensuing dismissal unfair.

The application of a criterion of sickness or injury to people who are absent from work as a result of accidents at work will not necessarily be unreasonable – Bartholomew and ors v The Mayor and Burgess of the London Borough of Haringey EAT 627/90. In that case it was argued that to include absences due to industrial injury at work under the criterion of absence due to 'sickness/injury' was unreasonable and unfair. The tribunal disagreed, holding that the criteria were reasonable in all the circumstances and applied equally and objectively to all employees. The EAT refused to interfere.

8.126 However, in Walsh v Homeserve Property Repairs ET Case No.1606356/09 a tribunal took the opposite approach. W was injured in a road traffic accident at work when travelling in a van driven by one of HPR's employees. He had to take 28 days off work and took further time off for subsequent treatment and medical examinations. He was later selected for redundancy, in part because of his high level of absence. A tribunal found that he had been unfairly dismissed, commenting that as HPR was vicariously liable for the accident and resulting time off work, it 'ill behoved them' to apply the scoring criteria for absence in a way that penalised W.

Whether or not a particular injury amounts to an 'industrial injury' may be a matter of dispute. However, so long as the employer's approach falls within the range of reasonableness, a tribunal is unlikely to interfere with it. For example, in Veitch v Kingspan Ltd ET Case No.1802555/09 V had an accident at work with a forklift truck in November 2007. He was discharged from hospital with painkillers but a few days later became distressed at work by flashbacks to the accident and his doctor signed him off work for 16 days with 'stress reaction'. Towards the end of 2008 K Ltd carried out a restructuring exercise and V was selected for redundancy. He claimed unfair dismissal on the basis that he had been given a low score for attendance primarily because of the time he had taken off suffering from stress, and that this should not have been taken into account because it was due to an industrial injury. However, the tribunal dismissed his claim. One reasonable interpretation of the term 'industrial injury' would be any injury sustained at work, but K Ltd's interpretation – that an industrial injury was a reportable injury under the Reporting of Injuries, Diseases and Dangerous Occurrences Regulations 1995 SI 1995/3163 – was not outside the range of reasonable interpretations. K Ltd acted reasonably in relying on the view of its safety manager that V's accident was not reportable because V had not sustained a physical injury that led him to being off work for three days or more.

Note that where an employee's poor health amounts to a disability, selection of **8.127** the employee for redundancy on health grounds might amount to disability discrimination under the Equality Act 2010 – see Chapter 9 under 'Discriminatory selection – disability discrimination'.

Manner of selection   8.128

In order that dismissals on the basis of any particular selection criteria are fair, the *application* of those criteria must be reasonable. For example, in Eurocasters Ltd v Greene EAT 475/88 – see 'Length of assessment period' above – it was the inappropriate application of otherwise fair selection criteria that made the employee's dismissal unfair.

There have been numerous cases where the absence of consultation or the **8.129** failure to offer alternative employment has made an otherwise fair dismissal unfair, but the actual application of the criteria themselves may make a dismissal unfair even before the question of consultation is addressed. Some examples:

- **Hattersley v Lucas Aerospace** ET Case No.13651/87: the employer introduced a redundancy selection procedure that involved a series of weighted criteria against which the employee was marked. The tribunal found that the choice of criteria and their relative weights was fair. However, the fact that H received only 50 per cent of the maximum points for attendance when his record was near-perfect meant that the criteria had not been 'reasonably, fairly and objectively applied' to him and his resulting selection was therefore unreasonable

- **Alexanders of Edinburgh Ltd v Maxwell and ors** EAT 796/86: selection was made on the basis of 'merit'. The selector was given no guidance and, although he did assess the employees under various headings, the tribunal found that there had been no attempt systematically to tabulate factors for comparison. The application of the selection criterion was therefore unfair

- **Rafferty and anor v JJ Boyle Ltd** EAT 193/89: the employer wished to make two of his six road-labouring staff redundant. The men worked in three squads of two, and the employer decided upon a selection criterion based on the productivity of each squad. Productivity was assessed on the basis

253

of the amount of materials consumed by each squad over a given period, the squad which had consumed the least materials being made redundant. While R accepted that productivity was a fair criterion, he claimed that its application was badly flawed. One of the other squads had the use of a far larger lorry and the squads had different work patterns. However, the EAT refused to overturn the tribunal's decision that the application of the criterion, though imperfect, was reasonable in the circumstances

- **Boulton and Paul Ltd v Arnold** 1994 IRLR 532, EAT: selection of employees was to be made in accordance with an agreed procedure. The criteria were performance, length of service, discipline and attendance. In carrying out the exercise, the employer took every day of absence into account including, in the case of A, an authorised doctor's visit of half an hour. As a result, A scored only three out of a possible ten points in relation to absence despite having no unapproved short-term absence or lateness on her record. On the basis of this score, A was made redundant. A tribunal held, among other things, that not only had the employer radically departed from the agreed procedure but that treating a half-hour authorised absence to see a doctor as absence for the purpose of the redundancy assessment was unfair. The EAT upheld these findings.

8.130 However, while tribunals are entitled to consider whether selection criteria were applied fairly, they should not examine the actual scoring unless there has been bad faith or an obvious error – Dabson v David Cover and Sons Ltd EAT 0374/10. In that case, the claimant had been made redundant following a selection procedure in which his skills had been marked against the requirements for two different posts, Transport Manager and Transport Assistant. For the managerial job he had been given two points out of two under the heading 'Ability to plan routes', but for the less senior job only one point out of two for 'Ability to assist with route planning'. The EAT accepted that this did not clearly demonstrate error. Relying on the industrial experience of the lay members, it noted that the particular skills for a junior post may be different from those required for a senior post. For example, the manager of a plumbing business may not be required to be a skilled plumber. It therefore rejected the claimant's argument that it was obviously inconsistent for him to be given different marks for essentially the same skill.

8.131 **'Double' marking.** It may be unreasonable for an employer to take the same matter into account in respect of more than one selection criterion. In Jeyanthikumar v Carclo Technical Plastics Ltd ET Case No.2303150/09, for example, a tribunal found that J's dismissal for redundancy was unfair on the basis of the selection criteria and the way they were applied. There were five criteria, including disciplinary warnings and quality of work. J's score for quality of work was reduced because she had received a verbal warning for unacceptable performance, but the same warning also reduced her score under the discipline criterion. The tribunal considered that this was neither proportionate nor fair.

Discriminatory application of selection criteria. Potentially discriminatory factors in the application of seemingly objective criteria may also result in unfairness (not to mention a discrimination claim). For example, in British Sugar plc v Kirker 1998 IRLR 624, EAT, K, who was partially sighted, was selected for redundancy after 20 years' service. In the assessments he scored zero under two heads – performance and potential. The tribunal found that K had not been marked objectively as his low scores did not reflect the true position. This made the dismissal unfair and the EAT upheld this finding. See further Chapter 9 under 'Discriminatory selection'. **8.132**

Analysing employee assessments
8.133

When faced with the task of selecting employees for redundancy, it is fairly common practice for employers to decide upon a number of different criteria against which the employees in the pool for selection should be assessed and then to allocate marks for each employee under each of those criteria. Once the selection has been made, those selected might feel that the marking or grading was not carried out accurately and complain that the resulting dismissal was unfair. The question which then arises is whether, and to what extent, the tribunal can lawfully scrutinise the employer's assessments of all those in the pool in order to discover any evidence that would substantiate the employees' claims.

In Buchanan v Tilcon Ltd 1983 IRLR 417, Ct Sess (Inner House), the Court of Session ruled that, where an employee makes a general complaint of unfair selection, the employer does not have to prove to a tribunal that its grading of employees was carried out accurately. In that case B was selected for redundancy mainly on account of his comparatively short service and poor attendance record. A tribunal found the dismissal unfair. To show reasonable selection, it said, an employer must prove the accuracy of the information on which it was based. On B's absenteeism, for example, the employer should have produced direct evidence of the retained employees' records, to satisfy the tribunal that their record was indeed not as bad as B's. The EAT, overturning this decision, held that the tribunal had imposed too high a standard of proof on the employer and so had erred in law. On appeal, the Court of Session held that where an employee's only complaint is unfair selection, all that the employer has to prove is that the method of selection was fair in general terms and that it was reasonably applied to the employee concerned. Where the tribunal, as here, had accepted that the senior official doing the selecting had made his decision fairly, using information he had no reason to question, to demand that he set up the accuracy of that information by direct evidence was unreasonable and unrealistic.

255

8.134 The Buchanan case was subsequently followed in Eaton Ltd v King and ors 1995 IRLR 75, EAT. There, four employees lodged complaints of unfair selection. One of the issues raised was the general fairness of the employer's application of the selection criteria. The manager, who was the only witness for the employer, had not carried out the assessments himself and was unable to explain in detail how the marks had been allocated to the employees concerned. In the tribunal's view, the absence of evidence as to how the marks had been arrived at made it impossible for it to decide that the selection criteria had been fairly applied to any of the claimants. Accordingly, it held that the employees had not been fairly selected. The EAT overturned the tribunal's finding. On a proper application of the principles established in the Buchanan case, all that the employer had to show was that it had set up a *good system of selection which had been reasonably applied*. In the EAT's view, there was no reason why the managers who took the decision to dismiss should not have relied on the information supplied to them by the supervisors who carried out the assessments, and the managers could not be expected to be able to explain each marking. Furthermore, there was nothing in the tribunal's findings to suggest that the assessments were not carried out honestly and reasonably. The EAT considered that, while there may be cases where an inference could be drawn from the markings that there was something unfair about the application of the selection process, this was not such a case. The EAT concluded that the tribunal had fallen into precisely the error which had been identified in the Buchanan case, and ruled that all four employees had been fairly dismissed. (Note that the EAT's decision in this case was overturned on appeal by the Court of Session on another ground – King and ors v Eaton Ltd 1996 IRLR 199, Ct Sess (Inner House).)

The observations in the above cases, that an employer need only demonstrate that it had established a good system of selection which had been administered fairly, were expressly approved by the Court of Appeal in British Aerospace plc v Green and ors 1995 ICR 1006, CA. That case examined a tribunal's powers to order discovery of assessment forms by claimants who made general complaints about an employer's selection process. At that particular stage in the proceedings the claimants were not able to prove that the documents sought were relevant to an issue which had already been raised. The employees appeared to be seeking the information to go on a 'fishing expedition' for specific instances of unfairness. The Court, in refusing to grant an order of discovery, noted that if a system of graded assessment were to function effectively, its workings were not to be subjected to over-minute analysis. That was true both at the stage when the system was actually being applied and when its application was being questioned at a tribunal hearing. The Court added: 'To allow otherwise would involve a serious risk that the system itself would lose the respect with which it is at present regarded on both sides of industry, and that tribunal hearings would become hopelessly protracted.'

In Taylor and ors v (1) BICC Brand Rex Ltd (2) BICC Cables Ltd EAT 651/94 **8.135** employees dismissed for redundancy complained to the EAT that a tribunal had made 'generic' findings (i.e. findings which applied equally to all the claimants) in coming to its conclusion that all had been fairly dismissed, and had failed to address the specific matters raised by the employees. In particular, a conflict of evidence over attendance and timekeeping records had not been resolved. This, in the employees' view, fell foul of the guidelines in Williams and ors v Compair Maxam Ltd 1982 ICR 156, EAT, that a tribunal should satisfy itself that it was reasonable to dismiss each individual employee and that the selection criteria had been applied fairly to each one of them. Again, the case turned on the degree of scrutiny required of the tribunal in such cases. Lord Justice Waite in the Green case (above) was quoted as saying: 'So in general the employer who sets up a system of selection which can reasonably be described as fair and applies it without any overt sign of conduct which mars its fairness will have done all that the law requires of him.' The EAT thought it plain that, in order for the claimants to succeed in this case, there needed to be some sort of unfair conduct on the employer's part which could mar the fairness of the system, such as evidence of bad faith, victimisation or discrimination. In the instant case the dispute was over whether warnings had been given or had lapsed and the EAT concluded that the tribunal had made no error of law.

The principle that tribunals should not subject redundancy selection criteria or the employer's application of them to undue scrutiny applies even where two groups of employees are scored separately and no system of moderation is used. In First Scottish Searching Services Ltd v McDine and anor EAT 0051/10 F Ltd acquired the business of two other companies, including SPH. TM and JM, who were formerly employed by SPH, transferred to F Ltd's employment. Before the acquisition, F Ltd indicated that it would probably need to make some redundancies after the transfer. The scoring matrix used by F Ltd in its subsequent redundancy exercise involved a mix of objective criteria – for example, disciplinary records and length of service – and subjective criteria such as interpersonal skills, performance, attitude and enthusiasm. F Ltd's employees (the 'pre-transfer employees') were scored by managers employed in F Ltd before the transfer while SPH employees, including TM and JM, were scored against the same matrix but by two SPH managers. TM and JM were identified as being at risk of redundancy whereas none of the pre-transfer employees was at risk. The EAT overturned a tribunal's decision that F Ltd's selection process was fatally flawed because there had been no system for moderating the scores of the two groups of employees. It considered that the tribunal had fallen into the trap of engaging in 'microscopic' or 'over-minute' examination of the type warned against by the Court of Appeal in British Aerospace plc v Green and ors (above) and by the EAT in John Brown Engineering Ltd v Brown and ors 1997 IRLR 90, EAT (see 'Duty to disclose assessments to employees' below). The EAT noted that the tribunal's main

257

criticism was that the method used by F Ltd did not incorporate a system for moderating the two sets of scores. However, the tribunal had not explained what it meant when it referred to 'moderating' the scores, and nor was there any basis for the tribunal's assumption that moderation would have increased the scores of TM or JM. The EAT concluded that the tribunal had been wrong to find that identification of a risk in the system meant that the dismissals were unfair. The tribunal had substituted its own view for that of a reasonable employer in deciding that there was a need for moderation.

8.136 However, where there is clear evidence of unfair and inconsistent scoring, any subsequent dismissals are likely to be unfair. In Wardle v Killingholme Stevedoring Ltd ET Case No.1807464/09, for example, a tribunal found that W's selection for redundancy was unfair because three managers had carried out the scoring exercise on supervisors from three different parts of the workforce. It was clear on examining the marks that one manager had consistently scored people lower than the other two and there had been no attempt to ensure consistency in the scoring. The tribunal observed that the difficulty was that a large number of the criteria were 'very subjective'; but the HR department could have spent time talking to the managers, collectively, before the scoring exercise was carried out, and reviewed the scores afterwards. Examples could have been used as a scoring exercise and the three managers could have discussed beforehand how they would go about the task.

8.137 **Documentary evidence.** In FDR Ltd v Holloway 1995 IRLR 400, EAT, the Appeal Tribunal ruled that an employee dismissed for redundancy was entitled to be given access to documents relating to the assessments of other employees who had been retained. The main reason for this finding was that the employee's allegations of unfairness were specific, in that he was able to point to a particular employee whom he claimed should have been selected for redundancy instead of him. While he had been employed for over four years, another employee doing comparable work had been retained after only a few months' service. He claimed that the employer had been in breach of the agreed procedure and that its selection criteria had either been unfairly applied or not applied in his case. The EAT held that the documents sought were clearly relevant to the issue of whether the employee had been unfairly dismissed and ordered the employer to disclose the information. Note, however, that the Court of Session has doubted (obiter) the correctness of this decision as, in its view, it is irreconcilable with the Court of Appeal's decision in British Aerospace plc v Green and ors (above) – King and ors v Eaton Ltd 1996 IRLR 199, Ct Sess (Inner House).

Nevertheless, there may be cases where the *absence* of documentary evidence indicates a lack of objectivity. In E-Zec Medical Transport Service Ltd v Gregory EAT 0192/08 G worked for a private ambulance service. An important part of the firm's business was transporting injured and sick holidaymakers who had been repatriated to the United Kingdom. During 2006 the company faced a downturn in this aspect of its work. It decided to restructure the site where G worked and to make four employees redundant out of a pool of 14. The selection process was supervised by the senior HR manager W, who allocated marks for service, absence, sickness days, sickness occasions, and discipline. This was done by reference to employees' personnel files. The remaining selection criteria – performance, commitment and attitudes, skill base, and team working – were assessed by the regional manager, D. The company adopted a scoring matrix with definitions for the various criteria. However, D did not use any records or objective evidence in arriving at his scores but relied on his personal judgement as a line manager and his experience of working with the employees in the pool. G obtained one of the lowest scores and was made redundant.

The employment tribunal accepted that it was not its task to subject the marking **8.138** system to microscopic analysis or to check that the system had been properly operated. While the choice of criteria fell within the range of reasonable responses, key aspects of the marking had been left to D's personal judgement; some of the criteria were not capable of measurement by reference to personnel records; and there was no evidence as to how the scoring had been arrived at. According to the tribunal: 'The absence of evidence before us as to how the scoring had been arrived at made it impossible to for us to decide that the selection criteria had been fairly applied and accordingly the claimant had been unfairly selected.' The EAT upheld the tribunal's decision.

Duty to disclose assessments to employees. The above cases were concerned **8.139** with the evidence an employer must produce at an unfair dismissal hearing to show that it had fairly applied the selection criteria. However, the question of whether the employee has a right to know how he or she fared in the assessment process may well arise prior to dismissal. A failure to disclose to an employee selected for redundancy the details of his or her individual assessments may give rise to a finding that the employer failed in its *duty to consult* with the employee. In John Brown Engineering Ltd v Brown and ors 1997 IRLR 90, EAT, the Appeal Tribunal held that the employer's refusal, as a matter of policy, to disclose the marks of those selected for redundancy rendered its internal appeal process a sham. The employees' subsequent dismissals were accordingly unfair for lack of proper consultation. The EAT pointed out that a fair redundancy selection process requires that employees have the opportunity to contest their selection, either individually or through their union. See 'Collective consultation' and 'Individual consultation' below.

The Brown case does not go so far, however, as to hold that employees should be entitled to compare their own scores with those of employees who have been retained. On this question the courts, while demonstrating a clear understanding of an employee's desire to answer the question 'Why me and not somebody else?', have taken the view that to require the employer to review the assessments each time someone selected for redundancy challenges his or her own marks, or those of other employees, is an intolerable burden. These decisions confirm the Court of Session's view in Buchanan v Tilcon Ltd 1983 IRLR 417, Ct Sess (Inner House), that, in general claims of unfair selection for redundancy, there is little scope for employees to challenge the fairness of an employer's decision to select a particular individual.

8.140 This logic was adopted in (1) Boal (2) Langley v Gullick Dobson Ltd EAT 515/92. There, employees complained that the consultation with them over their proposed dismissals for redundancy was rendered defective by the employer's refusal to disclose details of how their rivals for redundancy had been assessed. They argued that they could not challenge the decision to select them if they were unable to draw comparisons between the way in which they had been assessed and the way in which those retained had been assessed. In short, they could not answer the question 'Why me?' The EAT emphatically rejected these arguments. There was no legal authority for the proposition that consultation had to be as detailed as the employees claimed. The duty on the employer was to act reasonably within the terms of S.98(4). It could not be said that an employer was under a duty to provide an employee selected for redundancy with all the information on which the decision to dismiss had been based so that the employee could examine it, point out any mistakes that might have been made and require the employer to go through a revision exercise. If this were required, the employer would not be able to carry out the redundancy exercise at all; it would lead to an 'intolerably protracted and utterly impracticable process'. Moreover, the disclosure of such information to employees would involve breaches of confidentiality and would destroy the morale of both workers and management.

8.141 **Collective consultation**
As explained in Chapter 12, S.188 of the Trade Union and Labour Relations (Consolidation) Act 1992 (TULR(C)A) places employers under a statutory duty to consult 'appropriate representatives' – i.e. trade union representatives or, where no union is recognised, employee representatives – where collective redundancies are proposed. While this duty is not strictly relevant to unfair dismissal claims, it has nonetheless been taken into account by tribunals considering the question of reasonableness under S.98(4) ERA.

In Williams and ors v Compair Maxam Ltd 1982 ICR 156, EAT, the Appeal Tribunal stated that trade union consultation was a factor in assessing the reasonableness of a dismissal but that a failure to consult would not, of itself, render a dismissal unfair. The EAT stressed in Hough and ors (including APEX) v Leyland DAF Ltd EAT 76–77/89 that a finding of failure to consult in breach of S.188 did not automatically lead to a finding of unfair dismissal. But, it said, it was reasonable for the tribunal in that case to decide that, had the union been consulted, the redundancy dismissals might never have occurred.

While fair and proper consultation is a necessary ingredient of a fair dismissal, **8.142** whether the consultation is adequate in all the circumstances is a question of fact for the tribunal. However, some guidance as to what constitutes 'fair consultation' was provided in R v British Coal Corporation and Secretary of State for Trade and Industry ex parte Price and ors 1994 IRLR 72, Div Ct. Lord Justice Glidewell said that fair consultation means consultation when the proposals are still at the formative stage, adequate information, adequate time in which to respond, and conscientious consideration by an authority of the response. Putting it another way, Glidewell LJ stated that consultation 'involves giving the body consulted a fair and proper opportunity to understand fully the matters about which it is being consulted, and to express its views on those subjects, with the consultor thereafter considering those views properly and genuinely'. Although Glidewell LJ's comments were made in the context of the duty to consult collectively under S.188 TULR(C)A, they have been applied by the EAT in Rowell v Hubbard Group Services Ltd 1995 IRLR 195, EAT, and Pinewood Repro Ltd t/a County Print v Page 2011 ICR 508, EAT, and by the Court of Session in King and ors v Eaton Ltd 1996 IRLR 199, Ct Sess (Inner House), all of which are unfair dismissal cases.

In the King case the Court of Session applied Glidewell LJ's definition of 'fair consultation' to the facts of the case before it and overturned a tribunal's finding that there had been proper consultation with the unions. The Court found that, although there had been several meetings with the unions over the redundancies, these had taken place *after* the employer had formulated its proposals. There was no indication that the unions had had time to respond to the issues raised or that their views would have been considered. Nor had there been any specific reference at the meetings to the method of selection and this was a further pointer to the fact that the consultation had been flawed. The Court ruled that the redundancy dismissals were unfair for lack of consultation and because the employer had not shown that its method of selection was fair.

The question is always one of what is reasonable in the circumstances. In a **8.143** small workplace fewer formalities may suffice. In Milne v Distillers Company (Cereals) Ltd EAT 692/87, for example, all but one of the staff were members of the General, Municipal, Boilermakers and Allied Trades Union, with whom the employer had agreed the redundancy selection procedure. M challenged his dismissal for redundancy on the ground that, as a member of the Transport and General Workers' Union, his union had not been consulted. The EAT upheld a tribunal's rejection of the claim. Given the small size of the plant, the claimant must have been aware from an early stage of the redundancy situation. He had not asked his union to intervene and, moreover, had been individually consulted about his dismissal.

8.144 Individual consultation

Dismissals are more likely to be unfair for lack of individual rather than collective consultation. The 1972 Industrial Relations Code of Practice, which was repealed in June 1991, laid down principles for redundancy dismissals which included warning the employees concerned, considering voluntary redundancies and transfers, and offering assistance to those employees who were to be made redundant. Failure to comply with the Code was not itself unlawful, but was relevant to the question of whether an employer had behaved reasonably.

8.145   The principle of warnings and consultation is now so enshrined in the law that the repeal of the Code has made no practical difference to the obligation to consult. The importance of following proper procedures was made resoundingly clear by the House of Lords in Polkey v AE Dayton Services Ltd 1988 ICR 142, HL. In that case Lord Bridge stated that: 'In the case of redundancy... the employer will normally not act reasonably unless he warns and consults any employees affected or their representative, adopts a fair basis on which to select for redundancy and takes such steps as may be reasonable to avoid or minimise redundancy by redeployment within his own organisation.' Below, we summarise the facts in Polkey and another case to illustrate the point:

- **Polkey v AE Dayton Services Ltd** (above): P was dismissed for redundancy without his employer having made any attempt to consult him. A tribunal faulted the employer's breach of procedural fairness but decided that P had not been unfairly dismissed because he would have been dismissed even if the company had consulted him. The EAT and the Court of Appeal dismissed P's appeal but the House of Lords ruled that he had been unfairly dismissed. The question for the tribunal was whether the employer had acted reasonably in deciding that the reason for dismissing the employee was sufficient, not whether the employee would have been dismissed even if warning or consultation had taken place. Only if the employer could reasonably have concluded at the time of dismissal that the decision to dismiss would be unaffected by any consultation with the employee could a dismissal in breach of procedural fairness be reasonable

- **De Grasse v Stockwell Tools Ltd** 1992 IRLR 269, EAT: D was made redundant from his position as machinist in a very small company with no warning and no consultation. He gave evidence that, had he been consulted, he would have suggested being considered for a position of driver-handyman – a job he could have done and which was held by an employee with less service than he had. The tribunal appeared to apply the 'no difference rule', which Polkey had rejected, noting that the outcome would have been the same if a fair procedure had been followed and excused the employer's lack of adequate redundancy procedures on account of the size of the company. The EAT, applying Polkey, overturned this finding on the ground that the 'no difference rule' was no longer good law. Furthermore, consultation would have made a difference – D might have been considered for another post. Regarding the size and administrative resources of the company, the EAT acknowledged that S.98(4) ERA specifically referred to these factors as relevant to the determination of reasonableness. It accepted that size could affect the nature and formality of the consultation process but refused to accept that it could excuse a total absence of consultation.

Consultation 'futile'. The above cases confirmed, in general terms, that a **8.146** procedural impropriety in carrying out a dismissal would render the dismissal unfair. The only escape available to an employer was where it could reasonably have concluded that a proper procedure would be 'utterly useless' or 'futile'.

The question of whether an employer could reasonably have concluded that carrying out a proper procedure would be futile was for the tribunal to answer in the light of the circumstances known to the employer at the time of the dismissal. In Polkey, Lord Bridge expressed the view that such cases would be 'exceptional'. In practice, such 'exceptional' cases have generally (but not always) been those where, for various reasons, the employer has been bound to operate under some measure of secrecy. Two examples:

- **Hammond v BTB Mailing Services Ltd** ET Case No.7129/88: the claimant was made redundant after returning from sick leave. During his absence his job was made surplus by the installation of a computer and his employer, after consideration, decided that there was no alternative work available for him. The dismissal was found to be fair despite the lack of consultation as the employer had decided not to worry H with the issue of redundancy on account of his ill health. The employer had also decided, as it was entitled to on the facts known at the time, that consultation would have been futile

- **Speller v Golden Rose Communications plc** EAT 1360/96: S returned from her holiday to find that she had been dismissed from her post of marketing manager with a commercial radio station. A tribunal found that there were special circumstances justifying the complete lack of warning or consultation. The station was in dire straits, with all its advertising revenue frozen; there was a need for secrecy to avoid a knock-on effect on another station run by the company; and the employer had considered alternative employment but concluded there was nothing available. The EAT could find no grounds for overturning the tribunal's decision that the dismissal was fair.

Two examples where the defence failed: **8.147**

- **Poat v Holiday Inn Worldwide** EAT 883/93: the employer made P, a secretary, redundant without consultation when it reorganised its business in such a way that it no longer needed secretarial staff. There were no other suitable vacancies for her and a tribunal accepted the employer's argument that consultation would have made no difference to the decision to dismiss.

The EAT overturned this finding, however, on the ground that the tribunal had erred in failing to apply Polkey. The EAT mentioned the various practical purposes which consultation could have but also said that it was 'courteous and humane to consult people when you are thinking of making them redundant'

- **University of Glasgow v (1) Donaldson (2) McNally** EAT 951/94: D and M were made redundant when their fixed-term contracts, which were funded by an external body, came to an end. The university had a policy of not carrying out formal consultations in relation to externally funded posts, even though they generally consulted the relevant unions over impending redundancies. A tribunal found the dismissals unfair. The fact that the employees' posts were externally funded did not excuse the lack of consultation and the circumstances of the case did not amount to 'exceptional' circumstances as envisaged by Polkey. The EAT upheld that finding, saying that there was nothing in Polkey to suggest that consultation did not apply to fixed-term contracts – the fact that a contract is fixed term is only one factor to be taken into account in determining reasonableness. Nor could it be said that consultation would have been futile when there were vacancies in the university at the time of the dismissals.

8.148   One question that has arisen over the interpretation of Polkey is whether an employer must make a conscious decision that consultation would be futile in order to act reasonably. In Polkey itself, Lord Mackay said that if the employer could reasonably have concluded in the light of the circumstances known to it at the time that consultation or warning would be utterly useless, it might well be acting reasonably in failing to consult. One interpretation of this dictum is that the tribunal must consider what a reasonable employer might have done in the circumstances – the objective test. However, Lord Bridge, while agreeing with Lord Mackay, expressed the exception in different terms. He said that a dismissal might be fair despite the lack of proper procedure if 'the employer himself, at the time of dismissal, acted reasonably in taking the view that, in the exceptional circumstances of the particular case, the procedural steps normally appropriate would have been futile'. This seems to suggest that the employer must have made a deliberate decision not to consult the employee, and on reasonable grounds – a subjective test.

In Robertson v Magnet Ltd (Retail Division) 1993 IRLR 512, EAT, the Appeal Tribunal took the view that, on the basis of Lord Bridge's speech, the exception would normally apply only where the employer had considered and rejected the possibility of consultation. However, the Court of Appeal in Duffy v Yeomans and Partners Ltd 1995 ICR 1, CA, took a different view. Lord Justice Balcombe refused to accept that a redundancy dismissal must, as a matter of law, be unfair unless the employer has taken a deliberate decision not to consult. In his view, neither the wording of S.98(4) nor the judgment of Lord Mackay

264

supported that proposition. The tribunal must judge what the employer did and not what it might have done. It was what a reasonable employer could have done which had to be tested, so the tribunal must ask whether an employer, acting reasonably, could have failed to consult in the given circumstances.

Relationship with collective consultation. An employer should not assume **8.149** that individual consultation is unnecessary where consultation with the appropriate representatives (see 'Collective consultation' above) has taken place. In Alexanders of Edinburgh Ltd v Maxwell and ors EAT 796/86 unions had been consulted on impending redundancies, but a dismissal was nevertheless unfair for lack of individual consultation. There was evidence that the shop stewards involved in negotiations had been more concerned with protecting their own interests than those of the other union members. However, even in the absence of such evidence, the EAT has stressed in a number of cases that employers should not assume that employees are privy to consultation with their union over redundancies, and that they should themselves ensure that the staff are aware of what is going on – see, for example, T and E Neville Ltd v Johnson EAT 282/79 and Huddersfield Parcels Ltd v Sykes 1981 IRLR 115, EAT.

This will be particularly important where collective consultation is carried out in secret. In Williams v Nationwide Building Society ET Case No.1700172/10 NBS began a redundancy process in March 2009. The process was agreed with a union, but it was also agreed that it would be kept secret to protect the business and managers had to sign non-disclosure agreements. W was called to a meeting on 17 September 2009 during which she was advised that following selection her post was redundant. A tribunal found that W was unfairly dismissed because she was told of her dismissal in advance of any genuine consultation – consultation carried out with the union did not help her because it was subject to the non-disclosure agreement.

Just because a redundancy process is agreed with employee representatives **8.150** does not mean that it is necessarily fair, even if it is based on suggestions made by those representatives. In Swan v DB Schenker Rail (UK) Ltd ET Case No.1607553/09 the employee representatives made a suggestion during consultations, adopted by management, that there should be no selection between employees in one location because there were matching vacancies for each employee. The outcome of this was that S was left in a pool of one. Had the employer not accepted this proposal, S would have been able to compete with another employee for a vacancy. His dismissal was therefore unfair.

Even where an employee is involved in the collective negotiations as a representative, the employer should not neglect to consult that employee as an individual if he or she is to be made redundant. The Court of Appeal in Walls Meat Co Ltd v Selby 1989 ICR 601, CA, found the dismissal of a shop steward unfair because the employer had not given him the opportunity to negotiate his own position after he had agreed, as a union representative, the application of a LIFO procedure. The Court stated that good industrial practice involved a two-stage consultation – first with the union about the procedure to be adopted, and then with the individuals chosen under that procedure.

8.151 The relationship between collective and individual consultation was considered by the EAT in Mugford v Midland Bank plc 1997 ICR 399, EAT. In that case the employer was planning a major reorganisation which would result in some 3,000 redundancies. M was given a series of briefings on the details of the proposed reorganisation and on the criteria to be used in redundancy selection. M was subsequently selected for redundancy. There followed a number of meetings to discuss the possibility of redeployment but they came to nothing and M was dismissed. The tribunal found that, although there had been no real individual consultation with M, there had been full consultation with the union and that on balance the employer had fulfilled its obligation to consult and M's dismissal was fair. On appeal, the EAT noted that collective consultation often concentrated on such matters as selection criteria and general arrangements for redeployment and that unions seldom wanted to be involved in the actual selection of individuals for redundancy. The EAT added that, once individuals had been identified for redundancy, consultation between the employer and the individual employees became important, even if there had already been extensive consultation on a collective level. Nevertheless, the EAT pointed out that it was a question of fact and degree for a tribunal to decide whether the consultation that had taken place was so inadequate as to render the dismissal unfair. In the instant case the tribunal had been critical of the lack of individual consultation but had decided that such consultation as had taken place was adequate in all the circumstances. Although the EAT suggested that it might have taken a different view, there were no grounds for overturning the tribunal's decision. To rule that the tribunal had made an error of law would, said the EAT, have raised the need for individual consultation prior to a decision to dismiss into a prerequisite for a fair dismissal. In the EAT's view, there were no grounds for taking such a restrictive approach.

The Mugford case made it plain that the simple fact that the employer carries out collective consultation does not, of itself, excuse a failure to conduct individual consultations. Nevertheless, tribunals appear to be more willing to tolerate an attenuated process of individual consultation if the employer has already consulted with a trade union or workplace representatives. In Unipart Eberspacher Exhaust Systems Ltd v Keenan EAT 1473/00, for example, the EAT overturned a tribunal's finding that an employer should have conducted individual consultation regarding the selection criteria in addition to the collective consultation that had already been carried out over the same matter. The employer had agreed the criteria with an established employee forum that regularly discussed workplace matters with management. In those circumstances, the EAT held that the tribunal's decision was perverse.

Subject matter of consultation. If individual consultation is generally expected **8.152** of an employer, the inevitable question arises: consultation about what? To some extent, the subject-matter will depend upon the specific circumstances, but best practice suggests that it should normally include:

- an indication (i.e. warning) that the individual has been provisionally selected for redundancy

- confirmation of the basis for selection

- an opportunity for the employee to comment on his or her redundancy selection assessment

- consideration as to what, if any, alternative positions of employment may exist, and

- an opportunity for the employee to address any other matters he or she may have.

The purpose of consultation is not only to allow consideration of alternative employment or to see if there is any other way that redundancies can be avoided: it also helps employees to protect themselves against the consequences of being made redundant.

While the question of what constitutes fair and proper consultation in each **8.153** individual case is a question of fact for the tribunal, the EAT provided some guidance in Rowell v Hubbard Group Services Ltd 1995 IRLR 195, EAT. There, R was warned in a memorandum from her employer that redundancies would have to be made and it set out the selection criteria to be used. R then received a letter informing her that she had been selected and offering her the opportunity 'to discuss any matters arising from [the] letter'. When R claimed unfair dismissal, the tribunal held that the invitation to discuss the contents of the letter provided sufficient opportunity for consultation. On appeal, however, the EAT said that the letter could not be read as anything approaching consultation. In the EAT's view, there was no real consultation with R, nor any invitation to consult at any stage in the process. Since this was contrary to the procedural requirements laid down in Polkey, it overturned the tribunal's decision and held that R's dismissal was unfair.

In the course of its judgment, the EAT also referred to the comments of Glidewell LJ in R v British Coal Corporation and Secretary of State for Trade and Industry ex parte Price and ors 1994 IRLR 72, Div Ct (see 'Collective consultation' above), including the comment that consultation 'involves giving the body consulted a fair and proper opportunity to understand fully the matters about which it is being consulted, and to express its views on those subjects, with the consultor thereafter considering those views properly and genuinely'. The EAT took the view that those comments on the meaning of fair consultation were 'of assistance to employers when they have to consult with staff in the context of dismissal for redundancy or dismissal'. Although there were no invariable rules and the outcome of each case depended on its own facts, the EAT stated that 'when the need for consultation exists, it must be fair and genuine, and should... be conducted so far as possible as the passage from Glidewell LJ's judgment suggests'.

8.154 The Court of Session in King and ors v Eaton Ltd 1996 IRLR 199, Ct Sess (Inner House), similarly adopted Glidewell LJ's definition. It was also quoted with approval by the EAT in John Brown Engineering Ltd v Brown and ors 1997 IRLR 90, EAT. In that case the EAT stated that what is required in each case is a fair process which gives each individual employee the opportunity to contest his or her selection, either directly or through consultation with employee representatives. The EAT suggested that this involved allowing employees selected for redundancy to see the details of their individual redundancy selection assessments.

Where an employee has been identified as the only employee at risk of redundancy, a failure to consult properly with him or her as to whether a more junior employee should be included in the pool for selection may render his or her dismissal unfair, even if the employer had considered the matter – Fulcrum Pharma (Europe) Ltd v Bonassera and anor EAT 0198/10. In that case, the EAT agreed with the tribunal that the employer had been wrong to conclude, without any further or meaningful consultation as to the size of the pool, that the pool was one person because it was the manager's role that had to go. Although notes prepared by the employer clearly showed that it had considered the issue of pooling, this had not been discussed with the employee who was at risk. More than this was required in terms of consultation. For example, the EAT thought that it might be for the employer to determine within the consultation process whether the more senior employee would be prepared to consider the more junior role at a reduced salary. (This case is also discussed under 'Pool for selection – bumping' above.)

8.155 Some examples of cases where there was insufficient consultation:

- **Clark v Business Angels Bureau Ltd (t/a Advantage Business Aims)** ET Case No.1307384/07: C was employed by BAB Ltd as Investment Manager. During his absence on holiday in August 2007 BAB Ltd acquired another company and e-mailed staff stating that there would be changes in the way that the company was run, and that the job of the Investment Manager would change. C saw the e-mail for the first time on his return from holiday and at a meeting on his first day back at work he was told about the changes, but no mention was made of redundancy. On 3 September he was told by e-mail that his old job had disappeared, and that his new role was to be discussed with him the next day. At that meeting he was told that the basic salary for the new job would be considerably less than what he had been receiving. Following unsuccessful negotiations, C refused the alternative offer and was made redundant. A tribunal accepted BAB Ltd's contention that it was not incumbent on it to consult with C over the business decision, but held that there was still a requirement that it consult adequately and properly at an individual level as to how that decision would impact on C's position. C had been unfairly dismissed

- **Abela v UGO Foods Group Ltd** ET Case No.3303108/07: A was employed as New Product Development Executive Chef. In June 2007 he was called to a meeting and told that there was to be no further new product development for a while. However, the managing director assured him that he would remain in employment. He continued in his role and an external candidate was appointed to another role which might have been suitable for him. Ultimately, A was dismissed as redundant. A tribunal found that A's dismissal was unfair. The managing director was acting in ignorance of the employer's true financial situation when he assured A that his job was safe, and thereby deprived A of making an informed decision to apply for the alternative post

- **McLeod v Thresher Group Ltd** ET Case No.3301163/08 and another: M was employed as branch manager of TG Ltd's off-licence in Finchley. By 1 November 2007 TG Ltd had decided to close the Finchley branch. On 14 January 2008 M was instructed to arrange a meeting with all staff on 16 January, but was given no indication of the purpose of the meeting. At the meeting TG Ltd announced that the store was under threat of closure and invited consultation on alternatives. TG Ltd mentioned to M that there was a vacancy for a manager at another store but M knew that that store was also under threat of closure. There were weekly bulletins giving details of vacancies but not all posts were included. M was informed at a meeting on 15 February that he was redundant and the store closed the next day. A tribunal accepted that TG Ltd was entitled to take its own business decision about closure of the store and was not obliged to consult staff on that decision, but it was not reasonable or fair to tell staff they were being consulted about a decision that had already been taken. If employees had been informed in late 2007 that the branch was to be closed, consultation would have concentrated on possible alternative employment. There would then have been vacancies that would have been acceptable to M

- **Hampton v Yakult UK Ltd** ET Case No.3300509/10: H was employed as a field representative by Y Ltd in the United Kingdom. Field representatives in Ireland were made redundant and in August 2009 Y Ltd drew the attention of its UK employees to these redundancies and stated that a review of the UK operation was 'currently underway'. In fact, by this time it had decided that the role of field representative should cease and be replaced by a different type of work. On 14 October the UK field representatives were summoned to meetings where they were told they were redundant. A tribunal upheld H's claim of unfair dismissal. The single line notice stating that a review of operations was underway could not amount to a warning that redundancies were likely.

8.156 However, in Russell v DSG Retail Ltd ET Case No.2605368/09 a tribunal found that a relatively minor flaw in the consultation process was not such as to make the dismissal unfair. R was not expressly told in the letter advising him of his redundancy that he had the right to appeal, although it was mentioned in an employee support guide supplied to him and all other employees at risk of redundancy.

8.157 *Information to be provided.* The EAT underlined the importance of providing an employee with adequate information in order to give him or her the opportunity to challenge a selection for redundancy in Pinewood Repro Ltd t/a County Print v Page 2011 ICR 508, EAT. There, P, who had worked as an estimator for PR Ltd for 23 years, was told that he was at risk of redundancy. He was placed in a pool with two other employees and they each received a copy of the scoring matrix together with the standards and qualities that each level represented. However, P did not receive his actual scores. P scored the lowest and was invited to a consultation meeting at which he was given his scores. He raised a number of queries in relation to these, but was not provided with an explanation as to how they had been calculated. When his appeal against his redundancy selection was dismissed, P brought an unfair dismissal claim before an employment tribunal.

The tribunal found that P's redundancy dismissal was unfair on the basis that he did not have an opportunity during the consultation process to challenge his scoring since PR Ltd had not explained how the scores had been arrived at. On appeal, the EAT upheld this finding, stressing – after referring to Glidewell LJ's comments in R v British Coal Corporation and Secretary of State for Trade and Industry ex parte Price and ors (above) – that fair consultation involves the provision of adequate information on which an employee can respond and argue his or her case. This did not happen in the instant case. P should have been given the opportunity to challenge his scoring in relation to flexibility – particularly since this was an entirely subjective area.

8.158 However, the EAT did go on to note that further explanation of scoring may not be necessary in every case, especially where the scores relate to issues such as attendance, timekeeping, conduct and productivity. In essence, it is for a tribunal to decide whether an employee has been given sufficient information to challenge the scores given in a redundancy selection exercise. The EAT observed that in the modern climate much of this information would hopefully have been available to an employee via a previous appraisal process.

Another example:

- **Mills v European Metal Recycling Ltd** ET Case No.2500506/09: a tribunal found that M's dismissal for redundancy was unfair because he was not given the scoring matrix prior to his dismissal. The tribunal believed he should have been given the matrix and 24–48 hours to consider it, to enable him to bring forward points relevant to his selection before the meeting. The employer's failure to do so rendered the consultation not meaningful.

Employer's responsibility for selection. In one unusual case, a dismissal was found to be unfair because the employer had left the entirety of the selection procedure and consultation to the company to which the employee had been seconded. In Atlantic Power and Gas Ltd v More EAT 1125/97 M was employed by APG Ltd, a company providing services for rigs in the North Sea. The company had an agreement with a joint venture company, A/S Ltd, which was set up to provide services to Shell Oil. M and a number of other APG Ltd employees were seconded to A/S Ltd for the purposes of working on a particular rig. Shell's need for rig workers subsequently decreased and A/S Ltd began a selection process which led to M being 'de-seconded'. That in turn led to M's immediate dismissal for redundancy by APG Ltd. An employment tribunal found that the dismissal was unfair because the employer had no input whatsoever into the consultation and selection process, which was left completely to A/S Ltd, and the employer had taken no steps to satisfy itself that the selection made was reasonable. In the tribunal's view, this was a fundamental obligation of employers that could not be surrendered to any third party. The EAT upheld the tribunal's decision. It further pointed out that, even if the selection process carried out by A/S Ltd had been fair, the employer should at the very least have given M the chance to state why it should be somebody other than him who should be selected. **8.159**

Length and timing of consultation. Case law suggests that concern over the adequacy of consultation is likely to be particularly acute if an employee is kept in the dark until very late in the redundancy process. Three examples: **8.160**

- **Air 2000 Ltd v Mallam** EAT 0773/03; 0058/04: following a review of its IT department (in which M was employed as the e-solutions manager), A Ltd decided to advertise for the position of head of IT. M did not apply for the post. He was subsequently informed that his position was to be integrated with the senior position, and consultations took place as to whether there was an alternative position available. At a meeting in December 2002 he was told that he had been unsuccessful in his application for an alternative job and that, as a result, he was to be made redundant with immediate effect. His complaint of unfair dismissal was upheld by a tribunal on the ground that A Ltd had failed adequately to warn him of the possibility of redundancy during the departmental review, and had failed to consult him at that point about the deletion of his post. On appeal, the EAT observed that the fact that there has been adequate consultation in respect of one stage in a redundancy process – in this case, consideration for suitable alternative employment – did not necessarily mean that the tribunal was bound to find that consultation had been adequate overall. Nor was it the case that an employer is never under a duty to consult the employee about the commercial decision to delete his or her post but only about the consequences of that decision. The tribunal's conclusion in this case – that fairness required the employer to have consulted prior to the decision being taken to delete M's job – was one to which it had been entitled to come

- **Mofunanya v Richmond Fellowship and anor** EAT 0449/03: M was employed to work on the night-shift for a charity providing residential care for people with mental health problems. A female colleague worked with M on the night-shift. One of the patients in the care home, P, was a female who required intimate care and, for that reason, M's co-worker had always been female. The charity ran into financial difficulties and it was proposed that the number of night staff be reduced. Discussions took place over a substantial period – always during the day, when M was not at work – and eventually it was resolved that M should be made redundant rather than his co-worker, owing to P's need to be looked after by a female employee. Only then was M informed about the proposal, and, following a second meeting shortly afterwards, he was dismissed. A tribunal rejected his argument that his dismissal was unfair on account of the employer's failure to consult prior to making the decision to dismiss. On appeal, however, the EAT overturned that finding. At no stage during the lengthy consideration of the redundancy proposal did the employer take any steps to have personal discussions with the two people – M and his co-worker – who were intimately involved in the process. And when the decision to dismiss was eventually made, matters were thereafter rushed. There was no period of reflection to enable M to take in and assess what was being put to him and to consider his various options. The employer's decision did not, therefore, fall within the band of reasonable responses

- **Vose v Cert Octavian plc** ET Case No.3301548/09: V was given one hour's notice of a meeting following his return from leave, and was not told what the meeting was about. The meeting lasted for seven minutes: V was told he was redundant, asked to return company property and was told to leave immediately. A client was told that day that V had left and a notice was posted saying that he and some others had left the business. He was only invited to a consultation meeting after he wrote to CO plc complaining of unfair dismissal. At the time there was a vacancy that would have been suitable for him. He raised it with CO plc at the meeting and was told he could apply for the post. When he asked why he could not simply be offered the job, he was told this was not possible as CO plc was in the middle of an internal recruitment process. CO plc conceded that V's dismissal was unfair. The tribunal noted that CO plc's failure to consult prevented any proper discussion of the alternatives and led to a breakdown of trust and confidence.

The extent and length of consultation necessary will vary between cases **8.161** depending on the facts. In Hilton v BAT Building Products Ltd EAT 787/87, for example, the EAT upheld the decision of a tribunal that H's dismissal was fair despite the fact that there had been only one and a half days' consultation with him before the decision to dismiss was taken. He had chosen not to work out his month's notice and had made it clear that he was not prepared to be downgraded in order to remain in employment. In the circumstances, the tribunal was therefore entitled to reach the decision it did. Similarly, in Dudson v Deepdene School EAT 674/97 a school teacher received little consultation before being informed that she had been selected for redundancy. The tribunal nevertheless found her dismissal fair because the dismissal did not take effect for a further seven months, during which period the employee made no effort to apply for any alternative posts that were available within the school. The EAT upheld the tribunal's decision. It stated that, while consultation before dismissal is highly desirable and its absence will very often be critical, it is only one of many factors to be taken into account. According to the EAT, 'where there is ample opportunity for consideration after a decision as to redundancy but before its actual implementation, the weight to be attached to the absence of prior consultation may obviously be reduced'.

Note that the scope of the duty to warn and consult extends only to those employees who are the target of the proposed redundancy. An employer will not be penalised for failing to consult an employee at an earlier stage if the employee was not at risk of redundancy at that time but only becomes so as a result of subsequent knock-on effects of the original redundancies. In Byrne v Arvin Meritor LVS (UK) Ltd EAT 239/02 the employee accepted a new role having been made fully aware that the position was unlikely to last for more than a year. Once he was in his new role, his old job disappeared following a restructuring exercise, during which redundancies were made. At the same time, the employer's requirements for the work carried out by the employee in his new job disappeared sooner than expected. Although efforts were made to find alternative employment, none was found and he was made redundant. An employment tribunal rejected his contention that he should have been consulted at the time of the original restructuring and, on appeal, the EAT upheld that finding. No duty to consult arose in regard to someone who might in the foreseeable future be affected by a redundancy/restructuring. To impose such a duty would place much broader obligations on an employer to consider the potential economic consequences of redundancy than are required under the reasonableness test in S.98(4) ERA.

8.162 **Appeals.** As identified under 'Reason for dismissal – breach of statutory dismissal procedures' above, a key component of the (now repealed) statutory dismissal and disciplinary procedures (DDPs) contained in the Employment Act 2002 was the employee's right to an appeal. Where one of the DDPs applied (broadly speaking, where fewer than 20 redundancies were proposed in a 90-day period), a failure on the part of an employer to allow an employee to appeal against his or her dismissal led to that dismissal being deemed automatically unfair. Crucially, since all the steps in the statutory procedures were mandatory, an employer's failure to hold a meeting with the individual concerned prior to dismissal (Step 2) could not be rectified at the appeal stage – Davies v Farnborough College of Technology EAT 0137/07.

With the repeal of the DDPs, the situation with regard to appeals is governed by pre-2004 case law. This established that a failure by the employer to consult an employee before dismissal *can* be cured at an appeal hearing after the date of dismissal – Lloyd v Taylor Woodrow Construction 1999 IRLR 782, EAT. In that case L was one of two quantity surveyors employed by TWC at a site in South Wales. In September 1997, owing to a reduction in workload, TWC decided that one of the surveyors would have to be made redundant. It decided upon L on the basis of ad hoc selection criteria. It did not consult with L about the selection criteria but informed him at a meeting that he was 'potentially redundant'. He was dismissed in October. Eight weeks later L requested a meeting with management and he was informed for the first time of the primary selection criteria used, namely length of service, attendance, disciplinary record and capability/suitability for the post. In the light of this meeting, L appealed against the decision to dismiss him and a final appeal was heard in April 1998. Both appeals were treated by TWC as rehearings of L's case, and on both occasions the original decision to dismiss L was upheld. L claimed unfair dismissal.

8.163 The employment tribunal found that the consultation process was defective in that L was not informed of the selection criteria before TWC took the decision to dismiss him. Nevertheless, the tribunal decided that – despite the procedural defect – there had been no unfair dismissal because the defect had been corrected by TWC at the later appeal hearings, when L was given the opportunity to contest the criteria. L appealed to the EAT, arguing that, where a dismissal is on the ground of redundancy, a failure by the employer to consult with the affected employee about the selection criteria before dismissal cannot be cured by consulting at a later date and then holding appeal hearings. The EAT dismissed L's appeal, stating that the tribunal was entitled to find that the defect in consultation prior to dismissal had been cured by the rehearing at the appeal stages. It cited Whitbread and Co plc v Mills 1988 ICR 776, EAT, as clear authority for the proposition that a procedural defect at the dismissal stage may be cured at the appeal stage. In doing so, it rejected L's argument that a case of dismissal by reason of redundancy was distinguishable from cases of dismissal for conduct or capability such as occurred in the Whitbread case.

Note that the EAT in Whitbread held that procedural defects could only be cured where the appeal amounted to a complete rehearing of the matter, not simply a review of the original decision. However, this part of its decision was subsequently overruled by the Court of Appeal in Taylor v OCS Group Ltd 2006 ICR 1602, CA. In that case the Court held that it is irrelevant whether the appeal hearing takes the form of a rehearing or a review as long as the appeal is sufficiently thorough to cure the earlier procedural shortcomings – see IDS Employment Law Handbook, 'Unfair Dismissal' (2010), Chapter 6, under 'Disciplinary proceedings – the appeal'.

Alternative employment

8.164

The consideration of alternative employment for employees selected for redundancy will often be an important part of a fair and reasonable redundancy procedure. While the statutory mechanism for offering alternative or renewed employment is dealt with in detail in Chapter 3, we consider below some of the circumstances in which a failure to offer such employment can lead to a redundancy dismissal being rendered unfair.

Extent of obligation. In Thomas and Betts Manufacturing Ltd v Harding 8.165 1980 IRLR 255, CA, the Court of Appeal ruled that an employer should do what it can so far as is reasonable to seek alternative work. This does not mean, however, as the EAT pointed out in MDH Ltd v Sussex 1986 IRLR 123, EAT, that an employer is obliged by law to enquire about job opportunities elsewhere and a failure to do so will not necessarily render a dismissal unfair. Two examples:

- **Kilgallon and ors v Pilkington United Kingdom Ltd** EAT 0771/03: P Ltd sought to avoid compulsory redundancies by offering secondments to Spain on terms that each secondee would accept voluntary redundancy at the end of the secondment period. Following negotiations with the recognised trade union, a clause was inserted into the secondment agreement providing that 'should there be any other opportunities for further employment with [P Ltd] at the end of your secondment, you will have the opportunity to be given full consideration' (the consideration clause). K and others accepted secondment in September 1999 but were made redundant in September 2001 without any attempt being made to redeploy them pursuant to the consideration clause. They adduced evidence to show that during the secondment period, P Ltd had filled vacancies for professional engineers and other jobs had been taken by ex-apprentices in accordance with the priority accorded to them under a recruitment policy agreed with the union. The claimants unsuccessfully claimed that their dismissals were unfair as P Ltd had failed to consult about and offer alternative employment both in 1999 and at the end of the secondments. On appeal, the EAT held that the question of alternative employment did not arise in 1999 because the claimants had agreed to be seconded to Spain as an alternative to being made redundant. As for the position in September 2001 when their secondments ended, the tribunal had been entitled to find that the breach by P Ltd of its obligation under the consideration clause made no difference to the outcome in view of (i) the agreed policy favouring the recruitment of ex-apprentices, and (ii) the fact that the claimants were not suited to the other available positions

- **Allen and ors v The Manchester College** ET Case Nos.2411439/09 and others: a tribunal did not accept the claimants' submission that the college acted unreasonably in failing to redeploy them. Given the size of the college and diversity of the skills of its employees it would not have been reasonable to put recruitment on hold. While the college did not actively seek employment for those at risk of redundancy it did provide them with vacancy lists and its actions in this regard were not unreasonable.

8.166 These cases show that, in certain circumstances, an employer may be excused a failure to make efforts to redeploy employees rather than make them redundant. However, as a general rule, tribunals will expect an employer with sufficient resources to take reasonable steps to ameliorate the effects of redundancy, including giving detailed consideration to whether suitable alternative employment is available. Furthermore, in Fisher v Hoopoe Finance Ltd EAT 0043/05 the EAT suggested that an employer's responsibility does not necessarily end with drawing the employee's attention to job vacancies that may be suitable. The employer should also provide information about the financial prospects of any vacant alternative positions. A failure to do so may lead to any later redundancy dismissal being found to be unfair.

Even if an employer considers that an employee would not accept an alternative post, it may be unreasonable to exclude him or her from consideration for it without consulting him or her first. In Ward and anor v Mahle Filter Systems UK Ltd ET Case No.3102701/09 and another a tribunal found that the claimants' dismissals were unfair because a short-term post had arisen in a different part of the country and it was offered to one of the claimants' colleagues. It was only due to continue for a month, but in the event was extended for a further three months; it was unfair to exclude the claimants from consideration for the post, without consultation.

8.167 The potential consequences for an employer who entirely fails to consult or even consider the possibility of alternative employment are well illustrated by Stanco Exhibitions plc v Wright EAT 0291/07. W was unfairly dismissed from his post as an electrical foreman. At the liability hearing the tribunal concluded that although the company no longer employed electricians under contract (as opposed to sub-contract), W's history of being an employed electrician meant there was a possibility that he would have been kept on as an employed electrician, on a salary of £24,500, and that he should be compensated accordingly. On appeal to the EAT, the employer argued that the tribunal had erred in finding that the company ought to have created a new position of employment for W, when the company had in fact given up employing electricians directly. However, the EAT refused to interfere with the tribunal's decision, concluding that the tribunal had to consider whether on the balance of probabilities it was likely that W would have found a job within the company. Its conclusion was 'a realistic proposal' in the light of the evidence, including the fact that the company had originally employed electricians directly and that W was experienced.

Objectivity required? It should be noted that, when considering employees for **8.168** alternative employment, it would seem that there is no need to adopt the strict objectivity that is so important in the process of selection for redundancy. In Akzo Coatings plc v Thompson and ors; Thompson and ors v Akzo Coatings plc EAT 1117/94; 1037/95 a redundancy situation was created when the employer closed a depot where 45 employees worked. Most of the employees applied for alternative employment at two other depots. The employer drew up selection criteria for the available vacancies in consultation with the employees' union. Each employee completed a questionnaire and was interviewed by a panel. The candidates with the highest scores were offered the alternative jobs. Those who had not been offered alternative employment brought claims of unfair dismissal. A tribunal found that the criteria used to select the employees for alternative employment were insufficiently objective, fair and reasonable. For example, the procedure included a subjective assessment by each employee's immediate manager; there was no independent observer present at the panel interviews; and the selection criteria used differed from those originally published. The tribunal therefore concluded that the dismissals were unfair. The EAT overruled the tribunal, holding that the tribunal had misdirected itself by applying the guidelines set out by the EAT in Williams and ors v Compair Maxam Ltd 1982 ICR 156, EAT. Those guidelines were concerned with the formulation and application of objective criteria related to selection for dismissal from a pool where some employees would be retained and others would be dismissed. The guidelines did not apply to selection for alternative employment, where the issue was whether the employer had taken reasonable steps to find alternative employment for the employees. It was clear on the facts of this particular case that the employers had taken such reasonable steps and the EAT substituted a finding that the dismissals were fair.

Similar findings to that in Akzo were reached by other divisions of the EAT in the following cases:

- **Darlington Memorial Hospital NHS Trust v Edwards and anor** EAT 678/95: a tribunal found dismissals for redundancy unfair because, in offering alternative employment, the employer had not followed similar principles of fairness to those that apply to selection for redundancy. The EAT overturned this decision on the same grounds as Akzo. However, it added some gloss to that decision, suggesting that the selection process will need to meet at least some criteria of fairness

- **Look Ahead Housing and Care Ltd v Odili and anor** EAT 0437/07: in written tests and an interview for alternative posts, O and M fell well short of the required mark, but a tribunal considered that the employer ought to have offered them the posts because, among other factors, it had failed to take into account their past performance and because the interview process was subjective. The EAT overturned the tribunal's decision. The evidence did not entitle the tribunal to find that the jobs were so similar that any reasonable employer would have had regard to past performance. It also became too embroiled in the interview process. The EAT recognised that an interview process is always going to be to some extent a subjective exercise, but the evidence was that there had been a discussion beforehand about the questions to be posed and the kinds of answers that the employer was looking for. The case was remitted to a fresh tribunal for reconsideration

- **Jones v Northumberland County Council** EAT 0482/08: J challenged the fairness of an interview process for a newly created post, claiming that there should have been a pre-existing template or set of model answers, and that the interviewing panel should have been differently composed. However, the EAT upheld the tribunal's decision that the process was not unfair. The tribunal had found that proper assessments were made based on the answers given by both candidates. The questions were based on the job description and person specification, and raised for consideration issues pertinent to the job. The tribunal considered the lack of model answers, but did not find that this made the process unfair; it pointed out that it is impossible, if two people are being interviewed for the same job, completely to remove any subjectivity from the process.

8.169　However, while the strict objectivity required when selecting for redundancy is not necessary in relation to offering alternative employment, a degree of objectivity is nevertheless important. In Ralph Martindale and Co Ltd v Harris EAT 0166/07 two senior management posts – held by H and E – were to be deleted and a new position created. Both H and E applied for the new role, while applications were also sought from other internal candidates whose posts were not at risk of redundancy. E was appointed after the application of a matrix of subjective criteria drawn up by a director of RMC Ltd, and on the basis that his was a 'less insular' management style. A tribunal decided that, owing to its subjective nature, the process of offering alternative employment was not fair, and further that no reasonable employer would have opened the new post up to candidates other than H and E. On that basis it determined that H's dismissal was unfair. On appeal, the EAT concluded that the tribunal's decision was not at odds with Akzo (see above), and noted that the decision in Edwards (also above) supported the contention that minimum standards of fairness will apply. Tellingly, the EAT did not disapprove of the tribunal's criticism of the subjective nature of E's selection for the post.

Nevertheless, even where an employer fails to adhere to its own job description and person specification, and deviates from its stated interview process, in making a new appointment, a tribunal may still be entitled to conclude, on the evidence, that the process was fair – Morgan v Welsh Rugby Union EAT 0314/10. In that case M was employed by WRU to manage the development of premier-level rugby union football coaches. In 2008 WRU conducted a reorganisation, which involved amalgamating M's post with that of S, whose role had been to manage the development of community-level coaches. A new single post was created, for which M and S both applied. The job description and person specification provided that the appointee 'will be qualified to at least WRU Level 4 or equivalent' and that he or she 'will have an established reputation of developing elite coaches and within the field of coach education'. Following an interview process, S was appointed, and M was dismissed for redundancy. He brought a claim of unfair dismissal, which was dismissed, and he appealed to the EAT. He argued that in deciding to interview S, the appointment committee did not adhere to the job description or person specification. S was not qualified to the appropriate level and, unlike M, had no recent experience of training elite coaches. Furthermore, the committee did not adhere to the notified interview format. S was allowed to give an extended presentation, setting out a plan and vision for the post as opposed to addressing the agreed topic. As a result, he was not asked individual questions. The committee gave overall scores but did not score the presentation or questions individually.

The EAT observed that where an employer has to decide which employees from **8.170** a pool of existing employees are to be made redundant, the criteria will reflect a known job, performed by known employees over a period. Where, however, an employer has to appoint to new roles after a reorganisation, the employer's decision has to be forward-looking, centring on the ability of the individual to perform in the new role. This sort of selection is more likely to involve an interview process. A tribunal considering whether the process of appointment to a new role is fair simply has to apply S.98(4) – as the tribunal did in Ralph Martindale. The EAT stressed that the tribunal is entitled to consider how far an interview process was objective, but it should keep in mind that an employer's assessment of which candidate will best perform in a new role is likely to involve a substantial element of judgement. The majority of the tribunal did not commit an error of law in taking the view that WRU was not bound to adhere to the job description and person specification slavishly or precisely. If the appointment of a new manager had been external, the employer would not have been so bound. If a candidate had emerged who was outstanding but did not meet some aspect of the person specification, the employer would have remained entitled to appoint that candidate. Although this might seem unfair to other candidates who did meet the person specification, it would not follow that the employer's decision was unreasonable. In the EAT's view, WRU was entitled to interview internal candidates even if they did not precisely meet the job description, and it was entitled to appoint a candidate who did not precisely meet the person specification. Nor did the EAT think that the tribunal had erred in its approach to the interview process WRU had followed. Like the tribunal, the EAT criticised the panel's failure to mark the candidates in accordance with the original plan, but considered this a matter for the tribunal to take into account in its assessment under S.98(4), which it had done.

8.171 It should be noted, however, that while the same level of objectivity may not be required in appointing redundant employees to alternative posts, as compared with selecting them for redundancy in the first place, subjectivity in the process is more likely to raise questions of discrimination. In Rivkin v Mott MacDonald Ltd ET Case No.2408125/09, for example, R's post was selected for redundancy when he was aged 60, and his CV, which included his date of birth, was forwarded to managers of other divisions in an attempt to find suitable alternative work. One manager invited him to a meeting since he believed that if R was able to demonstrate his skills at interview, he could make a business case to employ him. Following an interview the division decided not to employ R, and he was made redundant. The manager claimed not to have known R's age, and said it had not therefore been a factor in the decision not to offer him a post. However, a tribunal found that although R's dismissal for redundancy was not on the ground of his age and was not unfair, the decision not to appoint him to the alternative post did amount to age discrimination. The fact that the manager claimed not to have known R's age before the interview, despite the fact that the notice of appearance said that he did, and that there had been a discussion during the interview about R's age and the time it would take to train him up led the tribunal to infer that age was a factor in the decision not to offer R a post in the division.

Discriminatory redundancy is discussed in Chapter 9.

8.172 **Group companies.** It may sometimes be appropriate for employers to consider the availability of alternative employment not only within the particular company in which the employee is employed but also within other companies in the same group. In Euroguard Ltd v Rycroft EAT 842/92 GTS Ltd, a security company, had two subsidiary companies, E Ltd and CIT Ltd. R worked as a personnel officer for E Ltd and was based in Glasgow. GTS Ltd had two other personnel officers in Scotland, one in Glasgow and one in Edinburgh. One of the three had to be made redundant and R was chosen. At the time of the redundancy CIT Ltd was looking for a personnel officer. R expressed an interest in the post and was interviewed but was not successful. Other candidates for the job underwent more rigorous assessment and psychometric testing before the selection was made. The tribunal took the view that E Ltd had a duty to take reasonable care to consider R for any other posts which might have been suitable and, on the facts, R's application for alternative employment with CIT Ltd had not been adequately considered. His dismissal was unfair for that reason. E Ltd appealed on the ground that E Ltd and CIT Ltd were independent companies, but the EAT took the view that there might be circumstances in which it would be appropriate to look beyond the immediate employer to other companies within the group when considering the availability of alternative employment. The affairs of the company in this particular group, at least in regard to the appointment and redundancy of staff at R's level, were closely integrated: the same individuals were involved and the same policy applied. The EAT concluded that the tribunal had been entitled to find R's dismissal unfair.

However, where there is evidence that the companies within a group operate autonomously, it will not be open to a tribunal to conclude that an employer should have allocated an employee to a vacant position within an associated company – Parfums Givenchy Ltd v Finch EAT 0517/09. In that case F was engaged on the beauty counter of PG Ltd's franchise in Selfridges department store in London. Separately branded, but part of the same group of companies, were Christian Dior and Guerlain. A single HR Manager presided over the HR functions of the three perfume divisions. On 28 August 2008 PG Ltd's franchise closed down. F applied for alternative vacancies within the group, but she was unsuccessful. She alleged that the HR managers had colluded in denying her a role. However, the EAT overturned a tribunal's decision to uphold F's unfair dismissal claim. It was not open to the tribunal on the evidence to find that PG Ltd had power to allocate F to a position in Guerlain or Christian Dior. The three companies operated autonomously, with their own HR and line managers, and it was the line managers who interviewed F. The highest it could be put was that PG Ltd was under a duty to assist F and to consider alternative work. The EAT remitted the case to a fresh tribunal.

Inferior position. It will not necessarily be unreasonable for an employer to **8.173** assume that an employee would not wish to accept an inferior position. The EAT suggested in Barratt Construction Ltd v Dalrymple 1984 IRLR 385, EAT, that 'without laying down any hard and fast rule' a senior manager who was prepared to accept a subordinate post rather than being dismissed should make this known to his or her employer as soon as possible. This case does not relieve employers from the obligation to consult employees, however, and in Hall v Times Furnishing Co Ltd EAT 267/87 a different division of the EAT found that the dismissal of a senior manager was unfair for lack of consultation. After failing to find him an equivalent position to that which he had held before, his employer dismissed him without discussing the possibility of offering him one of the inferior positions available.

8.174 **Unreasonable terms.** Where an alternative job is offered on unreasonable terms, the dismissal of an employee who refuses that offer will probably be unfair. In Elliot v Richard Stump Ltd 1987 ICR 579, EAT, the employer refused the employee a trial period in a new job. The EAT ruled that the ensuing dismissal was unfair, as it was unreasonable of the employer to offer the alternative job on those terms. This was despite the fact that, as a matter of law, the employee was entitled to a trial period (see Chapter 3 under 'Trial periods'). The EAT held that, where the terms of an alternative job offered were prima facie unreasonable, the employee's dismissal on refusing it would justify a finding of unfair dismissal.

In Sun Valley Poultry Ltd v Mitchell and ors EAT 164/96 E and her two colleagues worked as administrators. The employer embarked upon a large scale reorganisation that involved the merging of administrative departments and the loss of administrative jobs. The administrative jobs that would be available after the reorganisation were advertised internally, with employees from a number of departments being invited to apply. The stated qualifications for the new jobs included a requirement of A-level English and, if possible, another language. As E did not have A-level English she decided she had no chance of the job and sought employment elsewhere. Sometime later, however, she learnt that the A-level requirement was a mistake. A tribunal upheld the employee's claim of unfair dismissal. Upholding that decision, the EAT held that the tribunal had been entitled to find that the employer acted unfairly and outside the bounds of reasonableness in imposing the requirement for A-level English. Moreover, the removal of the requirement had come too late, as the employee had already secured employment elsewhere.

8.175 By contrast, if the employer imposes a condition on alternative employment which is reasonable, dismissal of the employee for refusing to accept it may be fair. In Bickerton v Central Office Ltd ET Case No.16132/95 B had a 'spiky' haircut and wore T-shirts, torn trousers and a heavily studded belt. The employer tolerated this style of dress but tried to keep him away from customers, some of whom had complained about his appearance. When the employer had to reorganise its business owing to severe financial pressure, B was made redundant. He was offered alternative work, but on the condition that he wore company livery. B refused and the employer modified the condition to his wearing 'suitable' clothing. B still refused and was dismissed. The tribunal found the dismissal fair as the employer's request was reasonable.

8.176 **Assessment at time of dismissal.** The question of timing is important here. Since the reasonableness of a dismissal is dependent on the situation known to the employer at the time of the dismissal, the appearance of an alternative job *after* the employee has been dismissed cannot make the dismissal unfair. In Octavius Atkinson and Sons Ltd v Morris 1989 ICR 431, CA, work became available only hours after the employee was dismissed on account of redundancy.

The Court of Appeal held that this made no difference to the question of fairness. However, where an employer knows that work will become available in a short time it may be unreasonable to dismiss an employee for redundancy.

By the same token, the fact that it subsequently transpires that the employee would not have accepted the alternative employment even if it had been offered to him or her will not prevent a finding of unfairness (although this may be a factor taken into account when the tribunal considers compensation). Thus, in Brown v Gavin Scott t/a Gavin Crawford EAT 149/87 the tribunal decided that there was no unfair dismissal, despite a failure to offer available alternative employment, because it found that B would not have accepted the offer in any event. The EAT overturned the decision and held that the dismissal was unfair for lack of consultation. Citing the decision in Polkey v AE Dayton Services Ltd 1988 ICR 142, HL (see 'Individual consultation' above), the EAT stated that the dismissal was unfair as the employer could not reasonably have decided at the time of the dismissal that consultation with B would have been 'utterly useless'.

9 Discriminatory redundancy

Sham redundancies

Victimisation

Discriminatory selection

Discrimination against part-time workers

Discrimination against fixed-term employees

In addition to claiming unfair dismissal (discussed in Chapter 8), an employee **9.1** selected for redundancy may argue that his or her dismissal was discriminatory. Most discrimination claims are brought under the Equality Act 2010 (EqA), although special provisions exist in respect of part-time and fixed-term workers (see 'Discrimination against part-time workers' and 'Discrimination against fixed-term employees' below). In this chapter we set out the main issues that can arise in the context of a redundancy claim. However, it is not intended to provide a comprehensive exposition of the law on discrimination, which is outside the scope of this Handbook. For detailed discussion of discrimination law under the EqA, see IDS Employment Law Guide, 'The Equality Act 2010', and our forthcoming IDS Employment Law Handbook, 'Discrimination in the Workplace' (2012).

The EqA does not contain any provisions that relate specifically to redundancy. **9.2** However, the employee may seek to rely on the Act where:

- the redundancy was a 'sham', in that the dismissal was not by reason of redundancy, but was instead by reason of age, disability, gender reassignment, marital or civil partnership status, pregnancy or maternity, race, religion or belief, sex or sexual orientation (the 'protected characteristics') and thus constituted direct discrimination

- the employee's selection for redundancy constituted victimisation for his or her bringing a discrimination claim or taking other action protected under the Act

- the application of the selection criteria, the failure to offer alternative employment, or any other aspect of the redundancy process, was influenced by a protected characteristic and thereby amounted to direct or indirect discrimination.

Note that whereas the rights to claim redundancy pay and unfair dismissal are limited to employees as defined by S.230 of the Employment Right Act 1996 (see Chapter 5 under 'Employees and excluded employees'), discrimination claims under the EqA can be brought by a more broadly defined category of worker – see IDS Employment Law Guide, 'The Equality Act 2010', Chapter 3.

9.3 **Uncapped compensation.** Unlike compensation for unfair dismissal, where there is a limit of (currently) £68,400 on the compensatory award, compensation for discriminatory dismissal is uncapped. In addition, tribunals may make an award for injury to feelings. Under the guidelines set out in Vento v Chief Constable of West Yorkshire Police 2003 ICR 318, CA, such awards generally range from £500 to £30,000.

An example of just how costly a discriminatory redundancy selection can be is afforded by Abbey National plc and anor v Chagger 2010 ICR 397, CA. In that case C, who was of Asian ethnic origin, was made redundant in a procedure that breached all of the Compair Maxam guidelines (see Chapter 8 under 'Unreasonable redundancy'), as well as the (now repealed) statutory dismissal procedure. In addition, his employer failed to respond to a race discrimination questionnaire, had not followed the Commission of Racial Equality's Code of Practice (since superseded by the Equality and Human Rights Commission's Code of Practice on Employment) on workforce monitoring, and had given no satisfactory explanation for facts which the tribunal found presented a prima facie case of race discrimination. The tribunal initially ordered that C be reinstated, but when the employer refused, it awarded C £2,855,659. Had the selection for redundancy merely been unfair on procedural grounds and not discriminatory, the maximum C could have recovered would have been £63,000 (the upper limit at the time). (The Court of Appeal subsequently remitted the case to the same tribunal to reconsider C's compensation on the ground that it had erred in failing to look at whether the award should be reduced to reflect the chance that C would have been dismissed in any event. However, it also went on to say that C could, in principle, recover 'stigma damages' to reflect the fact that employers – unrelated to the respondent – were unwilling to employ him because he had brought a discrimination claim.)

9.4 ## Sham redundancies

As discussed in Chapter 2 under 'Unreasonable redundancy', when determining the fairness of a redundancy dismissal tribunals are not normally entitled to investigate the reasons behind the redundancy situation. There is no need for employers to demonstrate that they were forced into making redundancies by economic circumstances: it will be sufficient if they have their own good commercial reasons for making the changes. This does not mean, however, that tribunals will always take the employer's stated reasons for the dismissal at face value. As discussed below under 'Discriminatory selection – reverse burden of proof', where an employee establishes facts from which discrimination can be inferred, the tribunal will look to the employer to provide a non-discriminatory explanation for those facts. Where consultation has been minimal, selection less than transparent and little effort made to offer the employee alternative employment, claims that a 'redundancy situation' was a sham – and the dismissal discriminatory – will be harder for an employer to rebut.

Some cases where tribunals have found 'redundancies' to be fabricated **9.5** and discriminatory:

- **Catton v Rye Street Coachworks Ltd** ET Case No. 3201204/08: on 7 February 2008 C told the daughter of her employer's proprietor that she was pregnant. On 11 February C was told that, because of a 'reshuffle', she was redundant. There had been no indication that there might be redundancies and no sign of any downturn in work. The employer claimed that the decision had been taken to make C redundant in December, but she had not been offered employment at another branch where a new employee was taken on in January 2008. In the absence of any evidence from the proprietor or his daughter, the tribunal found that the employer knew that C was pregnant when it made the decision to dismiss. There was no true redundancy situation and C was dismissed because she was pregnant. This was an act of sex discrimination

- **Birchall v Rapide Reprographics Ltd** ET Case No.2401876/09: while off work due to illness B discovered she was pregnant, and informed her employer on 31 October 2008. Later the same day the employer delivered a letter to her home saying they were commencing a 14-day consultation period for redundancy due to a down-turn in business. The letter said they were considering making about 11 people redundant, but in the event B was the only person dismissed. Although she was still off work ill she was fit to attend a meeting, but was not invited to do so. On 18 November she received a letter dismissing her. A tribunal found that the timing of the letter warning her of redundancy, the failure to meet her or consider alternative work and the fact that she was the only person made redundant all indicated that pregnancy was the true reason for dismissal

- **Lantsbury v Ebara International Corporation** ET Case No.2301433/09: L, who was aged 58, was employed as a field service engineer. EIC experienced a fall in orders and also wanted to reduce overheads in its UK operation, and so decided to lose one of its three field service engineers. It assessed the engineers and because L's score was lowest decided to select him for redundancy. He was called to a consultation meeting on 22 December 2008, where he was told he would be redundant with effect from 31 December. A tribunal concluded that the redundancy situation was not genuine; the need for UK-based engineers had not ceased or diminished. In any event the dismissal would have been unfair since EIC had decided who should be made redundant before the consultation period commenced, and neither of the other engineers was called to a consultation meeting. There was no

287

consideration of alternatives to dismissal or of alternative work. L was substantially older than the other two engineers, and EIC had recruited a much younger engineer in the USA in September. EIC had relied primarily on L failing to establish a prima facie case of discrimination and had no substantive defence to the claim of age discrimination. The tribunal drew the inference that L's dismissal was linked to his age and was discriminatory.

9.6 Victimisation

Victimisation is a self-contained form of discrimination under the EqA. S.27(1) provides that 'a person (A) victimises another person (B) if A subjects B to a detriment because (a) B does a protected act, or (b) A believes that B has done, or may do, a protected act'. 'Protected acts' for this purpose are any of the following:

- bringing proceedings under the EqA

- giving evidence or information in connection with proceedings under the EqA

- doing any other thing for the purposes of or in connection with the EqA, and

- making an allegation (whether or not express) that A or another person has contravened the EqA – S.27(2).

9.7 'Detriment' is not defined by the EqA but, according to the Equality and Human Rights Commission's Code of Practice on Employment, it would be 'anything which the individual concerned might reasonably consider changed their position for the worse or put them at a disadvantage' (para 9.8). It is clear that selection for redundancy could constitute a detriment, as the following cases demonstrate:

- **Fitness First Clubs Ltd v Drysdale** EAT 0195/08: the EAT upheld a tribunal's decision that an employee's selection for redundancy had been affected by her submission of a questionnaire under the Equal Pay Act 1970 (now the EqA)

- **Marshall v Veolia ES (UK) Ltd** ET Case No.2801214/09: on 23 September 2008 M and her manager had an argument. She gave evidence that he had launched into a tirade of abuse, including sexist language. She was signed off work suffering from stress and depression and did not return. She lodged a grievance, as a result of which her manager was given a written warning. M said she could no longer work with the manager, since she feared a repetition of the incident. On 12 December she was informed that she was at risk of redundancy. M was scored lowest of the people in the pool, and she was dismissed. However, a tribunal found that M's selection for redundancy was an act of unlawful victimisation. M had done a protected act by complaining

288

about her line manager and he was substantially involved in the redundancy process. She established a prima facie case that the decision to put her in a pool with two administrators even though she was a sales coordinator (and thus did not have the same skills) could have been made by reason of her protected act and her employer failed to prove the contrary

- **Hill v Smith Emmerson Ltd and ors** ET Case Nos.2601657/08 and another: H was practice manager for SE Ltd. In September 2007 SE Ltd invited her to become a partner in SEA LLP. The next day S informed SE Ltd that she was pregnant. In November SE Ltd offered her the choice of remaining an employee of SE Ltd or resigning and becoming a salaried partner with SEA LLP, with a consequent reduction in maternity entitlement. She elected to remain an employee of SE Ltd. Later that month SEA LLP asked H to relinquish her non-salaried LLP partner status to enable them to bring another partner into the business. H was distressed by this turn of events and made it clear that she wanted the status quo to remain. Notwithstanding her view, SEA LLP drew up an agreement to admit new partners and for H to resign as a partner. She made it clear that she thought this action was being taken because she was pregnant and submitted a grievance. She was removed as a partner in SEA LLP. On her return from maternity leave on 29 May, she was informed that she had been provisionally selected for redundancy. She unsuccessfully applied for another role and was dismissed. A tribunal found that H was unlawfully victimised by SE Ltd because she had made an allegation of discrimination.

9.8 For a fuller discussion of victimisation claims under the EqA, refer to IDS Employment Law Guide, 'The Equality Act 2010', Chapter 2, and our forthcoming IDS Employment Law Handbook, 'Discrimination in the Workplace' (2012).

Discriminatory selection **9.9**

Even where there is a genuine redundancy situation, a claim may arise where the employee considers that some aspect of his or her selection for redundancy was discriminatory. This may be because of the manner in which consultation was conducted (or because it was not conducted at all); because the employer failed to offer a suitable alternative vacancy to the employee; because of the application of discriminatory selection criteria; or for some other reason.

The two main forms of discrimination are direct discrimination and indirect discrimination. These are discussed in detail in IDS Employment Law Guide, 'The Equality Act 2010', Chapter 2; and in our forthcoming IDS Employment Law Handbook, 'Discrimination in the Workplace' (2012). Briefly, direct discrimination occurs where the employer treats an employee less favourably than it treats other employees because of a protected characteristic (i.e. on the

289

ground of age, disability, gender reassignment, marital or civil partnership status, pregnancy or maternity, race, religion or belief, sex or sexual orientation) – S.13 EqA. For example, the employer selects an employee for redundancy because of their age. Indirect discrimination occurs where, instead of selecting an employee for redundancy on one of the prohibited grounds, the employer applies a provision, criterion or practice that puts an employee who has a particular protected characteristic at a particular disadvantage when compared with persons who do not share that characteristic and the use of the provision, criterion or practice cannot be justified – S.19. For example, the employer selects employees for redundancy on the basis of 'last in, first out'. This criterion is potentially indirectly discriminatory on the ground of age, as younger employees tend to have less service and are thus more likely to be selected for redundancy.

9.10   However, an employer may be able to justify an indirectly discriminatory selection criterion (or any other indirectly discriminatory aspect of the redundancy selection process) if it can be shown to be a *proportionate means of achieving a legitimate aim* – S.19(2)(d). An example:

- **Ganesan v Opera Solutions Ltd** ET Case No.2203343/09: G worked for OS Ltd as a management consultant. Three redundancies needed to be made in the office in which G was based, and he was selected. He claimed, among other things, that his selection amounted to indirect race discrimination because one of the criteria related to language skills. G was of Indian/Tamil origin and said that people not of his national and ethnic origin would be more likely to speak other European languages. During the hearing he withdrew the claim. However, the tribunal noted that since it was necessary for management consultants to have language skills of a high level for some of OS Ltd's projects, it would have found the inclusion of this criterion to be a proportionate means of achieving a legitimate aim.

We discuss below some issues that are generic to discriminatory redundancies, before briefly considering three specific characteristics that raise particular issues with regard to indirect discrimination: pregnancy/maternity, age and disability. This is not intended to provide a comprehensive account of the law in this area, but rather to highlight some of the issues involved. For detailed discussion of discrimination law under the EqA, see IDS Employment Law Guide, 'The Equality Act 2010', and our forthcoming IDS Employment Law Handbook, 'Discrimination in the Workplace' (2012).

9.11   **Reverse burden of proof**

As observed in Chapter 2 under 'Presumption of redundancy', where an employee is claiming a redundancy payment, there is a presumption that he or she has been dismissed for redundancy unless the contrary is proved – S.163(2) ERA. However, where the employee is claiming that his or her selection for redundancy was discriminatory this presumption is not relevant and the so-called 'reverse burden of proof' applies. This does not mean that, once an employee alleges that his or her selection for redundancy was discriminatory, the employer must disprove it. Rather, if an employee can prove facts from which the tribunal could infer that discrimination has taken place, then the burden shifts to the employer to provide a non-discriminatory explanation for those facts. Reverse burden of proof provisions are now found in all strands of discrimination law – see IDS Employment Law Guide, 'The Equality Act 2010', Chapter 5, for details.

A simple allegation that an employee's selection for redundancy was discriminatory will be insufficient to shift the burden of proof. For example, in Hart v Anglia Newspapers Ltd ET Case No.1502625/08 a newspaper editor claimed that he was selected for redundancy on the ground of his age, because he was the oldest editor in the group of newspapers and one of the oldest of the sub-editing staff. However, a tribunal found that even if H was the oldest editor, which was unproven, there was nothing to infer that age-related factors lay behind the redundancy. H offered no evidence to advance his suspicion that age was a factor in his dismissal, and thus failed to make out a prima facie case sufficient to shift the burden of proof to the employer.

Once an employee has proven facts from which discrimination could be **9.12** inferred, employers are likely to find it harder to establish a non-discriminatory explanation for those facts in circumstances where they have failed to adopt a transparent and objective selection process (see also 'Sham redundancies' above). Two examples:

- **Obikwu and anor v British Refugee Council** ET Case Nos.1502553/06 and another: a tribunal found that the employer had abandoned its own policies in the way it selected people for redundancy and that the way in which interviews were scored was 'eccentric and lacking in transparency'. After the redundancy selection there were no black workers, and two white females were retained without undergoing a selection process. The employer failed to prove the absence of discrimination and so the claims of direct race discrimination were upheld, although the tribunal was satisfied that there was no conscious discrimination

- **Shaw v Symphony Group plc** ET Case No.2400697/09: S worked for SG plc as a business account manager and in April 2008 was one of its highest performers. S told SG plc in April that she was pregnant. She was not due to go on maternity leave until October, but SG plc began to transfer her accounts to other employees in July. S told SG plc she was unhappy about this, and decided to take her annual leave immediately before her maternity leave, making her last day at work 28 August. The market for SG plc's products deteriorated rapidly over the summer and on 24 September it decided to make up to 25 employees redundant nationwide. S was selected for redundancy and was dismissed on 24 October. A tribunal upheld her sex discrimination claim. In certain respects SG plc's criteria lacked objectivity, clarity and consistency. S was one of the top performers but was selected for redundancy before people who performed less well and SG plc failed to satisfy the burden of proving a non-discriminatory reason for dismissal.

9.13 Relationship between discrimination and unfairness

A dismissal that is discriminatory will almost certainly also be unfair under S.98(4) of the Employment Rights Act 2006 (ERA). Although the tests of discrimination and unfair dismissal are different, it is difficult to see how an employer could act 'reasonably' for ERA purposes while contravening discrimination legislation. An example of a redundancy dismissal that was both discriminatory and unfair:

- **British Sugar plc v Kirker** 1998 IRLR 624, EAT: K, who was partially sighted, was selected for redundancy after 20 years' service. In the assessments he scored zero under two heads – performance and potential. The tribunal found that K had not been marked objectively as his low scores did not reflect the true position. This made the dismissal unfair. The tribunal also found that the employer's attitude towards K's eyesight coloured its judgement of him in the redundancy selection process. It held that K had been treated less favourably as a result of the employer's prejudice and awarded him damages of just over £100,000 under the Disability Discrimination Act 1995 (now the EqA). The EAT upheld these findings and the award.

The reverse is not necessarily the case: unfair dismissals are not invariably discriminatory. However, where an employee's selection for redundancy has been found to be unfair, and discrimination is also alleged, the employer may find it harder to convince a tribunal that discrimination did not occur.

9.14 Positive discrimination

It should be stressed that while the EqA prohibits discrimination against employees on one of the protected grounds, it does not sanction preferential treatment on the basis of any of the protected characteristics. An employer who positively discriminates in favour of an employee because he or she has a protected characteristic will leave itself open to discrimination claims from other employees who do not share that characteristic and were thereby disadvantaged (except in the case of disability discrimination, which does not 'work both ways' – i.e. an employee cannot claim protection under the EqA on the ground that he or she is *not* disabled).

Nowhere was this more aptly demonstrated than in Eversheds Legal Services Ltd v De Belin 2011 ICR 1137, EAT, in which the EAT upheld a claim of direct sex discrimination brought by a man selected for redundancy from a pool of two. The other employee was a woman on maternity leave, who had been awarded a notional score for 'lock up', a measure of how quickly employees secured payment from clients for work completed. He received an actual score of 0.5 points for lock up, and 27 points overall, while she was given the maximum two points for lock up, and scored 27.5 points overall. The EAT upheld the tribunal's finding that the claimant had suffered less favourable treatment on the ground of his sex. The Appeal Tribunal rejected ELS Ltd's argument that it had a defence under S.2(2) SDA (now S.13(6)(b) EqA), which provides that no discrimination arises out of 'special treatment afforded to women in connection with pregnancy or childbirth'. The EAT decided that S.2(2) did not create a blanket exemption. The obligation could not extend to favouring pregnant employees or those on maternity leave beyond what was reasonably necessary to compensate them for the disadvantages occasioned by their condition. Given that there were less discriminatory ways of achieving a fair result, such as scoring both candidates as at an earlier date when they were both at work, awarding a notional maximum score was disproportionate.

A similar issue arose occurred in Obikwu and anor v British Refugee Council **9.15** ET Case Nos.1502553/06 and another. Two women on maternity leave were 'ring-fenced' for retention. The tribunal observed that 'those on maternity leave must take their selection or otherwise jointly with the rest of the workforce and be treated equally', commenting that the employer seemed to have got confused with the requirement to give preferential treatment in offering alternative work to women on maternity leave who have been made redundant (see below).

Alternative employment and positive discrimination. Preferential treatment **9.16** is possible, in limited respects, when offering suitable alternative employment to employees who have been made redundant. First, as discussed under 'Pregnancy and maternity leave' below (and in detail in Chapter 3 under 'Offers during maternity, adoption or paternity leave'), employers have a statutory responsibility to offer suitable alternative employment first to any employees made redundant while on maternity, additional paternity or adoption leave – even if this means that a person of the opposite sex is thereby denied it.

In addition, given that a non-disabled person cannot benefit from the provisions of the EqA, moving a disabled employee to the head of the queue for redeployment in a redundancy situation (but behind any employees on maternity leave, etc) will not incur liability in discrimination law, whereas moving people of a particular race or sex would. A tribunal might, in fact, consider it a reasonable adjustment to offer a disabled employee preferential treatment. In Kent County Council v Mingo 2000 IRLR 90, EAT, the Appeal Tribunal held that a policy which gave preferential treatment to redundant or potentially redundant employees by prioritising them for redeployment over employees who suffered incapability or ill health was discriminatory. In the EAT's view, the Council could have made a reasonable adjustment to the policy

293

to ensure that disabled employees received the benefit of priority consideration for deployment along with employees liable to be made redundant.

For more on disability discrimination, see 'Disability discrimination' below, and IDS Employment Law Handbook, 'Disability Discrimination' (2010).

9.17 Failure to offer alternative employment

Even where an employee's selection for redundancy is non-discriminatory, a failure to offer him or her a suitable alternative post may give rise to a successful discrimination claim. This may be in part because, as we discussed in Chapter 8 (in the section 'Unreasonable redundancy' under 'Alternative employment – objectivity required?'), a competitive selection process for a new role does not have to meet quite the same stringent standards of objectivity as selection for redundancy from a pool – and this may thereby leave more room for discrimination to 'creep in', or at least be more readily inferred and harder to rebut. For example, in Rivkin v Mott MacDonald Ltd ET Case No.2408125/09 a tribunal found that although R's dismissal for redundancy was not on the ground of his age and was not unfair, the decision not to appoint him to an alternative post did amount to age discrimination. The fact that the manager claimed not to have known that R was 60 before the interview despite the notice of appearance indicating to the contrary, and the fact that there had been a discussion during the interview about R's age and the time it would take to train him up, led the tribunal to infer that age was a factor in the decision not to offer R the alternative post.

As mentioned under 'Positive discrimination – alternative employment and positive discrimination' above and under 'Pregnancy and maternity leave' below, an employer will in some circumstances fall under a statutory duty to offer suitable alternative employment to an employee who has been made redundant. A failure to comply with this duty will lead to a finding of automatic unfair dismissal and may also be discriminatory.

9.18 Pregnancy and maternity leave

Selection of a woman for redundancy for a reason related to pregnancy or childbirth will amount to an automatically unfair dismissal – see Chapter 8 under 'Automatically unfair redundancy'. It will also constitute direct discrimination under S.18 EqA. Employers need to be particularly aware of the risk of treating employees on maternity leave as 'out of sight, out of mind', as this can lead to discriminatory selection. In Pickard v BSS Group plc t/a Buck and Hickman ET Case No.1310103/09, for example, P went on maternity leave in August 2008 and another employee covered some aspects of her work. However, by the end of 2008 changes in working processes meant that more junior staff had time on their hands, and they took on some of P's work. In February 2009 the employer decided to make redundancies. P was selected for redundancy because the employer believed there was no longer a need for her role. She was dismissed on 2 April 2009. A tribunal found that P's absence on maternity leave had a significant influence on the employer's decision-making. If she had remained at work her duties would not have been dispersed around the team and it would have become apparent to the employer that the roles of other team members had diminished more than P's had.

However, this does not mean that all pregnant employees dismissed as redundant will automatically succeed in a claim of unfair dismissal or discrimination. An employee will not succeed if she is selected for redundancy for a reason which is genuinely unconnected with her pregnancy. In one unusual case, Sewell v McCowen EAT 569/94, the office manager of a very small and unsuccessful firm took maternity leave and, during her absence, the employer found that it could manage without her. In view of the company's worsening financial difficulties, she was dismissed for redundancy without consultation because the employer was certain she would not have wanted to do any of the other jobs within the company. The EAT upheld the tribunal's conclusions that a genuine redundancy situation existed and that the employee's maternity absence was not a relevant factor in her dismissal. Moreover, she had not been discriminated against on the ground of sex. It also found that the lack of consultation did not render the dismissal unfair because consultation would have been utterly useless. However, the EAT did add that this was an exceptional case.

Application of discriminatory selection criteria. Employers may need to give **9.19** thought to adapting redundancy selection criteria to avoid indirectly discriminating against women on maternity leave. For example, pregnancy-related absence is commonly disregarded in selection based on attendance. Some consideration should also be given to the way in which flexibility is rewarded, since those with childcare responsibilities – predominantly women – may be adversely affected.

Employers also need to beware making assumptions about pregnant women or women on maternity leave. In Denysenko v Credit Suisse Securities (Europe) Ltd ET Case Nos.3200840/08 and another D was vice president responsible for Ukraine. In order to ensure her market was covered while she was on maternity leave she recruited a new employee, K, who began work in March 2006. Later that month D commenced maternity leave and her baby was born on 10 April. When she returned to work a year later there had been considerable management changes. D was told that K was to continue in his post, and at first they were both to cover the role. Then on 1 October she was put at risk of redundancy. She was selected and K was retained. The tribunal found that during the redundancy selection process the employer commented on her lengthy absence (on maternity leave) and made assumptions about D's ability as a mother to travel and work long hours when necessary. This amounted to direct discrimination.

9.20 However, employers also need to beware the danger of disadvantaging male employees in adapting potentially discriminatory selection criteria. In Eversheds Legal Services Ltd v De Belin 2011 ICR 1137, EAT (see 'Positive discrimination' above), the more favourable treatment of a woman on maternity leave in the redundancy selection exercise amounted to sex discrimination against the male claimant.

9.21 **Alternative employment.** As discussed in detail in Chapter 3, an employee who is made redundant while on maternity, adoption or additional paternity leave is entitled to be offered suitable alternative employment in preference to other employees – Reg 10 of the Maternity and Parental Leave etc Regulations 1999 SI 1999/3312 (MPL Regulations), Reg 23 of the Paternity and Adoption Leave Regulations 2002 SI 2002/2788 and Reg 28 of the Additional Paternity Leave Regulations 2010 SI 2010/1055. The employee does not have to 'apply' for such employment. In Bottomer v Chamberlains Estate Agents and ors ET Case No.1307016/08 four office managers were at risk of redundancy, but there was one only vacancy, for which all could apply. B, who was on maternity leave, did apply and was interviewed, but was not successful. The employer conceded that the failure to offer her the alternative post rendered her dismissal automatically unfair under the MPL Regulations, and the tribunal found that it also amounted to an act of discrimination.

A failure on the part of the employer to comply with these provisions will lead to a finding of automatically unfair dismissal, and, frequently, to a finding of discrimination under the EqA. Two further examples:

- **Hibbert v Mawdsley Brooks and Co Ltd** ET Case No.2411347/09: after H returned from maternity leave she was made redundant. A tribunal found that she was unfairly dismissed pursuant to the MPL Regulations and her dismissal amounted to sex discrimination. Her employer had restructured and had created a new post that incorporated part of H's job, and was very similar to it. The employee who had covered H's maternity leave applied for and obtained the new post in H's absence. The employer treated H less favourably on the ground of her maternity leave by failing to offer her the opportunity to apply for the new post

- **McKeith-Wellington v Denial.London Ltd and anor** ET Case No.3303074/10: M-W told D Ltd's director that she was pregnant in January 2010. In April D Ltd undertook a review of the business and decided that the line on which M-W worked should be discontinued, as it was not profitable. She was informed that her job was at risk of redundancy. At a consultation meeting D Ltd mentioned the possibility of creating a new sales manager role and gave M-W one day to indicate whether she was interested in being considered for it. On 15 May, however, when M-W was on maternity leave, D Ltd wrote to her saying it did not think she would be suitable for the role mentioned and on 4 June she was given notice of dismissal and offered a much more junior role. A tribunal found that M-W was entitled to be offered the sales manager role under the MPL Regulations. The director wanted someone who could start immediately and so did not want to wait until M-W returned from maternity leave. The dismissal was therefore also discriminatory on grounds of M-W's pregnancy and/or maternity leave.

It is important that the employer does not make discriminatory assumptions as to what alternative employment an employee will or will not accept, as the following cases demonstrate: **9.22**

- **Smulczyk v Eutopia Solutions Ltd** ET Case No.3303068/08: when S went on maternity leave in December 2007 she knew the division in which she worked was not economically viable. At a meeting with ES Ltd in July 2008 she was told that two of her colleagues were transferring to Dubai. She assumed that she might also be offered a transfer to Dubai, so discussed this with her husband. He was favourably disposed to moving to Dubai as his firm had a branch there. ES Ltd wrote to S on 1 August inviting her to a meeting to discuss the fact that her division had now closed and the possibility of her role being made redundant. She was on holiday at the time, and met ES Ltd on 5 September. At that meeting she was told she was to be dismissed as redundant. She informed ES Ltd that she was willing to be transferred to Dubai, which seemed to take the employer aback. ES Ltd wrote to confirm her redundancy terms, but made no mention of the possibility of a transfer to Dubai. She appealed, and in response ES Ltd stated that it had not offered her a job in Dubai because 'it was not considered that you would want to move there with your family'. A tribunal found that the decision to dismiss S was taken while she was on maternity leave without considering the option of a transfer to Dubai. The reason ES Ltd gave for not considering this was revealing and was discriminatory on its face

- **Morgan-Iqbal v Minster Care Management Ltd** ET Case No.1306805/08: M-I worked as regional manager of four care homes. She was also acting manager of one of the homes. On 7 February 2008 that home was inspected and given a very poor rating. On 3 March M-I told MCM Ltd she was pregnant, and shortly afterwards was off work for a week with a pregnancy-related condition. On her return she discovered that another manager had been moved into the home and she was increasingly sidelined. In May M-I was told she was at risk of redundancy. She was only offered jobs as a nurse in homes for which she had previously had responsibility. A tribunal drew an inference that MCM Ltd assumed M-I was not competent to perform as a manager because she was pregnant. There was a vacancy for a home manager at the time she was being consulted about redundancy but she was not even considered for it. The tribunal held that she had been discriminated against and she was awarded £15,000 for injury to feelings.

297

9.23   The statutory duty to offer suitable alternative employment to employees in certain circumstances creates an interesting quandary for employers who have only one alternative vacancy, and more than one employee on maternity leave, adoption leave, and/or additional parental leave. Does one type of leave trump another? To avoid allegations of discrimination, we suggest that an employer in such circumstances would be well advised to conduct an objective assessment of the two employees in order to determine who should be offered the available job, to demonstrate that the decision was not made on the ground of a protected characteristic.

For further discussion of discrimination in the context of pregnancy and maternity leave, see IDS Employment Law Handbook, 'Maternity and Parental Rights' (2009), Chapter 13.

9.24   ## Age discrimination

Traditionally, age was considered a legitimate factor to take into account in a redundancy exercise, and the right to claim a redundancy payment or unfair dismissal was subject to an upper age limit of 65. However, the prohibition on age discrimination – initially introduced by the Employment Equality (Age) Regulations 2006 SI 2006/1031 ('the Age Regulations') and now contained in the EqA – made many employers re-evaluate their redundancy selection procedures. A redundancy selection criterion or a selection process that directly or indirectly discriminates on the ground of age will be unlawful unless the employer can show that it is objectively justified – see below.

Two contrasting examples:

- **Walker and ors v DCE Consultants Ltd and anor** ET Case Nos.2301417/09 and others: W was a 38-year-old managing director. He referred in a meeting to the company as being top heavy with 'older, grey-haired consultants'. A redundancy exercise was started in August 2008. The employer applied a matrix to determine who should be selected for redundancy, which went through seven versions before finally being used to select the claimants, who were all in their 50s. Another consultant, who was in his 40s, had scored much lower in relation to performance indicators, but was retained. The claimants were dismissed as redundant. A tribunal drew the inference that the employer had changed the matrix to get the result it wanted and held that, on the basis of the comments made by W, the claimants were targeted for redundancy because of their age

- **King v Richard Lees Steel Decking Ltd** ET Case No.3500039/09: K was a highly skilled draftsman in his early 60s. When the company had to make redundancies the marking system included employees' ability to use draftsmen's tools. One such tool was the Tekla system, on which K had been trained but he had only used it for about a month before being transferred to another job where he did not use it. He therefore had very little experience of using Tekla and when the selection criteria were applied he received a low score. He was selected for redundancy and claimed that the selection exercise was tainted by age discrimination: of the ten draftsmen in the department, he, along with four other people in their 50s and 60s, was selected for redundancy while five people in their 20s and 30s were retained. The tribunal dismissed his claim. Tekla was made available to the entire workforce and the employer made serious efforts to ensure everyone was trained. However, three of the older employees did not want to go on the courses, and the issue was allowed to lie. This was not age discrimination; it was part of the workforce not wanting to improve their skills.

Ensuring that the terms of a redundancy policy do not fall foul of the prohibition on age discrimination is, however, simply the beginning. Employers must also ensure that the policy is applied in a non-discriminatory manner. An example: **9.25**

- **Mayor and Burgesses of the London Borough of Tower Hamlets v Wooster** 2009 IRLR 980, EAT: W, a long-serving Council employee, was on secondment to a registered social landlord, EEH. When his work there came to an end, the Council gave him 12 weeks' notice of dismissal for redundancy, but reassured him that that period would be used to try to find him alternative employment. EEH then offered to extend W's secondment until his 50th birthday when he would become entitled to an early retirement pension. This offer was rejected by M, the Council's director of housing management, with the words: 'If you are going to pay his salary then you can pay his bloody pension when he is 50. If he goes now we do save the pension.' W unsuccessfully applied for vacancies at the Council before taking voluntary redundancy. A tribunal upheld his unfair dismissal and age discrimination claims, finding that M's refusal even to countenance extending the secondment and her comments to EEH about 'saving the pension' showed that W's pensionable age was the 'tipping point' in the decision to dismiss him. Furthermore, had the Council followed a fair redundancy and redeployment procedure, W would have obtained a permanent post. The Council appealed against the tribunal's finding on age discrimination but the appeal was dismissed by the EAT.

Objective justification. As mentioned above, there is a 'justification defence' available to employers facing claims of direct or indirect age discrimination. However, the Government stated in the 'Coming of Age' consultation document on the draft Age Regulations that 'the test of objective justification will not be an easy one to satisfy... treating people differently on grounds of age will be possible but only exceptionally and for good reasons'. In order to benefit from the defence, the employer must show: **9.26**

- in a direct discrimination claim, that the less favourable treatment meted out to the claimant because of age was a proportionate means of achieving a legitimate aim – S.13(1) and (2) EqA

- in an indirect discrimination claim, that the provision, criterion or practice which placed persons of the claimant's age group at a disadvantage was a proportionate means of achieving a legitimate aim – S.19 EqA.

In practice, the success of an age discrimination claim in the context of redundancy selection often turns on the employer's ability to establish the justification defence. Below, we look at some examples of cases where employers have – with varying degrees of success – sought to argue that the adoption of an age-discriminatory criterion when making redundancy selections was a proportionate means of achieving a legitimate aim.

9.27 *Last in, first out.* Traditionally, one of the most common methods of selecting employees for redundancy has been the 'last in, first out' (LIFO) method. As explained in Chapter 8 under 'Unreasonable redundancy – selection criteria', what this means is that the employees with the shortest length of service are selected for redundancy first. From an employer's perspective, LIFO carries the benefit of minimising the level of redundancy payments which are, of course, determined by length of service.

While LIFO does not directly discriminate on the ground of age – it does not automatically follow that an employee with ten years' service will be older than an employee with three years' service – it clearly constitutes a provision, criterion or practice which will, generally speaking, adversely impact on younger workers. It follows, therefore, that an employer seeking to use LIFO as part of a redundancy selection exercise must be prepared to demonstrate that its use is objectively justified. If it cannot do so, the use of LIFO will be unlawful indirect discrimination. For example, in Catchpole and ors v DB Schenker Rail (UK) Ltd ET Case No.2509588/09 C and one other employee scored jointly in a redundancy selection exercise and the employer decided to use length of service as a tie-breaker to decide who should be made redundant. The other employee had longer service than C and so C was selected for redundancy. A tribunal upheld his claim of age discrimination. C was aged 34 and the other employee was 60. They were thus in quite different age groups and on the face of it the criterion of length of service was discriminatory. In the tribunal's opinion, the employer failed to justify its use as a proportionate means of achieving a legitimate aim. It used the criterion as a tie breaker because it was administratively convenient to do so, and that was not enough.

9.28 For the purposes of the justification defence, examples of what might arguably constitute a legitimate aim might include:

- encouraging and rewarding staff loyalty

- retaining skills and knowledge of the business that have been developed over time

- minimising costs in order to keep a company afloat.

It would be fair to assume that where LIFO is used as a part of a selection matrix that objectively takes into account the various qualities of staff considered for redundancy, it will be less of a challenge to show that its use and application is justifiable. This proposition draws support from a recent decision of the Court of Appeal in Rolls-Royce plc v Unite the Union 2010 ICR 1, CA, where the Court considered whether the use of length of service as a redundancy selection criterion was a proportionate means of achieving a legitimate aim. RR plc's redundancy policy, agreed collectively with the union, stipulated that an employee's length of service was a factor that would be taken into account in a redundancy selection exercise. In November 2007 RR plc announced that it was to start a redundancy consultation in its Derby factory. Concerned at the prospect of employees dismissed for redundancy bringing claims of indirect age discrimination in the employment tribunal, RR plc sought a declaration from the High Court that the length of service criterion could not lawfully be relied upon. Mr Justice Morison, sitting in the Queen's Bench Division, accepted that the criterion indirectly discriminated against younger workers. However, he decided that its inclusion was justified by the legitimate aim of bringing about redundancies peaceably.

9.29 The Court of Appeal, by a majority, upheld this decision. The Court held that the criterion's legitimate aim was to reward loyalty and create a stable workforce in the context of a fair redundancy selection process, and that the means adopted were proportionate. Lord Justice Wall thought that the most important factor indicating that the means were proportionate was that length of service was just one of many criteria used and was not determinative of the selection. The union's statement that all workers were supportive of the policy, the younger ones being aware that they were likely to benefit from it at some point in the future, was also a factor that carried weight.

Wall LJ was also satisfied that the length of service criterion qualified as 'legitimate employment policy' and a 'labour market objective' in accordance with Article 6 of the EU Equal Treatment Framework Directive (No.2000/78), which identifies specific circumstances in which age discrimination may be justified. He commented that 'to reward long service by employees in any redundancy selection process is, viewed objectively, an entirely reasonable and legitimate employment policy and one which a conscientious employer would readily and properly negotiate with a responsible trade union'.

9.30 *Cost considerations.* In Mayor and Burgesses of the London Borough of Tower Hamlets v Wooster (above) the claimant succeeded with his direct age discrimination claim where the employer's decision to make him redundant instead of redeploying him was motivated by a wish to avoid the additional costs of his becoming entitled to an early retirement pension. Surprisingly, the employer made no attempt to put forward a justification defence in that case

301

and the EAT did not therefore have to determine whether the need to keep costs down could amount to a legitimate aim and whether dismissing an employee to avoid such costs is a proportionate means of achieving that aim.

This issue cropped up again in Woodcock v Cumbria Primary Care Trust 2011 ICR 143, EAT, the facts of which were very similar to those found in Wooster. In Woodcock, W was employed in the public sector. His role was redundant and he would have been entitled to early retirement and enhanced pension benefits if employed at 50. Upon discovering the cost of these pension benefits – estimated to be between £500,000 and £1,000,000 – the Trust accelerated the redundancy process, bypassing the consultation stage entirely, and gave W 12 months' notice of dismissal shortly before his 49th birthday. W complained of direct age discrimination, among other things. The tribunal found that W had been directly discriminated against on the ground of his age. However, it went on to hold that the discrimination was justified as a proportionate means of achieving a legitimate aim – that of avoiding the additional costs that would be incurred if W reached pensionable age, coupled with depriving him of a 'windfall' (see Chapter 6 under 'Enhanced redundancy pay – enhanced scheme not modelled on statutory scheme' for a discussion of this factor as a legitimate aim). W appealed.

9.31 Before the EAT, W argued that the tribunal had found his discrimination to be justified purely on the basis of cost, and that this was contrary to the decision of the EAT in Cross and ors v British Airways plc 2005 IRLR 423, EAT (a case which went to the Court of Appeal on other grounds). The EAT found that, on the contrary, the tribunal had followed the 'costs plus' approach as set out in Cross – i.e. that cost is an admissible factor in determining whether discrimination is justified, but may not be taken alone. The perceived cost of delay was not the only justification advanced for the Trust's decision to give notice before the consultation meeting. There was also the consideration of preventing W receiving a 'windfall' – i.e. a benefit which he had no legitimate right to expect. Accordingly, ensuring that W was not employed when he turned 50 – and avoiding the corresponding loss to the Trust – was a legitimate aim going beyond the mere wish to reduce costs.

Mr Justice Underhill then went on to set out the Appeal Tribunal's thinking on the 'costs plus' orthodoxy and although his comments were obiter and are not binding on tribunals, they will no doubt carry some weight in future cases given that they were made by the President of the EAT. The EAT accepted that as a matter of both principle and common sense, considerations of cost must be admissible in considering whether a provision, criterion or practice that has a discriminatory impact may nevertheless be justified. Furthermore, it saw no principled basis for a rule that such considerations can never by themselves constitute sufficient justification. The adoption of such a rule would tend to involve parties and tribunals in an artificial game of 'find the other factor', producing arbitrary and complicated reasoning. Underhill P noted that deciding where 'cost' stops and other factors start is not always straightforward.

Disability discrimination

9.32

As identified in Chapter 8 under 'Unreasonable redundancy – selection criteria', there are potential pitfalls in using health and attendance records as a means of selecting employees for redundancy, since doing so may infringe the disability discrimination provisions of the EqA (previously found in the Disability Discrimination Act 1995 (DDA)). These prohibit, inter alia, direct and indirect disability discrimination and discrimination arising from a disability. They also impose a duty on employers to make reasonable adjustments. In this section we briefly explain the new concept of discrimination arising from a disability before turning to the application of the duty to make reasonable adjustments in a redundancy context. For a full discussion of disability discrimination law, see IDS Employment Law Handbook, 'Disability Discrimination' (2010), and our forthcoming IDS Employment Law Handbook, 'Discrimination in the Workplace' (2012).

Discrimination arising from disability. Under the DDA as originally 9.33 interpreted, it was generally assumed that where an employee's poor health or poor attendance was attributable to a 'disability' as defined, an employer's decision to select him or her for redundancy on health or absence grounds could amount to disability-related discrimination contrary to S.3A(1) of that Act. According to the Court of Appeal in Clark v Novacold Ltd 1999 ICR 951, CA, for disability-related treatment to be discriminatory under that provision, the individual must have been treated less favourably than other people to whom that disability-related reason did not, or would not, apply (and that treatment was not justifiable).

This approach set out in Clark was settled law until the House of Lords, in Mayor and Burgesses of the London Borough of Lewisham v Malcolm 2008 IRLR 700, HL, took a very different view of the comparative exercise required. Having considered the matter at length, a majority of their Lordships (Baroness Hale dissenting) reached the conclusion that Clark v Novacold was incorrectly decided. In their view, the appropriate comparator was a non-disabled person who was otherwise in the same circumstances as the disabled claimant. (Note that Malcolm was not an employment case; it concerned Part III of the DDA, which covered the provision of goods and services and the management and disposal of premises. However, the Part III definition of disability-related discrimination – their Lordships' focus in Malcolm – was the same as that contained in S.3A(1) and in Stockton-on-Tees Borough Council v Aylott 2010 ICR 1278, CA, the Court of Appeal confirmed that the narrower Malcolm approach applied equally in the employment field.)

303

9.34   The effect of Malcolm was to make disability-related discrimination harder, if not impossible, to prove, and after consultation the Government included a new provision in the EqA to replace disability-related discrimination. This provision – S.15 EqA – introduces the concept of 'discrimination arising from disability'. Unlike disability-related discrimination, S.15 does not require the disabled person to establish that his or her treatment is less favourable than that experienced by a comparator. It provides that a person (A) discriminates against a disabled person (B) if A treats B *unfavourably because of something arising in consequence of B's disability*, and A cannot show that the treatment is a proportionate means of achieving a legitimate aim. We therefore suggest that employers should once again be particularly careful when applying criteria that could adversely affect disabled employees.

For a more detailed discussion of S.15 EqA, see IDS Employment Law Guide, 'The Equality Act 2010', Chapter 2.

9.35   **Reasonable adjustments.** Under S.20(3) EqA (previously S.4A(1) DDA), an employer is under a duty to make reasonable adjustments where a provision, criterion or practice (PCP) of the employer's puts a disabled person at a substantial disadvantage in comparison with persons who are not disabled. A failure to comply with that duty will amount to discrimination – S.21. S.18B(2) DDA used to contain a non-exhaustive list of examples of what might amount to a reasonable adjustment. For example, in the context of redundancy selection, the list included 'modifying procedures for testing or assessment' and 'transferring [the employee] to fill an existing vacancy'. However, the list has not been reproduced in the EqA. Instead, the Equality and Human Rights Commission's Code of Practice on Employment (which contains statutory guidance on the EqA) states that what is a reasonable step for an employer to take will depend on the circumstances of each individual case (para 6.29). Although the EqA does not specify any particular factors that should be taken into account, the examples previously given in S.18B(2) DDA are likely to remain relevant in practice. Those examples are listed in para 6.33 of the Employment Code. The Code also suggests some further examples of reasonable steps that did not appear in the DDA, including adjusting redundancy selection criteria.

In addition to the list of examples contained in S.18B(2), S.18B(1) DDA set out a number of factors tribunals should consider when determining reasonableness, including the effectiveness of a proposed step. These factors have not been replicated in the EqA but are likely to continue to be relevant, given that the majority of them are now listed in para 6.28 of the Employment Code as examples of factors that a tribunal *might* take into account when considering reasonableness. In other words, it will not automatically be an error of law for a tribunal to fail to consider, for example, the effectiveness of an adjustment, so

304

long as it has adequately considered whether the proposed adjustment would be reasonable.

However, it is unlikely to be 'reasonable' to alter redundancy selection criteria **9.36** if the alteration would still result in the claimant being selected – Lancaster v TBWA Manchester EAT 0460/10 (discussed under 'Omitting or altering selection criteria' below). The difficulty for employers, of course, is that it is often not until the reasonable adjustment has been applied that it is possible to know if the employee would still be selected for redundancy; so the ratio in Lancaster should probably not be relied upon to excuse taking action, unless the outcome has been researched and can safely be predicted. However, an employer may rely upon the case at tribunal to avoid an injury to feelings award being made against it.

Below, we discuss various reasonable adjustments that have been proposed in the context of redundancy selection, and the extent to which these have been considered by tribunals to fulfil the employer's duty under S.20(3) EqA.

Discounting disability-related absences. It seems safe to assume that **9.37** discounting disability-related absences when selecting for redundancy could amount to a reasonable adjustment, given that the Employment Code suggests adjusting redundancy selection criteria as an example of a reasonable step. Some examples of cases brought under the DDA:

- **Cox v City Centre Training (Northern) Ltd** ET Case No.2504232/06: C was diagnosed as suffering from diabetes in 2004. In 2005, CCT Ltd began a redundancy consultation and C was selected following the application of selection criteria which included attendance, despite C's having been off sick with an ingrown toenail for the duration of the consultation exercise. At a meeting, C expressed the view that the problems with his toenail were a result of his diabetes and offered to obtain medical advice to prove it. CCT Ltd, however, proceeded to dismiss C later that week. A tribunal found that the problems with C's toe and the ensuing absence were both related to his disability. In the circumstances, the tribunal took the view that a reasonable adjustment would have been to discount the absences which were related to C's disability. In addition, it formed the view that fatigue caused by diabetes had impacted negatively on C's performance, thus harming his scores in the selection process. In the tribunal's view, CCT Ltd had ignored the issue of C's disability, had displayed an ignorance of the effects of the condition, and had carried out a dismissal that was both discriminatory and unfair from beginning to end

- **Robson v Domino UK Ltd** ET Case No.1400506/09: R was employed as a salesman. In autumn 2006 he was diagnosed as diabetic and he also began to suffer from what was later diagnosed as chronic fatigue syndrome. He had a long period of absence from April 2007 to January 2008. He came back on a phased return for two months and was not given any sales targets for five months. In October 2008 D UK Ltd began consulting its employees about redundancy. R was selected on the basis of the scoring criteria. His scores were adversely affected by his absence: D UK Ltd had looked back only over the previous 12 months, when R had either been absent or doing reduced work for much of the time. His manager told him that his drive and energy had been reduced since his illness and that D UK Ltd needed the best people to cope with the extra work resulting from the cuts in the workforce. R's disability discrimination claim was upheld. The tribunal found that the effects of his disabilities reflected adversely upon his work prior to selection and that it would have been a necessary and reasonable adjustment for the employer to increase his scores to remove the disadvantage.

9.38 *Trial period.* It may be a reasonable adjustment to offer an employee a trial period in a new role. In Lee v University of Westminster ET Case No.2201292/08 L, who suffered from epilepsy, was assessed as being unsuitable for redeployment into a new role that was being considered. The University offered him redeployment on a trial period as an alternative to redundancy. However, he was then absent due to substantial ill health for some months. When he recovered he asked to be put on the trial period, but the University decided that because of his absence he was even more unskilled for the role and that it would be too much of a business risk to put him in it. His employment was terminated with effect from 31 March 2008. A tribunal upheld his claim of disability discrimination. The tribunal was hesitant about whether offering a trial period on the employee's return to work could be a reasonable adjustment, but accepted the parties' shared view that it was.

9.39 *Delaying consultation pending health assessment.* In Aubury v SP Group Ltd ET Case No.1316697/09 A fell ill in June 2008 with a neurological condition. In September 2008 he returned to work on a phased basis, resuming full-time work in February 2009. An occupational health report in January stated that he was fit to fulfil his role, but without overtime or unusual hours, and that he should be fully fit within three to six months. By June 2009 the employer had to embark on a redundancy programme. A was selected for redundancy and he claimed that he was discriminated against on the ground of his disability because he was still not functioning fully as a result of his illness and this was not taken into account. His claim was upheld in part: the employer applied the selection criteria and then considered A's objections to his scoring without having an up-to-date assessment of his health. The employer should have made a reasonable adjustment by delaying the consultation and decision-making process until such a report was obtained so the full impact of his disability could be considered. However, the employer had made a reasonable adjustment in assessing A over a period of nine months rather than 12, and in comparing his scores against a period of 12 months before his illness and attributing an extra mark to him as a result. Even had the employer obtained such a report, he would still have been selected for redundancy. A was awarded £2,000 for injury to feelings. (Note that, following the EAT's decision in Lancaster v TBWA Manchester (above), the tribunal's finding that it would have been a reasonable adjustment to delay the consultation and decision-making process until a health report was obtained is questionable, given that on the facts it would have made no difference to his selection. However, we suggest that taking such action may well be considered a reasonable adjustment in a different case.)

Extending assessment period. It may be a reasonable adjustment to extend the **9.40** period for assessment, where a disabled employee has been absent for considerable periods; and/or to extend the time over which the redundancy process itself is implemented. In Kelly v Land Rover ET Case No.1311339/09 K suffered from physical disabilities and as a result had two long periods of sickness absence. In January 2009 LR embarked upon a restructuring process as a result of which redundancies became necessary. The selection criteria included performance over the past three years. K did not score well, as he had been absent for half of the three-year period and as a result few people had recent knowledge of his skills and abilities, and he was selected for redundancy. A tribunal found that K had been put at a substantial disadvantage when compared to any of his non-disabled colleagues who were not absent during the assessment period. LR could have carried out a number of reasonable adjustments such as extending the three-year period, extending the timescale over which the process was carried out and allowing K a full interview process.

Omitting or altering selection criteria. In Lancaster v TBWA Manchester EAT **9.41** 0460/10 L, a senior art director at an advertising and marketing agency, suffered from a panic and social anxiety disorder that amounted to a disability for the purposes of the DDA (now EqA). Following the loss of a major contract, L was at risk of redundancy. He was placed in a pool of three and scored against selection criteria about which he had not been consulted. L's initial score was 198, compared to 298 and 299 for the other two senior art directors. Following his dismissal for redundancy, L brought various claims, including one of disability discrimination. The basis of this was that the application of three of the redundancy selection criteria – all of which required communication skills and relied on the subjective views of the scorers – was a provision, criterion or practice (PCP) which placed him at a substantial disadvantage due to his disability. He therefore contended that TBWA was obliged to make a reasonable adjustment to the selection process by omitting those criteria. As an alternative argument, L identified the PCP which disadvantaged him as the entirety of the selection criteria, and argued that the adjustment TBWA should have made was adopting a more objective set of criteria such as attendance and length of service. The tribunal rejected both contentions: since L had failed to establish that either of his proposed adjustments would or could have prevented his being selected for redundancy, they could not be considered reasonable.

L appealed to the EAT, arguing among other things that the tribunal gave undue regard to the question of whether the two proposed adjustments would have removed the disadvantage L suffered. The EAT held that the tribunal had been entitled to find that the removal of the three offending selection criteria would not have been a reasonable adjustment. When considering if an adjustment is reasonable, a tribunal was obliged by S.18B(1)(a) DDA to take into account the extent to which that adjustment 'would prevent the effect in relation to which the duty is imposed'. The tribunal had done so, and concluded that the removal of the criteria would not have made a difference because L would still have scored the lowest of the candidates. As for the second proposed adjustment – the replacement of all selection criteria with purely objective measures – the EAT held that the tribunal had been entitled, in light of the creative and senior level of the post held by L, to find that the wholesale replacement of selection criteria could not have prevented his redundancy. (Note that S.18B(1)(a) was not re-enacted in the EqA. However, most of the factors listed in that subsection, including the one referred to by the EAT, are now listed in para 6.28 of the Equality and Human Rights Commission's Code of Practice on Employment, which contains statutory guidance on the EqA.)

9.42 **Alternative work.** As discussed under 'Positive discrimination' above, a disabled employee may have grounds for arguing that it would amount to a reasonable adjustment for him or her to be prioritised for alternative available employment. Even if that is not the case, employers should always consider the possibility and in doing so should be careful not to make assumptions about a disabled employee's ability to perform alternative work without consulting him or her first. In Steers v S Walsh and Sons Ltd ET Case Nos.3201805/09 and another a tribunal upheld an employee's claim that his selection for redundancy amounted to unlawful direct discrimination on the ground of his disability because, among other things, his employer had failed to discuss with him the possibility of alternative employment and offered work to another employee that he could have performed because it made assumptions about his multiple sclerosis without checking whether those assumptions were correct.

9.43 ## Discrimination against part-time workers

Employers in straitened circumstances may wish to make part-time workers redundant as it is usually more cost effective to make a part-time worker redundant than to cut the hours of another, full-time worker. However, employers considering such action must ensure that they do not fall foul of the Part-time Workers (Prevention of Less Favourable Treatment) Regulations 2000 SI 2000/1551. These provide that a part-time worker has the right not to be treated by his or her employer less favourably than the employer treats a comparable full-time worker as regards the terms of his or her contract, or by being subjected to any other detriment by any act, or deliberate failure to act, by his or her employer – Reg 5(1). It applies where:

- the reason for the treatment is that the worker is a part-timer

- the treatment is not justified on objective grounds – Reg 5(2).

This right is in addition to the right not to be unfairly selected for redundancy for exercising rights under the Regulations that is found in the Employment Rights Act 1996 (see Chapter 8 under 'Automatic unfair redundancy – part-time and fixed-term work').

9.44 The DTI (now BIS) guidance notes on the Regulations (URN 02/1710) state specifically that the Regulations give part-time workers the right to be treated no less favourably than comparable full-timers with respect to redundancy selection, unless the different treatment is objectively justified. Two examples of cases in which employees successfully claimed discrimination on this basis:

- **McGuinness v North Estates Ltd** ET Case No.2400578/08: a tribunal found that a part-time administrator was selected for redundancy because she worked part time. Another administrator who worked part time was also made redundant, whereas a full-time employee doing similar work was retained, and there was no evidence that the employer had considered retaining the part-time employees

- **Clarke v Brookside (1998) Ltd t/a Nottingham Volkswagen and anor** ET Case Nos.2600301/09 and another: C was employed as a fleet sales executive. Following a period of maternity leave she worked for three days a week. In April 2008 B Ltd recruited a new fleet sales manager to whom C was to report. The tribunal accepted C's evidence that he made comments about her being the 'part-time department' and 'a baby machine'. Following a downturn in business C was informed in October 2008 that she was at risk of redundancy. As she was pregnant she asked if she could bring forward her maternity leave and take a year's leave to give the market time to recover, but B Ltd rejected that proposal and she was dismissed as redundant later that month. A tribunal found that C was discriminated against on grounds of her gender and part-time working arrangement.

9.45 However, in Vij-Solanki v IDT Global Ltd ET Case Nos.2203531/08 and another V's claim of less favourable treatment on the ground of part-time status was dismissed. In June 2008 V's employer had to make redundancies, and V, who worked three days a week, was selected. She claimed, among other things, that in being selected for redundancy and dismissed she had been less favourably treated than her full-time colleagues. However, the tribunal found that apart from a remark that V did not show the same 'commitment' as the others in her pool, there was nothing in the selection exercise which could have led it to believe that V's status as a part-time worker was the reason for her treatment.

309

The employer had demonstrated its willingness to accommodate flexible or part-time working in agreeing to V's two requests to reduce or change her hours following periods of maternity leave. The tribunal was satisfied, notwithstanding the comment regarding her commitment, that V's selection for redundancy was because she scored lower than her colleagues, and that there was no evidence that her scores were tainted by her part-time status. It noted that in fact it would have suited the employer's 'budgetary imperatives' to have selected a full-time worker rather than V for redundancy.

Note that discriminatory selection for redundancy on the ground of an employee's part-time status may also give rise to an indirect sex discrimination claim, given it is predominantly women who work part time – see IDS Employment Law Handbook, 'Sex Discrimination' (2008).

9.46 ## Discrimination against fixed-term employees

The Fixed-term Employees (Prevention of Less Favourable Treatment) Regulations 2002 SI 2002/2034 provide specific protection for fixed-term employees. They provide that it is unlawful for an employer to treat a fixed-term employee less favourably because of his or her fixed-term status as regards the terms of his or her contract, or by subjecting him or her to any other detriment by any act or deliberate failure to act, than the employer treats comparable permanent employees, unless the difference in treatment can be objectively justified – Reg 3.

According to the BERR guide to the Regulations, 'Understanding fixed-term contracts', this means that fixed-term employees should not be selected for redundancy purely because they are on fixed-term contracts, unless this can be objectively justified. Where, for example, a fixed-term employee has been brought in specifically to complete particular tasks or to cover for a peak in demand, it is likely that an employer could objectively justify selecting him or her for redundancy at the end of the contract. The guide also states that where length of service is the main criterion for redundancy selection, the same criteria should apply to fixed-term employees as to comparable permanent employees, unless differences are objectively justified.

9.47 In Hopkins v City University ET Case No.2204178/08 the employee failed to establish that his selection for redundancy was on the ground of his fixed-term status. H was employed in a senior administrative capacity on a series of fixed-term contracts from 18 June 2007 to 30 September 2008. One of the main reasons for his appointment was to ensure oversight at a senior level of a reorganisation programme. A consequence of the reorganisation was that H's role was disestablished and replaced by a similar role of COO, which was advertised externally. Following the competitive recruitment procedure an external candidate was appointed and H's last fixed-term appointment was not renewed, meaning that he was dismissed for redundancy. He claimed that he had suffered a detriment on the ground of his fixed-term status by the University creating the COO role, advertising the post externally, and subsequently dismissing him. However, a tribunal dismissed his claim. The decision to create the position of COO was part of the restructuring exercise, and had nothing to do with H personally. H could not point to a valid comparator, but in any event the decision to advertise the COO role externally had nothing to do with H's fixed-term status: it was because the role was judged to be of critical importance and the University was anxious to ensure that the best possible candidate was appointed. The same policy applied to other COO roles in the University. His dismissal was the inevitable consequence of H losing the competition, and was not discriminatory. The tribunal concluded that even had it found discrimination under Reg 3(1), it would have found H's treatment justified under Reg 3(3)(b). The University was entirely justified in seeking to recruit the best possible candidate for a senior role, and H at the time gave them every reason to think he agreed with the decision to advertise the role externally.

9.48 The right not to be treated unfavourably under Reg 3 is in addition to the right not to be unfairly selected for redundancy for exercising rights under the Regulations that is found in the Employment Rights Act 1996 (see Chapter 8 under 'Automatic unfair redundancy – part-time and fixed-term work').

The Fixed-term Employees Regulations are discussed in detail in IDS Employment Law Supplement, 'Fixed-Term Work' (2003).

10 Enforcement

Statutory redundancy payments

Unfair dismissal

Contractual redundancy payments

Fast-track claims

Most redundancy payments are paid by the employer at the time of dismissal. **10.1**
But what happens if there is a dispute between employer and employee as to
the employee's entitlement to a redundancy payment, the amount of
redundancy pay due, or the legitimacy of the employee's selection for
redundancy? If the parties cannot come to an agreement on the matter, the
employee may be forced to bring proceedings in an employment tribunal to
settle the dispute. In this chapter we examine the procedural requirements for
bringing a statutory redundancy pay claim or for claiming unfair redundancy.
We also consider various procedural issues relating to claims for contractual
redundancy payments.

Statutory redundancy payments   10.2

Any question as to an employee's right to a statutory redundancy payment, or
as to the amount of any payment made, should be referred to an employment
tribunal under S.163 of the Employment Rights Act 1996 (ERA). Claims for
statutory redundancy payments fall under the exclusive jurisdiction of
employment tribunals and cannot be brought in the civil courts. While a full
examination of the procedural requirements for bringing tribunal claims falls
outside the scope of this Handbook, it is worth noting a couple of basic points.
First, all claims to employment tribunals must be made on a specified form, the
ET1, while all responses to claims must be on form ET3. Failure to use the
correct form will lead to the claim or response being inadmissible. Secondly,
claims for redundancy payments are one of the jurisdictions under which an
employment judge may sit alone (i.e. without lay members) – S.4(3)(c)
Employment Tribunals Act 1996. A detailed exposition of employment tribunal
procedure can be found in IDS Employment Law Handbook, 'Employment
Tribunal Practice and Procedure' (2006).

Time limits   10.3
Section 164 ERA sets out the time limits for presenting a claim under S.163.
The general rule is that an employee will lose entitlement to a statutory

313

redundancy payment unless one of the following four events occurs before the end of a period of *six months* beginning with the relevant date:

- the payment is agreed and paid – S.164(1)(a)

- the employee makes a written claim for the payment to the employer – S.164(1)(b)

- the question as to the employee's right to, or the amount of, the payment has been referred to an employment tribunal – S.164(1)(c). (Note that a claim is 'referred to a tribunal' when it is physically received at the tribunal office, not when it is posted – Secretary of State for Employment v Banks and ors 1983 ICR 48, EAT), or

- the employee presents a claim of unfair dismissal to a tribunal under S.111 ERA – S.164(1)(d).

10.4 The 'relevant date' in this context means the effective date of termination of employment (EDT) and is defined in three ways:

- where the employee's contract of employment is terminated by notice (whether given by the employer or the employee), it is the date on which the notice expires

- where the contract is terminated without notice, it is the date on which termination takes effect

- in relation to an employee who is employed under a limited-term contract which terminates by virtue of the limiting event without being renewed under the same contract (see Chapter 1 under 'Expiry of limited-term contract'), it is the date on which the termination takes effect – S.145(2).

10.5 There are two special features of the relevant date in the context of the time limit for tribunal claims:

- if the employee accepts an offer of alternative employment with a trial period and then leaves or gives notice or is dismissed during the trial period, the relevant date is the date the employment comes to an end and not, as in other contexts, the date the original contract ended – S.145(4)(a)

- if the employer dismisses summarily or with insufficient notice, the relevant date is the date upon which the termination takes effect. It is *not* deemed to be the date upon which proper notice ought to have been given, as it is for certain other purposes by virtue of S.145(5). If an employee who is entitled to the maximum statutory notice of 12 weeks is summarily dismissed on 15 March, the six-month period still expires on 14 September. No account is taken for this purpose of the notice the employee ought to have been given.

It is crucial to note that a period of six months beginning with the relevant date *includes* that date. Thus, six months beginning with 15 March ends on 14 September and not, as the unwary often think, on 15 September.

Section 164(1) provides that one of the specified events must occur before the **10.6** end of the six-month period beginning with the relevant date. There seems no reason on this wording why the event should not take place before the relevant date itself so that an employee could, for example, make a claim for a redundancy payment while still working out his or her notice of dismissal. The EAT, however, held in Watts v Rubery Owen Conveyancer Ltd 1977 ICR 429, EAT, that a claim will be premature and invalid if it is made before dismissal takes effect. This decision was followed by another division of the EAT in Pritchard-Rhodes Ltd v Boon and anor 1979 IRLR 19, EAT.

The correctness of the Watts decision has long been the subject of debate – especially since S.111(3) specifically permits an unfair dismissal claim to be presented during a notice period, and this is one of the events specified in S.164(1). However, the decision was recently endorsed by the EAT in Foster v Bon Groundwork Ltd 2011 IRLR 645, EAT, a case concerning issue estoppel. In the course of the proceedings, an issue arose as to whether the principle that a claim for a redundancy payment can only be pursued after the expiry of the notice period remained good law. In the EAT's view, it clearly did. According to Mr Justice Silber, 'Parliament has not changed the law on this when it could have done so when introducing the provision for unfair dismissal.'

Extending the time limit. Under S.164, an employee's right to a redundancy **10.7** payment does not necessarily expire at the end of the six-month period if none of the specified events has taken place. If during the six months immediately following the initial six-month period he or she makes a written claim for payment to the employer or refers a redundancy pay claim to a tribunal or presents an unfair dismissal complaint to a tribunal, then the tribunal has a *discretion* to award a redundancy payment. This discretion is to be exercised if it appears to the tribunal to be *just and equitable* that the employee should receive a redundancy payment having regard to the reason shown by the employee for his or her failure to take any of the specified steps earlier and to all the other relevant circumstances – S.164(2) and (3).

Subject to two exceptions relating to mediation in cross-border disputes and death of the employee (discussed below), there is no discretion to extend the time limit beyond the second six-month period and a claim received even one day after the combined 12-month period will be irrevocably out of time. This is the case even where the employee is in no way at fault. In Crawford v (1) Secretary of State for Employment (2) Colmore Depot 1995 IRLR 523, EAT, C failed to apply for a redundancy payment when his employer's business, which was in receivership, was sold. This was because all the parties, including the Secretary of State, assumed that there had been a transfer under the Transfer of

Undertakings (Protection of Employment) Regulations 2006 SI 2006/246 (TUPE). Over a year later it became clear that there had not been a transfer and C applied to the Secretary of State for a redundancy payment. This was refused on the ground that his claim was out of time. The EAT agreed. It rejected C's claim that it should consider the spirit and intention of the legislation and that time should only begin to run against C when it became clear that there had been no transfer. The EAT recommended that employees of companies that become insolvent should make provisional claims for a redundancy payment from the employer and the Secretary of State promptly to cover themselves in the event that the insolvent undertaking is not transferred to a third party under TUPE.

10.8 *'Just and equitable'.* In deciding whether it is just and equitable to award a redundancy payment outside the normal six-month time limit, a tribunal should take account of all the relevant circumstances – S.164(3)(b). The EAT considered this provision in Paul v C and J Stone Ltd EAT 209/80, where a tribunal had refused to consider a claim presented four days out of time. In the EAT's view, the statutory words involved the tribunal taking some account of the merits of the employee's claim – i.e. how likely he or she was to succeed in a claim for a redundancy payment if it allowed the claim to proceed – and there was certainly no error of law in it doing so. The EAT went on to say that 'the circumstances under which this Appeal Tribunal would feel able to interfere with a discretion exercised by [a] tribunal are rare indeed'. Thus, there will normally be no point in appealing against a tribunal's decision on this issue unless there has been a clear misdirection in law.

The EAT did find an error of law in Smith v Humber Ship Repairing Ltd and ors EAT 366/85. S's claim had been late because of faulty advice from his union. The tribunal relied on the case of Dedman v British Building and Engineering Appliances Ltd 1974 ICR 53, CA, and said simply that any remedy S might have lay against his union advisers. The EAT pointed out that the Dedman case concerned the time limit for an unfair dismissal claim. The statutory test for this is whether it was 'reasonably practicable' to have brought the claim in time, not the very different test of whether the tribunal considers it 'just and equitable' to award a redundancy payment outside the six-month time limit. The case was remitted for the tribunal to think again.

10.9 Four cases where late claims have been allowed:

- **Gadd v Maiseys (Kenilworth) Ltd** ET Case No.5994/78: the employer and the company accountants promised several times to do something about a redundancy payment but then refused to pay after the six-month time limit had passed. The employee referred her claim to a tribunal promptly after the refusal

316

- **Taylor v Secretary of State for Employment** ET Case No.14939/95: T, who was made redundant upon her employer's bankruptcy, applied to a tribunal for a redundancy payment just within the discretionary 12-month limit. The tribunal took account of the fact that T had been given incorrect advice and information and had waited patiently for the outcome of certain disputed matters

- **Ratcliffe v (1) Chillingtons Developments (By the Official Receiver) (2) Secretary of State for Employment** ET Case No.27278/83: R, a company director, knew that the company was insolvent when he was dismissed for redundancy. He waited for the company to go into liquidation – which took about eight months – before claiming a redundancy payment from the official receiver. The tribunal thought it was reasonable for him to wait and see what happened when the company went into liquidation

- **Nixon v DMB Contractors Ltd** ET Case No.4733/85: N was employed for about five years on a succession of contracts in between which he was laid off. He did not claim a redundancy payment until ten months after the expiry of the last contract. A tribunal decided that he had been continuously employed and that it was just and equitable to award a redundancy payment because he expected to be re-employed and had kept in touch with the employer.

10.10 *Mediation in EU cross-border disputes.* Since 20 May 2011, the time limit for enforcing a redundancy payment claim may be extended where the parties are engaged in mediation to resolve a cross-border dispute and that mediation started before the time limit was due to expire – Ss.164(4) and 207A(5). If, in these circumstances, the normal time limit for bringing a tribunal claim under S.164(1)(c) or the extended time limit under S.164(2) would expire before the mediation ends or less than eight weeks after it ends, the time limit will be extended to the end of eight weeks after the mediation ends – Ss.164(4) and 207A(6). A cross-border dispute is one in which at least one of the parties is domiciled or habitually resident in a Member State of the European Union other than that of any other party – Article 2 EU Cross-border Mediation Directive (No.2008/52).

10.11 *Death of employee.* If the employee dies during the period of six months beginning with the relevant date, the period is extended to one year beginning with the relevant date – S.176(7)(a). Where no claim has been brought on behalf of the deceased employee by the end of that period, it would seem possible, by virtue of S.164(2), for the tribunal to extend the time limit by an additional six months if it considers it just and equitable to do so. If the employee dies after the first six-month period, but before the end of the following six months, the second six-month period, during which the tribunal has a discretion whether or not to award a redundancy payment, is extended to one year – S.176(7)(b).

If there is no personal representative to pursue a claim on behalf of a deceased employee's estate, the tribunal has the power to appoint an 'appropriate person' for this purpose. This may be a person authorised to act in connection with the claim by the employee before his or her death. Alternatively, it may be the surviving spouse, civil partner, child, parent or sibling of the deceased – S.206(4) and (5).

10.12 **Subsequent claims.** Section 164 states that an employee will not be entitled to a redundancy payment unless one of the specified events has taken place within the six-month period beginning with the relevant date. But if one of the specified events has occurred within the six-month period, there is no time limit for presenting a subsequent claim to a tribunal. Two illustrations:

- **Bentley Engineering Co Ltd v Crown and Miller** 1976 ICR 225, QBD: M was dismissed and paid a redundancy payment, based on eight years' service, within six months. Nearly two years after his dismissal he made a claim to a tribunal that the payment should have been based on 23 years' service. The High Court held that there was nothing in the wording of S.164 to prevent his doing so

- **Germain v Harry Taylor of Ashton Ltd** ET Case No.51738/95: G was made redundant in February 1974. He sent a letter to his employer five months later asking for his redundancy pay. He received a cheque for £580 but discovered, in June 1995, that he had been paid only half the amount to which he was entitled. A tribunal found that, since G had made a claim in writing for redundancy pay within six months of the relevant date, his claim could proceed to a full hearing.

10.13 **Written claim to employer.** One of the events that secures the right to a redundancy payment is where the employee has made a claim for the payment in writing to the employer within the six-month time limit – S.164(1)(b). Employees may not always frame written claims with legal precision, however. In Hetherington v Dependable Products Ltd 1971 ITR 1, CA, the Court of Appeal said that any notice in writing should be construed liberally in favour of the employee. In that case the only written communication within the time limit was a letter from a union representative to the employer asking 'when it would be convenient for me to come along and meet your Mr Ditchburn re the position of Mr Hetherington, who was made redundant whilst off on the sick'. The Court of Appeal said that – even on a liberal construction – this could not be construed as a claim for a redundancy payment. It appeared to be no more than a request to discuss the possibility of an ex gratia payment. The Court stated that it would have been different if the letter had asked for a meeting to discuss a redundancy payment to Mr Hetherington.

In Price v Smithfield and Zwanenberg Group Ltd 1978 ICR 93, EAT, the Appeal Tribunal refined the Hetherington test and said that 'the test which ought to be applied is that the notice or the writing relied on must be of such a character that the recipient would reasonably understand in all the circumstances of the case that it was the intention of the writer or, if it is written on behalf of the employee, the employee to seek a redundancy payment'. In that case there had been a meeting with the employer at which, among other things, the employee's entitlement to a redundancy payment had been discussed. The notice relied on was a letter from the employee's solicitors to the employer saying: 'So far I have not heard from you in respect of Mr Price's claim for wrongful dismissal including his claim for a redundancy payment.' The EAT said that the letter was a sufficient indication that the employee was seeking a redundancy payment.

10.14 Note that, prior to 6 April 2009, submitting a written claim – or, to use the statutory language, a 'grievance' – was a mandatory requirement before an employee could bring a tribunal claim for a redundancy payment (see 'Grievance procedures' below).

10.15 **Unfair dismissal complaints.** Another of the events that secures the right to a redundancy payment is the presentation of an unfair dismissal complaint within the six-month time limit – S.164(1)(d). 'Presentation' occurs when the claim form is actually delivered to the tribunal office, not when it is posted or e-mailed. But the time limit for presenting an unfair dismissal complaint is actually three months (see 'Unfair dismissal' below), not six months (unless the tribunal decides that it was not reasonably practicable to present the complaint in time and that it was presented within a reasonable period thereafter) – S.111(2). However, the EAT has held that an unfair dismissal complaint presented outside the three-month limit will still entitle the employee to a redundancy payment if it was presented within the six months specified in S.164(1) – Duffin v Secretary of State for Employment 1983 ICR 766, EAT. Mr Justice Browne-Wilkinson thought that the normal limitation period of six months for redundancy payment claims should still apply where the claim has been mistakenly identified as an unfair dismissal claim, provided, of course, that the employee has actually been dismissed because of redundancy.

10.16 **Lay-off and short-time.** The normal statutory time limit does not apply when an employee's claim for a redundancy payment is based on a spell of lay-off or short-time working. The very different rules that apply to lay-off and short-time claims are fully explained in Chapter 4. There are, however, circumstances in which a claim that is apparently based on a period of lay-off or short-time is in reality, or is converted into, an 'ordinary' redundancy claim:

- the statutory scheme for lay-off and short-time redundancies only applies when the employer has a contractual right to lay off or impose short-time working. If an employer has no contractual right, imposition of a lay-off or of short-time working will be a fundamental breach of contract entitling

319

the employee to resign and claim to have been constructively dismissed for redundancy

- the statutory scheme for lay-off and short-time redundancies does not apply at all if an employee has been dismissed – S.151. If an employee serves a notice of intention to claim based on a spell of lay-off or short-time working and the employer responds by dismissing him or her, the employee can only claim a redundancy payment on the basis of an express dismissal for redundancy.

In both these circumstances, the employee's claim will in fact be a 'normal' redundancy claim so that the normal time limit of six months will apply.

10.17 Grievance procedures

Until fairly recently, an employee complaining about payment or partial payment of redundancy pay was required to put that complaint in writing to the employer and wait 28 days before bringing a tribunal claim. Failure to do so deprived the tribunal of jurisdiction to hear the claim – S.32 Employment Act 2002.

However, this statutory procedure was repealed in April 2009, although transitional arrangements set out in the Employment Act 2008 (Commencement No.1, Transitional Provisions and Savings) Order 2008 SI 2008/3232 meant that it continued to apply in certain circumstances beyond 6 April 2009 – see IDS Employment Law Supplement, 'Disciplinary and Grievance Procedures' (2009), Chapter 1, under 'Transitional provisions'. A failure to pay redundancy pay, or a partial payment, is a one-off event so if it occurred on or before 5 April 2009, the statutory grievance procedures apply. If it occurred on 6 April 2009 or later, they do not.

10.18 It is worth noting that the compensation adjustments, set out in S.31 of the 2002 Act, were also repealed in April 2009. That section provided that, where a statutory grievance procedure applied but was not completed before proceedings were begun and the non-completion was wholly or mainly attributable to a failure by either the employer or the employee, this would result in the increase or reduction of an employee's tribunal award.

10.19 Acas Code of Practice. When the statutory disciplinary and grievance procedures were repealed in April 2009, a new Acas 'Code of Practice on Discipline and Grievance' took their place. While the Code does not apply to redundancy dismissals, it *does* apply to redundancy payment claims under S.163 ERA. Accordingly, although an employee is no longer required to present a written grievance to his or her employer before bringing a tribunal claim, his or her failure to initiate a grievance in accordance with the Code could mean that any payment he or she receives is reduced by up to 25 per cent. Likewise, an employer's failure to deal with the grievance as the Code requires could result in an increase of up to 25 per cent.

The provisions of the Acas Code are discussed in depth in IDS Employment Law Supplement, 'Disciplinary and Grievance Procedures' (2009).

Non-payment

10.20

Section 7 of the Employment Act 2008 inserted a new S.163(5) into the ERA giving employment tribunals the power to award additional financial loss to employees who have brought a successful claim for a redundancy payment where that loss is attributable to the employer's non-payment. The amount that a tribunal can award must be 'appropriate in all the circumstances'.

Unfair dismissal

10.21

An employee aggrieved at his or her selection for redundancy may bring a claim of unfair dismissal. Like claims for redundancy payments, unfair dismissal claims fall under the exclusive jurisdiction of employment tribunals. The circumstances in which a redundancy dismissal may be unfair are discussed in Chapter 8. In this chapter, we briefly consider the time limit and other procedural requirements that apply to an unfair dismissal claim. For a more detailed discussion of the law governing unfair dismissal generally, see IDS Employment Law Handbook, 'Unfair Dismissal' (2010).

Time limit

10.22

Unlike claims for redundancy payments, where the time limit for bringing the claim is six months (see 'Statutory redundancy payments – time limits' above), claims of unfair dismissal must be brought within *three months* of the end of employment (unless not reasonably practicable). This is enshrined in S.111(2) ERA, which states that a tribunal will not consider a complaint of unfair dismissal unless it is presented:

- before the end of the period of three months beginning with the effective date of termination (EDT) – S.111(2)(a) (the rules governing the EDT are the same as those governing the 'relevant date' for redundancy payments – see 'Statutory redundancy payments – time limits' above), or

- within such further period as the tribunal considers reasonable in a case where it is satisfied that it was not reasonably practicable for the complaint to be presented before the end of that period of three months – S.111(2)(b).

These two provisions are subject to S.111(3), which states that, where a dismissal is with notice, tribunals may consider a complaint if it is presented before the notice period expires.

10.23 **Mediation in EU cross-border disputes.** Since 20 May 2011, the time limit for bringing an unfair dismissal complaint may be extended where the parties are engaged in mediation to resolve a cross-border dispute and that mediation started before the time limit was due to expire – Ss.111(2A) and 207A(2). If, in these circumstances, the normal time limit under S.111(2)(a) would expire before the mediation ends or less than four weeks after it ends, the time limit will be extended to the end of four weeks after the mediation ends – Ss.111(2A) and 207A(3). A cross-border dispute is one in which at least one of the parties is domiciled or habitually resident in a Member State of the European Union other than that of any other party – Article 2 EU Cross-border Mediation Directive (No.2008/52).

10.24 **Reasonably practicable.** As with redundancy payments, the time limit for unfair dismissal claims is subject to tribunals' discretion to extend time in certain circumstances. However, unlike redundancy payments, the discretion applies not where it is 'just and equitable' to extend time, but where it was not 'reasonably practicable' for the claimant to present the claim within three months of the EDT. A full consideration of the circumstances in which a tribunal can exercise this discretion falls outside the scope of this Handbook but can be found in IDS Employment Law Handbook, 'Employment Tribunal Practice and Procedure' (2006), Chapter 3, under '"Not reasonably practicable"'.

10.25 ## Disciplinary and dismissal procedures

Prior to 6 April 2009, employers and employees alike were obliged to follow the statutory disciplinary and dismissal procedures introduced by the Employment Act 2002 and a failure to do so could have dire consequences. For more information on the now-repealed procedures, including the consequences of non-compliance, see Chapter 8 under 'Automatically unfair redundancy – breach of statutory dismissal procedures'.

The procedures were repealed in 2009 and replaced by the Acas 'Code of Practice on Discipline and Grievance'. However, unlike the statutory procedures, the Acas Code does not apply to redundancy dismissals (although it does apply to redundancy payment claims – see 'Statutory redundancy payments – grievance procedures' above).

10.26 ## Qualifying service

As explained in Chapter 5 under 'Qualifying service', the right to a statutory redundancy payment is limited to those employees who have at least two years' continuous service. By contrast, the right to claim unfair dismissal is subject to a qualifying period of only one year's continuous service. In addition, there are a number of circumstances giving rise to automatically unfair dismissal, in respect of which there is no qualifying period (see further IDS Employment Law Handbook, 'Unfair Dismissal' (2010), Chapter 10).

The shorter qualifying period for unfair dismissal is particularly relevant to employees who have between one and two years' service: they will be able to challenge their selection for redundancy via the medium of unfair dismissal, but they will be unable to claim a statutory redundancy payment. For employers, this emphasises the importance of following a fair selection procedure and not simply choosing for redundancy those employees who are ineligible for a statutory payment (see further Chapter 8).

Consultation on increasing qualifying period. In early 2011, the Government 10.27 announced its plans for reforming access to the employment tribunal system. These plans, which are set out in full in the consultation document 'Resolving workplace disputes', include a proposal to increase the minimum qualifying period for unfair dismissal claims to two years. The consultation closed in April 2011 and the Government's response is expected by the end of the year.

Compensation
10.28

Tribunal awards for unfair dismissal are normally split into two parts – the basic award and the compensatory award. However, in cases where a statutory redundancy payment has been made, and provided that the payment has been correctly calculated (see Chapter 6 under 'Statutory redundancy pay scheme'), an employee who successfully establishes that his or her redundancy was in fact unfair will not normally be entitled to the basic award element. The formula used to calculate the basic award is identical to that used to calculate redundancy payments and the statutory regime makes it clear that employees are only entitled to one, not both – see S.122(4).

But in certain circumstances (which are set out in Chapter 8 under 'Automatically unfair redundancy') a minimum basic award for unfair dismissal of, currently, £5,000 applies – S.120(1) ERA. Where a minimum basic award applies and it exceeds an employee's entitlement to a redundancy payment, the employee will be entitled to the difference.

Compensation for unfair dismissal is generally subject to a statutory cap, 10.29 currently set at £68,400. There are, however, a number of types of automatically unfair dismissal where the cap does not apply, meaning that a claimant can recover the full extent of his or her loss – see further Chapter 8 under 'Automatically unfair dismissal'.

Contractual redundancy payments
10.30

Many employers offer enhanced redundancy pay as part of their benefits packages. However, if an employer declines to make such a payment, the employee will need to demonstrate that the enhanced scheme forms part of his or her contract of employment. It may be that the contract of employment expressly refers to the scheme, or it could be incorporated by implication. On the other hand, the employer may contend that the scheme is not contractual and simply indicates the employer's policy, subject to the exercise of discretion. A more detailed examination of enhanced redundancy pay can be found in Chapter 6 under 'Enhanced redundancy pay'. For consideration of the general principles of contract law, including the incorporation of contractual terms, see IDS Employment Law Handbook, 'Contracts of Employment' (2009), Chapters 1 and 2.

Where an employer's enhanced redundancy scheme is contractual, an employee's entitlement to a payment under that scheme arises on the termination of employment. As a result, claims for contractual redundancy pay fall under employment tribunals' limited jurisdiction to hear contract claims granted by the Employment Tribunals Extension of Jurisdiction (England and Wales) Order 1994 SI 1994/1623 (the 1994 Order), as well as being actionable in the civil courts. Generally speaking, an employee will be better served bringing the claim in a tribunal as costs will only be awarded where the claim is misconceived or vexatious. However, there are some circumstances – for example, where the amount claimed exceeds £25,000 – in which a civil court claim may be preferable.

10.31 Time limits

There is a vast difference between the time limit for claims in employment tribunals and that for claims in the civil courts. An employee claiming a contractual redundancy payment in an employment tribunal must normally present his or her claim within three months of the effective date of termination (EDT) or, if there is no EDT, within three months beginning with the last day upon which the employee worked in the employment which has terminated – Article 7 of the 1994 Order. By contrast, an employee has six years from the date of breach of contract to lodge a claim in the county court or High Court in England and Wales – S.5 Limitation Act 1980, or five years to lodge a claim with the Sheriff Court or Court of Session (Outer House) in Scotland – S.6 Prescription and Limitation (Scotland) Act 1973.

10.32 **Effective date of termination.** The EDT for the purposes of contractual redundancy pay claims is the same as for statutory redundancy pay claims, namely:

- where the employee's contract of employment is terminated by notice (whether given by the employer or the employee), it is the date on which the notice expires

- where the contract is terminated without notice, it is the date on which termination takes effect

- in relation to an employee who is employed under a limited-term contract which terminates by virtue of the limiting event without being renewed under the same contract, it is the date on which the termination takes effect. (Note, however, that the inclusion of contractual redundancy schemes in limited-term contracts is extremely rare.)

In most redundancy situations, the employee's contract will be terminated with notice, meaning that the time limit starts to run from the end of the notice period. This is the case so long as the employer gives notice – it does not matter if the employee is not expected to work for all of the notice period.

Date of breach of contract. If the contractual redundancy scheme specifies a **10.33** date or event upon which any payments under the scheme will be made, then it is only once that date has passed that the employer could be said to be in breach of contract by not making the payment. Where the contract is silent as to when such a payment will be made, it falls to the court to determine when the obligation to pay arose. While there is significant scope for academic debate on when a breach occurs, in practical terms the entitlement to a redundancy payment arises upon the dismissal of the employee. Therefore, a court would be likely to find that the breach occurred either on or immediately after the employee's dismissal.

Public sector cases. In addition to the general contractual jurisdiction afforded **10.34** by the 1994 Order, tribunals may have to consider claims made under contractual, as opposed to statutory, redundancy schemes in the public sector in two circumstances:

- where the claimants are Crown servants who are excluded from the statutory scheme but have the right to refer questions of entitlement under an analogous scheme to a tribunal – S.177 ERA

- where the claimants have rights under an alternative scheme because they have been contracted out of the statutory scheme through an exemption order – S.157 ERA.

The statutory time limits for redundancy payments do not necessarily apply in **10.35** these circumstances. In Greenwich Health Authority v Skinner 1989 ICR 220, EAT, S was excluded from the statutory scheme as being a Crown servant and she received a contractual redundancy payment in December 1986. She presented a claim disputing the amount to a tribunal in January 1988. The employer objected that this was out of time. The terms of her contractual scheme imposed an obligation to claim from the employer within six months of the cessation of employment, but then simply said that if an employee was dissatisfied the matter could be referred to a tribunal. The EAT held that the statutory time limit only applied to claims under the statutory redundancy scheme. The terms of S's contractual scheme, which was what governed her rights, did not impose any express time limit for a reference to a tribunal. It followed that the time limit for a claim was the general limitation period of six years for a contractual claim imposed by the Limitation Act 1980. It is probable

325

that the same reasoning would apply in a case covered by an order under S.157. (Note that the corresponding limitation period in Scotland is five years, not six.)

10.36 Grievance procedures

Prior to 6 April 2009, contractual redundancy pay claims were subject to the statutory grievance procedures, which required an employee making a complaint about payment or partial payment of redundancy pay to put that complaint in writing to the employer and wait 28 days before bringing a tribunal claim. Failure to do so deprived the tribunal of jurisdiction to hear the claim – S.32 Employment Act 2002.

Following the repeal of the statutory grievance procedures in 2009, employers and employees are now expected to observe the grievance procedures contained in the Acas 'Code of Practice on Discipline and Grievance', which applies to breach of contract claims brought in employment tribunals. An unreasonable failure to comply with the provisions of the Code may result in an adjustment to the amount of compensation awarded – S.207A Trade Union and Labour Relations (Consolidation) Act 1992.

The provisions of the Acas Code are discussed in depth in IDS Employment Law Supplement, 'Disciplinary and Grievance Procedures' (2009).

10.37 Compensation limit

While employment tribunals have jurisdiction to hear breach of contract claims following termination of employment, there is a statutory limit of £25,000 on the amount of damages that they can order a party to pay – Article 10 of the 1994 Order. If an employee has a contractual right to a redundancy payment in excess of this figure, he or she is not prevented from pursuing a claim in the tribunal, but will not be able to recover any more than £25,000. There is also a potential trap for employees pursuing such claims in the tribunal and intending to recover any further amount owing in the ordinary civil courts:

* **Fraser v HLMAD Ltd** 2006 ICR 1395, CA: F succeeded in his wrongful dismissal claim in an employment tribunal and was awarded £25,000 in damages, although the tribunal had assessed his loss at £80,000. However, when he brought an action in the High Court to recover the amount by which his damages for wrongful dismissal exceeded the tribunal's statutory maximum, the High Court held that he was barred from doing so by 'cause of action estoppel' and struck out the claim. The Court of Appeal upheld the High Court's decision.

10.38 Thus, employees claiming contractual redundancy payments of over £25,000 should bring the whole claim in the county court or High Court (or the Sheriff Court or Court of Session in Scotland). An employee cannot claim the first £25,000 in the tribunal and then rely on the tribunal's finding of breach of contract to secure any monies outstanding in the civil courts, since the cause of action (in this case, breach of contract) will have been extinguished upon the tribunal's reaching its decision.

Fast-track claims 10.39

Claims for redundancy payments are made and dealt with in much the same way as any other tribunal claim, subject of course to the fact that it is one of the jurisdictions in which an employment judge may sit alone without wing members. See IDS Employment Law Handbook, 'Employment Tribunal Practice and Procedure' (2006), for an in-depth study of employment tribunal procedure.

There have been proposals to allow certain claims to be dealt with under a 'fast-track' procedure, under which a small number of relatively straightforward monetary claims, including claims for breach of contract and redundancy payments, would be dealt with by employment judges 'on the papers', i.e. without a hearing. However, while the power to dispose of claims without a hearing – either with the parties' written consent, or where the respondent did not contest the claim or had failed to enter a response – is provided for in S.7(3A), (3AA) and (3AB) of the Employment Tribunals Act 1996, the detail of the new procedure was left to regulation and at the time of writing no regulations have been made. Consultation on the necessary secondary legislation took place in the summer of 2008 – see 'Dispute Resolution: Secondary legislation consultation', July 2008 (URN 08/1049), but the Government's proposal failed to draw strong support. Many of those responding doubted that the new procedure would bring the envisaged cost and time savings, and noted that the existing procedure of an employment judge sitting alone on simple cases worked well – see 'Dispute Resolution Secondary Legislation – Government response to consultation', December 2008 (URN 08/1491). As a result, the Government decided not to go ahead with secondary legislation to enable a written determinations process.

11 Time off during notice period

Section 52 of the Employment Rights Act 1996 (ERA) gives employees under **11.1** notice of dismissal for redundancy a right to reasonable time off with pay during working hours, either to look for work or to make arrangements for training for future employment. A tribunal can make a modest financial award against an employer who unreasonably refuses to allow such employees time off or who allows time off but refuses to pay for it.

Who is protected? **11.2**

The right to time off to look for work only applies to employees, so the self-employed are excluded.

Employees **11.3**
Crown employees are specifically given the right to time off – S.191 ERA, as are Parliamentary staff – Ss.194 and 195. Certain categories of employee are not covered, however. They are:

- members of the armed forces – S.192

- merchant seamen and women and share fishermen and women – S.199(2) and (4) (although seafarers employed on ships registered under S.8 of the Merchant Shipping Act 1995 are covered provided that the ship is registered as belonging to a port in Great Britain, that under his or her contract the employee does not work wholly outside Great Britain, and that he or she is ordinarily resident in Great Britain – S.199(7) and (8))

- those in the police service, or having the powers and privileges of a constable – S.200.

Employees who 'under [their] contract of employment' ordinarily work outside **11.4** Great Britain used to be excluded from the right to time off (and from other rights contained in the ERA, including the right to claim unfair dismissal) by virtue of S.196. However, S.196 was repealed by the Employment Relations Act 1999, leaving the ERA silent with regard to its territorial scope. The House of Lords in Lawson v Serco Ltd and two other cases 2006 ICR 250, HL, cleared up some of the uncertainty by holding that the statutory right to claim unfair dismissal ordinarily covered 'employment in Great Britain'. It is strongly arguable that this test should also apply to the right to time off under S.52, along with all the other rights that used to be excluded by virtue of S.196. See Chapter 5 under 'Employees and excluded employees – overseas employment' and IDS Employment Law Handbook, 'Unfair Dismissal' (2010), Chapter 2, under 'Exclusions from right to claim – working abroad' for further details.

11.5 Qualifying period

In order to qualify for the right to time off, employees must have been continuously employed for at least two years on whichever is the later of the following dates: the date when notice expired, or the date notice would have expired if the statutory notice due under S.86(1) ERA had been given – S.52(2). Provided that an employee has at least two years of continuous employment, he or she will qualify for the right regardless of how many hours he or she works.

11.6 Notice of dismissal

As noted above, the right to time off applies to employees who are under notice of dismissal for redundancy. This means the employee must have received an indication of the actual date when the employment will terminate: a mere warning that redundancies are likely to occur will be insufficient. Also, the reason for the dismissal must actually be redundancy. If the employee loses his or her job for some other reason not involving a redundancy situation – for example, due to a reorganisation of the business – he or she has no statutory right to time off. However, the fact that the employee is not entitled to a redundancy payment (for example, because the employee has unreasonably refused an offer of suitable alternative employment) does not affect the right to time off – Dutton v Hawker Siddeley Aviation Ltd 1978 ICR 1057, EAT.

11.7 Request for time off

It seems that an employee must actually request the time off before he or she can be entitled to it (although there is no specific requirement to this effect in the ERA itself). This point arose in Ryford Ltd v Drinkwater 1996 IRLR 16, EAT, albeit in the context of the right to take time off for trade union duties under S.168 of the Trade Union and Labour Relations (Consolidation) Act 1992. There, D, who was due to work a night shift from 6 pm to 6 am, stopped work at midnight because he had to attend a meeting about pay at 10 am the following day. R Ltd deducted £30.66 from his pay for the six hours he did not work. The employer accepted that D's absence from work was for union duties. It did not, however, consider that it was in breach of its duty to allow him time off. Although D claimed to have put in his request two hours before he started the night shift, R Ltd said that it did not know that he had made such a request. D was supposed to get permission from C, the works director, but, according to C, D had not asked him for permission. The EAT held that an employer can only 'fail to permit' time off if it is aware that a request for time off has been made. Therefore the employee had to establish, on the balance of probabilities, that a request for time off was made, that it came to the notice of the employer's appropriate representatives, and that the employer either refused or ignored it.

Reasonable time off   11.8

The employee is entitled to 'reasonable' time off which the employer must not 'unreasonably refuse'. The ERA itself does not define what is meant by 'reasonable' but, essentially, a balance must be struck between the needs of the employee to seek work or arrange training against the needs of the employer to get the work done. The following factors are likely to be relevant:

- the length of the employee's notice period

- when the employee put in the request for time off

- local difficulties in finding employment

- the provisions of any redundancy procedure agreement which deals with the question of time off

- the effect of the employee's absence on health and safety

- the effect of the employee's absence on the running of the business – for example, there may be production targets which might be affected by the employee's absence or, where large-scale redundancies are involved, the employer may wish to retain some control over how many employees have time off at any one time.

There do not appear to have been any instances where it has been held that the **11.9** employer was reasonable in refusing any time off at all, even where the employer's business is in serious financial difficulties. Such difficulties, may, however, reasonably give rise to the imposition of restrictions as to when and how much time is taken off.

Nothing in the ERA says that an employee must produce evidence of appointments before being granted time off to look for work. Such evidence will be no more than a relevant consideration in deciding whether a refusal to grant a particular request for time off was reasonable – Dutton v Hawker Siddeley Aviation Ltd 1978 ICR 1057, EAT. A tribunal followed this approach in Hasler v Tourell Precision Engineers Ltd ET Case No.11431/83, holding that the employer acted unreasonably in making it a condition of taking time off that the employee had a firm lead to follow up. Such a rule, it said, would even prevent

331

the employee from visiting a job centre in working hours during his or her notice period. Conversely, in Seldon v The Kendall Co (UK) Ltd ET Case No.14442/85 the tribunal rejected a claim under S.52 where the evidence showed that the employee had ignored job vacancies in his own area, preferring instead to travel further afield to make speculative enquiries. He had also refused extra work offered by his present employer. The fact that he had no definite lead to follow on his travels had fuelled his employer's suspicions that his search for work was not genuine and its refusal to allow time off was, therefore, reasonable.

11.10 Working hours

The right is to take reasonable time off during 'working hours', which are defined in S.52(3) ERA as being 'any time when, in accordance with [the employee's] contract of employment, the employee is required to be at work'. This means that an employer will not be able to require an employee simply to rearrange his or her hours or make up for lost time elsewhere – see, for example, Ratcliffe v Dorset County Council 1978 IRLR 191, ET.

In Hairsine v Kingston upon Hull City Council 1992 ICR 212, EAT, the Appeal Tribunal considered the meaning of 'working hours' in the context of the right to take time off work to perform union duties under what is now S.168 of the Trade Union and Labour Relations (Consolidation) Act 1992 (TULR(C)A). There, H worked a basic 39-hour week on a shift pattern. He applied for permission from the Council to attend a union-organised course for shop stewards. In a letter formally granting permission to attend the course, the Council stated that 'day release with pay will be granted where H would normally be at work'. The letter emphasised that, when not on the course, H was to report for work in the usual way. H's course fell on a day when he was rostered on a late shift, from 3 pm to 11 pm. The course ran from 9 am to 4 pm. Having attended the course, H travelled to work, arriving at 4.40 pm. He worked until 7 pm and then went home. The Council paid H from 3 pm until 7 pm (i.e. for four hours' work) but did not pay him for the hours from 7 pm to 11 pm, which he did not work. H argued that the course he attended was the equivalent of an eight-hour shift and he was therefore entitled to be paid for those eight hours whether or not he attended work in the evening.

11.11 The EAT held that H's contention could not be supported. It referred to what is now S.173 TULR(C)A, which states that 'working hours' should be taken to be 'any time when, in accordance with his contract of employment, [the employee] is required to be at work' (identical wording to that used in S.52(3) ERA). The EAT stated that if 'working hours' were intended to mean the mathematical number of hours which the employee was contracted to work during any given day, then the phrasing of this provision would have been quite different. In the instant case, the hours before 3 pm during which H attended the course did not constitute 'working hours' since his shift was not scheduled to start on the day of the course until that time. And the hours from 4 pm to 11 pm that he was required to work did not count because the course had ended by that time and time off during those hours was not therefore required to enable him to carry out trade union activities.

Cases on the definition of working time under the Working Time Regulations 1998 SI 1998/1833 may also be relevant. So, for example, employees who are required to be at the employer's premises while on call are likely to be entitled to time off to look for work during that period because it constitutes working time. However, employees who are not required to be on the employer's premises while on call will probably not be entitled to time off during that period because it does not constitute working time – see Landeshauptstadt Kiel v Jaeger 2004 ICR 1528, ECJ; Sindicato de Médicos de Asistencia Pública (SIMAP) v Consellería de Sanidad y Consumo de la Generalidad Valenciana 2001 ICR 1116, ECJ. A degree of caution needs to be exercised here, since statutory 'working time' is not necessarily the same as contractual 'working hours'. For more information as to the definition of 'working time' see IDS Employment Law Handbook, 'Working Time' (2009).

Right to be paid

11.12

An employee who takes time off under S.52 ERA is entitled to be paid at the 'appropriate hourly rate' for that time off (subject to a maximum overall entitlement). The appropriate hourly rate is the amount of a week's pay divided by:

- the number of normal working hours in a week as specified in the contract of employment – S.53(2), or

- where the number of normal working hours varies from week to week, the average number of normal working hours, calculated by dividing by 12 the total number of the employee's normal working hours during the 12-week period ending with the last complete week before the day on which notice was given – S.53(3). The calculation date for this purpose is the date on which the employer's notice was given – S.225(2).

For more information about 'a week's pay' and 'normal working hours' see IDS Employment Law Handbook, 'Wages' (2011), Chapter 10.

The maximum entitlement during the whole of the employee's notice period is **11.13** two fifths of one week's pay (S.53(5)), and an employee will have no further entitlement to paid time off once that maximum has been reached. There is, however, no ceiling on the amount of a week's pay as there is when, for example, calculating redundancy pay (where the current limit on a week's pay is £400) – S.227. It follows that if an employee earns £1,200 per week, his or her maximum entitlement for time taken off during the notice period is £480.

Note that S.52 does not place any limit on the *amount* of time off that may be taken, provided that the time off is reasonable. It is only the *payment* for that time that is subject to the two-fifths maximum. In theory, then, an employee may be entitled to more than two fifths of a week off to look for work. In practice, however, an employee who has already taken two fifths of a week off would not have an effective remedy if refused further time off as it is not possible to claim compensation once the maximum entitlement due under the ERA has been paid.

11.14 ## Complaining to a tribunal

If an employer unreasonably refuses to allow time off or fails to pay what is due, the employee may complain to a tribunal – S.54(1) ERA. The complaint must generally be presented within three months of the day on which it is alleged that time off should have been allowed, although a tribunal may extend this time limit by a further reasonable period if it is satisfied that it was not reasonably practicable for the complaint to be presented in time – S.54(2). (The time limit may also be extended where the parties are engaged in mediation to resolve a cross-border dispute and that mediation started before the time limit was due to expire – Ss.54(2A) and 207A(2).)

If the employee's complaint is successful, the tribunal must make a declaration to that effect and order the employer to pay the amount which it finds to be due to the employee – S.54(3). If the employer has allowed time off but refused to pay for it, the amount due is the appropriate hourly rate for the time off (subject to the maximum discussed above). If the employer has unreasonably refused time off, the amount due is that which the employee would have received if the request had been granted. This means that an employee who was refused time off and who stayed at work can be paid twice for the same period of time, once for working and once under the tribunal's award. As the tribunal said in Hasler v Tourell Precision Engineers ET Case No.11431/83, this is in the nature of a bonus for the employee and a penalty for the employer. If the employer does pay some of the amount due, it goes towards discharging the employer's liability and the tribunal can only award the amount by which it falls short of the appropriate sum – S.53(7). However, the amount awarded should not be affected by the fact that the employee receives a contractual redundancy payment which is more generous than the statutory redundancy entitlement.

11.15 Finally, S.203 invalidates any provision that purports to exclude or limit the right to time off (unless incorporated into a valid compromise agreement or an agreement reached under the auspices of an Acas conciliation officer) – see further IDS Employment Law Handbook, 'Employment Tribunal Practice and Procedure' (2006), Chapter 9.

334

12 Collective redundancies

Scope of duty to consult

Timetable for consultation

The consultation process

'Appropriate representatives'

Special circumstances defence

Complaints about breach of S.188

Notification

The statutory duty on employers to inform and consult the workforce about **12.1**
proposed redundancies, which is contained in S.188 of the Trade Union and
Labour Relations (Consolidation) Act 1992 (TULR(C)A), was introduced in
order to implement the mandatory provisions of the EU Collective Redundancies
Directive (No.75/129), which was subsequently replaced by the EU Collective
Redundancies Directive (No.98/59). S.188 was significantly amended by the
Trade Union Reform and Employment Rights Act 1993 and the Collective
Redundancies and Transfer of Undertakings (Protection of Employment)
(Amendment) Regulations 1995 SI 1995/2587 ('the 1995 Regulations') in
order to bring it further into line with the provisions of the Directive. The 1995
Regulations were introduced in response to the ECJ's ruling in Commission of
the European Communities v United Kingdom 1994 ICR 664, ECJ, that the
UK provisions failed properly to implement the 1975 Directive on a number of
points. The most significant finding of the ECJ was that the UK provisions were
in breach of the Directive in that they did not require an employer to consult
where there was no recognised trade union.

Although the 1995 Regulations purported to fill the gaps in the UK consultation
requirements, they were highly controversial, not least because they permitted
employers to bypass consultation with a recognised union and consult instead
with 'employee representatives'. Moreover, there were many who argued that
S.188 remained in conflict with the 1975 Directive in that the provisions for the
consultation of 'employee representatives' were insufficiently detailed and
permitted an employer to evade its obligations to consult. Although a legal
challenge on these grounds failed in R v Secretary of State for Trade and
Industry ex parte Unison and ors 1996 ICR 1003, Div Ct, the Government
nonetheless decided to make further amendments to the consultation provisions.
Among other things, these amendments – which were introduced by the
Collective Redundancies and Transfer of Undertakings (Protection of

Employment) (Amendment) Regulations 1999 SI 1999/1925 ('the 1999 Regulations') – compelled an employer to consult with a recognised trade union where there is one. The amendments also tightened up the provisions on the election of employee representatives.

12.2 Over the past decade, the procedure for handling collective redundancies has remained unchanged. However, in May 2011, the Government announced that it was looking at the collective redundancy rules as part of its review of 'employment red tape'. In particular, it was considering whether to make changes to the collective redundancy consultation periods. This was in response to employers' concerns that the minimum 90-day consultation period, which applies where the employer is proposing to dismiss as redundant at least 100 employees in a 90-day period, is hindering their ability to restructure efficiently. The Directive does not provide for minimum periods of consultation – only that consultation must start 'in good time'. No concrete proposals for change have yet been published but are expected towards the end of 2011.

Statutory references in this chapter are to sections of the TULR(C)A, as amended, unless otherwise stated, while references to 'the Collective Redundancies Directive' are to the 1998 Directive, which is in effect a consolidation of the 1975 Directive as amended by Directive 92/56. References to 'BIS' are references to the Department for Business, Innovation and Skills, which was created by the merger of the Department for Innovation, Universities and Skills and the Department for Business, Enterprise and Regulatory Reform in June 2009, and thereby became the competent Government department in respect of collective redundancy matters.

12.3 ## Scope of duty to consult

Section 188(1) TULR(C)A states that 'where an employer is proposing to dismiss as redundant 20 or more employees at one establishment within a period of 90 days or less, the employer shall consult about the dismissals all the persons who are appropriate representatives of any of the employees who may be affected by the proposed dismissals or may be affected by measures taken in connection with those dismissals'.

Before a change of wording introduced by the 1999 Regulations, the duty was to consult only the representatives of the employees whom the employer proposed to dismiss. Now the duty is to consult with any employees who *may be affected* by the proposed dismissals, or by measures taken in connection with those dismissals, whether or not the employer proposes to dismiss them. The amendment recognises the fact that there are employees whose jobs are not directly threatened but who may nevertheless be either directly or indirectly affected by the proposed redundancies.

Exclusion of small-scale redundancies 12.4

An employer's duty to consult only arises where it is proposing to dismiss 20 or more employees at one establishment within a period of 90 days. The meaning of 'establishment', and questions concerning the number of proposed redundancies, are discussed under 'Timetable for consultation' below.

Employees only 12.5

The obligation to consult on collective redundancies only arises in respect of 'employees' as defined by S.295(1) TULR(C)A. This includes apprentices but excludes Crown employees, those serving in the armed forces, House of Lords and House of Commons staff, those in police service, 'short-term' employees (i.e. those employed under a contract for a fixed term of three months or less or for a specific purpose not expected to last for more than three months and who have actually worked for three months or less) and share fishermen and women – Ss.273, 274, 277, 278, 280, 282 and 284. It should be noted that the provision in S.285 excluding employees working overseas from the right to be consulted was repealed by the Employment Relations Act 1999. However, employers are not under a duty to notify the Secretary of State of proposed redundancies in respect of employees who ordinarily work outside Great Britain – see 'Notification' below.

Meaning of 'employer' 12.6

Section 295(1) TULR(C)A provides that the obligation to consult on collective redundancies falls on the 'person by whom the employee... is employed'. The obligation, and liability for failure to comply, therefore falls on the employer which employs the employees affected by any proposed redundancies. This is the case even if the decision on redundancies is taken by another company controlling the employer, for example, where the employer is part of a group of companies. In Akavan Erityisalojen Keskusliitto AEK ry and ors v Fujitsu Siemens Computers Oy 2010 ICR 444, ECJ, the ECJ clarified that the obligation to consult will always lie with the subsidiary company which employs the workers and never with the parent company irrespective of whether the decision in connection with collective redundancies was made by the parent or the subsidiary – see under '"Proposing to dismiss" – who proposes to dismiss?' below.

Definition of 'dismissal' 12.7

For the consultation obligations to apply, it must be shown that the employer is actually proposing to 'dismiss' at least 20 employees. 'Dismiss' and 'dismissal' are to be construed in accordance with the Employment Rights Act 1996 (ERA) – S.298 TULR(C)A. These terms therefore cover the expiry of limited-term contracts and constructive dismissals (S.95 ERA) but not short-time or lay-off situations.

12.8 **TUPE transfer.** In circumstances where it is proposed that an undertaking, or part of an undertaking, is to be transferred to another employer, then – provided the Transfer of Undertakings (Protection of Employment) Regulations 2006 SI 2006/246 (TUPE) apply – there will be no dismissals, although the separate duty to consult contained in those Regulations will arise. However, if TUPE does *not* apply, then employees' contracts are likely to be terminated on the transfer and so a proposal for a transfer will potentially give rise to the obligation to consult on redundancy.

12.9 **Alternative employment.** It has been established that redeployment may amount to a 'dismissal' for the purposes of the collective consultation provisions – Hardy v Tourism South East 2005 IRLR 242, EAT. There, the employer decided to close one of its offices as part of a restructuring, but initially estimated that, of the 26 employees at that office, only 12 would be made redundant with the rest being redeployed. An employment tribunal held that the employer's hope that some of the employees would be redeployed meant that it had not been proposing to dismiss 20 or more employees in total, and hence that the collective consultation provisions had not been triggered. The EAT, however, overturned the tribunal's decision on appeal. In its view, an employer proposes to 'dismiss' an employee if, on an objective consideration of what it says or writes, it is proposing to withdraw the existing contract from the employee, or to depart so substantially from it that it amounts to a withdrawal of the whole contract. The EAT thought it sufficiently clear from the tribunal's findings of fact that this test was met in this case, and so substituted a decision to that effect. The EAT in Hardy did not have before it extensive details of the redundant employees' existing contracts. However, it did note that there was no suggestion on the employer's part that the employees were subject to a mobility clause. It was therefore clear that any redeployment could not be within the terms of the existing contracts, and so would be tantamount to a dismissal.

By contrast, in Home Office v Evans 2008 ICR 302, CA, the Court of Appeal held that an employer was entitled to rely upon a mobility clause in employees' contracts in order to relocate them within the terms of their existing contracts, thus avoiding making them redundant upon the closure of their place of work. E and L were employed by the Home Office as immigration officers based at Waterloo International Terminal (WIT). In 2004 the Home Office decided that immigration control there was no longer required, and initially considered applying its redundancy procedures (which largely reflected the obligations under the TULR(C)A). Having taking legal advice, however, it decided to enforce the mobility provisions contained in employees' contracts of employment. E and L were informed that they would be transferred to Heathrow. They resigned and claimed unfair constructive dismissal.

In the tribunal's view, the closure of immigration control at WIT automatically **12.10** triggered a 'redundancy notice' under E's and L's contracts, together with the relevant consultation obligations. It conceded that the Home Office had a choice between invoking the mobility provisions and making redundancies. However, that choice had to be made at the time the obligation to consult arose and, once made, the employer could not then change its mind. The Court of Appeal disagreed, holding that the employer had not 'dodged' between implementing contractual redundancy procedures and invoking the mobility clause. From the time of its announcement that the employees' workplace was to close, the employer made it clear that it would relocate the affected employees in accordance with their contracts. Accordingly, there had been no proposal to dismiss the claimants as redundant, and the Home Office had not acted in breach of contract in respect of consultation. E and L had not been constructively dismissed and their claims were rejected.

Voluntary redundancies. Voluntary redundancies can amount to 'dismissals' **12.11** for collective consultation purposes. In Optare Group Ltd v TGWU 2007 IRLR 931, EAT, the Appeal Tribunal upheld a tribunal's finding that employees who applied and were accepted for voluntary redundancy were 'dismissed', and so should have been included in the total number of employees whom the employer proposed to dismiss as redundant. Their inclusion raised the total number of redundancy dismissals to 20, meaning that the employer's failure to consult collectively was a breach of S.188. It must be stressed, however, that again this decision turned on its own facts – it is for tribunals to decide whether there has been a consensual termination of employment, in which case there would have been no proposal to 'dismiss', or whether, as here, the employees have volunteered *to be dismissed as redundant*, in which case they must be included in the calculation under S.188.

Definition of 'redundancy'
12.12

The proposed dismissals must be on the ground of redundancy, as defined by S.195(1) TULR(C)A, in order for the duty to consult to arise – S.188(1). It is important to note that, as a result of amendments introduced by the Trade Union Reform and Employment Rights Act 1993, the definition of 'redundancy' for collective consultation purposes differs significantly from the ERA definition for the purpose of individual claims for redundancy payments or unfair dismissal – for which see Chapter 2 under 'Definition of "redundancy"'. S.195(1) provides that 'references to dismissal as redundant are references to dismissal for a reason not related to the individual concerned or for a number of reasons all of which are not so related'. This broadly echoes the definition to be found in Article 1 of the Collective Redundancies Directive.

The difference between the definitions of individual and collective redundancy has potentially important implications. If, for example, an employer wants to introduce a change in terms and conditions but cannot secure the agreement of employees to the change, the usual course is to terminate existing contracts and issue new ones incorporating the desired variation. These facts would be unlikely to fall within the ERA definition of 'redundancy', and so would not give rise to statutory redundancy payments (although they may give rise to unfair dismissal claims). Under the S.195 definition of 'redundancy', on the other hand, such dismissals – not being related to the individuals concerned – would trigger the S.188 statutory consultation procedure, requiring the employer to negotiate with the appropriate representatives of the employees with a view to reaching an agreement before imposing the new contracts. In GMB v Man Truck and Bus UK Ltd 2000 ICR 1101, EAT, the employer gave employees notice of dismissal and then offered them re-engagement under new terms. The EAT held that the duty to consult applied despite the fact that the employer never intended the employees to lose their jobs and that the employees continued to work uninterrupted throughout.

12.13 Note that, for the purpose of proceedings brought under the redundancy consultation provisions, there is a presumption that a dismissal, or proposed dismissal, is for redundancy – S.195(2). Further note that the consultation requirements will still apply even if the employees concerned are not entitled to redundancy payments by reason of an agreement to that effect – Association of University Teachers v University of Newcastle-upon-Tyne 1987 ICR 317, EAT.

12.14 Timetable for consultation

To reiterate, S.188 TULR(C)A provides that an employer proposing to dismiss as redundant 20 or more employees at one establishment within a period of 90 days or less must consult the appropriate representatives of the employees affected by the redundancies. Consultation must begin 'in good time' and must in any event begin:

- where 100 or more redundancies are proposed at one establishment within a 90-day period, at least 90 days before the first of the dismissals takes effect, and

- otherwise, at least 30 days before the first dismissal takes effect – S.188(1A).

12.15 'In good time'

The requirement to begin consultation 'in good time' derives from Article 2(1) of the Collective Redundancies Directive, which does not set out any specific time limits. It was introduced by the 1995 Regulations in place of the previous requirement to consult 'at the earliest opportunity'. In Newspaper Publishing plc v NUJ EAT 0164/97 the EAT thought that there was unlikely to be any significant distinction between the two phrases, holding that, on the facts of the case, both would require consultation to begin within 24 hours of the date that redundancy dismissals were proposed. However, in Dewhirst Group v GMB

Trade Union EAT 0486/03 the EAT appeared to accept that the change was a deliberate move by the Government to reduce the obligation on employers to the bare minimum required by the Directive, and that 'in good time' is therefore a less stringent requirement than 'at the earliest opportunity'.

A comparison of the following two cases – one decided before and one after 1995 – seems to support the view that the change of wording is significant. In a pre-1995 case, GKN Sankey Ltd v National Society of Metal Mechanics 1980 ICR 148, EAT, the employer decided at the end of May to close its factory on 15 September. It began consultation with the union on 5 June, thus providing for the statutory 90 days. The EAT found that, in the circumstances, consultation had not begun 'at the earliest opportunity', i.e. at the end of May, and the employer was therefore in breach of S.188, even though it had observed the applicable statutory consultation period. In the post-1995 case, Amicus v Nissan Motor Manufacturing (UK) Ltd EAT 0184/05, redundancies were initially proposed in October but consultation with appropriate representatives did not begin until January. The EAT accepted that 'in good time' means no more or less than time sufficient for fair consultation to take place, working back from the final date, which is the first date for dismissal. Furthermore, this should not involve a mechanistic, arithmetical or calendar approach – what is 'good time' depends on many factors, including the number of staff and unions involved, and what is a reasonable amount of time for unions to be able to respond to proposals and make counter-suggestions. On the facts of the case, counting back from the date of the eventual dismissals the following June, the EAT was satisfied that consultation had taken place 'in good time'.

12.16 In any event, employers should ensure that they begin the consultation process early enough to enable meaningful consultation to take place. In complex cases, this may mean that consultation would need to start more than 30 or 90 days before the first dismissal takes effect (see 'Minimum statutory consultation periods' below) in order to be 'in good time'.

Minimum statutory consultation periods **12.17**

As explained under 'Timetable for consultation' above, while employers are under an overriding duty to begin consultation 'in good time', S.188(1A) sets out *minimum* periods of consultation. To recap, these are:

- where 100 or more redundancies are proposed at one establishment within a 90-day period, at least 90 days before the first of the dismissals takes effect, and

- otherwise, at least 30 days before the first dismissal takes effect.

These minimum periods are intended to ensure that the parties have sufficient time within which to consult by specifying a date by which consultation must have started. They do *not* dictate how long the consultation should take. In other words, the 30- or 90-day requirements do not require that the parties consult for 30 or 90 days. It is therefore possible for collective consultation to take place over a shorter period of time. However, the employer's proposals must still be at a formative stage when consultation begins, and the union must be given sufficient time to make a meaningful contribution. For example, in Amicus v Nissan Motor Manufacturing (UK) Ltd (above), the EAT held that the employer, which started consultation well before the applicable 30-day minimum requirement, complied with S.188(1A), even though consultation with the trade union effectively lasted only two weeks.

12.18 But where the employer has reached agreement with the appropriate representatives before the end of the minimum consultation period, it should not be tempted to then bring forward the date of any agreed dismissals. If it dismisses before the statutory consultation period is up, it will be in breach of S.188. (The only exception is if there are 'special circumstances which render it not reasonably practicable' for the employer to comply, but in this situation the employer must still comply to the extent that it is reasonably practicable to do so in the circumstances – see 'Special circumstances defence' below.)

12.19 **'Proposing to dismiss'**
The duty to consult arises where the employer is 'proposing to dismiss' for redundancy. Historically, courts and tribunals have taken the view that this phrase implies that some sort of decision must have been made. For example, in Association of Patternmakers and Allied Craftsmen v Kirvin Ltd 1978 IRLR 318, EAT, the Appeal Tribunal stated that, for it to be said that an employer is 'proposing to dismiss', 'the employer must have formed some view as to how many are to be dismissed, when this is to take place and how it is to be arranged'. In that case the employer was in financial difficulties and attempts were made to sell the business. When the last prospective purchaser withdrew, a receiver was appointed who immediately gave redundancy notices to the workforce. The union argued that the duty to consult arose when the employer contemplated, or should reasonably have contemplated, the possibility of redundancies. The EAT, however, held that the employer only proposed to dismiss on the day the last potential purchaser vanished and the receiver was appointed. Before that, redundancies were merely a contemplated possible event, so there was no breach of the consultation requirements.

However, while the TULR(C)A imposes the duty to consult at the point that an employer *proposes* collective redundancies, Article 2(1) of the Directive requires consultation 'where an employer is *contemplating* collective redundancies' (our stress). And in MSF v Refuge Assurance plc and anor 2002 ICR 1365, EAT, the Appeal Tribunal accepted that the difference in wording makes the TULR(C)A more restrictive than the Directive requires – 'proposing to dismiss' refers to a state of mind that is much more certain and further along in the decision-

342

making process than mere contemplation. The EAT thus confirmed that the TULR(C)A does not comply with European law.

The EAT's conclusion in MSF is supported by the European Court of Justice's **12.20** decision in Junk v Kühnel 2005 IRLR 310, ECJ. The Junk case focused on the timing of consultation in relation to the notice of dismissal (on which see 'Timing of dismissal notices' below), but the ECJ also considered the point at which the duty to consult arises. It noted that 'the case in which the employer "is contemplating" collective redundancies and has drawn up "a project" to that end corresponds to a situation in which no decision has yet been taken'. It went on to state that the wording of the Directive indicates that 'the obligation to consult and to notify arise, prior to any decision by the employer to terminate contracts of employment'. Thus, as a matter of European law, the obligation to consult arises before the employer has set its mind on dismissal. This interpretation of the Directive is unimpeachable as a matter of common sense – any consultation that takes place once an employer has already decided to dismiss would be little short of a sham – but creates something of a dilemma for UK courts and tribunals, which have to resolve the conflict between clearly worded EU and UK legislation.

In this regard, the EAT has attempted to give the wording of S.188 some degree of 'purposive' construction. In Scotch Premier Meat Ltd v Burns and ors 2000 IRLR 639, EAT, for example, it held that a company considering two possible courses of action as to its future, one of which would involve effecting redundancy dismissals, the other of which would not, was 'proposing to dismiss' for S.188 purposes. According to this interpretation, it would seem that while the duty under the TULR(C)A does not arise until there is some specific proposal for dismissals, it can arise (as the Directive requires) before the employer's mind is committed to a definite course of action. However, more recently the EAT has required something more specific in order for dismissals to be 'proposed' for collective consultation purposes. In UK Coal Mining Ltd v NUM (Northumberland Area) and anor 2008 ICR 163, EAT, Mr Justice Elias, then President of the EAT, noted that the collective consultation duty will not arise 'when the closure is mooted as a possibility but only when it is fixed as a clear, albeit provisional, intention'. This interpretation seems to be closer to the wording of the TULR(C)A than to the ECJ's clear statement of principle in Junk. However, Elias P considered all of the relevant case law – including Junk – on the point, and so his comments can be taken to hold some authority.

The European Court revisited the question of when an employer can be said to **12.21** be 'contemplating' collective redundancies in Akavan Erityisalojen Keskusliitto AEK ry and ors v Fujitsu Siemens Computers Oy 2010 ICR 444, ECJ. There the Court held that an employer's duty to consult under Article 2(1) of the Directive is triggered once a strategic or commercial decision compelling it to contemplate or to plan for collective redundancies has been taken and not when such a decision is merely contemplated. In the ECJ's view, there were clear disadvantages to a premature triggering of the obligation; for example, restricting the flexibility available to undertakings when restructuring, and causing unnecessary uncertainty for workers about their job security. The ECJ also considered that, should consultation begin when decisions that may lead to redundancies are merely contemplated, the relevant factors to be taken into account during the course of that consultation would not be known. In such circumstances, the objectives of the consultation listed in Article 2(2) of the Directive – avoiding termination of employment contracts, reducing the number of workers affected, and mitigating the consequences – could not be achieved. Moreover, the ECJ held that the obligation to start consultation was not dependent on the employer being able to supply to workers' representatives information of the type listed in Article 2(3)(b), such as the reasons for the projected redundancies, the numbers and categories of employees to be made redundant, the period over which the projected redundancies are to be effected and the selection criteria to be used. In the ECJ's view, the wording of the Directive clearly envisaged such information being provided *during* consultations, but not necessarily at the time they start.

Unfortunately the decision in Akavan is not without its problems and at certain points the ECJ appears to blur the distinction between the triggering of the obligation to consult and the obligation to start consultation. This was recognised by the Court of Appeal in United States of America v Nolan 2011 IRLR 40, CA, and as a result the Court decided that a reference to the ECJ was necessary to clarify when the consultation obligation under the Directive arises. While the ECJ had already addressed the issue in Akavan, the Court of Appeal considered that decision to be 'unclear'.

12.22 In Nolan, the commanding officer of a US army base in Hampshire informed the civilian workforce on 24 April 2006 that the base would close at the end of September 2006. In early June management wrote to the Local National Executive Council, which represented the employees, stating that final decisions on redundancies would be made at the end of June, following consultation. On 30 June, around 200 civilian employees received notice of dismissal and the dismissals took effect at the end of September. One of those made redundant, N, made a claim for a protective award on the basis that workforce representatives had not been consulted as required by S.188. An employment tribunal upheld her claim, finding that, as the decision to close the base inevitably meant mass redundancies, consultation should have commenced before the decision was made, given that there could be no meaningful consultation afterwards. According to the tribunal, this view was reinforced by the EAT's decision in UK Coal Mining Ltd v NUM (Northumberland Area) and anor (above), handed down after the tribunal's initial deliberations. On appeal, the EAT took the view that the UK Coal Mining case required consultation over the decision to close a workplace where it would inevitably lead to redundancies and upheld the protective award. However, it remitted the case to the same tribunal on other grounds. The USA again appealed arguing, among other things, that the ECJ's decision in Akavan Erityisalojen Keskusliitto AEK ry and ors v Fujitsu Siemens Computers Oy (above), handed down after the EAT's decision in UK Coal Mining, showed that the latter decision had interpreted the consultation obligation under the Directive too widely.

In deciding to refer the matter to the ECJ, the Court of Appeal stated that it found the reasoning in Akavan 'difficult to follow'. In the Appeal Court's view, it was not clear whether the ECJ had stated that the consultation obligation arises (i) when an employer proposes, but has not yet made, a decision that will foreseeably or inevitably lead to collective redundancies; or (ii) only when such a decision has actually been made and the employer is proposing consequential redundancies. The Court was able to cite parts of the ECJ's judgment supporting each of these constructions. Since the issue at stake was too important to risk adopting the wrong interpretation, the Court concluded that a reference to the ECJ to clarify when the consultation obligation arises under the Directive was necessary. (Note that at the time of going to press (November 2011), no hearing date before the ECJ has yet been set.)

12.23 In many cases the difference between 'propose' and 'contemplate' will be of little more than semantic interest. Now that employers are obliged to consult 'in good time' rather than 'at the earliest opportunity', the need to pinpoint the precise moment at which the duty to consult arises is diminished. This is because deciding whether consultation was undertaken 'in good time' is likely to involve focusing on the date of dismissal, and looking at what happened up to that date, rather than on the date on which the duty to consult was triggered. In fact, as noted under 'In good time' above, the EAT endorsed this approach in Amicus v Nissan Motor Manufacturing (UK) Ltd (above). Thus, there is support for the proposition that so long as the consultation process does not begin so late that proposals for dismissal have effectively been cast in stone, there should be no grounds for complaint to a tribunal that the process did not begin until some time after the possibility of mass redundancies was first mooted. This must, however, be subject to the overriding requirement that consultation is 'meaningful'.

Note that, as we discuss in 'The consultation process – subject matter of consultation' below, following the decision of the EAT in UK Coal Mining Ltd v NUM (Northumberland Area) and anor (above), employers are obliged to consult over the economic reasons behind a redundancy situation. Thus, 'in good time' indicates that consultation must begin early enough for representatives to be able to have a real opportunity to affect the decision to make redundancies.

12.24 **Who proposes to dismiss?** Aside from the rather ephemeral issue of the difference between 'contemplation' and 'proposal', there are some more practical issues to consider. The legislation is couched in terms of the employer's contemplating or proposing dismissal, with no clarification of who, in a corporate entity, is to be taken as doing the thinking.

The EAT considered this issue in Leicestershire County Council v Unison 2005 IRLR 920, EAT, highlighting the difference, in some organisations, between 'officers' who propose courses of action, and 'politicians' who decide on them. In that case, a tribunal had found that a 'proposal' within the meaning of S.188 had been made by officers of the Council nearly a month before being ratified by a formal political decision of the Council's employment committee. The tribunal, having considered the reality of proposing and deciding on redundancies within the Council, concluded that not only a proposal but also the decision to dismiss had been made by the Council officers prior to the confirmation by the employment committee. The EAT upheld this decision. (Note that part of the EAT's decision was appealed to the Court of Appeal – 2006 IRLR 810, CA – but this aspect of its judgment was untouched.)

12.25 Similarly, in Dewhirst Group v GMB Trade Union EAT 0486/03 an employer's decision to close one of its manufacturing sites constituted a proposal to dismiss, notwithstanding that in order to be carried out, the proposal needed to be approved by the company group of which the employer formed a part.

12.26 *Parent company.* In Akavan Erityisalojen Keskusliitto AEK ry and ors v Fujitsu Siemens Computers Oy (above), the ECJ considered how a parent company's involvement in the process that leads to collective redundancies can impact on the employer's obligation to consult. Article 2(4) of the Directive provides that the obligation to consult only applies to the employer and not the parent company controlling the employer. According to the ECJ, this means that where the decision that will lead to redundancies is taken by the parent company, the obligation does not arise until such time as the parent company identifies the subsidiary which will be affected by the redundancies. In the Court's view, to conclude otherwise would be to strip the obligation to consult of any meaning: until the subsidiary is identified, it is not possible to identify means of avoiding, reducing the number of, and mitigating the consequences of, collective redundancies.

That said, where the parent company has identified the subsidiary which is likely to shed jobs and fails immediately and properly to inform it of a decision that may or will lead to collective redundancies, it is the subsidiary that must bear the consequences. Furthermore, in light of the decision in Junk v Kühnel 2005 IRLR 310, ECJ (see 'Timing of dismissal notices' below), the consultation procedure must be concluded by the subsidiary affected by the collective redundancies before that subsidiary, on the direct instructions of its parent company or otherwise, terminates the contracts of the employees who are to be affected by those redundancies.

Company wound up. In some cases where a financial crisis is the cause of the **12.27** redundancies there may be a question as to whether S.188 applies at all. In the case of In re Hartlebury Printers Ltd and ors (in liquidation) 1992 ICR 559, ChD, it was held that the duty to consult did not arise where redundancies were the result of a court order requiring the winding up of the company, contrary to the wishes of the administrators. In such circumstances it could not be said that the dismissals were ever 'proposed' within the meaning of S.188. Mr Justice Morritt emphasised, however, that S.188 did apply to circumstances where the administrator of an insolvent company proposes dismissals. This is because an administrator acts as an agent of the employer, so that the administrator's proposals must be regarded as having been made by the employer.

In MSF v Refuge Assurance plc and anor 2002 ICR 1365, EAT, Mr Justice Lindsay, then President of the EAT, commented that the interpretation of S.188 in Hartlebury 'may be vulnerable as representing a construction of the Directive so as to make it consistent with the domestic legislation rather than, as is required, the other way round'. Having said that, Hartlebury has not been expressly overruled, and so the possibility still remains of an employer escaping liability under S.188 where the decision to close down a company's operations is made by a court.

Ascertaining the number of redundancies

12.28

In determining how many employees an employer is proposing to make redundant within the meaning of S.188, no account may be taken of any employees in respect of whom consultation *has already begun* – S.188(3). Thus, if an employer is already consulting on 70 proposed redundancies (which, as noted above, would require a minimum 30-day consultation period) and a further 30 redundancies are proposed a few days later, it is not possible to add the two groups together and claim that the threshold of 100 proposed redundancies has occurred and the 90-day minimum consultation period applies to all. If, however, consultation has not started in respect of the 70 employees, the two groups may be added together. S.188(3) would not apply in these circumstances and the company would have 'proposed' 100 redundancies – see, for example, TGWU v Nationwide Haulage Ltd 1978 IRLR 143, ET.

As noted under 'Scope of duty to consult' above, in ascertaining the number of dismissals proposed account must be taken of all those affected, potentially including some employees whom the employer has no intention of dispensing with. For example, this should include all those whose terms and conditions might be changed as a result of any reorganisation (Hardy v Tourism South East 2005 IRLR 242, EAT) and those whom it is proposed should be dismissed and immediately re-engaged (GMB v Man Truck and Bus UK Ltd 2000 ICR 1101, EAT).

12.29 Where the employer staggers proposed dismissals (and has not yet begun consulting), the question often arises as to whether – provided they occur within a 90-day period – the dismissals should be aggregated. If, for example, the employer proposes to make over 100 employees redundant but, for a variety of reasons, decides that the employees should leave gradually in batches, the obligation is to consult with the employees at least 90 days before the first dismissal takes effect. If, however, the employer did not intend to make a second batch of redundancies when the first batch was initially proposed, it may not be caught by S.188 where each batch involves fewer than 20 employees.

In Rae and ors v Beaumont Legal ET Case Nos.1810229/08 and others the downturn in the housing market had a detrimental impact on BL's workload. On 4 April 2008, it dismissed four employees with short service by reason of redundancy and, three days later, announced that it expected to make a further ten employees redundant. In the event, nine employees left by the end of May. In June, BL decided that an additional 12 employees were to be made redundant. The employees argued that BL was now under an obligation to consult collectively. The tribunal disagreed. In its view, BL conducted two discrete redundancy exercises. The first took place in April and concluded by May, at which stage BL did not contemplate making any further redundancies. The subsequent decision that more jobs needed to go was triggered by the impact of the fall in the housing market on the company's cash flow. The tribunal found that BL was not trying to evade its obligations under the TULR(C)A.

12.30 By contrast, in Jones and ors v Sunlight Service Group Ltd ET Case Nos.1200582/09 and others an employment tribunal found that the employer deliberately divided a large group of redundancies into two batches to avoid more onerous obligations to consult under the TULR(C)A. SSG Ltd, which suffered a downturn in business in 2009, announced that it was to close its plant at Wellingborough with a loss of 89 jobs, which triggered a 30-day consultation period. However, the tribunal found that the company had deliberately reduced the number of employees being made redundant, and thereby brought down the consultation costs, by making ten staff redundant immediately after the decision to close the plant was taken. This was a calculated breach of its S.188 duty.

12.31 ## Meaning of 'establishment'
The requisite number of dismissals must be proposed 'at one establishment' in order to engage the consultation obligations under S.188 TULR(C)A. The leading decision on the meaning of 'establishment' is Rockfon A/S v Specialarbejderforbundet i Danmark acting for Nielsen and ors 1996 ICR 673, ECJ, a case referred to the ECJ by the Danish national court. The ECJ held that 'establishment' is a term of Community law and cannot be defined by reference to the laws of the Member States. Rather, in every jurisdiction it must be understood as meaning, depending on the circumstances, the unit to which the

redundant workers are assigned to carry out their duties. It is not essential for the unit in question to have a management which can independently effect collective redundancies.

The employer in Rockfon was seeking to evade the consultation requirements by centralising the responsibility for dismissals so that all employees could be considered as working at one establishment, as, under Danish law, the larger the workforce in a particular establishment, the higher the number of proposed redundancies needed to trigger collective consultation. Such an approach would be of no use to UK employers seeking to avoid the consultation requirements, since the UK legislation has adopted the alternative formula provided by Article 1(1) of the Directive for defining collective redundancies, whereby the consultation requirement is triggered if 20 employees are to be made redundant at one establishment, regardless of the size of the workforce at that establishment. Thus UK employers would be prone to argue not that all the employees are employed at a single establishment, but that the redundant employees were in fact employed at different establishments. Nevertheless, the principle of the ECJ's decision suggests that any attempt by a UK employer to divide the employees' 'establishment' for the purposes of S.188 will be as unsuccessful as the Danish employer's attempts at aggrandisement.

12.32 Rockfon was subsequently endorsed in Athinaiki Chartopoiia AE v Panagiotidis and ors 2007 IRLR 284, ECJ. In that case the European Court applied the Rockfon principles to a case referred to it by a Greek court, confirming, among other things, that:

- the term 'establishment' is to be defined broadly so as to limit the instances of collective redundancy to which the Directive does not apply

- an establishment, in the context of an undertaking, may consist of a distinct entity, having a certain degree of permanence and stability, which is assigned to perform one or more given tasks, and which has a workforce, technical means and a certain organisational structure allowing for the accomplishment of those tasks

- the entity in question need not have any legal, economic, financial, administrative or technological autonomy in order to be regarded as an establishment

- it is not essential for the unit in question to be endowed with a management that can independently effect collective redundancies in order for it to be regarded as an establishment.

12.33 Prior to Athinaiki, the EAT had the opportunity to consider how Rockfon applies to UK cases. The following two cases gave rise to contrasting decisions:

- **Mills and Allen Ltd v Bulwich** EAT 154/99: B was employed by MA Ltd from 1993 until her dismissal for redundancy in 1998. She was based in the company's Manchester office and was a manager in the direct sales team, which sold poster sites to businesses. MA Ltd planned a reorganisation of the sales force in which it was initially envisaged that the entire direct sales team staff would be dismissed as redundant. In the event the company dismissed 24 employees around the country, all members of the direct sales team. A tribunal held that MA Ltd had breached S.188 by failing to undertake consultation, and the EAT upheld that decision. While the company had treated the Manchester direct sales department as a distinct entity, the redundancies were directed solely to that department nationwide, and so the tribunal had been entitled to find that the department was a single establishment in which more than 20 employees were made redundant. The nationwide team was capable of constituting the 'unit to which the workers made redundant are assigned', within the meaning of Rockfon

- **MSF v Refuge Assurance plc and anor** 2002 ICR 1365, EAT: although a tribunal found that redundant insurance field workers were assigned to their local branch offices, it concluded that the establishment in question was not the individual branch office, but the entire field staff. The EAT, however, overturned that decision, as it did not accord with the principle laid down in Rockfon that 'establishment' means the unit to which workers are assigned.

12.34 Both cases demonstrate that the decision is ultimately one for the tribunal to reach on the facts of the particular case. More recently, tribunals have tended to adopt a broad definition of 'establishment' – as advocated by the European Court in Athinaiki – where employers have tried to avoid their obligations under S.188 in cases of multi-site redundancies. Two examples:

- **Tierney-Rymer v Sainsbury's Supermarkets Ltd** ET Case No.1803829/09: T-R worked for SS Ltd, a national chain of supermarkets, as a community food and health adviser. All advisers promoted healthy eating to a variety of community-based groups in a particular geographical area. They were given a large supermarket in that area as their 'home store' for Inland Revenue purposes and to allow them access to office facilities, but they were not managed in any way by the store. In 2008, SS Ltd made 34 advisers, including T-R, redundant but decided that it was not required to carry out collective consultation. The tribunal disagreed, finding that the advisers were effectively organised as a national team and thus a distinct entity within SS Ltd; they were not subject to the branch management structure and only had a tenuous link to their home stores. Accordingly, SS Ltd had made more than 20 employees redundant at one establishment

- **Fairhurst v Stephens LLP** ET Case Nos.2406673/09 and another: S, a firm of solicitors, proposed to dismiss as redundant up to 60 employees across its five offices. It argued that each office was a separate establishment, which meant that its S.188 duty was not triggered. The tribunal noted, among

350

other things, that management decisions were made centrally, e.g. by a staff committee attended by senior partners and employees from all the offices, and found that the firm as a whole formed one establishment for the purposes of S.188.

Bringing forward the dismissal date

The EAT has been astute to avoid a potential problem that might arise in respect of the statutory periods of consultation where the redundant employees choose to leave early. Suppose, for example, that an employer proposing to dismiss over 100 employees starts consultation the statutory 90 days before the date it is proposed that the first dismissal will take effect, but some or all of the employees volunteer to leave before that date. If the employer allows them to do so, is the employer in breach of its consultation duties? After all, consultations have now started less than 90 days before the first dismissal. The EAT has held that in these circumstances there is no breach because the relevant date in S.188(1A) is the date proposed for the first dismissal to take effect, and not when the first employee actually leaves – E Green and Son (Castings) Ltd and ors v ASTMS and anor 1984 ICR 352, EAT; TGWU v RA Lister and Co Ltd EAT 436/85.

Timing of dismissal notices

One matter that often causes confusion is the relationship between the employer's duty to consult under S.188 and the duty to give proper notice to the employees to terminate their employment contracts. These are, of course, separate issues: redundancy dismissals must be effected in accordance with both the statutory consultation procedure and with the provisions as to notice contained in statute or employees' individual contracts.

The UK courts and tribunals have long insisted that consultation must begin before dismissal notices are sent out – see NUT v Avon County Council 1978 ICR 626, EAT. Furthermore, it is generally held that an employer cannot legitimately send out dismissal notices on the day after consultation began. For example, in TGWU v Ledbury Preserves (1928) Ltd 1985 IRLR 412, EAT, the Appeal Tribunal said that 'there must be sufficient meaningful consultation before notices of dismissal are sent out. The consultation must not be a sham exercise; there must be time for the union representatives who are consulted to consider properly the proposals that are being put to them.' But this approach still leaves open the possibility that in a long consultation procedure (i.e. 90 days), so long as the consultation has reached a meaningful stage, notice of dismissal can be given towards the end of the consultation process but before it actually finishes. So, an employer undertaking a 90-day consultation might validly give a month's notice of dismissal after 60 days, so that dismissals take effect at the end of the statutory consultation period but no later.

12.37 The ECJ considered the issue in Junk v Kühnel 2005 IRLR 310, ECJ. In that case, the Court was asked to rule on the meaning of 'redundancy', as it appears in the Directive, in the context of German law. The relevant provisions of domestic legislation used two words for termination of employment: 'Kündigung', referring to a party's declaration of intention to terminate the employment relationship; and 'Entlassung', referring to the actual cessation of the employment. The existence of a legal distinction between the two meant that, under German law, a redundancy did not occur on the date on which the employer declared its intention to terminate the contracts of employment, but on the date when the individual periods of notice of redundancy expired. Accordingly, an employer was able to enter consultation (and notify the relevant authority) *after* declaring its intention to terminate employment, since it would be doing so before the actual cessation of employment. The Berlin Labour Court queried whether this was compatible with the Directive.

The ECJ held that it was not. It considered that Articles 2–4 of the Directive must be construed as meaning that the event constituting redundancy consists of the declaration by an employer of its intention to terminate the contract of employment. An employer is not entitled to give notice of termination until *after the conclusion* of the consultation procedure set out in Article 2, and after notification of the projected collective redundancies to the competent public authority as provided for in Articles 3 and 4 (see 'Notification' below). The ECJ took the view that notification to a worker that his or her contract of employment has been terminated is the expression of a decision to sever the employment relationship, and the actual cessation of that relationship on the expiry of the period of notice is no more than the effect of that decision. Thus, for the purposes of the timing of the consultation procedure set down in the Directive, a redundancy dismissal must be deemed to take place on the day the employer gives notice, and not on the day that that notice expires. In other words, running the consultation period alongside the notice period is incompatible with the Directive.

12.38 At first glance, the Junk decision has significant implications for UK law. However, as we noted above, while the TULR(C)A sets down minimum consultation periods of 30 or 90 days, the Directive does not. All the Directive requires is that consultation begins 'in good time' and with a view to reaching an agreement. With this in mind, BIS, in its guidance 'Redundancy consultation and notification' (URN 06/1965), states that redundancy notices may be issued when 'the consultation has either resulted in agreement with employee representatives, or has otherwise reached its conclusion', and that this may be before the 30- or 90-day period has run its course. In other words, there is no reason why an employer cannot give notice of dismissal, taking effect at the end of the minimum period, once the actual substance of the consultation has been completed. Take the example given above of an employer undertaking a 90-day consultation. If, by the 60-day point, all possibilities of avoiding redundancy

352

have been explored and exhausted, the employer may still issue notices of dismissal taking effect 30 days later. The Directive, as interpreted by Junk, is satisfied because the substantive consultation and the notice period do not coincide. Moreover, the employer will also have abided by its TULR(C)A obligations – consultation began at least 90 days before the first dismissal 'takes effect' for S.188 purposes. To clarify, BIS takes the view that, regardless of Junk, the date on which a dismissal 'takes effect' under S.188 is the date of termination rather than the date on which notice of dismissal is given.

The same principle would presumably apply where an employer is undertaking a 30-day consultation (i.e. where it is proposed to dismiss as redundant between 20–99 employees within 90 days). However, unless employees' notice periods are very short and the consultation is over very quickly, there will inevitably be overlap between the notice period and the substantive consultation process, such as to render the procedure incompatible with the Directive. In these cases, it might be safer to hold off on issuing notices of dismissal until consultation has run for 30 days. While this will result in added expense for the employer at a bad time, avoiding the risk of a protective award arguably makes that a price worth paying – see 'Complaints about breach of S.188 – protective awards' below.

When does consultation end? 12.39

The TULR(C)A does not expressly set out when consultation is deemed to finish, which left the EAT to grapple with this issue in Vauxhall Motors Ltd v TGWU 2006 IRLR 674, EAT. In that case, VM Ltd proposed in January 2003 to dismiss 400 'temporary' employees engaged on 12-month fixed-term contracts at one of its plants, with the first dismissal taking effect on 25 April 2003 and the last on 5 September 2003. On 24 January 2003, VM Ltd gave notification of its intentions to the Secretary of State on the standard form HR1 (for which, see 'Notification' below); wrote to the TGWU, enclosing a copy of that form and providing further information about the proposals; and began consultation (all as required by Ss.188 and 193 TULR(C)A). The consultation was successful, with the temporary employees' contracts being extended, and the proposed redundancies thus avoided. However, 46 of the temporary employees remained at risk of redundancy and, on 11 March 2004, VM Ltd successfully applied to the Department for Trade and Industry (now BIS) for a six-month extension to the HR1 registered the year before. On 23 September the company told the union that there was no redundancy situation in relation to the remaining temporary employees. However, four days later it wrote to the DTI, explaining that the planned termination dates for the temporary employees was, by agreement with the union, extended to 22 October to allow for further consultation. With that letter the company lodged a new HR1, identifying 345 permanent staff for redundancy. The union was not given a copy of this. The company subsequently refused to add the

353

remaining 46 temporary employees at risk of redundancy to the consultation process for the proposed 345 redundancies. On 26 November 2004 the temporary employees were dismissed.

On a complaint by the union, a tribunal found VM Ltd in breach of S.188. In its view, the relevant date for the purposes of considering whether VM Ltd had complied with its S.188 obligations was 27 September 2004, when the second HR1 was sent to the DTI. VM Ltd's refusal to include the 46 remaining temporary employees in the larger redundancy exercise meant that it had failed to engage in meaningful consultation or to provide the union with relevant information, as required by S.188. The EAT overturned that decision on appeal. It was common ground that the requirement to provide information to the union was complied with in January 2003, along with the S.193 duty to send an HR1 to the DTI. The question was whether there came a time when the S.188 compliance was spent. The EAT agreed with the tribunal that S.188 does not have an unlimited shelf-life. Where, for instance, a company in grave financial difficulties serves a S.188(4) letter on a union and consultation begins, but redundancies are prevented because the company receives a large order, consultation ends at that point. If a year later the order is fulfilled with nothing to replace it, so that the employer needs to consider redundancies again, the original S.188 notice is spent and a fresh round of consultation is required.

12.40 However, the situation in the instant case was very different. The tribunal had in fact found that there had been an ongoing dialogue between the company and the union about the status, extension and transfer of the temporary employees from January 2003 up until their eventual dismissals in November 2004. The tribunal, however, had confused matters and accordingly misdirected itself by holding that a second wave of consultation should have begun when the second HR1 was sent to the DTI in accordance with S.193. Had it confined its deliberations to the requirements of S.188, as it should have done, it would have found that there had been a seamless and meaningful consultation process from January 2003 right up until the date of the eventual dismissals; the 'elastic' of the S.188 compliance had not, therefore, been broken.

The Vauxhall decision should not be taken as laying down a general principle that a consultation procedure remains valid for a considerable period. Rather, it emphasises that tribunals' focus should be on the substance of a consultation rather than the timetable within which it takes place. The reference to 90 days in the TULR(C)A does not mean that, if consultation extends beyond that period, it must restart. So long as the consultation is meaningful, and deals with the same employees and the same prospective redundancies, there should be no grounds for finding a breach of S.188 simply because the dismissals only take effect some time after the procedure was instituted.

The consultation process

12.41

The nature of the consultation required of employers under S.188 TULR(C)A was changed by the Trade Union Reform and Employment Rights Act 1993 (TURERA) to bring that section into line with the Collective Redundancies Directive. S.188(2) now provides that the consultation must include consultation about ways of:

- avoiding the dismissals

- reducing the numbers of employees to be dismissed, and

- mitigating the consequences of the dismissals

and must be undertaken by the employer 'with a view to reaching agreement with the appropriate representatives'.

Meaningful consultation

12.42

The final requirement – that the objective of the consultation must be agreement – does not mean that both parties have to end up entirely satisfied with the outcome. The final decision on redundancies is one for the employer to take, and economic factors will often have to prevail over employees' interests. However, this requirement does mean that the consultation must at least be meaningful. In Susie Radin Ltd v GMB and ors 2004 ICR 893, CA, an employer found to be 'going through the motions' of consultation was held to be in breach of S.188, which, in the words of Lord Justice Peter Gibson, imposes an 'absolute obligation on the employer to consult, and to consult meaningfully'. The ECJ in Junk v Kühnel 2005 IRLR 310, ECJ, took a similar view, based on the same wording in Article 2(1) of the Directive, holding that the words 'with a view to reaching an agreement' connote an obligation to negotiate.

The Government, in the BIS guidance 'Redundancy consultation and notification' (URN 06/1965), confirmed that there is no obligation for agreement to be reached, but that 'genuine' consultation 'with a view to reaching agreement' is required. This means that employers must engage actively with employee representatives when discussing options such as alternative work patterns, job share proposals, etc. The process 'should continue until the issues have been aired and parties have had a reasonable amount of time to comment on information provided and the proposals or counter-proposals which have been made'. The guidance also notes that it is important for employers and representatives to show that they have acted reasonably throughout their dealings, and suggests that as a matter of good practice, signed copies of any meeting minutes should be kept.

Substance of the consultation

12.43

The amendments made to S.188 by the TURERA fundamentally changed the basis upon which consultation takes place. Courts and tribunals tended to take

355

a fairly narrow view of the sort of consultation employers were required to undertake under the unamended S.188. Although the EAT insisted that consultation must not be a 'sham' – see, for example, TGWU v Ledbury Preserves (1928) Ltd 1985 IRLR 412, EAT – consultation was largely restricted to the procedure for handling redundancies which the employer had already decided upon.

Since 1995, however, courts and tribunals have not shied away from imposing progressively more onerous consultation obligations on employers. One of the leading cases on the substantive requirements of S.188(2) since the TURERA amendments, Middlesbrough Borough Council v TGWU and anor 2002 IRLR 332, EAT, established that the three features of redundancy consultation set out in S.188(2) – namely, consultation about ways of avoiding the dismissals, reducing the numbers to be dismissed and mitigating the consequences of the dismissals – are to be viewed disjunctively as three separate, mandatory duties of consultation. So, while an employer might genuinely consult with the unions about ways of reducing the number of employees to be dismissed and mitigating the consequences of those dismissals, it may still fail in its duty to engage in genuine consultation as to the principle of whether or not to declare redundancies at all, and so breach S.188. Furthermore, it is not open to an employer to argue that consultation about ways of avoiding the dismissals would, in the circumstances, be futile.

12.44 **Reasons for redundancies.** It was long thought that consultation need not be concerned with the economic background to the redundancy situation. In Securicor Omega Express Ltd v GMB 2004 IRLR 9, EAT, for example, the Appeal Tribunal held that there was no breach of S.188 when an employer did not consult with trade unions over redundancies arising from workplace closures until the decision to close the workplaces had already been taken. The employer had satisfied S.188 by consulting about ways of avoiding the dismissals that could result from the closures, reducing the number of employees to be dismissed, and mitigating the consequences of those dismissals. Although the consultation had to be fair and meaningful, and not a sham, there was no obligation on the employer to consult about the necessity of closing the workplaces in the first place.

However, this view – that the reasons behind a redundancy situation do not need to feature in employers' negotiations with employee representatives – was rejected by the EAT in UK Coal Mining Ltd v NUM (Northumberland Area) and anor 2008 ICR 163, EAT. There, an employer's decision to close a coal mine gave rise to an obligation to consult under the TULR(C)A. Although some consultation was instigated, the employer gave the union representatives a misleading reason for the closure, citing health and safety considerations rather than the economic concerns that were the true motivating factor. A tribunal found that there was a breach of S.188. The employer appealed, arguing that, since cases such as Securicor had established that there was no duty to consult about the reasons for a redundancy situation, giving a misleading reason for the closure could not affect the validity of the consultation procedure. The unions resisted that argument and cross-appealed, asserting that the authorities were wrong to rule out consultation about the reasons for redundancy.

The EAT agreed with the unions. In its view, Article 2(2) of the Collective **12.45** Redundancies Directive clearly requires consultation over a decision to close a plant, and had the Directive been properly implemented then the TULR(C)A would say this. The EAT recognised that there was an issue over whether the TULR(C)A could be interpreted to incorporate this requirement. However, it felt that the obligation to consult over avoiding proposed redundancies 'inevitably involves engaging with the reasons for the dismissals, and that in turn requires consultation over the reasons for the closure'. The EAT went on to note that, strictly, it is the proposed dismissals that are the subject of consultation rather than the closure itself, and that if the employer planned a closure but believed that redundancies could be avoided then there would be no obligation to consult under the TULR(C)A over the closure. Realistically, however, this would be an exceptional case, and where closure and dismissals are inextricably linked (as they almost always are), the duty to consult over the reasons for the closure arises.

Although the focus of the UK Coal Mining ruling was on workplace closures, there is no reason why the logic of the decision should not extend to any case of restructuring that might lead to multiple redundancies. As noted under 'Scope of duty to consult – definition of "redundancy"' above, 'redundancy', within the meaning of the TULR(C)A, is not limited to instances where there is a reduced need for work of a particular kind, and can include fundamental changes in terms and conditions tantamount to a dismissal. In such cases, following UK Coal Mining, the reasons for such changes will have to be open to scrutiny. It is also worth noting that the lay members of the EAT in UK Coal Mining expressed the view that, in practice, the decision would not alter industrial arrangements very much, since most employers already inform union representatives about their reasons for considering the need to close a plant and are prepared to respond to union observations on the matter.

It should be noted that the decision in UK Coal Mining has recently come **12.46** under scrutiny in United States of America v Nolan 2011 IRLR 40, CA, which concerned the USA's decision to close a military base in Hampshire. The USA argued that, following the ECJ's decision in Akavan Erityisalojen Keskusliitto AEK ry and ors v Fujitsu Siemens Computers Oy 2010 ICR 444, ECJ, the Collective Redundancies Directive did not require consultation over a decision (including the reasons) to close a plant. The Court of Appeal accepted that, if Akavan is indeed authority for a narrower interpretation of the Directive, it followed that the UK Coal Mining decision was wrongly decided. However, as fully explained under 'Timetable for consultation – "proposing to dismiss"' above, the Appeal Court found the reasoning of the European Court in Akavan 'difficult to follow' and therefore decided to make a reference to the ECJ to clarify its ruling. At the time of writing (November 2011), no hearing date has yet been set.

12.47 Disclosure of information

Meaningful consultation between the employer and the appropriate representatives about a collective redundancy situation presupposes that the representatives have some knowledge of the employer's plans. As the BIS guidance 'Redundancy consultation and notification' (URN 06/1965) notes, the 'representatives will need enough information about the employer's proposals to be able to take a useful and constructive role in the process of consultation'.

12.48 Section 188(4), which closely resembles Article 2(3) of the Directive, sets out the information that the employer must give to the representatives for the purposes of the consultation. It states that the employer must disclose in writing to the appropriate representatives:

- the reasons for its proposals

- the numbers and descriptions of employees it proposes to dismiss as redundant

- the total number of employees of that description employed at the establishment in question

- the proposed method of selecting the employees who may be dismissed

- the proposed method of carrying out the dismissals, including the period over which the dismissals are to take effect, and

- the proposed method of calculating the amount of any redundancy payments to be made (other than statutory redundancy pay) to employees who may be dismissed

- the number of agency workers working temporarily for and under the supervision and direction of the employer

- the parts of the employer's undertaking in which those agency workers are working, and

- the type of work those agency workers are carrying out.

12.49 The final three categories of information were added by the Agency Workers Regulations 2010 SI 2010/93 with effect from 1 October 2011. Employers use temporary agency workers for a number of reasons, often to cover for short-term absences among its permanent staff but also to fill job vacancies on a longer-term basis. The use of agency workers in the employer's business will usually be a topic for discussion when the parties come to consult about ways to avoid or mitigate any proposed dismissals – with appropriate representatives likely to suggest that the number of temporary staff should be reduced first before the dismissals of any permanent staff are considered.

Recipients of information. In order to comply with S.188(4), the information **12.50** must be given to the appropriate representatives. However, as we will discuss under 'Appropriate representatives' below, there is one exception to this. S.188(7B) provides that, if the employees have been invited to elect representatives but have failed to do so within a reasonable time, the employer must instead give the information required under S.188(4) directly to each affected employee.

Timing of disclosure. Section 188 does not expressly state when the information **12.51** must be given, and it was thought initially that it must be disclosed *before* the consultation begins – E Green and Son (Castings) Ltd and ors v ASTMS and anor 1984 ICR 352, EAT. However, the EAT revisited this issue in Securicor Omega Express Ltd v GMB 2004 IRLR 9, EAT. Considering S.188(4) in the light of Article 2(3) of the Directive, which requires the information to be given 'in good time during the course of the consultations', the EAT concluded that, in so far as the Green case requires a S.188 notice to be given before consultation begins, the judgment should not be followed. In its view, 'the service of a S.188 notice should not be a question of procedural or substantive bar wholly, but should form part of the wider question as to whether there has, in a particular case, been fair consultation'.

The issue of when, for the purposes of Article 2(3) of the Directive, the necessary information should be supplied to workers' representatives was considered by the ECJ in Akavan Erityisalojen Keskusliitto AEK ry and ors v Fujitsu Siemens Computers Oy 2010 ICR 444, ECJ. There, the European Court stressed that the wording of the Directive clearly envisioned such information being provided during consultations – the obligation to supply all the information required does not necessarily have to be fulfilled at the moment when consultation begins. Moreover, the rationale behind the provision was to enable workers to participate in the consultation process as fully as possible, which meant that the employer had to keep workers informed of developments and supply them with all the relevant information that became available at different times during the consultation process.

Adequacy of information. In MSF v GEC Ferranti (Defence Systems) Ltd **12.52** (No.2) 1994 IRLR 113, EAT, the EAT held that there is no rule that failing to provide full and specific information under each of the S.188(4) heads must in all cases be treated as non-compliance with the statute. The EAT suggested that the headings are not necessarily of equal importance in every case and could not necessarily be treated as separate and distinct. The seriousness of the default, and whether it is such as to amount to non-compliance with S.188, is a question of fact for the tribunal. The later judgment in Securicor Omega Express Ltd v GMB (above) suggests that, in any event, even if a failure to provide adequate information amounts to non-compliance, the remedy may be adjusted to reflect the seriousness of the default. There, the S.188(4) notice was inadequate in that it contained no mention of the total number of employees at the establishment in question or the proposed method of calculating the redundancy payments. However, these were technical failures and the EAT decided that a nominal protective award of one day's pay was appropriate in the circumstances.

Section 188(4) does not lay down any guidance as to how specific and detailed the information must be. Article 2(3) of the Directive, however, says that the purpose of providing the employees with the information is to 'enable workers' representatives to make constructive proposals'. This suggests that a fairly high level of detail is required. Employers will be reluctant to disclose information that they consider sensitive, especially information that pertains to their financial circumstances. However, following the ruling in UK Coal Mining Ltd v NUM (Northumberland Area) (above), to the effect that employers must consult over the reasons behind a redundancy situation, they may have little choice. Furthermore, as Mr Justice Elias, then President of the EAT, noted in that case, the Information and Consultation of Employees Regulations 2004 SI 2004/3426, which impose general information and consultation obligations on all businesses with 50 or more employees, arguably require a similar level of disclosure.

12.53 It has been suggested that the S.188(4) list of information that the employer is required to give may not be exhaustive. Article 2(3) of the Directive requires that employers shall, in good time during the course of consultations, provide representatives with 'all relevant information' but there is no comparable requirement in the TULR(C)A. However, in GMB v Amicus and ors 2003 ICR 1396, EAT, the Appeal Tribunal opined that the draftsman can be taken to have assumed that 'all relevant information' would be contained in the matters set out in S.188(4) and that perhaps the reason for the omission was a wish for precision and clarity. If the EAT is correct about this, then this suggests that tribunals should resist the urge to attempt to interpret S.188(4) purposively and so read in notification requirements that are not set out in black and white.

12.54 **Adequacy of HR1 notice.** In MSF v GEC Ferranti (Defence Systems) Ltd (No.2) (above) the employer claimed to have satisfied the requirements of S.188(4) when it sent the union a copy of the HR1 form used to notify the Secretary of State of redundancies under S.193 – see 'Notification' below. The HR1 indicated the total number of proposed redundancies, the occupational groups affected and the number by which each group would be reduced, although the employer stressed that these figures were 'a best estimate only' and could change dramatically. In meetings with management, the union emphasised the importance of knowing what categories of employees would be affected and two weeks later, on 26 September, the union was given a more detailed breakdown of the redundancies by sector. On 7 October the employer issued the union with a list identifying the numbers and descriptions of the persons to be made redundant by reference to job category and location. An employment tribunal held that consultations began when the union received the HR1. On appeal, the EAT stressed that the question of whether sufficient information had been supplied depended on the facts and circumstances of the particular case. However, the EAT stated that the tribunal had failed to give any proper consideration to the question and had not provided any reasons for its decision. It held that the information in the HR1 was inadequate and that the employer only complied with S.188(4) when it provided the further information on 26 September.

Delivery of information. The information should be either given to the appropriate representatives or posted to an address notified by them to the employer or, in the case of trade union representatives, posted to the main or head office of the union – S.188(5). The question of what constitutes effective delivery of the information arose in NALGO v London Borough of Bromley EAT 671/91. In that case the information regarding proposed redundancies was sent to the union's office by hand on 19 December. When the employer's messenger entered the office he found it occupied by a woman who said that the relevant union officer was not in but that she would pass the delivery on to him when he returned. In the event, the union officer did not receive the information until 31 December. No explanation for the delay could be found and the identity of the woman to whom delivery was made could not be established. The EAT held that the information had nevertheless been properly delivered when it was handed into the union's office, not when it finally reached the relevant official. A delivery is effected for the purposes of S.188(5) when the information is given to an individual whom the deliverer reasonably believes has authority to receive it. **12.55**

Duty to give representatives copy of HR1 — 12.56
There is one further information right enjoyed by employee/trade union representatives. Whenever an employer is proposing redundancies on a scale that triggers the consultation procedures of S.188, it will be under a duty to notify the Secretary of State of those redundancies – S.193(1) and (2) (see 'Notification' below). In addition to notifying the Secretary of State, S.193(6) provides that the employer must give a copy of the notice (usually termed an HR1 form) to each of the representatives who are to be consulted under S.188. There does not appear to be any remedy in the case of an employer who fails to comply with this requirement, however.

12.57 **Access to employees and facilities**

Finally, in relation to the consultation process, note that an employer must allow the representatives with whom it is consulting access to the affected employees and must afford those representatives such accommodation and other facilities as may be appropriate – S.188(5A). This requirement is also important as a matter of good practice and as a means of achieving meaningful consultation. As the BIS guidance 'Redundancy consultation and notification' notes, the speed of the consultative process depends partly upon the resources devoted to it. Representatives should be able to work more quickly where they have access to good facilities to undertake their work and communicate with employees.

12.58 ## 'Appropriate representatives'

The Collective Redundancies Directive requires Member States to introduce legislation obliging employers who are contemplating redundancies to consult with 'workers' representatives'. However, S.188 TULR(C)A originally required employers to consult only where the employees were members of a recognised trade union. Therefore, an employer who did not recognise a trade union did not have to comply with the statutory consultation requirement. This was declared unlawful by the ECJ in Commission of the European Communities v United Kingdom 1994 ICR 664, ECJ, and accordingly the 1995 Regulations amended S.188 so that employers were placed under a duty to consult with the 'appropriate representatives' of the affected employees. One aspect of this amendment which raised many eyebrows at the time was that it had the effect that, even where the employer recognised a trade union, it was able to bypass that union and consult instead with employee representatives if it saw fit. This controversial aspect of the consultation provisions was subsequently removed by amendments introduced by the 1999 Regulations, which ensure that a recognised trade union can no longer be lawfully left out of the consultation process.

12.59 Section 188 now defines the 'appropriate representatives' of the affected employees with whom the employer must consult as follows:

- if the employees are of a description in respect of which an independent trade union is recognised by the employer, then the 'appropriate representatives' are the representatives of the trade union – S.188(1B)(a)

- in any other case (i.e. where the employees are not represented by a union recognised by the employer), the employer can choose to consult either: (i) employee representatives who were appointed or elected by the affected employees for a purpose other than redundancy consultation but 'who (having regard to the purposes for and the method by which they were appointed or elected) have authority from those employees to receive

362

information and to be consulted about the proposed dismissals on their behalf'; or (ii) employee representatives elected by the affected employees for the purposes of redundancy consultation (the election must be in accordance with S.188A(1) – see below) – S.188(1B)(b).

12.60 We shall consider each of these categories of representatives in turn. However, in determining the 'appropriate representatives' within their organisation for the purposes of redundancy consultation, employers may find it useful to consider the following, necessarily sequential, questions:

(1) is an independent trade union (or more than one) recognised in respect of *all* the affected employees? If the answer is 'yes', the employer *must* consult with the recognised union(s)

(2) if the answer to (1) is 'no', is an independent trade union (or more than one) recognised in respect of *some* of the affected employees? If the answer is 'yes', the employer must consult with the recognised union(s) *and* either existing employee representatives who have authority to consult on behalf of affected employees who are not represented by a union or with employee representatives specially elected for that purpose

(3) if the answer to (2) is 'no' because there is no independent trade union recognised at the employer's workplace, the employer must either consult with existing employee representatives who have authority to consult on behalf of affected employees or with employee representatives specially elected for that purpose.

Trade union representatives

12.61 The effect of S.188(1B) is that, if affected employees – or, to use the words of the statute, employees 'of a description' – are represented by a recognised, independent trade union, the employer must inform and consult representatives of that trade union, as opposed to other employee representatives. This is reflected and expanded upon in the BIS guidance, 'Redundancy consultation and notification' (URN 06/1965), which states that where affected employees 'are represented by an independent trade union recognised for collective bargaining purposes, the employer must inform and consult an authorised official of that union... The employer is not required to inform and consult any other employee representatives in such circumstances, but may do so voluntarily if desired.'

12.62 'Independent' and 'recognised' trade union. Section 188(1B) does not compel an employer to consult with the representatives of a trade union unless that union is 'independent' and 'recognised'. Both concepts are discussed in detail in IDS Employment Law Handbook, 'Trade Unions' (2000), but for present purposes it suffices to set out the basic statutory requirements that must be met.

12.63 *Independence.* The law acknowledges that, for trade unions to carry out their functions properly, they must be truly independent of employers. There is a statutory definition of 'independence', found in S.5 TULR(C)A, which provides that a union is independent if it is not under the domination or control of an employer, and not liable to interference by an employer (arising out of the provision of financial or material support or by other means) tending towards such control.

Note that a listed trade union – that is, one found on the list of unions maintained by the Certification Officer – may apply to the Certification Officer under S.6(1) TULR(C)A for a certificate stating that it satisfies the statutory definition of independence.

12.64 *Recognition.* Put simply, 'recognition' is the process by which an employer accepts a trade union as being entitled to act on behalf of a particular group (or groups) of workers for some purpose. S.178(3) TULR(C)A provides that a recognised trade union is one that is recognised 'by an employer, or two or more associated employers, to any extent, for the purposes of collective bargaining'. 'Collective bargaining' encompasses negotiations relating to or connected with one or more of the following:

- terms and conditions of employment, or the physical conditions in which any workers are required to work

- engagement or non-engagement, termination or suspension of employment

- allocation of work between workers or groups of workers

- disciplinary matters

- a worker's membership or non-membership of a trade union

- facilities for trade union officials, and

- machinery for negotiation or consultation, and other procedures, relating to any of the above matters, including the recognition by employers or employers' associations of the right of a trade union to represent workers in such negotiation or consultation or in the carrying out of such procedures – S.178 TULR(C)A.

Recognition can be either voluntary on the part of the employer or compulsory under the complex scheme contained in Schedule A1 to the TULR(C)A, which is discussed at length in IDS Employment Law Handbook, 'Trade Unions' (2000), Chapter 5.

12.65 **No need to be member of recognised union.** It is important to note that S.188(1B) does not stipulate that a trade union representative can only be an 'appropriate representative' for the purposes of redundancy consultation where the affected employees are, in fact, members of the union. Instead, the provision makes it clear that the affected employees must be 'employees... of a description' in respect of which the union is recognised by the employer. It is therefore the *class* or *category* of employees that the union represents that is relevant here, not whether any particular employee is a member of the union.

It follows from this that an employer may be obliged to consult a union even if the employees to be dismissed or otherwise affected by the dismissals are not actually members of that union. In Governing Body of the Northern Ireland Hotel and Catering College and anor v NATFHE 1995 IRLR 83, NICA, the employer recognised two independent trade unions for collective bargaining purposes in respect of its college lecturers, the NATFHE and the NASUWT. When two lecturers at one of the employer's colleges faced redundancy, the employer consulted with their union, which was the NASUWT. The NATFHE argued that it should have been included in the consultation because it was recognised by the employer in respect of employees 'of a description' whom it proposed to dismiss, i.e. college lecturers, even though it had no members at that particular college. The Court, examining the relevant Northern Ireland provision that mirrored S.188(1B) (but which has since been repealed), agreed. In its view, if Parliament had intended to limit the requirement to consult to a case where the employee was a member of the recognised union, it would have been simple to state that in clear terms. Moreover, the Court pointed out that, even though the union may not be concerned to protect individual non-members, it may be interested in preserving the jobs being made redundant. The NATFHE should accordingly have been consulted over the proposed redundancies.

Union 'representatives'. Any consultation must take place with 'representatives' **12.66** of the trade union, which are defined by S.196(2) as officials or other persons authorised by the trade union to carry on collective bargaining with the employer. Employers should therefore ensure that they are consulting with persons who have the appropriate authority to conduct negotiations for the trade union. The BIS guidance, 'Redundancy consultation and notification' (URN 06/1965), notes that an appropriate trade union official could be a shop steward, a district union official or a national or regional official.

In GMWU v Wailes Dove Bitumastic Ltd 1977 IRLR 45, ET, a tribunal held that an employer fully complied with S.188 when it consulted a shop steward about redundancies, and other union officials had no right to any further consultation. In that case the employer consulted the recognised shop steward with whom it customarily negotiated. Sometime later it notified the union's regional organiser that redundancies were anticipated. The regional organiser demanded a meeting with the employer but this was refused because consultation had already taken place with the shop steward. The tribunal held that consultation with the shop steward was sufficient and that there was no need for the employer to have consulted the regional organiser too. The BIS guidance appears to confirm this approach, noting that once information and consultation has gone ahead with an appropriate official, the employer is not required to inform and consult any other employee representatives, but may do so voluntarily.

12.67 Employee representatives

Where there is no recognised union, or the affected employees are not of a description in respect of which an independent trade union is recognised, the employer must consult with 'employee representatives'. As we mentioned under 'Appropriate representatives' above, the employer has a choice between consulting existing employee representatives or employee representatives that have been elected by the affected employees specifically for the purposes of the consultation. Regardless of which route the employer decides to take, the employee representatives must be employed by the employer at the time of their election or appointment – S.196(1).

12.68 Existing employee representatives

One option, then, is for the employer to inform and consult 'employee representatives appointed or elected by the affected employees otherwise than for the purposes of [redundancy consultation], who (having regard to the purposes for and the method by which they were appointed or elected) have authority from those employees to receive information and to be consulted about the proposed dismissals on their behalf' – S.188(1B)(b)(i).

The employer may therefore consult through an existing consultative body, such as a staff council, even though the existing employee representatives were not appointed or elected for the specific purpose of being consulted about proposed redundancies. What matters is that these employee representatives have suitable authority from the affected employees to consult about that issue on their behalf. The BIS guidance, 'Redundancy consultation and notification' (URN 06/1965), notes that 'their remit and method of election or appointment must give them suitable authority from the employees concerned' and regard should be had to 'the purposes for and the method by which they were appointed or elected' – S.188(1B)(b)(i). The guidance goes on to state, by way of example, that a committee specifically established to consider the operation of a staff canteen would not be the appropriate body with which to consult about redundancies among sales staff, but it may well be appropriate to consult a committee, such as a works council or staff forum, which is regularly consulted about the company's financial position and personnel matters.

12.69 In United States of America v Nolan 2011 IRLR 40, CA, the employer argued that N was not an 'appropriate representative' within the meaning of the TULR(C)A because, having been elected to the Local National Executive Council (LNEC) following the announcement of redundancies, she had not been elected by the affected employees 'otherwise than for the purposes of

[S.188]'. Rather, she had been specifically elected for that purpose, which meant that she fell within S.188(1B)(b)(ii) and her election would then have to satisfy the detailed electoral requirements set out in S.188A (see 'Election of employee representatives' below). As those requirements had not been met, she had no standing to claim a protective award under S.189 (see 'Complaints about breach of S.188' below). The EAT was not convinced that this was what actually happened in the case. It thought that, while it was overwhelmingly likely that the LNEC's work from the date of N's election would be concerned with the proposed redundancies, N might have been elected to deal with a variety of matters relating to those redundancies, including but not limited to consultation under S.188, in which case her election as an employee representative would be valid. However, the tribunal had not made the necessary findings of fact to determine whether N had been validly elected for the purposes of S.188(1B)(b)(i), and the issue was remitted to the tribunal. On appeal, the Court of Appeal upheld the EAT's decision.

ICE Regulations. Usually, employee representatives elected under the **12.70** Information and Consultation of Employees Regulations 2004 SI 2004/3426 (the ICE Regulations), which apply to businesses with at least 50 employees, will satisfy the description of existing representatives set out in S.188(1B)(b)(i). The BIS guidance states that this will be the case. However, this is subject to the proviso that the remit of the representatives elected under the ICE Regulations is sufficiently broad. The ICE Regulations give free rein to employers and employee representatives to agree the issues on which representatives will be entitled to be informed and consulted. In the event that the agreement does not extend to redundancy and/or reorganisation, the representatives may not be competent to undertake consultation under the TULR(C)A.

Although employers and employees are free to negotiate any type of information and consultation agreement under the ICE Regulations, there is a standard agreement that applies where such negotiations prove fruitless. The standard agreement is set out at Regs 18–20 and expressly covers decisions likely to lead to a redundancy situation, as defined by the TULR(C)A – Reg 20(1)(c)(i). However, when the S.188 duty to consult arises, the employer is free to comply with its duties under the TULR(C)A *instead of* those under the ICE Regulations, provided that the employer notifies the ICE representatives in writing of its intention to do so – Reg 20(5). Thus, an employer may choose to conduct elections for employee representatives specifically for the redundancy consultation rather than go along with the default agreement in place under the ICE Regulations.

For more information on the ICE Regulations, see IDS Employment Law Supplement, 'Information and Consultation Regulations 2004' (2005).

12.71 **Election of employee representatives**

If there are no trade union or appropriate employee representatives already in existence, then it will be necessary to elect employee representatives specifically for the purpose of redundancy consultation. The employer may also decide to elect new employee representatives where it does not want to use existing ones, perhaps because it is unsure as to whether the latter have authority to consult on behalf of the affected employees. Any election that ensues should be conducted in accordance with the detailed list of requirements for the election of employee representatives set out in S.188A.

12.72 Section 188A(1) provides that:

- the employer must make such arrangements as are reasonably practical to ensure that the election is fair

- it is the employer's responsibility to determine the number of representatives to be elected. The employer must ensure that there are sufficient representatives to represent the interests of all the affected employees, having regard to the number and classes of those employees

- the employer must determine whether the affected employees should be represented either by representatives of all the affected employees or by representatives of particular classes of those employees

- before the election the employer must determine the employee representatives' term of office. The term of office must be long enough to enable the information and consultation process to be completed

- the candidates for election as employee representatives must, on the date of the election, be affected employees

- no affected employee may be unreasonably excluded from standing for election

- all those who are affected employees on the date of the election are entitled to vote

- the employees may vote for as many candidates as there are representatives to be elected to represent them or their particular class of employee

- so far as is reasonably practicable, voting must be in secret and the election should be conducted so as to ensure that the votes are accurately counted.

12.73 Furthermore, S.188A(2) provides that if, following an election, one of the successful candidates ceases to act as an employee representative and any of the employees are no longer represented as a result, then another election must be held – in accordance with S.188A(1)(a), (e), (f) and (i) – to elect a new employee representative.

The legislation is silent as to how many representatives must be elected, but states that this will depend on the number and classes of affected employees. Given the use of the word 'representatives' in the plural throughout Ss.188 and 188A, it seems likely that a single representative will not be sufficient. To some extent, the number of employee representatives the employer chooses will depend on whether it decides that, in accordance with S.188A(1)(c), affected employees should be represented either by representatives of all the affected employees or by representatives of particular classes of employee who may be affected by the proposed dismissals. The latter may increase the overall number of employee representatives, but has the obvious advantage of ensuring that the interests of each group of affected employees is represented.

12.74 In Robson v Domino UK Ltd ET Case No.1400506/09 the tribunal found that the employer unreasonably excluded an employee from standing for election as a representative in breach of S.188A(1)(f). D Ltd proposed to make a number of redundancies across its business, triggering the S.188 duty to consult. It then invited all affected staff to apply for election as employee representatives. D Ltd wished to appoint two employee representatives for its sales team and R put himself forward. However, his application was rejected on the basis that D Ltd wanted the representatives to be from the Cambridge Head Office (R worked from home) because that was where most of the affected employees were likely to be based and where the consultation meetings would take place, and where photocopying and other facilities were more readily available, and it did not wish to take R out of the 'sales loop' while consultation was ongoing. The tribunal found, having regard to the company's statement that all affected employees were entitled to stand for election, it was not reasonable for it to reject R's application. Furthermore, R was told to stop acting as a salesman during the consultation month, most of the company's sales staff were not based in Cambridge, and the tribunal did not think that the cost of the arrangement or the convenience of having people in head office could outweigh employees' rights under S.188A.

12.75 **No need to hold ballot.** The statutory requirement to 'elect' representatives pursuant to S.188A was scrutinised by the EAT in Phillips v Xtera Communications Ltd 2011 IRLR 724, EAT. XC Ltd, a technology company, intended to close its Harold Wood site, thereby triggering the collective redundancy consultation obligations. It decided that two employee representatives would be needed and the staff provided the names of two volunteers. Another person then volunteered and the company agreed to proceed with three employee representatives. No staff objected to this process of selection. Following his redundancy, P complained that XC Ltd was in breach of its duty to consult under the 1992 Act because it failed to hold an 'election' for the employee representatives as required by S.188A.

369

The EAT rejected his complaint, holding that XC Ltd had complied with S.188A because the provision could not be interpreted as forcing an employer to hold a ballot where the number of candidates precisely matched the number of available places for elected representatives. The statutory scheme's aim is to ensure that in larger-scale redundancy situations the interests of the employees are collectively represented by those of their number whom they have chosen to represent them. The function of S.188A is to ensure a fair process for identification of those representatives by way of election. But it could not be said that Parliament intended to compel the employer to conduct a ballot in every circumstance. Where, as in this case, the number of candidates precisely tallies with the number of representatives to be elected, the employer would only expend valuable time and resources on a wholly unnecessary exercise. It therefore concluded that the statute does not require a ballot in an uncontested election.

12.76 The Appeal Tribunal did acknowledge that the absence of a requirement to hold a ballot may enable an employer to 'rig' the nomination process – for instance, by identifying 'favoured "yes men"' among its staff and encouraging them to stand for election and then creating a matching number of vacancies for employee representatives. That said, it was adamant that S.188A(1) itself contains sufficient protection against manipulation of this sort in that S.188A(1)(a) requires that the employer must make arrangements 'to ensure that the election is fair'.

12.77 Delay in electing representatives. There are specific provisions for dealing with the potential delaying effect of having to elect representatives prior to consultation. S.188(7A) provides that where an employer has invited any of the affected employees to elect employee representatives, and the invitation was issued in time to allow the employees to elect the representatives before the date when the consultation is required to begin, the employer shall be taken to have complied with the obligations if it consults or informs as soon as is reasonably practicable after the election. What this means is that if the employer misses the 30- or 90-day consultation period because it is waiting for representatives to be elected, then this will not amount to a breach of S.188 so long as the employees have been given sufficient time to elect representatives and the employer has consulted as soon as possible after the election. No light is thrown on what is an appropriate time to allow for an election to take place, which will be a question of fact for the tribunal to decide. If other employee elections are conducted among the workforce, the timescale for these may be relevant here.

12.78 Duty to inform individuals. Note that S.188(7B) provides that if affected employees, having been invited by the employer to elect representatives, fail to do so within a reasonable time, the employer must provide each affected employee with the information set out in S.188(4) (see 'The consultation process – disclosure of information' above).

Statutory protection for appropriate representatives 12.79

Elected employee representatives, and candidates for such elections, enjoy certain rights and protections under the Employment Rights Act 1996 (ERA). These are the right to time off to fulfil their duties and the right not to be selected for redundancy, to be dismissed or to suffer a detriment for a reason connected with their status or activities as employee representatives – see Ss.47(1), 61–63, 103 and 105 ERA. Trade union representatives who are also employees enjoy similar rights under the TULR(C)A – see Ss.146, 152, 153 and 168 TULR(C)A.

In addition, S.47(1A) ERA gives employees the right not to be subjected to a detriment by any act, or any failure to act, by the employer done on the ground that the employee participated in an election of employee representatives. The wording of this provision appears wide enough to protect both the organisers of elections and those who vote in them, as well as the actual candidates.

Section 47 does not apply if the detriment in question amounts to a dismissal 12.80 – S.47(2). This is because dismissal is dealt with separately in S.103 ERA. S.103(1) provides that it is automatically unfair to dismiss an employee on the ground that he or she performed or proposed to perform any of the functions or activities of an elected employee representative or of a candidate in an election for such representatives. S.103(2) extends this protection to those participating in the election of representatives. It provides that a dismissal will be regarded as unfair if the principal reason for the dismissal 'is that the employee took part in an election of employee representatives' for collective redundancy purposes.

Special circumstances defence 12.81

There is a 'defence' open to employers which have failed to comply fully with the information and consultation requirements of S.188 TULR(C)A. S.188(7) provides that if there are 'special circumstances which render it not reasonably practicable' for an employer to comply with a requirement to:

- begin consultation in good time and within the applicable 30- or 90-day period (S.188(1A))

- consult about ways of avoiding or reducing the dismissals and mitigating their consequences (S.188(2)) or

- disclose information to the appropriate representatives for the purposes of consultation (S.188(4)),

the employer need only take such steps towards compliance with that requirement as are reasonably practicable in the circumstances. The onus is on the employer to show both that there were special circumstances and that it took all reasonably practicable steps – S.189(6).

371

12.82 **What are 'special circumstances'?**

There is no definition of 'special circumstances' in the TULR(C)A. In Clarks of Hove Ltd v Bakers' Union 1978 ICR 1076, CA, the Court of Appeal held that a 'special circumstance' must be something 'exceptional', 'out of the ordinary' or 'uncommon'. Indeed, since the purpose of the consultation requirements is to allow planning for, and consultation on, a redundancy situation, in order to constitute special circumstances making it not reasonably practicable to consult fully, the situation must usually be unexpected or have very specific and unusual characteristics.

Even where special circumstances are shown, these do not absolve the employer from complying with those requirements in respect of which compliance *was* reasonably practicable or which were not affected by the special circumstances. The employer must still take all steps towards compliance as are reasonably practicable in the circumstances of the case. In Shanahan Engineering Ltd v Unite the Union EAT 0411/09 SE Ltd, an engineering construction firm contracted to work on a new power station, was urgently required by its client, Alstom, to reduce the number of workers it had on site to alleviate health and safety problems caused by congestion and ground conditions. Within three days, SE Ltd had selected around 50 employees for redundancy according to agreed selection criteria and dismissed them with one week's notice. The EAT agreed with a tribunal's finding that 'special circumstances' applied to relieve the employer of the obligation to undertake the full 30-day consultation over collective redundancies, but that it should still have made some attempt at consultation. The EAT stated: 'The instructions given by Alstom made it inevitable that the workforce on the contract would have to be reduced; but it remained for Shanahan to decide whether employees should be dismissed for redundancy, how many employees should be dismissed, when they should be dismissed, and what if anything ought to be done to mitigate the consequences of dismissal. These were proper matters for consultation; it was the aim of the legislation that there should be consultation with a view to agreement if possible on these issues.'

12.83 Below we consider some of the more common situations in which employers plead special circumstances. It is worth noting that while some of these may not be 'special' enough to excuse lack of consultation, they may nevertheless be taken into account by a tribunal when considering the remedy for breach of S.188 – see 'Complaints about breach of S.188 – protective awards' below. There is one situation which will *never* amount to special circumstances and that is where the decision leading to the proposed dismissals is taken by 'a person' who controls the employer (e.g. a parent company) and that person fails to provide the employer with the necessary information. We deal with this exclusion from the scope of S.188(7) first.

Exclusion from the defence. Although the TULR(C)A does not define 'special **12.84** circumstances', it does specify one situation which *cannot* constitute a S.188(7) defence in respect of a failure to consult. This is where 'the decision leading to the proposed dismissals is that of a person controlling the employer (directly or indirectly)' and that person fails to provide 'information' to the employer. S.188(7) provides that the employer cannot rely on that failure as a special circumstance excusing lack of compliance with S.188. This provision, which was introduced by the Trade Union Reform and Employment Rights Act 1993, derives from the Directive.

The scope of this exclusion from the 'special circumstances' defence was considered by the EAT in GMB v Amicus and ors 2003 ICR 1396, EAT. Its key conclusion was that 'information' referred to in S.188(7) includes not just the specific information the employer is required to give to employee representatives under S.188(4), but also any information that an employer needs in order to begin a redundancy consultation process. The employer in that case therefore could not rely on the 'special circumstances' defence where there had been a delay in its receipt of information about a decision leading to proposed dismissals taken by a controlling undertaking.

The EAT set out a practical example to show how the exception operates. It **12.85** described a hypothetical situation where a parent company decides that a wholly-owned subsidiary operating one plant with 100 employees must cease trading. The parent company makes that decision on day one, but does not inform its subsidiary until day 90. The subsidiary ceases trading on day 91 and dismisses all of its employees on that day. Owing to the operation of the exception contained in the second part of S.188(7), the subsidiary would not be permitted to rely upon the parent company's delay in notifying it of its decision as a reason for non-compliance with its statutory consultation obligations. The EAT went on to explain that if the parent company's delay in informing its subsidiary were only 30 days, it would be only the delay of 30 days which would fall to be ignored for the purposes of the special circumstances defence. The EAT further explained that if, in this second situation, the dismissals could not be avoided before a further 60 days had elapsed (meaning that the 90-day consultation period could not have been achieved in any event), the parent company's decision to close the plant might still amount to 'special circumstances' rendering the subsidiary's compliance with S.188 not reasonably practicable.

Insolvency and financial crises. Many redundancies are the consequence of **12.86** difficult financial circumstances, which may themselves lead to insolvency. In Clarks of Hove Ltd v Bakers' Union (above), the Court of Appeal pointed out that insolvency is not on its own a 'special circumstance'. Far from being 'exceptional' or 'out of the ordinary', insolvency is in fact a fairly common occurrence. In the Court's view, whether special circumstances exist will depend entirely on the cause of the insolvency. If, for example, sudden disaster strikes a company, making it necessary to close, then plainly that would be capable of being a special circumstance, and that is so whether the disaster is physical or financial. But where the insolvency is due to a gradual running down of the company, a tribunal is entitled to conclude that there are no special circumstances. The facts of the Bakers' Union case were that the company was in financial difficulties and required about £100,000 to meet its obligations. Because of an adverse report on its affairs, a crucial loan was refused. The last hope that some of the company's shops might be sold off proved to be ill-founded and redundancy notices were sent out. The Court of Appeal upheld the tribunal's finding that these facts disclosed no special circumstances.

Similarly, in GMB v Messrs Rankin and Harrison (as joint administrative receivers of Lawtex plc and Lawtex Babywear Ltd) 1992 IRLR 514, EAT, the EAT held that the dismissal of workers to make an insolvent company more attractive to investors, and the subsequent closure of the workplace when no buyer came forward, were incidents common to any form of receivership or insolvency. They were by no means sufficiently unexpected or out of the ordinary as to constitute special circumstances excusing the employer's failure to consult. And in In re Hartlebury Printers Ltd and ors (in liquidation) 1992 ICR 559, ChD, it was held that the fact that a company is under an administration order is not in itself a special circumstance.

12.87 Even if redundancies do flow from a sudden, unexpected event, that event must be looked at in context to see if its ramifications justify dispensing with the requirements of S.188. For example, in Industrial Chemicals Ltd v Reeks EAT 0076/04 the employer was not permitted to rely on the special circumstances defence where the reason for redundancy dismissals was the loss of a large contract for the supply of a particular chemical called 'SAP'. The chemical was produced at a plant by a workforce of 61 employees. The decision to withdraw the SAP contract was made on 7 August, and in letters written on 15 August IC Ltd informed the workforce that it had taken the view that SAP production would have to stop on 16 August. It therefore considered that the majority of the employees would be made redundant immediately (albeit with notice), although some 19 staff would be retained for a short period in order to finalise some work on the contract. The employer cited the 'speed and critical nature of developments' culminating in the loss of the SAP contract as the reason why it had not been reasonably practicable to undertake TULR(C)A consultation. However, a tribunal – whose decision the EAT upheld – considered that the chronology of events and the employer's circumstances fell a long way short of the special circumstances envisaged by S.188(7). It noted that although IC Ltd had trade debts of £5 million, the company held large amounts of assets and had turnover of £62 million per year. In the tribunal's view, IC Ltd had reached an entirely commercial decision to cut all future loss flowing from the SAP plant at the earliest opportunity, and had proceeded on the assumption that the sudden cessation of production excused its consultation obligations. However, the company had provided insufficient information to the tribunal to justify that assumption.

There are cases, however, where financial crises have been held to constitute special circumstances. In Hamish Armour (Receiver of Barry Staines Ltd) v ASTMS 1979 IRLR 24, EAT, a company ran into financial difficulties and, having already received one government loan, applied for another in December. On 12 January this was refused, although an alternative source was suggested. When this too was refused on 3 February the company went into receivership. Four days later the receiver dismissed the workforce without notice. The EAT held that there were special circumstances. It thought that an application for a second government loan in these circumstances was sufficiently special to make it not reasonably practicable to provide the information required by S.188(4) until the outcome of the application was known.

In USDAW v Leancut Bacon Ltd (in liquidation) 1981 IRLR 295, EAT, the **12.88** Appeal Tribunal followed the Hamish Armour approach and held that special circumstances existed where a withdrawal of a takeover offer by a third party led to a bank immediately placing an ailing company in receivership. Although receivership might not be unusual in such circumstances, the financial deterioration was sufficiently sudden to be a special circumstance.

Unexpected loss of work. In Howlett Marine Services v AEEU EAT 253/98 a **12.89** tribunal found that special circumstances existed where the employer was entirely unexpectedly told by the contractor to whom it provided labour that staff cuts would be needed. The tribunal found that the decision made by the contractor was out of the ordinary, exceptional and uncommon. This was particularly so as the project on which the employees were engaged was expected to last for several months more and the amount of work involved had increased rapidly since the start of the project, to the point where overtime was being worked. However, the contractor then repeated its instruction to de-man a week later. The tribunal found that, in respect of that second instruction, special circumstances could not be said to apply – in the light of the first order from the contractor to cut staffing levels, the second order could not have been entirely unexpected. The EAT upheld this approach on appeal.

Ignorance. The employer's mistaken belief that it is not obliged to consult is **12.90** not a special circumstance, even when it relies on Government advice – UCATT v H Rooke and Son (Cambridge) Ltd 1978 ICR 818, EAT.

Keeping the closure or takeover a secret. In NUJ v The Western Times **12.91** Company Ltd ET Case No.7819/87 a tribunal held that the employer's need to keep the closure of a newspaper secret, in order to avoid a considerable loss of immediate advertising revenue, was not a special circumstance. The tribunal said that most trading companies faced with large-scale redundancies could apply the same argument.

─────── **375**

12.92 **Problem industries.** In some industries – like construction and shipbuilding – workers are sometimes taken on for specific jobs in the knowledge that when the job is completed redundancies will be necessary. In Amalgamated Society of Boilermakers, Shipwrights, Blacksmiths and Structural Workers v George Wimpey ME and C Ltd 1977 IRLR 95, EAT, a case concerning redundancies at a building site, the impossibility of forecasting exactly when redundancies would occur was held to be a special circumstance excusing failure to consult.

12.93 **National security.** It seems plausible that matters of national security may be exempt from consultation obligations by virtue of S.188(7). In United States of America v Nolan 2011 IRLR 40, CA, the Court of Appeal conjectured that a decision not to consult over an operational decision of military sensitivity – in that case, the closure of a military base – would probably enable a sovereign state to plead the 'special circumstances' defence. However, the Court did not have to decide the issue because the USA had not advanced the defence.

12.94 Complaints about breach of S.188

A complaint that an employer has failed to comply with S.188 TULR(C)A should be brought under S.189, as amended by the 1999 Regulations. Under the amended provisions, the persons entitled to bring a complaint seeking a declaration and a protective award are:

- in the case of a failure relating to the election of employee representatives, any of the affected employees or any of the employees who have been made redundant. In these circumstances it is for the employer to show that the S.188A requirements for election have been satisfied – S.189(1)(a) and (1B)

- in the case of any other failure relating to employee representatives, any of the employee representatives to whom the failure related – S.189(1)(b)

- in the case of failure relating to representatives of a trade union, by the trade union – S.189(1)(c)

- in any other case, by any of the affected employees or by any of the employees who have been dismissed as redundant – S.189(1)(d).

If there is disagreement as to whether an individual was an appropriate representative for the purposes of S.188, the employer has the burden of satisfying the tribunal that the individual had the authority to represent the affected employees – S.189(1A).

12.95 A complaint under S.189 must be made either before the date on which the last of the dismissals takes effect or during the period of three months beginning with that date. However, tribunals have a discretion to allow complaints within such further period as they consider reasonable if it was not reasonably practicable to present the complaint within three months – S.189(5). The

376

reference to 'reasonably practicable' echoes the language used by the ERA in relation to time limits for bringing, among other things, unfair dismissal claims. The case law on reasonable practicability in that respect will therefore be highly relevant to claims under the TULR(C)A – see IDS Employment Law Handbook, 'Employment Tribunal Practice and Procedure' (2006), Chapter 3.

Right to claim   12.96

As will be obvious from the different categories set out in S.189(1) (above), whether or not an individual has standing to bring a claim in respect of an employer's failure to observe the requirements of S.188 depends on the kind of failure at issue. The relationship between failures related to employee representatives, under S.189(1)(a) and (b), and failures 'in any other case' under S.189(1)(d), was considered by the Court of Appeal in Mercy v Northgate HR Ltd 2008 ICR 410, CA. There, M, who was dismissed as redundant, brought a claim for a protective award in respect of the employer's failure to provide information to the elected employee representatives. The tribunal made the award but, on appeal, the EAT overturned that decision on the basis that M had no standing to claim under S.189. In so doing, it rejected M's argument that the failure was within the 'any other case' category of S.189(1)(d). Rather, the failure was one relating to employee representatives and so fell within S.189(1)(b), meaning that only the employee representatives could bring a claim. The Court of Appeal approved the EAT's decision. Where a complaint under S.189 relates to the *election* of an employee representative, any affected employee (including, in this case, M) would have standing under S.189(1)(a). However, where employee representatives are appropriately in place – as they were here – a complaint about a failure relating to them can only be brought by them. The proper approach would have been for M to raise his complaint with the employee representatives, who, if they could obtain no redress from the employer directly, could have brought the claim.

This interpretation would appear to accord with the Collective Redundancies Directive. In Mono Car Styling SA v Odemis and ors 2009 3 CMLR 47, ECJ, the European Court held that the Directive's provisions on consultation were essentially 'collective' in nature and therefore intended to be enforced by employee representatives rather than by the employees themselves. Thus, provided employee representatives (assuming they exist) can bring a claim, it would seem that national provisions limiting or setting conditions on an individual employee's right to do so will not contravene the Directive.

Impact on protective award. Section 189(1) is also relevant to the extent of the   12.97
tribunal's power to make an award for breach of S.188 (known as a 'protective award' – see 'Protective awards' below). Such an award may only be made in favour of those who have been dismissed as redundant *and* in respect of whom a complaint under S.189 has been proved. Since a trade union can only bring a claim in respect of those employees it represents, the protective award which

results only benefits those employees – TGWU v Brauer Coley Ltd 2007 ICR 226, EAT. The Appeal Tribunal noted that where there are non-union employees, representatives of whom have also not been consulted, they must make their own claims, although there is nothing to stop a claim being made simultaneously by a trade union and individual employees.

Similarly, if a protective award is made in favour of an individual claimant, it cannot be extended to other employees who, although affected by the employer's failure to consult, were not party to the proceedings brought by that claimant. In Independent Insurance Company Ltd v Aspinall and anor 2011 IRLR 716, EAT II Ltd went into provisional liquidation in June 2001 and made 351 employees – including A and his fellow claimant – redundant at the company's offices in Cheadle. In accordance with Ss.188 and 188A, II Ltd was obliged to consult and provide information to either employee or trade union representatives, and to arrange for the necessary elections, but it failed to do so. It followed that those employees faced with redundancy were entitled to a protective award under S.189. A large number of claims were stayed because of proceedings in the Companies Court, and when an application for a protective award made by some of the dismissed employees was finally heard, a number of them were struck out, settled or dismissed.

12.98 When A made his claim, he did not attempt to seek an award in respect of his fellow employees in a similar situation, and nor did his fellow claimant. Nevertheless, the employment tribunal made a protective award that applied to the claimants and all employees at the Cheadle office. At a subsequent review of its decision, the tribunal did not accept the employer's contention that the claimants lacked standing to bring in effect what amounted to a representative action, noting that S.189(3), which defines what a protective award comprises, states that it is an award in respect of 'one or more descriptions of employees'.

II Ltd appealed to the EAT. Relying on the Brauer Coley case among other things, it argued that it was necessary to construe the phrase 'description of employees' in the case of an individual claimant as referring to that individual only, rather than an entire class of which he or she was one. The EAT agreed. Ss.188–189 give representative rights to trade unions and elected representatives only. The effect of the tribunal's decision was hopelessly anomalous, as it would enable other employees – whose cases were dismissed, struck out, or not even brought – to benefit. Furthermore, it would be impossible for an employer to defend proceedings or to consider which defences might arise in relation to different individual employees. The statute had to be read in its context and regard had to be paid to the fact that Parliament would not have intended to produce such anomalies. Accordingly, II Ltd's appeal was allowed and the tribunal's protective award in respect of employees other than the claimants was set aside.

These cases demonstrate that anyone with legal standing to bring a claim under **12.99** S.189 can only obtain a protective award to benefit those he or she properly represents – either individually or collectively. However, what of those employees who, although represented for the purposes of S.188, are excluded from the scope of a protective award for one reason or another? Are they able to bring their own claims under S.189 in these circumstances? Or do they have any other course of redress? These issues were considered by the EAT in Harford and ors v Secretary of State for Trade and Industry EAT 0313/07. WF Ltd was placed in administrative receivership and its employees dismissed between 3 and 26 May 2006. The GMB union, which represented *all* of WF Ltd's manual workers, obtained a protective award in respect of employees who were dismissed on 3 or 5 May 2006 only – the dates on which its members were dismissed. A number of employees who were dismissed on other dates subsequently made an application to the Secretary of State for payment of a protective award out of the National Insurance Fund (see Chapter 7). The application was refused, and they brought a claim against the Secretary of State before an employment tribunal.

The same employment judge who sat alone in the GMB case heard their tribunal claim. He found that the employees were not covered by the protective award granted by him in the GMB case. Furthermore, he deduced from the documents before him that the employees were not manual workers (or union members), and could accordingly not benefit from the protective award made in the GMB's favour. For this reason, he refused to review, or extend the scope of, the original protective award.

On appeal, the EAT took issue with the judge's finding that the employees were **12.100** not manual workers, and thus not represented by the GMB union for the purposes of S.188. The judge appeared to have assumed that they were managerial or technical staff without raising this issue with their representative. The question of whether all or some of them were manual workers was accordingly remitted to the same judge.

The Appeal Tribunal went on to note that the protective award in the GMB case was limited in scope: only manual workers dismissed on 3 or 5 May 2006 could take advantage of it. The employees in question, assuming that they were indeed manual workers, could therefore not benefit from the award, as they had been dismissed on other dates. Their options in these circumstances seemed limited – particularly as they were by then out of time to make a free-standing claim under S.189(1)(a) or (d) (subject to being granted an extension of time). However, the EAT doubted in any event whether either provision would be available to employees who were represented by a trade union. Once a trade union was recognised in respect of any affected employees, S.189 appeared to require that only that union could bring a claim under the section. That said, the EAT thought it unnecessary to decide the point.

379

12.101 Instead, the EAT held that the employees who had missed out under the terms of the protective award could apply to the employment tribunal under rule 10(2)(r) of the Employment Tribunal Rules of Procedure, contained in Schedule 1 to the Employment Tribunals (Constitution and Rules of Procedure) Regulations 2004 SI 2004/1861, for the judge to allow them to be joined (out of time) as parties to the GMB case because they had an interest in the outcome of the proceedings. They could then apply, under rule 34 of the Tribunal Rules, for the decision in that case to be reviewed in the interests of justice so as to cover dismissals on other dates, and for any consequent protective award to be recoverable from the Secretary of State.

Although the majority of employees are likely to be dismissed at the same time when a company becomes insolvent, it is not uncommon for a small number of employees to be kept on for a short period in order to conclude the company's business and assist the representatives of the receivers. Any protective award obtained by the appropriate representatives in respect of the initial redundancies only would therefore leave those who have been dismissed later in the unenviable position of having to apply to the tribunal themselves to rectify the scope of the original award.

12.102 Protective awards

If a tribunal finds that an employer has acted in breach of S.188, it *must* make a declaration to that effect and *may* make a 'protective award' – S.189(2). A protective award is an award of pay to those employees who have been dismissed as redundant, or whom it is proposed to dismiss as redundant, and in respect of whom the employer has failed to comply with the requirements of S.188 – S.189(3). There seems to be something of an anomaly here. S.189(3), which was not altered by the 1999 Regulations, makes it clear that for an employee to be covered by an award, he or she must be an employee whom the employer has dismissed or has proposed to dismiss as redundant. Yet an important change introduced by the 1999 Regulations is the extension of the right to consultation to all 'affected' employees. That is, an employer is now required to consult not only in respect of employees whose jobs are threatened, but also in respect of those who are otherwise 'affected' by the redundancy situation – see 'Scope of duty to consult' above. Thus it would seem that, as the legislation currently stands, an 'affected' employee who does not fall within the scope of S.189(3) has the right to be consulted and the right to bring a complaint of failure to consult, but no right to receive a protective award.

12.103 Protected period. The award is for a 'protected period', beginning with the date on which the first of the dismissals to which the complaint relates takes effect, or the date of the award (whichever is the earlier), and continuing for however long the tribunal decides is 'just and equitable' – S.189(4). The Act gives tribunals no guidance as to how to exercise their discretion over the length of the protected period, or whether to make an award at all, except to say that

380

they should have regard to the 'seriousness of the employer's default'. However, there is a maximum limit on the protected period of 90 days.

The protective award is subject to the 90-day maximum in all cases. This is the result of an amendment made by the 1999 Regulations. Previously, S.189(4) related the protected period to the numbers of employees that the employer proposed to dismiss, so that an award of 90 days was only possible in cases where 100 or more employees were to be dismissed. In all other cases, the protected period was limited to 30 days. The amendment removed that distinction for the purpose of the protective award. In Newage Transmission Ltd v TGWU EAT 0131–32/05 the EAT expressly rejected the contention that, despite the amendment, the maximum award in a 30-day consultation period should still be 30 days. The employer there argued that if a 90-day protective award is proportionate to an employer's breach of the 90-day consultation period, then the same maximum award is disproportionate where the consultation period is 30 days. The EAT rejected that argument, noting that a protective award is punitive rather than compensatory, and so should be subject to the maximum compensation permitted by Parliament.

Quantification of protective award

12.104

Where a protective award has been made, remuneration must be paid to all employees who have been, or are to be, made redundant and who are of a description specified by the tribunal – S.190(1). The rate of remuneration is one week's pay for each week of the protected period – S.190(2). A week's pay is as defined by Ss.220–229 ERA and is explained in IDS Employment Law Handbook, 'Wages' (2011), Chapter 10. There is no ceiling placed on the amount of a week's pay for these purposes. If an employee would not have received any pay under the contract while employed, he or she is not entitled to anything under the protective award – S.190(4). This would apply to employees who are on unpaid leave or on strike – see, for example, Cranswick Country Foods plc v Beall and ors 2007 ICR 691, EAT.

In Canadian Imperial Bank of Commerce v Beck EAT 0141/10 the EAT held that, for the purpose of calculating a protective award, a week's pay should refer only to the employee's basic salary and not to any discretionary bonus. B had argued that the discretionary bonus constituted the bulk of his remuneration package and that to exclude it from the concept of 'a week's pay' would be to largely deprive the protective award of any real deterrent effect. Although S.221(2) ERA provides that a week's pay for these purposes is 'the amount which is payable by the employer under the contract of employment', B had contended that the effectiveness of EU law would not be guaranteed unless account was taken of his discretionary bonus. The EAT accepted that there might be cases in which an employee's basic salary is so small that it could be said that failing to include a discretionary bonus or commission payments in a week's pay would deprive a protective award of any deterrent effect. However, it did not consider that any such principle applied in B's case. It could not be said that the protective award of £45,000 in this case did not penalise the employer. The EAT noted that B's basic annual salary of £125,000 was 'not an insignificant sum', even if it was much less than he might ultimately have received as a remuneration package in respect of that year had he remained in employment. Moreover, at the time of his dismissal he had not yet become entitled to have any decision made as to whether he should receive a bonus, let alone how much that bonus should be or what form it should take.

12.105 Note that the set-off provisions once contained in S.190(3) were repealed by the Trade Union Reform and Employment Rights Act 1993 (TURERA). Under those provisions, where the employee received any payment from the employer under his or her contract of employment, or by way of damages for breach of that contract, for any part of the protected period, that payment went towards discharging the employer's liability to pay remuneration under the protective award. Conversely, the protective award could go towards discharging the employer's contractual liability in respect of the protected period. The effect of S.190(3) was that a three-month payment in lieu of notice could wipe out a maximum protective award altogether, thus allowing an employer to disregard the statutory provisions. The ECJ in Commission of the European Communities v United Kingdom 1994 ICR 664, ECJ, held that these set-off provisions deprived the protective award of its practical effect and deterrent value and were in breach of the Directive.

12.106 Length of 'protected period'

As stated above, the protective award will be calculated by reference to a 'protected period', which is of whatever length the tribunal decides is 'just and equitable', up to a maximum of 90 days – S.189(4).

Before 2004 courts and tribunals were unclear as to the purpose of the protective award, and hence of how to calculate the protective period. Most leading authorities inclined towards the view that the award was designed to be compensatory in respect of the failure to consult. However, that still left room for uncertainty as to exactly what the award was meant to compensate, especially in cases where employees suffered no actual loss. Thankfully, that debate has been conclusively laid to rest by the Court of Appeal's decision in Susie Radin Ltd v GMB and ors 2004 ICR 893, CA, where the Court made it clear that the protective award is designed to be punitive rather than compensatory.

12.107 **Award is punitive, not compensatory.** In Susie Radin, a tribunal found that the respondent employer had failed in its duties in respect of a collective redundancy situation when it had provided none of the information required under S.188(4) and had simply 'gone through the motions' of the consultation. The tribunal made an award for a protected period of 90 days. The employer appealed unsuccessfully to the EAT, and again to the Court of Appeal, against the level of the award, arguing that the purpose of the award was to compensate employees and that, in the circumstances, consultation would not have made any difference. The Court of Appeal rejected that argument, endorsing the tribunal's approach, and went on to give guidance on how tribunals should exercise their discretion under S.189. It noted that S.188 imposes an absolute obligation on employers to consult meaningfully over proposed redundancies, and that S.189 is designed to ensure that such consultation takes place by providing a sanction against a failure to comply. Nothing in the TULR(C)A links the award to any loss suffered by employees. Thus, the focus should be on the employer's default and its seriousness.

Relevant factors. The Court in Susie Radin condensed the above principles **12.108** into five factors that tribunals should have in mind when applying S.189:

- the purpose of the award is to provide a sanction, not compensation

- the tribunal has a wide discretion to do what it considers just and equitable, but the focus must be on the seriousness of the employer's default

- the default may vary in seriousness from the technical to a complete failure both to provide the required information and to consult

- the deliberateness of the failure may be relevant, as may the availability to the employer of legal advice about its obligations under S.188

- how the tribunal assesses the length of the protected period is a matter for the tribunal, but a proper approach where there has been no consultation is to start with the maximum period of 90 days and reduce it only if there are mitigating circumstances justifying a reduction to an extent to which the tribunal considers appropriate.

In the years since Susie Radin was decided, this case has been applied many **12.109** times by tribunals and courts without being greatly expanded. It therefore remains the definitive guidance on S.189. Attention should be drawn, however, to the EAT's decision in Amicus v GBS Tooling Ltd (in administration) 2005 IRLR 683, EAT, in which it considered the issue of 'deliberateness' in some detail. In that case, GBS Ltd had made efforts to give the union sufficient information and keep it informed in general terms of the economic circumstances that eventually gave rise to collective redundancies. However, employees were dismissed the day after the proposal to dismiss was crystallised with no consultation whatsoever. Following Susie Radin, the tribunal made a 70-day protective award, finding that efforts made by GBS Ltd to involve the union before the proposal to dismiss arose amounted to a mitigating factor justifying a reduction from the maximum. The EAT refused to interfere with that decision on appeal. It held that GBS Ltd's efforts at keeping the union informed 'put [it] into a different category from the employer who had either deliberately, or

383

recklessly, or even negligently, taken no steps whatever to inform the employees or the unions of the problems that might and/or were imminently going to arise'. So, in assessing deliberateness, tribunals should consider whether an employer has been secretive, misguided, or has simply failed to disclose information at the right time and in the right context.

Two other points are worth noting from the GBS Tooling decision. First, the EAT confirmed that a tribunal can take into account the employer's actions *before* the duty to consult arises. It expressly rejected the union's argument that the only mitigating factors that a tribunal can take into account are those arising during the statutory consultation period, i.e. after dismissals are 'proposed'. Secondly, the EAT underlined that futility – i.e. that consultation would have made no difference to the outcome – is not a factor to be taken into account under S.189. Rather, it thought that if consultation were genuinely futile, perhaps because the future of the business is out of the employer's hands, that might be relevant to making out a S.188(7) 'special circumstances' defence (see 'Special circumstances defence' above).

12.110 In Smith and anor v Cherry Lewis Ltd (in receivership) 2005 IRLR 86, EAT, the Appeal Tribunal identified some additional factors tribunals should *not* take into account. It overturned a tribunal's decision not to make a protective award on the basis that, since the employer would by reason of insolvency be unable to pay, the making of an award would be completely ineffective as a sanction against the employer. The tribunal had erroneously viewed the sanction as retributive rather than punitive or dissuasive. The EAT underlined the need for the tribunal to focus on the extent of the employer's default in exercising its discretion. The tribunal in the present case had therefore erred in taking into account the employer's inability to pay and the likelihood that the burden of paying the awards would fall onto the Government, both of which were irrelevant factors.

Note that the main thrust of Susie Radin – that tribunals should start at a 90-day protective period and reduce this if there are mitigating circumstances – only strictly applies where there has been no consultation at all. Although Susie Radin underlines that tribunals have a wide discretion under S.189 to make an award that is 'just and equitable', and are therefore entitled to make a full 90-day award even where there has been some attempt at consultation, we would suggest that this will be a rare case. Mr Justice Elias, then President of the EAT, has commented since Susie Radin that 'if there has been some consultation, however limited, then the tribunal is compelled thereby to reduce the compensation below the maximum. No doubt that is true where such consultation as does take place is more than minimal' – UK Coal Mining Ltd v NUM (Northumberland Area) and anor 2008 ICR 163, EAT. So, although the tribunal ultimately has a generous discretion to make such award as it thinks fit, it will generally have to 'give credit' for an employer's attempts to comply with S.188.

Below we give some further examples of factors that tribunals and courts have considered when determining the length of the protective period.

Employer giving misleading reasons. In UK Coal Mining Ltd v NUM **12.111** (Northumberland Area) and anor (above), the employer falsely told the trade unions that a colliery was being closed for health and safety reasons, when the real reason was economic. The tribunal took the view that there had been a very serious and fundamental failure to consult, and that the limited consultation about various marginal issues did not in any material way mitigate the seriousness of the conduct so as to compel it to reduce the protective period below the maximum 90 days. On appeal, the EAT refused to interfere with the tribunal's exercise of its discretion.

Employer's willingness to negotiate. In Leicestershire County Council v **12.112** Unison 2006 IRLR 810, CA, a tribunal found that there had been an intentional and total failure to consult in respect of one group of employees who were to have their pay downgraded, and so awarded the full 90 days. By contrast, in respect of a second group, whose rights to pay supplements and overtime were to be adversely affected, the tribunal noted that the Council had eventually offered to consult with the union, and the union had failed to take up that offer. Because of this, the tribunal limited the protected period for the latter group to 20 days. On the Council's appeal, the EAT held that the tribunal had failed fully to take into account the mitigating circumstances in respect of this group – the evidence of the Council's approach to the enhancement group was impressive, in that it did not seek simply to consult, but also to negotiate with a view to avoiding the dismissals. The EAT therefore substituted a protective period of ten days. However, the Court of Appeal allowed a further appeal by the union against the EAT's reduction of the protective award. Neither view – ten or 20 days – was perverse. Although a different tribunal might have awarded ten days, the tribunal in the instant case had correctly applied Susie Radin, and so its decision should not have been disturbed.

Trade union's reluctance to cooperate. In GMB v Lambeth Service Team Ltd **12.113** and anor; TGWU v Lambeth Service Team Ltd and anor EAT 0127/05; 0129/05 the EAT held that a tribunal was entitled to take a union's obstructive approach to statutory consultation into account when assessing the correct protective period. The tribunal had found evidence of the union's refusal to cooperate and, unlike in Susie Radin, this was not a case of an employer wholly failing to discharge its duty to consult. The company's initial failure to supply information had been quickly rectified and the union had chosen not to respond to the information provided. In the EAT's view, the Susie Radin guidance did not require the tribunal to focus solely on the employer's default but rather to take

385

into account 'all the circumstances' in order to make an award that was 'just and equitable' under S.189(4).

12.114 Trade union's acquiescence. In Lancaster University v The University and College Union 2011 IRLR 4, EAT, the Appeal Tribunal upheld a tribunal's decision to reduce a protective award in respect of an employer's failure to undertake collective redundancy consultation where the failure had effectively been condoned by the recognised trade union. The redundancies, which arose from the expiry of fixed-term contracts, had happened regularly for over ten years and the union had only recently begun to complain about the consultation procedure. According to the EAT, the tribunal was in effect saying that, because of the history, the employer may not have been fully alert as to the need for collective consultation and only became aware over a period of time. In other words, it had been 'lulled into a false sense of security' by the union. It had not been unreasonable for the tribunal to take that into account. The EAT therefore declined to interfere with the tribunal's decision to make a reduced protective award of 60 days' pay. It was relevant that the EAT placed weight on the fact that the employer's failure to consult was not deliberate. The EAT was less convinced that a union's previous acceptance – even if long-standing – would, by itself, be a mitigating factor, if the employer was well aware of its obligation to consult.

12.115 Attitude of employer. If an employer not only fails to consult but also acts in an uncooperative and obstinate way, a maximum award is likely to result. In General and Municipal Boilermakers Trade Union and ors v Swan Hunter Shipbuilding and Engineering Group (in administrative receivership) ET Case No.39135/94 and other cases a tribunal found that there had been a 'total and wilful' default and made a maximum award of 90 days.

12.116 Partial compliance. In TGWU v Purnell Colours Ltd COET 1130/99 the employer wrote to the union saying redundancies would be inevitable but, because of special circumstances (see 'Special circumstances defence' above), it was impossible to give exact details or to consult as S.188 required. The tribunal found there to be no special circumstances, but that the letter was a partial compliance with S.188. This, it concluded, should be taken into account when making the protective award. Similarly, in (1) NUT (2) NATFHE v South Glamorgan County Council ET Case Nos.37142/93 and another the local authority conceded that it had breached S.188. Nevertheless, the tribunal found that there had been several meetings with affected employees and union representatives and that the union was partly responsible for the failure to commence the statutory consultation process. The tribunal considered these circumstances were significant mitigation and made an award of 28 days rather than the maximum 90.

12.117 Third party pressure. In Shanahan Engineering Ltd v Unite the Union EAT 0411/09 the EAT held that the tribunal had failed to justify its reasons for granting a protective award of 90 days. SE Ltd, an engineering construction firm contracted to work on a new power station, was urgently required by its client, Alstom, to reduce the number of workers it had on site to alleviate health and safety problems caused by congestion and ground conditions. Within three days, Shanahan had selected around 50 employees for redundancy according to agreed selection criteria and dismissed them with one week's notice. While those 'special circumstances' (see 'Special circumstances defence' above) did not entirely excuse the failure to consult, they still operated as a mitigating factor, which the tribunal should have taken into account in assessing the seriousness of the default and in deciding the level of the protective award. The tribunal should also have had regard to the fact that consultation could have taken place over a shorter period of time, although the EAT stressed that this did not mean that the award should be tailored to the length of time consultation would have taken. The EAT remitted the case to the same tribunal to reconsider the length of the protective award.

Start date of 'protected period'

12.118

The 'protected period' starts when the first of the dismissals takes effect or from the date of the award if this is earlier – S.189(4). There have been conflicting interpretations of this provision. In GKN Sankey Ltd v National Society of Metal Mechanics 1980 ICR 148, EAT, the Appeal Tribunal considered that the period began when the first dismissal actually took place, irrespective of the original proposed date. This meant that if an employer persuades an employee to leave before the proposed date of dismissal, the protected period starts then. In theory, the protected period could therefore end before the other employees were made redundant on the original proposed date.

Another division of the EAT, in TGWU v Ledbury Preserves (1928) Ltd (No.2) 1986 ICR 855, EAT, considered this to be a wrong approach, however. In that case, the proposed date of termination of the employees' contracts of employment was 31 December but one employee left on 28 October. The tribunal held that the 30-day protected period began to run on 28 October, which meant that it ended before the other employees were dismissed. The EAT overruled the decision and held that the protected period should begin when the first dismissals were expected to occur in accordance with the original proposals. (This view was supported by another EAT decision, E Green and Son (Castings) Ltd and ors v ASTMS and anor 1984 ICR 352, EAT.)

The difference between the two approaches should be of much less significance 12.119 now that the S.190(3) set-off provisions have been repealed. Previously, the problem with the GKN Sankey approach was that it enabled an employer to lessen the impact of a protective award by persuading an employee to leave early. Since double payment was not allowed, the effect of a protective award would be largely nullified because the period of the award would coincide with the period during which the remaining employees continued to be employed and paid under their contracts. Following the removal of S.190(3), and the established punitive rather than compensatory approach to protective awards following Susie Radin Ltd v GMB and ors 2004 ICR 893, CA (see 'Length of protected period' above), there are far narrower grounds on which an award may be reduced, and so identifying the period in respect of which the award is made has become much less important.

12.120 Losing a protective award

Where an employee is employed during the protected period and he or she is fairly dismissed for a non-redundancy reason, or unreasonably terminates the employment contract, then he or she is not entitled to remuneration under the award in respect of any period during which he or she would otherwise have remained employed – S.191(1). Note that it is the wider definition of redundancy in S.195(1) that applies here, so that an employee will not be deprived of the award if the dismissal was for a reason or reasons 'not related to the individual concerned' – see 'Scope of duty to consult' above. Furthermore, if an employee unreasonably refuses an offer of suitable alternative employment, then he or she loses the protective award for the period during which he or she would, but for the refusal, have been employed – S.191(2) and (3). If the employee accepts such an offer, he or she has four weeks (or longer, if agreed in writing) to try out the new job. If the employee reasonably leaves during that time, he or she will still be entitled to the protective award – S.191(4)–(7). For more details on an employee's right to refuse alternative employment, see Chapter 3 under 'Suitability and reasonableness'.

Note that if an employee to whom a protective award relates dies during the protected period, the award has effect in that employee's case as if the protected period ended on his or her death – S.190(6).

12.121 Enforcing an award

An employee in respect of whom a protective award was made may bring a complaint under S.192 that the employer has failed, wholly or in part, to comply with the award – S.192(1). Note that it is the employee, not the representatives, who must enforce the protective award. The complaint must be made within three months of the last day on which the employer failed to pay the proper remuneration, unless it was not reasonably practicable to present it within that time – S.192(2).

12.122 **Enforcing awards on insolvency.** The issues of insolvency and redundancy commonly coincide, as the former will often lead to the latter. Employees made redundant on an insolvency will inevitably face difficulties recovering back pay, redundancy payments and protective awards from the insolvent company. In so far as protective awards are concerned, it has been established that such awards are 'provable' debts in liquidation, meaning that they can be claimed against the insolvent company out of its remaining assets – Day v Haine and anor 2008

ICR 1102, CA. Under the Insolvency Rules 1986 SI 1986/1925, debts are provable whether they are 'present or future, certain or contingent' as at the date of liquidation – rule 12.3(1). The Rules specifically state that debts which arise after the date of liquidation can only be claimed against the company if they arise 'by reason of [an] obligation incurred before that date' – rule 13.12(1). The Court of Appeal in Haine held that, where there has been a failure to consult under S.188, the tribunal realistically has no discretion not to make a protective award. Therefore, a failure to consult gives rise to a contingent liability at the time the failure occurs, even though no actual award is made until a tribunal determines the matter.

Note that Part XII of the Employment Rights Act 1996 (ERA) offers some protection to employees of an insolvent company by permitting them to apply to the Secretary of State for payment of certain debts, owed to them by their insolvent employer, out of the National Insurance Fund. These provisions are primarily designed to allow employees to claim arrears of pay, but 'pay' for these purposes is defined to include awards made in respect of a protected period – S.184(1)(a) and (2)(d) ERA. The amount that the Secretary of State can be obliged to pay is, however, limited to eight weeks' pay, capped at £400 per week.

Notification

12.123

The statutory duty to notify the Secretary of State of proposed redundancies is imposed by S.193 TULR(C)A. If an employer proposes to dismiss as redundant 100 or more employees at one establishment within 90 days or less, it must give notice to the Secretary of State at least 90 days before the first dismissal takes effect. If it proposes to dismiss 20–99 employees at one establishment within such a period, it must give notice at least 30 days before the first dismissal takes effect – S.193(1) and (2). Notice must be in writing and, where there are representatives to be consulted under S.188, a copy of the notice must be given to each representative – S.193(6).

The Collective Redundancies (Amendment) Regulations 2006 SI 2006/2387 amended S.193, from 1 October 2006, to make clear that notification to the Secretary of State must be given *before* the employer gives notice to terminate an employee's contract of employment in respect of any of the dismissals. This amendment was made in response to the ECJ's decision in Junk v Kühnel 2005 IRLR 310, ECJ, that, for the purposes of the Collective Redundancies Directive, a redundancy occurs when an employer gives notice of termination of employment contracts, and not when that notice expires. The amendment therefore makes clear that an employer may not wait until the notice period has already begun to run before notifying the Secretary of State.

Notification is not necessary in respect of redundancies affecting Crown employees, those serving in the armed forces, House of Lords and House of

389

Commons staff, those in police service, 'short-term' employees (i.e. those employed under a contract for a fixed term of three months or less or for a specific purpose not expected to last for more than three months and who have actually worked for three months or less), share fishermen and women, and employees who ordinarily work outside Great Britain – Ss.273, 274, 277, 278, 280, 282, 284 and 285.

Where an employer has already notified the Secretary of State of one set of redundancies, those redundancies do not count again if a further set of redundancies is notified – S.193(3). If, for example, an employer notifies the Secretary of State of a proposal to dismiss 70 employees for redundancy and then finds it necessary to dismiss a further 35, this counts as two separate proposals to dismiss, each of which requires 30 days' notification, and not as a proposal to dismiss 105 in total, which would require 90 days' notification.

12.124 Notification is to the address specified by the Secretary of State for the establishment concerned. Where there are representatives to be consulted under S.188, the notice must identify those representatives and state the date when consultation began. It must also be in the prescribed form and contain such particulars as the Secretary of State requires – S.193(4). The prescribed form – HR1 – can be obtained from the Redundancy Payments Office or downloaded from The Insolvency Service's website (www.insolvency.gov.uk). After receiving the notice, the Secretary of State may by written notice require the employer to produce further information – S.193(5).

If there are special circumstances which make it not reasonably practicable for the employer to comply with its obligations under S.193, it should take such steps as are reasonably practicable – S.193(7). Ignorance of the law is not a 'special circumstance' which will excuse a failure to comply – Secretary of State for Employment v Helitron Ltd 1980 ICR 523, EAT. Nor, where the decision leading to the proposed dismissals is that of a person controlling the employer (either directly or indirectly), is a failure by that person to provide the necessary information to the employer – S.193(7). 'Special circumstances' for these purposes will be defined by reference to the same defence available in respect of a failure to consult under S.188 – see 'Special circumstances defence' above.

12.125 Failure to give notice to the Secretary of State as required by S.193 is a criminal offence punishable on summary conviction by a fine not exceeding level 5 on the standard scale (currently £5,000) – S.194(1). However, failure to provide the appropriate representatives with a copy of the S.193 notification seems to have no consequences.

Case list

(Note that employment tribunal cases are not included in this list.)

A

B

393

I

J

Index